WINSTON CHURCHILL

WINSTON CHURCHILL

A BIOGRAPHY

By
René Kraus

SECOND EDITION ENLARGED

16 ILLUSTRATIONS

J. B. LIPPINCOTT COMPANY
PHILADELPHIA   NEW YORK

To Audrey, the inspiration,
in gratitude

CONTENTS

Part I—The Man

Part II—The Voice

ILLUSTRATIONS

PART I

The Man

CHAPTER I

Family Chronicle

LIFE moves in a circle. Him to whom it gives that highest happiness, harmony, it brings back to his starting-point, and to the starting-point of many who went before—fathers and forefathers. The blood of generations renews itself; the destiny of centuries is resurrected. Beginning and end blend into one.

In the beginning was the soil. And the house upon it. Blenheim Palace is an Italian castle, surrounded by an English park. Blenheim embodies in stone all the remembrances of Woodstock, the soil of the oldest English culture. Here the Roman generals built their winter villas two thousand years ago. For a thousand years and more Woodstock has been a focal point of English life; it was noted before the Norman Conquest. Here Saxon, Norman, Plantagenet kings held court. Blenheim was already a borough when the Domesday Book was being compiled. The park housed the wild beasts of Henry I. In the Civil War Woodstock House was held for King Charles until at last it was ravaged by the roundheads.

Winston Churchill, a Captain of Horse, rose up against the roundheads. The defeat of Charles I ruined him. He retired to the home of his wife—who incidentally was a niece of George Villiers, Duke of Buckingham—near Axminster. There a son was born to him. After the Restoration he was knighted. Sir Winston adopted the Spanish motto, *Fiel pero desdichado,* "Faithful, but unfortunate," which today still is the device of the Dukes of Marlborough. Charles II took the gentle hint, and made the faithful Sir Winston Clerk Controller of the Green Cloth, a resplendent office in the Royal Household. At the same time he appointed him one of the earliest fellows of the Royal Society.

Winston Churchill certainly inherited the blood of his ancestor and namesake, born in 1620. The latter too fought with sword and word and pen. He was in Parliament for Lyme Regis. He was so busy that he forgot about making money. He died happy and penniless, proud of his voluminous historical work, *Divini Britannici, being a remark upon the lives of all the Kings of this Isle from the year of the world 2855 unto the year of Grace 1660.* The book, indeed, did not receive unmixed praise. It was dedicated to Charles II, "who came when everybody thought that the monarchy had ended," and upheld the King's right to raise money without the consent of Parliament so fiercely that those remarks had to be eliminated from later editions. It also had more lasting values. It recalls Tacitus' *Imperium et libertas.* Two thousand years or so later the great Disraeli was to remark, "Imperium et libertas—not bad as a programme for a British Ministry." And the Primrose League, the all-powerful Conservative organization that still guards the Grail of the Tories (it was founded by Lord Randolph Churchill, the father of our hero), took the phrase for its motto.

Macaulay, it is true, says of Sir Winston Churchill, "He made himself ridiculous by publishing a dull and affected folio," a judgment that probably had much to do with spoiling our own Winston Churchill's taste for Macaulay; and Gardiner calls him "brilliant but erratic."

Those were the very two judgments that Winston Churchill the younger was to hear all his life. Here was the same problem. He too is waging a struggle "when everybody thinks that the Monarchy has ended." He too is an unconditional King's man; when the British crown reaches the gravest personal crisis of modern history, he proves it. He too is an M.P. for life, and all his life a poor man. He too is a historian and author. He too lives for the marvelous union of *imperium et libertas.* He too would rather proclaim his faith with a sharp and shining phrase than in long-winded effusions. He has become famous for remarks that are pointed but not wounding, just as was the first Winston Churchill, who expressed the everlasting foundations of war in such sayings as "Soldiers move not without pay; no song, no supper, no penny, no paternoster. . . ." And finally he too, the old gentleman who is still Young Churchill, has always been the butt of mild derision from specialists and experts.

It is a classic example of tradition. And yet it was really only Sir Winston's son who founded the tradition of the house. John Churchill, the greatest of England's soldiers, became the First Duke of Marlborough. Queen Anne presented him with Blenheim Palace, the estate of Woodstock, and a dukedom. In private life the glorious general came to be a paterfamilias so thrifty that all over the country people called him "the meanest man in England."

While still Marquess of Blandford, the seventh Duke of Marlborough married the Lady Frances Anne Emily Vane, eldest daughter of the third Marquess of Londonderry. We must not completely pass over the family chronicle. Grandpapa was the first unforgettable impression in little Winston's life. And the noble relationships and intermarriages must be clearly before our eyes if we are to understand the full meaning of Winston Churchill's revolt against his class and then his half-hearted return to the Conservative house of his fathers—undoubtedly the most important two events, psychologically, in his life.

It was the old, early Victorian period. (It is characteristic that Winston Churchill, the lifelong rebel, constantly describes himself as a child of the Victorian Era. The further his years advance, the more longingly he looks back.) Houses were still full of children. The ducal grandparents supplied themselves with eight —five sons, three of whom died early, and six daughters. Randolph Henry Spencer-Churchill came into the world in London on February 13, 1849.

We must devote a moment to him. Although he died early, Lord Randolph was to influence the whole growth and nature of his son. In all his roamings Winston Churchill has never devoted himself so completely to any mission as to the self-imposed task of being his father's executor.

The similarity between father and son is sometimes startling. To begin with, both were bad students. "To tell you the truth," the Duke wrote to his son Randolph at Eton, "I fear that you yourself are very impatient and resentful of any control, and while you stand upon some fancied right or injury, you fail to perceive what is your duty, and allow both your language and manner a most improper scope."

No question of where Winston got his revolutionary temperament. No question either of where his indifference to the requirements of school came from. One inclines toward mistrust of the world-famous English public school system with its centuries of tradition—of course quite the opposite of public, since it trains only the best of a privileged caste—when one observes its real failure with such brilliant specimens as Lord Randolph and Winston Churchill in two successive generations. True, all over the world some of the worst students are the greatest successes in life. On the other hand Mr. Winston Churchill regrets to this day that he adapted himself so ill to the social structure of his school. The road to the university was thus closed to him, and he confesses that the older he grows, the more deeply he misses the years of academic leadership and discussion.

In the celebrated biography of his father that Winston Churchill published in 1905, he writes: "At Eton he gained neither distinction in games nor profit from studies. He had learned to row and swim without aspiring to renown, and as for cricket and football he heartily detested them both."

Lord Randolph failed in his entrance examinations for Oxford, although a private tutor had coached him. He had to work for six months under the Reverend Lionel Dawson Damer at Cheddington, near Aylesbury, before he could take the examinations a second time, on this occasion with success.

Whatever young Lord Randolph may have lacked in studiousness and sporting spirit he amply made up for in dash and charm.

"There was not a boy in school," says Brimsley Richards in *Seven Years at Eton,* "who laughed so much and whose laughter was so contagious. There was scarcely one who was so frolicsome. His preferred method of descending a staircase was to skate down it with a rush, and if he had to enter the room of another boy, he would sooner bound against the door and force it open with his shoulder than go through the stale formality of turning the handle." Another chronicler of school-days, T. H. S. Escott in his biography of Lord Randolph, recalls: "He was addicted to dressing loudly, and I vividly recollect his appearance one day in a daring violet-coloured waistcoat."

Perhaps this overflow of youthful spirits was due to a secret knowledge or premonition of the end so near. Lord Randolph Churchill was quite early crippled by paralysis, and for a whole year he died by inches. A meteoric rise and fall gave him scarcely half a life to live—though a life in which every day was filled to the brim. Unquestionably this insatiable hunger for life passed on to the son. Otherwise Winston Churchill could not have squeezed half of his deeds and adventures into the sixty-five years that now lie behind him, in a life that still remains full of expectation.

At Oxford Lord Randolph became more famous as "a very bold and able horseman who also took the greatest interest in hunting," than as a student. He was nearly the most popular young man in Oxford, but he only squeaked through with his degree in history and law by the skin of his teeth. Nevertheless he was sent on the Grand Tour around Europe in 1870. This was another social triumph. Three years later—His Young Lordship now almost twenty-four, a finished man of the world—he spent the summer at Cowes. H.M.S. *Ariadne* lay at anchor, and in honor of the Tsarevitch and his exalted consort the commandant gave a ball on board. Of course Lord Randolph attended, although he was a poor dancer. These dizzy waltzes made him positively seasick. Even this tendency to seasickness his son, the regenerator of the British navy, inherited from him.

Lord Randolph danced the opening quadrille with a dark-haired young beauty to whose mother he had just been introduced by a friend. As it transpired between *Avant les messieurs!* and *Arrière les dames!,* she was Miss Jennie Jerome of New York City, aged nineteen. An American. How interesting! How peculiar!

The quadrille was followed by the inevitable waltz. "Let's sit it out. Or rather let's walk it out," Lord Randolph suggested. Waltzes made him seasick.

Outside the moon was shining on the deck of the *Ariadne.* A nineteen-year-old debutante of New York City would not be taken in by nonsense about seasickness. But the nonsense of the moon no girl has yet resisted. They walked three times around the deck.

When they came back to the ballroom, Lord Randolph said to his friend Colonel Edgecomb: "See those two girls standing with their mother? The dark one I'll make my wife!"

The dark one took a little longer to announce her decision. First the two had to encounter each other on a morning stroll, thanks to a lucky accident—one of those whims of fate that seem unfortunately to have gone out of fashion since the Victorian Era. Then he had to come to dinner—that same evening, of course—and listen raptly to the playing of the two sisters. For two minutes the young couple were left alone in the park of "Rosetta Cottage," where the Jerome ladies were stopping. And when Lord Randolph politely took his leave, Jennie confessed to her elder sister, "I think I shall marry our new friend."

Pictures taken about that time show a young girl of rarely harmonious beauty. It was not then customary to be photographed with sparkling rows of teeth and an expressionlesss poster smile. From her yellowed snapshots Miss Jennie Jerome looks at us reflectively, almost with melancholy. The playful ringlets in which she wears her rich, dark hair are the only piece of coquetry that a young lady allows herself. Above a conspicuously high, regular forehead arch strong, almost masculine eyebrows. The eyes are large, dark, full of mute interrogation. The face is slim, the nose

Grecian except for a funny little point that abruptly jumps out. The girl keeps her lips firmly closed. The short, prominent chin she must have inherited from a very energetic father. The figure, of medium stature and light as a feather, is clad in the evening gown of the time—black silk, high-necked, long sleeves flowing with folds and ruching and ribbons, bell-shaped, trailing. A heavy black silk dress such as this betrays no secrets. It asks riddles. Of such stuff is the young American made who is to be for decades one of the most-courted women of royal London.

Who is she, and whence does she come?

Lord Randolph wrote to his father on August 20, 1873, that he had found his happiness, the daughter of a certain Mr. Jerome. "This Mr. Jerome is a gentleman who is obliged to live in New York to look after his business." (The seventh Duke of Marlborough would scarcely have understood living in America for any other reason.) "I don't know what he is. He is reputed to be very well off, and his daughters, I believe, have very good fortunes, but I don't know anything for certain. He generally comes over for three or four mouths every year. Mrs. Jerome has lived in Paris for several years and has educated her daughters there. They go out in society there, and are very well known."

As a matter of fact Mr. Leonard Jerome was a prominent figure in America. He was publisher and co-editor of the *New York Times,* a big man in politics and at the race tracks. Winston Churchill has obviously inherited so many qualities from his American grandfather that it is worth while tracing these sources.

Leonard Jerome was the descendant of a certain Timothy Jerome who emigrated from England in 1717, and settled in the village of Pompey, in the colony of New York. Leonard, after graduating from Princeton College, moved to Rochester. Here he married a Miss Hall. In 1854 Jennie, Winston Churchill's mother, was born to the couple. She was but two years old when the Jerome family moved to New York City. Here the father, who had been very successful even in Rochester, among other things founding a paper that still survives as the *Rochester Demo-*

crat and Chronicle, built what has been called an American career. He made a fortune, lost it, made a second and greater one. Later in life he owned the controlling interest in the Pacific Mail Line. As a newspaper publisher and in the real-estate business he had fantastic successes. By the time the Civil War broke out he was a leading citizen.

For a time the views that he maintained on the Civil War in his *New York Times* were decidedly unpopular. There was daily danger of the mob's storming the building. Leonard Jerome remained unperturbed. He armed himself and his staff, turning his offices into a fortress defended by artillery. Once he had actually to beat off the rabble, not without bloodshed. With all his patriotic passion Jerome never sank to the level of a mere politician. He subscribed half his fortune to the Federal war funds.

When the national crisis passed, he devoted himself by preference to his two interests as a Maecenas—the promotion of art and sport. He was among the founders of the Academy of Music in New York, helped to start an opera, and had Jenny Lind, Adelina Patti, and other great singers of the time as frequent guests at his house in Madison Square.

Next to it stood the Manhattan Club House, which Leonard Jerome built. Incidentally he organized the Jockey Club, and was for many years its vice-president. The turf was more than his hobby; it was the great passion of his life. Jerome Park, the first American race track, was named after the "king of the American turf." An impressive figure with sharply chiseled profile, endless moustaches, and sharp eagle eyes, he drove about New York on the box of his own carriage with a team of six horses.

This free citizen in the American era of giants had no objection to his daughter's marrying a British lord. No doubt he would have preferred American grandchildren who might grow up to be men of his own kind; naturally he could not foresee how true the offspring would be to his vigorous, onrushing, unyielding, lavishly gifted American type. But he was one of those fathers who can reconcile themselves. He never tolerated tyranny, and never exer-

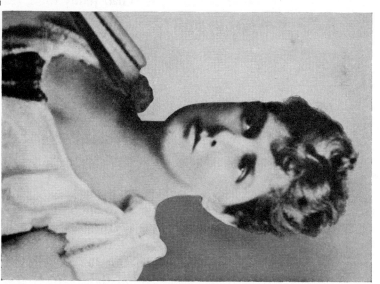

LORD AND LADY RANDOLPH CHURCHILL

cised it. Even when his wife took her daughters to Paris just before the outbreak of the Franco-Prussian War for the final polish that young girls could obtain only in the vicinity of the Empress Eugénie, he foresaw with resignation the disaster of European marriages for the children. All right, let it be this Lord Randolph Churchill, the Duke of Marlborough's son.

But when he heard that the British duke was making difficulties, the king of the American turf pounded on the table. Whose business was it to talk of mésalliances when the most beautiful girl in New York condescended to an English country squire?

On his father's and on his mother's side Winston Churchill comes of generations of arrogant, haughty, stiff-necked forebears— but at the bottom of their hearts they were good-natured and thoroughly generous souls. He springs from the typical Anglo-American cousinly battle. When he came to New York for his first American lecture tour, in December, 1900, white-haired Mark Twain introduced him to the audience with the kindly joke, "Ladies and gentlemen, I give you the son of an American mother and an English father—the perfect man!"

Of course the lovers were not to be intimidated by parental protests. Although Mrs. Jerome at once returned from Cowes to Paris with her daughters, and all correspondence was strictly prohibited, the couple wrote to each other regularly. Even in these early letters Jennie showed that she was to be the uncrowned queen of the Mayfair salons. No crumb of the gossip of Paris in that autumn of 1873 escaped her critical attention. Bazaine stood trial for his life, Gambetta revolutionized the Assembly. All the drawing-rooms of Paris were heavy with bittersweet mysteries. Lord Randolph replied that he would love her forever, and that the hare-coursing was good, but the grouse-shooting not very.

After an eternity of five weeks' separation he was able to write that at last everything would be all right. The Duke had implored him to contest Woodstock, the hereditary constituency, in the coming elections. Only he, the young darling of the countryside, could snatch the seat from the Liberal influences to which, oh, horrors!, even the incumbent Member, the Duke's younger brother, was not altogether inaccessible. Very well, replied Lord Randolph, he would sacrifice himself on the altar of Parliament, but only if Papa stopped objecting to the American marriage. It was a gentlemen's bargain, kept to the letter.

"Public life has no great charms for me," wrote Lord Randolph in telling his sweetheart the glad news, "as I am naturally very quiet and hate bother and publicity, which, after all, is full of vanity and vexation of spirit. Still it will have greater attraction for me, if I think it will please you."

Why must even true love lie? Public life not only turned out to have great charms for Lord Randolph Churchill; public life enslaved him. To it he sacrificed his life, every penny of his money, his health, his happiness. But no one understood this better than the woman in his life who became his most enthusiastic helper. Later she accompanied him to all his meetings, canvassed for him tirelessly, sometimes even stood on the platform herself. A ditty made the rounds in England:

> Bless my soul, that Yankee lady,
> Whether day was bright or shady,
> Dashed about the district like an oriflamme of war.
> When the voters saw her bonnet
> With the bright pink roses on it
> They followed as the soldiers did the helmet of Navarre.

The Duke, it must be said to his credit, felt the magic of his future daughter-in-law the moment he saw her. As if to apologize for his previous imperviousness, the old cavalier personally went to Paris on behalf of his son's suit. He took her to his veteran heart on the spot.

Now there was only Father Jerome on the other side still to be soothed. He bore no grudge; he was merely a little dogged. He displayed obstinate American views about a married woman's property, and made some propositions that Lord Randolph considered derogatory. All right, replied the young lord by letter, "I am determined to earn a living, in England or out of it, a course in which, I am bound to say, she thoroughly agrees with me." The old American fighter for freedom was not prepared, after all, to risk his daughter's having to depend on a "living in England or out of it." For the first time in his life he yielded— even with a grin, it is reported, and smiling his satisfaction. Twenty-four hours after the arrival of Lord Randolph's ultimatum, the last points of difference were settled.

On the fifteenth of April, 1874, the marriage of Lord Randolph Churchill and Miss Jennie Jerome was performed at the British Embassy in Paris.

On the third of December, 1874, the *Times* of London printed among its birth notices the following:

> "On the 30th November at Blenheim Palace, the Lady Randolph Churchill, prematurely, of a son."

The heir of British courtiers, marshals and dukes, the descendant of American puritans and burgess kings, the child of a father who was fated to illumine English politics like a meteor and a mother who was to be a radiant fixed star in the London firmament, the bearer of a heritage of endless, breathtaking struggle, victory, glory, had no time to waste. Winston Churchill began as a seven months' child. From the hour of his birth they called him "Young Man in a Hurry."

CHAPTER II

Problem Child

"And with a withering volley he shattered the enemy's line . . ."

Baby was now four years old. Baby had slightly bat ears; he was a funny rather than a beautiful baby. No matter, slightly bat ears might make it easier to drink in the music of these grandiose words. Sixty years later Winston Churchill can still hear the tones in which the old gentleman in his red uniform, glittering gold, uttered the magic-sounding sentence, "And with a withering volley . . ." His Grace, Grandfather, was unveiling the Lord Gough statue. It was the first impression that has survived in Winston Churchill's life. Even as a four-year-old, Baby was receptive to magic words. No wonder he has become the greatest living word-wizard in the English language.

The first winter of his eventful life "Winnie," as he was to be called for the next few decades, spent at Blenheim Palace. Then his parents moved to the town house at 50, Grosvenor Square, in London. The Duke of Marlborough became Viceroy of Ireland, and took along his son as secretary. The Churchill family moved into a house called The Little Lodge, directly across from the Viceregal Palace. Jennie, still feeling a little strange amid all the splendor, kept rather to herself at the official receptions. But now she was a Churchill. The men and women of that house can never help being the center of things. Lord D'Abernon, later British ambassador at Berlin, describes one of these receptions of the Duke's in his memoirs: "No eyes were turned on the Viceroy and on his consort, but all on a dark, lithe figure, standing somewhat apart and appearing to be of another texture to those around her, ardent, translucent, intent, more of the panther than of the woman in her look, but with a cultivated intelligence unknown to the jungle."

Jennie preferred to spend her free time with her husband, hunting, and the child remained largely under the care of Mrs. Everest, the nurse. She was the first friend Winston Churchill ever had, and for long years the only one. Today her picture hangs on the wall of his studio in Chartwell, as it did in the bachelor flat he used to occupy in Mayfair.

Mrs. Everest lived in constant fear of the Irish Fenians, who were quite capable of kidnapping the children of the "English oppressors." One day Winnie rode out on his donkey, accompanied by his nurse. In the distance a somber procession of dark-uniformed men appeared. Probably it was a marching troop of soldiers. Mrs. Everest, however, convinced they were Fenians, was terribly agitated. Her agitation communicated itself to the donkey, which bucked and threw its light burden. Winnie suffered a brain concussion. No more characteristic introduction to Irish politics could possibly have been contrived.

Mrs. Everest had a sister living in Ventnor whose husband was a prison warden. He told the lad about prison revolts, and how he himself had often been attacked and injured by the convicts. The sympathy that these tales aroused in the budding revolutionary was naturally directed toward the convicts. In later years Churchill recalled that these stories had remained vividly in memory when he became Home Secretary, and thus responsible for the English penal system. They led him to an inclusive prison reform. To them too he owed one of the greatest, if unintentional, humorous successes of his life. This was the famous affair of the Dartmoor Shepherd. (Dartmoor, of course, is the English Sing Sing.) The new Home Secretary was so full of the convicts' misery, which had haunted him since childhood, that he released an old shepherd who had been sentenced to a long term for a series of thefts from the offertory boxes. The particular character of the thefts seemed almost sacrilegious, and the man's pardon was interpreted as an anti-religious measure on the part of the Home Secretary, who was just going through his most violently radical stage. Naturally Churchill would return the blow with interest. All over the country he proclaimed the old shepherd a victim of the social order, who had to steal because he had never got a square chance in his life. Churchill himself found the man a job at Wrexham. But the old fellow did not last long. A few days after his "reformation" he was caught stealing again, and it proved that Mr. Churchill's martyr had been an incorrigible thief for years.

With the warden of Ventnor little Winston often went walking along the cliffs. One day they saw a splendid ship passing by with all sails set, only two or three miles from shore. "The *Eurydice*," said his companion proudly, "the training ship." Suddenly the heavens darkened. Such a hurricane broke loose as occurs but once a century in those temperate climes. The boy got home wet to the skin. Next day he heard that the *Eurydice* had capsized and gone to the bottom with three hundred soldiers and sailors on board. The divers went down to bring up the corpses; some of them fainted at seeing the fish eating the drowned. Winston had nightmares; he saw ghosts at night. He was a high-strung child.

Next came learning to read and write. There would be a governess—the boy awaited her as some figure of dread. Mrs. Everest, the nurse, tried to soften the shock. She brought in a book, *Reading Without Tears*, which the lad was to study in preparation for the lessons with the governess. But there was no reading without tears. The child fought desperately against the crooked, senseless shapes that were pounded into him, the letters and numbers. The letters were tolerable at a pinch; after a while they would take on shape, and assume some silly meaning or other. But figures? Never! Even in the nursery he showed that all through his school career he was going to fail in mathematics.

When the dreaded governess finally arrived, the boy ran out of the house, and hid away in the woods. It took hours to catch him. Then he was put to the treadmill. In vain he appealed to his beautiful mother. Mamma had no time. She quite agreed with the governess' strict methods. Besides, the horse was already neigh-ing impatiently at the door. On big, aristocratic thoroughbreds of the finest strain Jennie and her Lord hunted through the Irish woods. Children belonged at home, under supervision. "She made a brilliant impression on my childhood's eye," Churchill remem-bered of his mother. "She shone for me like the Evening Star. I loved her dearly—but at a distance."

Thus lonely children grow up, timid and scared amid viceregal pomp. For that matter, the pomp even then was rather superficial. The Duke had to spend all his money on entertaining the Irish in Dublin. His wife contributed to and collected for the Famine Fund.

The Irish came to the receptions; they made use of the Fund. Nobody said thank you. Clouds gathered darkly on the horizon.

The clouds, dark and menacing, descended even on Winnie's nursery. He was seven years old, and now it came time to take leave of the magic lantern, the real steam engine, and the thou-sand lead soldiers, wearing the uniforms of all the British services and regiments, that were more his playmates than his playthings. Off to school!

He would simply love school. There would be a great many other little boys, and wonderful adventures besides. Some boys grew so fond of school that they hated to come home for the holi-days. Just ask your older cousins!

The cousins said nothing, but grinned.

He started on the journey of life with fourteen pairs of socks and three half-crowns. With these possessions his beautiful Mamma delivered him to St. James' School, Ascot. She had scarcely taken leave of the headmaster, frozen in respect, before the latter's manner changed. He drew himself up as well as his stoop would allow. His wrinkled face darkened into an utterly authoritarian glare: "Have you any money with you?" The three half-crowns vanished into a drawer. True, Winnie was carefully given a receipt. Then they handed him his first Latin book. He must learn to decline *mensa*.

So far as education went, St. James' School was the last gasp of an antediluvian era. It had electric light, a revolutionary innovation at that time. It had a carefully chosen student body, with only ten boys in each form, all aspirants for Eton; it had the manner of Eton; its masters wore cap and gown. The school was fashionable and expensive. Each week in the library a number of boys were flogged until they were raw. Discipline demanded it.

The very first day, Winnie came dangerously close to the library. *Mensa,* vocative, his form master explained, meant "O table!" "You would use that in addressing a table," he said.

"But I never do," replied the boy.

"Next time you will be punished very, very severely!" With these words ended his introduction to the humanities.

Little Winston was not to be cowed. Never would he learn Latin, he vowed.

Of course they tried to introduce him by means of the cane to the beauties of the classical world. Once when he was thrashed too roughly he kicked the headmaster's hat to pieces. They beat him again. He was impertinent, stubborn, sulky. Why, the child even stole. Flogging again. His naughtiness became legendary.

Here the anti-disciplinarian was born. Traces still remain. H. G. Wells said of him many years later, "There are times when the evil spirit comes upon him, and then I can only think of him as an intractable little boy, a mischievous, dangerous little boy, a knee-worthy little boy. Only by thinking of him in that way can I go on liking him."

Untamable fury was stored up in the lad when discipline grew yet stricter. He would have revenge. When he was bigger he would come back to Ascot and publicly chastise the headmaster. He was still far too small for his great rage. After two years—the only two unhappy years of his life, as he later described them— he had a complete physical breakdown.

One question kept gnawing at his soul: why did not his father come to deliver him? After all, his father was the greatest and handsomest man in the world; he could come striding like a god.

WINSTON CHURCHILL AT THE AGE OF SEVEN

But his father was long since in the grip of politics. Politics will devour even the greatest and handsomest man in the world. Not until a serious illness attacked the child did his parents take him from the terrible boarding-school.

Lord Randolph had evidently forgotten his own school-days. He regarded his underdeveloped son with a troubled eye. To a friend he introduced him with the words, "Not much of a boy yet . . . But he's a good'n, a good'n . . ."

A summer trip with his parents to Bad Gastein, the Austrian spa, restored the boy's health to some extent. But his condition still required rest and care. He was therefore sent to Brighton, where the family physician, the then celebrated Dr. Robson Roose, was in practice. The child had to be under constant medical supervision. At the same time he was put into a school conducted by two elderly ladies of Brighton. This was a much more unpretentious boarding-school; there was neither the electric light nor the caning library of St. James' School. Instead there was an atmosphere of friendliness and sympathy quite new to the boy. For a little while he remained obdurate. Eva Moore, the actress, who was teaching dancing at Brighton just then, recalls Winston with the words, "A small red-headed pupil, the naughtiest boy in the class. I used to think him the naughtiest small boy in the world. He was cheeky in a specially annoying way, but smart. Games did not attract him, but theatricals. He constructed a toy theatre and produced *Aladdin*."

Indeed it was at this time that the histrionic element awoke which distinguished Churchill for years. Today it is long since extinct. The sacred flame needs no further Bengal lights. But it cannot be denied that until quite late in his youth he felt most at ease in the glare of the lights. He had his first dramatic success in a school performance of Colman's *Heir at Law*, in which he played Dick Dowles. His elocutionary gifts attracted general attention, though he did lisp slightly. This impediment gave him a good deal of trouble later. Like Demosthenes, Churchill, the greatest orator of his land and age, had to struggle painfully for speech.

Other early arts and sciences now came to him like a breeze. In French classes he did not have to say "O table!" Consequently he learned French very easily. Verses stuck in his youthful memory if he but read them once or twice. History began to fascinate him.

An attack of double pneumonia put the lad in bed. At that time double pneumonia was still a fatal disease, especially when the patient was a weakly, delicate child. But Winston pulled through. "He has a charmed life," said the doctor. The phrase was to follow Churchill wherever he went.

During his convalescence the nine-year-old began to take an interest in politics. He came to it in an odd way, a regular Churchill way. To occupy him on Sundays he was allowed to look through the old volumes of *Punch*. He not only looked them through, he devoured them. He was most deeply fascinated by the cartoons. Here he met the world, its great figures and events. Probably the portrayal of contemporary history in caricatures made a special appeal to the boy's rather scurrilous inclinations. The cosmogony he built up from the yellowing pages of *Punch* was not always a true one. For instance Gladstone, the great Liberal statesman, then the answer to all cartoonists' prayers, was usually portrayed as Julius Caesar, an august being crowned with myrtle, a sort of glorified headmaster. Later he learned that Julius Caesar was far from an august being, but instead, in Winston Churchill's own words, "the caucus manager of a political party, a wicked adventurer whose private life was a scandal, and that he had absolutely nothing in him that any respectable Victorian could tolerate."

The Franco-Prussian War and the American Civil War were also made vivid by *Punch*. He saw France defeated—a beautiful woman in distress, resisting, sword in hand, a blonde and apparently irresistible Germania. Young Churchill wanted to help the French.

In the American Civil War Mr. Punch was at first against the

South. He showed Miss Carolina about to whip a naked slave, a sort of Uncle Tom. On other pages the Yankees, decorated with long red noses, were running in the direction pointed by a signpost marked *To Canada*. Finally a picture showed North and South, two haggard, worn-out men, grappling as they moved toward an abyss labeled Bankruptcy. In the end, indeed, Britannia very sadly laid a wreath on Lincoln's grave.

In the course of his career Churchill himself became the favorite of the cartoonists. Not hundreds but thousands of drawings and caricatures show him with his two trade-marks, which have made him as familiar as the walrus moustache did his father, the monocle Joe Chamberlain, and the pipe Mr. Baldwin. One of these two trade-marks is the wart-shaped nose—which, however, is nothing but a malicious yet ineradicable invention. The other is a tiny hat on an excessively broad skull. The wart nose that they have attached to him Churchill might endure. But he has grave objections to the Charlie Chaplin hat. He tells how the hat legend originated. There is no denying that he once wore a hat too small for him by mistake while walking with his wife on the beach at Southport. Unfortunately a news photographer was on hand. From that day forward the cartoonists sealed the fate of Churchill's head and hat. In vain he points out tirelessly that his headgear is furnished by the best hatter in London. He had his trade-mark and his idiosyncrasy. At bottom he does not mind. A statesman no longer assaulted by the cartoonists is done for, he thinks with worldly wisdom. And as he was always a poor Latin scholar, he renders *Oderint dum metuant!* in his own private, tolerant fashion: "Let them laugh so long as they love." Which to some degree distinguishes him from the dictators, even as Supreme War Lord.

Even while he was educating himself on *Punch* he remained an ill-behaved boy, self-willed and refractory. The school paper that he founded before he was nine was of course called *The Critic*. Only one number appeared, however. He demonstrated his critical talent when he met Rider Haggard at the home of his aunt, Lady Leslie. Rider Haggard, the author of *She* and *King Solomon's Mines,* was then at the height of his fame. Young Winston, however, was by no means awestruck in his presence. "What do you mean by this passage in your new book?" asked the boy, quite without shyness. "I don't understand it."

Mr. Haggard examined the passage, and did not understand it either. Of course a masculine friendship at once developed out of that incident. Rider Haggard sent Winnie his newest work, and the latter thanked him with a most gracious holograph: "Thank you so much for sending me *Allan Quatermain.* It was so good of you. I like it better than *King Solomon's Mines;* it is more amusing. I hope you will write a great many more books."

An untamed, arrogant, presumptuous child, people said. No wonder—he was the son of the most conspicuous man in England.

After the Easter holidays of 1888 he took his entrance examinations for Harrow. He had been intended for Eton; but the climate there, with its everlasting fogs, was too unhealthy for the sickly boy. He was a little hurt by what he considered discrimination in the choice of schools. That the examination was no great success seemed to him less tragic. He had hoped to shine in his favorite subjects—history, poetry and essay-writing. Instead the examiners were painfully curious about his knowledge of Latin and mathematics. In the Latin paper, alas, he could not answer a single question. His mathematics did not seem to be much better. But Winston had the good fortune to find in the head of Harrow a great teacher with a deep knowledge of the boy soul. At this time Dr. Welldon, later Bishop of Calcutta and Dean of Durham, and for many years young Churchill's friend, was headmaster. Dr. Welldon was not unreasonable about his students' Latin prose at the expense of everything else. He knew a personality when he saw it, even in embryo form. Of his favorite pupil he was later to write: "Winston Churchill was not perhaps a boy who distinguished himself in the popularly accepted lines of public school life. He was not prominent in Latin and Greek scholarships or in mathematics or in natural science, nor again was he a prominent athlete as a cricketer or football-player. But not long after his entrance he attracted notice by his historical knowledge and his literary power, and he was among the Harrow boys of my time the most expert in the use of the foils. It would be wrong to pretend that he did not give the masters a good deal of trouble, but I think I may claim to have always felt, as I feel now, a great faith in him. I do not mean that I anticipated the full brilliance of his future life, but it is my deliberate judgment that he showed in his schooldays at Harrow the unmistakable promise of distinction."

One did need the kind heart of a Dr. Welldon to feel this promise of distinction immediately. For in the beginning Winston was ranked among the worst pupils. He stood but two from the bottom of the whole school. And as these two disappeared almost immediately, he was soon the last in order.

He managed to make the best of even this setback. It is an especially characteristic Churchill feature that bad always turns out to be good for him. At least he is able to interpret it so. Since he remained so long in the lowest form, his more gifted companions were taught Latin and Greek and similar splendors, while he was constantly taught English and English again. And in the person of a Mr. Sommerville he found an English teacher of uncommon stature. They continually practised English analysis. And when in later years his more gifted companions who had got prizes for Latin verses and Greek prosody could not write a simple English sentence to earn their bread and make their way, Winston Churchill could not quite keep a grin off his broad face.

Even in childhood he could see his own path marked out ahead, with all its wanderings and diversions. The visionary gift that was later to distinguish him, more than any other quality, from the great mass of mankind must already have been developed at least in rudimentary form by the time he said, at twelve, "Of course I will become a soldier while there is any fighting to be done. After that I shall have a shot at politics." Quite independently he went to the great throat specialist Sir Felix Semon. He must lose his lisp: "Cure the impediment in my speech, please. Of course I am going into the army first. But as a Minister later, I can't be haunted every time by the idea that I must avoid every word beginning with an S."

At thirteen he astonished the swim attendant at Marylebone baths by enquiring whether the good man was Conservative or Liberal. To a swim attendant in those happy days of course parties were a matter of complete indifference. "What?" Winston jumped. "You pay rates and taxes and don't bother about politics? Why, you ought to stand on a box in Hyde Park and tell people things!" For that was what he himself, at thirteen, wanted to do. Then he threw out his chest: "My father was Chancellor of the Exchequer, and I mean to be the same one day!"

His father had just thrown all England into uproar. On December 23, 1886, in two lines the *Times* reported the great event:

> "Lord Randolph Churchill resigned the offices of the Chancellor of the Exchequer and Leader of the House of Commons, and retired altogether from the Government."

Hidden behind these dry lines was at once a personal tragedy and a political event of the first order. Lord Randolph had been the founder of what he himself had christened "Tory Democracy." The aim of his life was to inspire the ruling classes of England with the progressive spirit. At the same time he himself was a restless, harried soul, the personal darling and political *enfant terrible* of the Tories, who gave him the highest posts in the kingdom even in youth, but refused again and again to follow his leadership. None was so tireless as he in denouncing Gladstone, the great Liberal statesman, in rousing England, in inflaming Ulster. He stood for religious and economic reconciliation between the two parts of Ireland, but he would never have agreed to a partition of the United Kingdom. "Ulster will fight, and Ulster will be right!" was his most celebrated slogan. Paradoxically it was his son, years later, who contributed more than any other man to conciliation with Ireland, and was certainly more hated than anyone by the Ulstermen.

Lord Randolph's whole life was a struggle with ill health. He smoked cigarettes "till his tongue was sore" to soothe himself. He was capable of feats requiring uncommon strength, but in reaction suffered grave fits of exhaustion and despondency. "He gallops till he falls," his wife said of him, remembering their early years of riding together.

His mother, the Duchess of Marlborough, wrote after his early death: "He had a wonderful faculty of making firm friends, who remained through his life devoted to him. He was very constant and decided in his attachments, and outspoken—often imprudently —in his likes and dislikes. This enabled him to succeed in life, but also often brought him into trouble . . . Alas, had I been a clever woman, I would have had more ability to curb and control his impulses, and I should have taught him patience and moderation. Yet at times he had extraordinary good judgment, and it was only on rare occasions that he took the bit between his teeth, and then there was no stopping him."

These lines read as if written about young Winston Churchill, not about his father. An almost uncanny likeness unites the two men.

There was no stopping Lord Randolph when he lost patience over a ridiculous trifle, and—perhaps in hysteria, perhaps already in the shadow of death—tossed away his brilliant career.

Among his ideas for modernizing Tory rule was an anti-militarist passion that was to be part of the early political heritage of Winston Churchill, the born soldier. Winston, like Lord Randolph, was one day to be a pacifist in the captain's saddle. Winston, however, was to have time to overcome this disease of childhood. Lord Randolph had no time. As Chancellor of the Exchequer he waged a furious struggle against the expenses of the Service Departments. He forced upon the First Lord of the Admiralty, Mr. George Hamilton, a reduction of £700,000. Mr. W. H. Smith, Secretary for War—a peaceful bookseller in civil life, and memorable through his caricature as Admiral Porter in Gilbert and Sullivan's "Pinafore"—on the contrary demanded an increase of £300,000. The subject of dispute was ridiculously small—not even one per cent of the total Army and Navy Estimates, which amounted together to £31,000,000. But Lord Randolph was looking for a fight. "I am pledged to large reductions," he declared. "If these things can be done in the Admiralty, the attitude of the War Office becomes intolerable."

He used up his strength in constant explosions. In addition, he was being squeezed by poverty at home. As a younger son he had but a small inheritance. As a political idealist he had never earned a penny. Soon only the dowry from New York would be left. But naturally Lord Randolph would never touch his wife's money.

Nevertheless rumors pursued him. High society did not understand his morbid intensity. A gossip campaign discovered the meanest motives for his strange behavior. Clubs abused him. The press censured him. The great Lord Salisbury, the Prime Minister, tried in vain to come to an understanding with his young right-hand man. When the House passed the Army Estimates according to the War Office demands, Lord Randolph recklessly chucked the whole business. Queen Victoria was grievously offended when she learned of her Chancellor's retirement.

A schoolboy at Harrow shared with burning heart and feverish cheeks in these struggles, which took place at what was for him an infinitely remote distance. Later he was to say of his father, with great understanding: "Lord Randolph Churchill was a Chancellor of the Exchequer without a budget, a Leader of the House of Commons but for a single session, a victor without the spoils. No tangible or enduring records—unless it be the Burma Province —exist of his labours, and the great and decisive force which he exerted upon the history of the Conservative and Unionist party might be imperfectly realized by a later generation. No smooth path of patronage was opened to him. No glittering wheels of

royal favour aided and accelerated his journey. Like Disraeli he
had to fight every mile in all his marches."

Words cannot tell how the boy Winston wanted to help his
father in every fight on every march. But naturally Lord Randolph gave him no opportunity; he was still far too young. The
battles for which the lad already felt the call had to be fought on
the football field, where he raged with the war-cry, "St. George,
St. Dunstan and the Devil!" Once at the swimming-pool he saw
an unfamiliar schoolmate, temptingly small of stature. Naturally
he flung him into the water from behind. To his horror it turned
out that he had laid hands on the person of a Senior.

The Senior, Leopold Amery by name, generously forgave him.
The two were fellow-correspondents in the Boer War. For more
than a generation they sat together as faithful friends in Parliament. Today Mr. Amery and Churchill are fellow Cabinet members.

Young Winston let out all his pent-up energy in riding, swimming and fencing. It was all simply a release, not boyish delight
in play; so much he himself knew. Still, he had no objection to a
good game of Indians. Once the redskins, two elder cousins,
chased him across a bridge. The paleface could escape only by
jumping off the bridge, which was held at both ends by the foe.
In falling he would grab the branches of a tree, he hoped. He
hoped in vain. He fell thirty feet, and landed on stones.

Once again he proved to have a charmed life. By rights he
should have shattered his skull. Instead he merely broke his right
shoulder. True, he did have to wear plaster casts for six months,
and his shoulder has never been right since. But when a man is
lucky, even an accident is good fortune. A few years later, at the
celebrated Omdurman cavalry assault, he was unable to use his
sword. And so, while cavalry sabers flashed around him, he shot
his way out with a brand-new Mauser pistol. No howling dervish
with the curved scimitar of the Prophet ventured too near him.

Winston Churchill spent three of his four and a half years at
Harrow in the Army Class. That he was to enter the service was

soon decided. Lord Randolph was pained to think that his boy
was too dull for the bar, which would really have been his paternal
desire. The father was faced with a puzzle: Why was Winston, a
noisy, alert lad, so feeble in his scholastic performances? He wrote
excellent compositions. Sometimes he wrote too pointedly. *The
Harrovian,* the school paper, had to censor one of his contribu-
tions radically because his language was not suited for publication.
But his Latin translation he had to get done by a classmate. In
return he dictated the latter's English essays to him.

The headmaster, Dr. Welldon, took a personal interest in the
promising lad who unfortunately was such a backward scholar.
Three times a week he gave him private tuition before evening
prayers.

But when the time arrived for the entrance examinations for
Sandhurst, the English West Point, Winston Churchill failed. He
failed a second time. At the third attempt he felt safe in English
and chemistry. French seemed tricky to him, although he had a
natural talent for the language. He spent six months in a grim
effort to master mathematics, his weakest subject. Up and at the
enemy where he is most dangerous, was his watchword even then.
All at once sines, cosines and tangents became his daily pabulum.
According to his own confession he has heard not a word of
these specters since Sandhurst. They vanished from his memory
as suddenly as he had conjured them up.

Once again a stroke of luck decided the outcome. He knew that
in the third examination, just ahead of him, he would have to
draw from memory the map of some part of the Empire. Unfortunately Great Britain is truly great, and consists of many parts.
He put bits of paper into his hat, each bearing the name of a
dominion or a crown colony. With eyes closed he drew the slip
marked New Zealand. New Zealand he studied.

In the examination the examiner said, "Draw us a map of
New Zealand on the board."

CHAPTER III

Knight Errant

W INSTON CHURCHILL was now a gentleman cadet, and so life began for him. Once again it began with a touch of bitterness. He barely qualified for a cavalry cadetship at Sandhurst. Service in the cavalry was no doubt more glamorous than in the infantry, but also immensely more expensive. Naturally the competition for infantry commissions was stiffer. But anyone who had to take his examinations three times, and then got through more by luck than good management, could be thankful to "get his horses."

So at least his father felt. Lord Randolph looked with anxiety to the future. His own means were almost, his health was completely, exhausted. On a journey to South Africa he had just tried to repair his finances by purchasing gold shares. This was the day of colonial investments. The great gentry could not earn their living at home. They belonged to politics—an honor, not a trade— and to their clubs. Joe Chamberlain was just sending his son Neville (the younger son, too slow-witted for politics) to the island of Andros in the Bahamas. Here he was to raise hemp—it would be a gold mine. It turned out a catastrophe. Young Neville stubbornly held on for seven years of self-denial—and self-deception. The fact that the entire capital, £50,000, was already lost he simply declined to realize.

Money did not grow on trees in South Africa either. The worried Lord Randolph pointed out to his offspring, "In the infantry one has to keep a man; in the cavalry, a man and a horse."

Papa did not even know that you have to keep two official chargers in the cavalry, and two hunters besides, to say nothing of a string of polo ponies. But let worries be worries and cares be cares; Winston Churchill was mad about horses. Into old age he has remained true to that passion. Riding is more than a sport to him; it is a part of his credo. "No one ever came to grief—except to honorable grief—through riding horses," he once said. "No hour of life is lost that is spent in the saddle. Young men have often been ruined through owning horses, or through backing horses, but never through riding them. Unless, of course, they break their necks, which, taken at a gallop, is a very good death to die."

In the eighteen months he spent at Sandhurst he became a celebrated horseman. Even at Harrow he had been an excellent fencer, taking the Public School championship in fencing. He was not sport-mad in the new-fangled way; he was an old-fashioned cavalier. His father, though he "galloped through life until he fell" himself, did not understand all this. He warned his son not to become a "social wastrel."

If his father had understood him better, Winston would probably have been spared all the compulsion, the forms and conventions of Harrow, into which he fitted so badly. The system may be all right for the average sons of the English upper class. In fact Harrow, like Eton, has turned out generations of brilliant youngsters. But Winston Churchill was neither average nor a son of the English aristocratic class alone. The American heritage was deep in his being. Like a regular Yankee lad he would have liked to be apprenticed as a bricklayer's helper, or run errands, or help his father dress the windows of a greengrocer's shop. That was what he dreamed of while he was wearing the broad-brimmed straw hat of a Harrow boy. A practical craving for action was deep in the nature of the old-fashioned cavalier-in-the-making. Indeed he would have liked to help his father in politics, too. But when he suggested that he might at least be useful to the secretary, Lord Randolph merely gave him a long look that made the boy shiver.

It was only when Winston made good at Sandhurst that things

changed a little. First Lord Randolph took the youngster to the
Empire Theatre to see the acrobats and jugglers and lion-tamers,
then to Lord Rothschild's house at Tring, where the young people
of the Conservative Party gathered, and finally, highest honor of
all, to see his old racing friends. At last father and son would
grow to be friends. If only there was a little time.

There was no time.

Winston not only made good, he made very good indeed. In
Tactics and Fortifications, the most important two subjects at
Sandhurst, he was soon ahead of all his classmates. In Topography,
Military Law, Military Administration, the rest of the curriculum,
he held his own. When he was tired by long hours of study and
parades, he was still never too tired to plunge into the strategical
works that his father sent him as a sign of approval. You had only
to loose rein and curb, and he would go the right way of his own
accord.

Of course there were escapades. At least it seemed at the time
as if they were escapades. Today, almost fifty years afterward, we
can see his public mission proclaiming itself even in his pieces
of boyish tomfoolery.

The battle of the Empire Theatre was the noisiest of these
pranks. His father had first taken him there. The Empire, accordingly, was sacred ground, despite the acrobats, jugglers and lion-
tamers round about. Here a sort of promenade for young people
of both sexes, who even took occasional alcoholic refreshment at
the bars, developed in the large space behind the dress circle.
Naturally the Sandhurst cadets were always on hand, particularly of a Saturday evening.

But Mrs. Ormiston Chant was against it. She was a puritan
crusader, and she started a fierce campaign against the promenade
at the Empire Theatre and the bars on both sides. In those happy
days all London could get excited over such a problem. A long
series of letters to the newspapers supported the clean-up. On
the other side an "Entertainment Protection League" formed,

determined to defend the rights of man and civic self-determination even at the bar.

The puritans succeeded in getting a sort of barricade put up between the promenade at the Empire and the row of bars. But they reckoned without the Sandhurst cadets. One evening a large group of the young gentlemen appeared, the barricade was torn down amid general enthusiasm, and naturally Winston Churchill celebrated the deed of liberation in a resounding address. It was his maiden speech. The occasion was a mere excuse for him to rise to the higher regions of politics. "You have seen us tear down these barricades tonight; see that you pull down those who are responsible for them at the coming election!" he blared, altogether Lord Randolph's son. He had, incidentally, prepared his speech with great care, taking pains to have as few words as possible beginning with S.

Next day most of the papers printed leaders about the storming of the barricades at the Empire Theatre. For the first time Winston Churchill was the hero of London.

He finished his studies at Sandhurst, with honors, eighth in a group of a hundred and fifty.

"Did you get your horses?" his father, already a dying man, asked him.

Certainly, he had got his horses all right. He was commissioned to the Fourth—the Queen's Own—Hussars, who had recently come back to Aldershot from Ireland. The regimental commander was Colonel Brabazon, an old friend of the family. Lord Randolph did grumble a bit at his old friend. "He had no business to turn the boy's head about going into the Hussars." He had still not quite given up hope of getting the boy into the 60th Rifles, whose commander, the Duke of Cambridge, had promised to open a back door to his own regiment, and thus to the infantry.

It was one last disappointment. On January 24, 1895, Lord Randolph Churchill died of paralysis at his mother's home. It was a gentle, painless death, really a dropping off to sleep. Winston stood by his father's deathbed. "The dunce of the family will take revenge on the whole pack of curs and traitors!" he vowed. He saw his life's work clearly before him: the name of Lord Randolph Churchill must be cleansed in the sight of his enemies and persecutors, his reputation rehabilitated, the country made to realize that it had not understood one of its greatest and most gifted sons.

In the end, Fate had other intentions. Lord Randolph Churchill sank into oblivion. A greater task awaited Winston Churchill.

From now on the regimental commander stood in loco parentis to Winston. The two were mysteriously linked, for Colonel Brabazon too had a lisp. In his case, indeed, it was not an impediment, but sheer grandeur. "The gwass is veddy gween!" was more or less how he talked. The Colonel showed special kindness to his youngest sub-lieutenant, although in general he was considered a strict disciplinarian. The two remained friends for twenty years, until Brabazon's death.

Outwardly Colonel Brabazon was nothing but a brilliant soldier and a man of the world. At court, in the clubs and drawing-rooms of Mayfair all doors opened before him, and all hands reached out to greet him. He was an intimate of the Prince of Wales, later King Edward. As he was also an officer famous throughout the army, who had won his spurs and medals in every conceivable colonial war, the earth bowed down to him. He took this quite for granted. "Wheah is the London twain?" he once asked the stationmaster at Aldershot. "Unfortunately gone, Colonel." "Gone? Bwing anotha one!"

Inwardly these perfectly polished super-gentlemen have a way of being less serene. Colonel Brabazon was a passionate bookworm, able to recite by heart pretty nearly all the famous poetry in the English language—something that he would of course never have admitted. Even less would he have admitted that he, the disciplinarian, was guilty of a long-continued mortal sin against discipline. For more than thirty years he wore a little imperial under his lower lip, whereas the Queen's Regulations, Section VII, expressly state, "The chin and the under lip are to be shaved." Of course the army made an exception of Colonel Brabazon, the darling of gods and men—until his regiment was transferred from Ireland to Aldershot. There Sir Evelyn Wood was in command, and he made no exceptions. Hearing one day that the irresistible Brabazon has publicly criticized some measure of his, he sent orders for the Colonel "to appear at his next parade shaved in accordance with the regulations."

The imperial fell. But Brabazon did not commit suicide; he bore his cross with a smile. Only thereafter nobody was allowed to mention the name of the commandant of Aldershot in his presence.

Such was the man who introduced Winston Churchill into the army of the Queen.

It was a kindly, a joyful introduction. Some happy, carefree months followed. From March to November of 1895 the young officer had the time of his life. Daily he enjoyed the thrill and the charm in the glittering jingle of a cavalry squadron maneuvering at the trot. Every day he was excited anew when the squadron was put to a gallop. The stir of the horses, the clank of their equipment, the thrill of motion, the tossing plumes, the sense of incorporation in a living machine, the suave dignity of the uniform—all these his own words—intoxicated him. The cavalier in him was swept off his feet. That he knew. What he did not know was that the artist in him was also stirring. The picture of the redcoats on white horses in the green countryside stamped itself deep on his consciousness. Years later he was to try to express those glowing colors in oil.

He himself was now as handsome as a picture. The little red-head had grown up into a sandy-haired youth with his hair parted on the left, according to regulations. From his mother he had inherited the high forehead, the prominent brow, the eyes full of inquiry, though usually brightened by a sly twinkle. The slim, aristocratic face with the mobile, blood-filled lips came from Father. There was nothing to hint that in the course of decades that face would grow disturbingly round. The youngest lieutenant of Her Majesty had his picture taken in a gold-laced tunic lavishly decorated with epaulettes, clasps and tassels. In his right hand he held his helmet. His left rested on the sword-pommel, not forgetting the kid glove between hand and pommel.

He was the favorite of the officers' mess. They were all a crowd of good companions, gay, well-bred, proud. They were the officers —this was what made them so proud—of the only cavalry division in the Kingdom. The Germans at that time had twenty cavalry divisions. But no one in Aldershot bothered his head about that. After all, there would never be another European war. Too bad. People ought to have gone back to the system of mediaeval combat. In those days the lords stepped out in front of their ranks, and disposed of the matter among themselves in knightly fashion. The world belonged to the better rider and swordsman.

Now, with the nineteenth century coming to an end, the world had become considerably more sordid. Even to extract a commission in some Indian punitive expedition you had to use all the craft and guile at your command. You needed pull, connections. There was no other road to heroism, a medal, and a spot of glory in the officers' mess. That path was jammed. Everyone wanted to slip through. None succeeded so brilliantly as the youngest sublieutenant of the Queen's Own Hussars.

There were three subjects of conversation: war, sport, and the questions of religion and irreligion. Of course these were purely theoretical questions. They could never be immediate and burning ones until the bullets were whistling around your head. What a shame that they would never hear such music!

Among Winston Churchill's companions of youth some fell in the Boer War, and the great majority in the first World War. Only two or three battered veterans are still alive. These, gouty, but indestructible, are now hunting through the townships where they are pensioned, in search of Hitler's parachute raiders.

The young English officers, unlike their German colleagues, did not live a narrow, secluded, barrack-yard existence. Nor were they, like them, regarded as beings of a higher order. No British

Prime Minister would confess, as the Imperial Chancellor von Bethmann-Hollweg did, that the greatest pride of his life was his position as a reserve major in the Landwehr, the National Guard. But in England promising subalterns were welcome guests in political society. It was not at all unusual for a man to move from the barracks to the House of Commons.

Young Churchill's celebrity soon spread beyond Aldershot. He was invited to a party at Devonshire House after the Ministerial banquet. Here he met Mr. George Curzon, the newly appointed Under Secretary of State for Foreign Affairs. Mr. Curzon was later to be a great British statesman, Viceroy of India, Chief of the Foreign Office. In 1895 he was still a rather bashful young man who nevertheless explained to Second Lieutenant Churchill on the evening of their first meeting that although his position was a small one, he hoped, as the representative of the Foreign Office in the House of Commons, to have a share in making the foreign policy.

Winston Churchill was much agitated on hearing this. Was some other youth to make a swift career ahead of him under his very nose? A few days later he himself gave his companions a small dinner, and the toast he proposed was to "Those yet under twenty-one years of age who in twenty years will control the destinies of the British Empire."

It was a farewell party. For in Cuba a rebellion had broken out against Spanish rule. It was such a chance as could no longer be found in the Empire at all. The seven seas were sunning themselves in deceptive peace. But after seven months' peaceful soldiering Winston Churchill was tired of peace. A friend of his father's, Sir Henry Wolff, was serving as British Ambassador at Madrid. Through Wolff's mediation Churchill was invited by the Captain-General of Spain, the famous Marshal Martinez Campos, to join in his expedition to suppress the rebellion.

And so Churchill could make comfortable—well, not exactly comfortable, but cheap—use of the ten weeks of leave that he had coming to him from his regiment. Having spent all his money on

EARLY MILITARY CAREER

Winston Churchill at the age of twenty-one in the uniform of the Fourth
Hussars

polo ponies he could not afford a hunting trip to Africa in any case.

All of his money meant, aside from the ridiculously small pay of a lieutenant, a yearly allowance of five hundred pounds from his mother. He knew that Lady Randolph, now a widow, could not easily save this sum from out of her dowry, the only capital she had left after the death of her husband. Lady Randolph at forty was as fascinating as on the day of her debut; but if it costs money to be a beautiful woman, it costs even more to remain a beautiful woman. Winston's relationship with his mother was now like that between brother and sister, and he was resolved not to be an expense to her much longer. Had he not been a first-class writer at school? He offered himself to a penny paper as Cuban war correspondent. He sent home five travel articles, at five pounds each. It was to be a few years yet before he got $2500 per article, making him the highest-paid journalist in the world next to Lloyd George, even $500 ahead of the Duce, who has never forgiven Churchill his advantage.

Early in November, 1895, Churchill left for Havana. He had to change boats at New York. And so for the first time he saw his mother's home city. A friend of the Jerome family, Mr. Bourke Cockran, was waiting for him at the pier, and looked after the young visitor with good old-fashioned American hospitality.

Bourke Cockran was a remarkable man. His huge skull, gleaming eyes and mobile countenance physically reminded young Churchill of the portraits of Charles James Fox. Mr. Cockran's physical appearance was impressive enough; the impression was strengthened the moment he opened his mouth. It was the first time that Winston Churchill had ever heard the dynamic American language from the mouth of one of its best speakers in that age. Even during his early days he had a fine ear for the power of language, which later was to be his own special weapon. He had never heard such conversation as Mr. Cockran's "either in point, in rotundity, in antithesis, or in comprehension." Even decades later he still felt that he had never met another speaker with the acuteness and individuality of this American politician.

Originally Bourke Cockran was a Democrat and a great man in Tammany. Mr. Bryan's Free Silver campaign drove him into the Republican camp, where he soon stood out as a leader. Still, when the currency issue was out of the way, he returned to his old party. Of course both sides reproached him with inconsistency. But Mr. Cockran always hotly denied this accusation. "Frequently recurring to the first principles of the American Constitution," he declared, his complete scheme of political thought permitted him to present a sincere and effective front in every direction according to changing circumstances. He was individualist, democrat, capitalist—but above all a Free-Trader, adhering to the one doctrine that united all the others. Throughout his life he fought against socialists, inflationists, and protectionists; and indeed Bourke Cockran's life was one endless fight.

This New York politician, more than any other one man, served as Winston Churchill's model. He too left his traditional party, and later returned to it. He too was individualist, democrat, capitalist—though without capital—and Free-Trader above all. He too has battled throughout his career against socialists, inflationists and protectionists. And he too has maintained with all his might the lifelong opinion that "first principles" are what count, and not the changing needs of parties.

But years were still to pass before this realization matured in his mind. Meanwhile the two young Englishmen took a look at New York by day and night. For in the company of our knight errant there was another adventurous officer, Reginald Barnes, who was to be a Divisional Commander in France during the first World War.

Arrived in Havana, the two young subalterns were treated as members of an important mission, sent at a time of stress by a mighty power and old ally. The harder they tried to clear up the apparent misunderstanding, the more profound was the respect surrounding them. They had no objections when this respect took the form of delivering immense shipments of oranges and boxes of pitch-black cigars to their hotel. But they felt out of place when they were honored as the secret emissaries of Great Britain. After all, their expedition was a mere private matter.

Here Winston Churchill was mistaken. To the Spaniards there was no such thing as a private matter when the fate of their crown colony, the Pearl of the Antilles, was in question. With an astonishment that gradually grew into a sort of admiration, the English officer learned that the idea of colonies was not, as he had supposed, a British monopoly. Other nations felt their colonial missions equally strongly, even though they might not accomplish that mission with the same imperialist genius. He made note of this Cuban lesson, and at the outbreak of the second World War Churchill was among the champions of the thesis that the natural wealth of the earth should be accessible to all nations and peoples.

Otherwise he did not find much that was admirable about the Spanish expedition. In his first travel letter he wrote: "While the Spanish authorities are masters of the art of suppressing the truth, the Cubans are adepts in inventing falsehoods." Nor was he much charmed with the secret devices that were used in this war. He referred to the rebels' intention to fire the sugar-cane crop by means of phosphorus, thus starting a conflagration without exposing the culprits to detection. Such fighting methods were not taught at Aldershot; he thought them unworthy of a gentleman. He was not to have a much higher opinion of the dive bombers, parachute-flyers and Fifth Columnists when the time came. He would even have some apology to make to the half-naked and half-starved Cuban rebels when he found himself confronted with Mr. Hitler's methods.

His second story as a war correspondent dealt with the difficulty of finding his own army. Only after infinite complications and confusion did he succeed in joining the mobile column under the command of General Valdez, which had just left Santa Clara for Sanctus Spiritus. Between the two towns were forty miles of road flanked on both sides by the rebels. "They are everywhere and nowhere," declared a friendly Spanish lieutenant who answered to the surprising name of Juan O'Donell, and was a son of the Duke of Tetuan. "Fifty of our horsemen can go where they please—two can't go anywhere."

It was really a bandit war—petty criminal fighting for a great cause. This led Churchill in his second report to make a remark whose spirit he has remained true to all his life: "I sympathize with the revolution—not with the revolutionaries!"

The *Daily Graphic* published his five reports simply with his initials, with no signature.

Sitting down to a very simple dinner, which however was served in polished grandeur, the English war tourist explained to the Spanish Dukes' sons and other Señores why he sympathized with the revolution. After all, it was the Cubans' own country, and they wanted to be free men, and—

—and ping, ping, enemy bullets whizzed from ambush about the officers' table. The Señores jumped up in panic. Only Winston Churchill did not stir. On the contrary he bit heartily into his cold drumstick. He bent down to do so. A bullet flew over his head, missing him by a hair. Had he really a charmed life?

Or was he thus imperturbable and wise even in youth? "I feel ridiculously old," he wrote to his mother the following day. It was his twenty-first birthday.

He took home another lesson from the expedition. It struck him that the Spanish infantry was able to march eighteen or nineteen hours a day in that murderous climate without looking in the least weary by evening. What was the reason? The siesta, of course! The day was carefully divided up: eight miles' march in the early hours of the morning, ending by nine o'clock. Then breakfast, an important meal with coffee and stew for the troops, and the greenest of grass for the horses. Then the siesta—sleep until two o'clock. Then marching until darkness. Winston Churchill acquired the siesta habit. He has found it most useful in the crises he has been through. As First Lord of the Admiralty in the first World War he discovered he could add two hours to his working day by taking a short nap after lunch. It is only in the present war that he has surrendered the habit of a lifetime. The old man in a hurry has not another second to lose.

As if in belated celebration of his twenty-first birthday, the following day brought the first skirmish of any consequence. Of course Churchill and his English companion marched immediately beside the general who led the infantry attack. The rebels let the Spanish troops come up to within three hundred yards; then white puffs of smoke began to go up all along the edge of the woods, and the first casualties fell around Churchill.

The infantry replied with rapid fire. They slunk up to the deadly forest at the double, Churchill still in the first rank, as cool as if he were quite uninvolved, admired the fighting spirit of the Spanish soldiers. Excellent troops, he said, but still they were not likely to bring the Cuban adventure to a speedy end. He stood in the midst of the fire-spouting jungle, as casual as if it were the parade ground of Aldershot. Hearing the rattle of Mauser pistols around him, he realized that the rebels had fled, and that there were merely a few of those left behind being liquidated. Of course methodical pursuit of the enemy was not possible in the impenetrable primeval forest.

General Valdez' column reached its goal at La Jicotea. The two English subalterns' leave had expired. When Churchill bade good-bye to General Martinez Campos the latter hung the Order of Military Merit, First Class, around his neck.

Twenty years later Don Alfonso, King of Spain, bestowed on him still another order for services in Cuba to the army of the kingdom. As he did so, the monarch whispered: "Allow me the pleasure. I am delighted to honor an Englishman. You know, the common people and I are the only ones in Spain who love England."

For Winston Churchill the Cuban adventure always had meaning. Not because of the rain of bullets in whose midst he stood. Since that time more things than bullets have rained around his head. No, it was because this was his first irruption into print.

CHAPTER IV

India

SUDDENLY writing became very important to him. The young officer regarded the art of the pen not as a departure from the art of soldiering, but rather as its complement. Twenty-year-old Churchill was basking in the sunset of an intellectual age. Great gentlemen poured out their intellect (never uncivilly or intrusively close to genius), their mellowness and cultivation upon quite petty questions. Heads of foam bubbled up from Ciceronian periods. Over table conversations in which political enemies were the best of friends, you thought yourself almost in Athens, if not in Paris.

Winston Churchill was not yet able to produce essays or learned dissertations. He lacked the years at Oxford, and was beginning to feel it. So he resolutely wrote a vigorous short story, "Man Overboard." The magazine where it appeared remarked in a note that the author was not the famous Winston Churchill—an American novelist now long past the peak of his fame—but the son of Lord Randolph Churchill. He was never to find time for a second attempt. All his life, by his own confession, he has remained a would-be author of short stories. But there was a novel in his head. It turned out to be a slender book on which he worked almost four years. At the end of the four years *Savrola* appeared, first in *Macmillan's Magazine*, then in an American book edition, and finally as a book in England.

Savrola is remarkable not as a literary work, but as a youthful confession. Churchill gave it the sub-title, "The tale of a revolution in Laurania." Laurania—which stands for some Ruritania—is a republic, and young Savrola revolutionizes it. In Savrola Win-

ston Churchill is depicting himself. When he got home to London
he set up in bachelor quarters that corresponded to a hair with
the dwelling of his hero. He portrayed himself even down to the
way he smoked a cigarette. Winston at twenty-one was immensely
occupied with himself. Shortly before, he had made the naive
confession: "I am not selfish. Self-centered? Maybe."

Now he had a short breathing-spell. In the spring of 1896 the
regiment marched from Aldershot to Hounslow, where it awaited
its departure to India. The officers of the Fourth Hussars were
to remain for fourteen years in India. Six months of preparation
—or really home furlough—was none too much for this. Meanwhile London was preparing for the Diamond Jubilee, to come
the following year. It was a brilliant summer season, the first
young Churchill had been through. His Aunt Lilian even invited
him to a dinner for the Prince of Wales at her castle, Deepdene.
It was an intimate little affair for fourteen people. But when
Churchill missed his train, with the next one not leaving for an
hour, the party had to sit down to table thirteen strong. Of this,
however, His Royal Highness would have none. The Prince of
Wales, punctual to the minute according to his habit, had appeared at eight-thirty. The young man in a hurry appeared breath-
lessly at twelve minutes to nine, having flung himself into evening dress in his train compartment, to the great astonishment
of his fellow-travellers.

"Don't they teach you to be punctual in your regiment, Winston?" asked the Prince of Wales in a very grave tone, looking at
his friend Colonel Brabazon, the regimental commander.

Next day this was the talk of all London. And indeed what
should they talk of? The dark shadows rising in South Africa
were no table conversation, after all. The German Emperor, who
had just sent off the famous Kruger telegram—another case of
Prussian saber-rattling—could scarcely be mentioned in polite
society at all any more.

In late autumn they set off for India. The troop-ship took
twelve hundred men from Southampton to Bombay harbor in

twenty-three days. It was a hot and fatiguing voyage. Churchill, going at his furious pace as always, could not wait to get ground under his feet again. He jumped ashore from the little boat that brought in the passengers so violently and unluckily that he altogether smashed his right shoulder, already injured by the childhood accident. It is unfortunately on record that he uttered most unchristian oaths. What was to become of his polo career in the Indian Army?

Of course polo was the main thing. It began every day at five in the afternoon. This was the hour that all the white officers in the brown empire eagerly awaited. Until eight o'clock dinner they raced hither and thither on their ponies, dripping sweat and oblivious of the world. The meal came at eight-thirty in the Casino. The regimental band played, and glasses clinked. Then they sat in the moonlight, smoking in silence until eleven. And so to bed.

This was the life for a gentleman in the Indian Army, even though most of the officers were never entirely free of money worries. The pay was fourteen shillings a day, plus three pounds a month for the maintenance of the horses. On this, however, each man had to maintain a little army of colored boys, and keep up an appearance no less lordly than that of His Excellency Lord Sandhurst, the General. Young Churchill could not go far on his five hundred pounds a year allowance. Besides, he was more than tired of accepting the money from his mother. He began to reflect.

Reflection carries one far afield. Mr. Churchill himself does not know how the philosopher in him happened to awake precisely in the camp of the Fourth Hussars in Bangalore, India. But it is a fact that it was here, in the midst of a group of carefree young officers, under a dark-blue southern sky, that a fierce intellectual hunger came upon him. Someone in the party mentioned the Socratic method, and suddenly the puzzle jumped at the young officer: this Socrates must have called into being something very explosive. Otherwise there could not have been a choice between

his life and the life of the Athenian Executive. Why had his
fame lasted through the ages? There was nothing about it in the
Manual of Arms.

Winston Churchill wished that he had a Socrates of his own,
a teacher to whom he could listen every day, and whom he could
cross-question. Of course he never found one—not in Bangalore,
nor anywhere else ever. He earned his own intellectual development by the sweat of his brow. Probably the most remarkable, if
also the most neglected, drama in the man's growth is the way
in which he consolidated and buttressed his rich life of action
by constant intellectual struggle with himself. He had no mental
stimulation from outside, no partner to play ball with. The brilliant conversational artists of Oscar Wilde, the acutely arguing
shadows of G. B. S. were not upon his stage. He had to build up
his own ethics, his understanding of men and things, and finally
the wisdom of his old age, from inside outward.

Probably his mother still understood him best. A brilliant
social career in London had not dulled her native American per-
ceptions. She had enjoyed only the fashionable education of a
well-bred lady of the good old days. But when her son wrote from
India that he wanted something to read she realized at once that
he meant neither the Bibliothèque Rose nor yellow-backed railway novels. She remembered how Lord Randolph had positively
lived in Gibbon's *Decline and Fall of the Roman Empire.* He had
been able to recite whole pages by heart. His own style was
strongly under the influence of the historian.

She sent her son Dean Milman's eight-volume edition. It was
the first scholarly work that Winston Churchill ever devoured.
His regret at the lack of a university education now became fully
conscious. Nevertheless his inborn realism prevented him from
overestimating one-sided intellectualism. The school system had
not been good for him personally. If he were to write his own
Republic, he said later, he would require sons to learn a trade
at seventeen or eighteen, or to work in the fields or in a factory,
with plenty of poetry, song, dancing, drill and gymnastics in their

spare time, and only the superior and most worthy ones should enjoy the coveted privilege of higher education, which would thus no longer be cheapened. This sounds very much like Platonic idealism. (Winston Churchill, who has never learned any more Greek than the alphabet, is fundamentally a Hellenic spirit.)

He plunged into Plato's *Republic* and the *Politics* of Aristotle, edited by Dr. Welldon, his headmaster at Harrow. He studied Schopenhauer, Malthus, Darwin. Philosophy led him to religion. The trifling conversations of the officers' mess took on a deeper meaning. The young gentlemen, living here in (no doubt very comfortable) banishment, all asked, each in his own time, what was the meaning of it all. Was there a survival after death? Had we ever been here before? Would we meet again beyond? Did some higher providence care for the world, or were things just drifting on somehow?

Religious visionaries were something that the Hussars' camp at Bangalore produced but seldom. In the English army people agreed that what counted was to try one's best to live an honorable life, do one's duty, be faithful to friends and kind to the weak and poor. Honor, fairness, and tolerance, not denomination, were important.

At church parade Lieutenant Churchill sometimes would march to the Roman Catholic church, sometimes to the Protestant. It made little difference to him, although he came of a family that had always suspected the Pope of standing behind the Fenians. Not too many years before, Grandfather, the Duke of Marlborough, had written to Winston's father: "Your aunt who is with us now is most unhappy. For I fear she is a Roman Catholic at heart and does not like to say so. If this be true it would be much better for her to declare her mind, and then, of course, however we might be grieved, the matter would never be alluded to in conversation."

This atmosphere of well-bred, philanthropic intolerance was the one Churchill had been bred to. In Harrow they trained him to be a patient churchgoer. In India he began to ask questions, to doubt. This doubt was strengthened by books—*The Martyrdom of Man,* by Winwood Read, Lecky's *Rise and Influence of Rationalism* and *History of European Morals*—and above all by the skepticism of the great Gibbon. He was on his way to becoming an atheist of the sort that was springing up like weeds at the turn of the century. But coming for the first time under the fire of the Indian rebels, he asked his Maker for special protection after all, and he was very grateful to the Lord for bringing him back safe and sound to tea at camp.

The oftener and the more closely perils encircled Churchill—and from now on they would be repeated ever more frequently—the more his rationalistic arrogance evaporated. As for everything else in his life, he had also to work for his own faith. And once again we see his wonderful growing: belief in fairness and punctiliousness turning into faith in Providence, from which all fair play springs. When Winston Churchill defends the Square Deal today, he is the champion not merely of the Empire alone. He feels himself wholly impregnated by his timeless mission; he is a warrior of God.

He did not realize all this himself in those days. In his first year of Indian service he regarded himself as above all a polo champion. The tournament for the Golconda Cup at Hyderabad took place six weeks after the arrival of the 4th Hussars. In the first round the 4th Hussars' team encountered the representatives of the famous Golconda Brigade, the bodyguard of the Nizam of Hyderabad. The Golcondas were the dead-sure winners of the tournament. All Hyderabad was gathered around the field. A review of the entire British garrison preceded the match. The elephants saluted by raising their trunks as they paraded past the polo teams. A vast concourse of Indian spectators formed a thoroughly expert audience. All of colonial society, from the Viceroy to the last white man, was in attendance. Everyone felt sorry for the 4th Hussars, who would have the misfortune to be put out of the tournament after the very first match.

The team of the 4th Hussars, with Lieutenant Churchill at center, first beat the Golconda killers nine to three, then all the other teams in rapid succession. Awaking from the intoxication of victory, Churchill remembered that he could scarcely play polo at all, because he had a broken right shoulder.

The hot season began. Now came three months' summer furlough in England. On the boat Churchill made the acquaintance of Colonel Ian Hamilton, twenty years his senior. Here developed the first of those lifelong friendships that were to bind Winston Churchill with men so much older than himself. Odd how the veterans regarded the young man in a hurry as their equal. From now on Ian Hamilton was to accompany Churchill in all his roamings. Years later, when England regarded him as an apostate for going over from the Conservative to the Liberal Party, Ian Hamilton was to be one of the few diehard fire-eaters who stood up for him. "He will come back. His colour is true blue" (the Conservative color), "none of these modern synthetic dyes." As they were sailing through the Red Sea in 1897, and passionately arguing about the new Graeco-Turkish conflict, neither of them knew that a ne'er-do-well village boy in the Austrian frontier community of Braunau am Inn was just committing his first pocket-pickings. Forty years later Ian Hamilton was to call on the sneak thief—an arrived man by now—and, returning, to tell his friend Winston: "I can't see what you have against this man Hitler. He's wonderful, he's charming. He is a great man, incapable of lying, and he wants nothing but peace." Of course when General Hamilton made this acute analysis he was, it must be admitted, past eighty years old.

There is no furlough from world events. Scarcely had Churchill arrived to breathe the gentle air and tread the green lawns before he read in the paper that the Pathan tribesmen on the Indian frontier were in revolt, and that a Field Force of three brigades under Sir Bindon Blood was to go out after them. Sir Bindon Blood, past ninety, died last year. During his lifetime he bore the name of "The Father of the British Army." Young Churchill had

already met him at Deepdene, his Aunt Lilian's house; of course
he had immediately wrung from the old warrior a promise to take
him along when it should really mean serious action—as serious,
that is, as these ridiculous little campaigns that Churchill hoped
to spend his life at could ever be.

From the green lawns of Goodwood he went to the next train.
He got a connecting vessel at once. Before reporting to Sir Bindon
he found opportunity to get hired by the *Allahabad Pioneer,* a
leading English-language newspaper in India, as a war correspondent. His mother meanwhile arranged in London for his reports
to appear also in the *Daily Telegraph* (then still a popular penny
paper, not the semi-official organ it is today), again at five pounds
per article.

Churchill was a reporter with journalism in his blood. He made
friends with Major Deane, an officer of the India Intelligence Service, and went with this wily politician in uniform to visit the
rebellious tribal leaders, several of whom proved to be not altogether averse from taking bribes. As a result he was better and
more quickly informed of many occurrences at the scene of war
than his own General Staff. His reports regularly scooped the
official army reports of General Sir Bindon Blood.

Nor can it be said that he was a bashful reporter. In the *Pioneer*
we read, from his own pen: "The courage and the resolution of
Lieutenant Winston Churchill, 4th Hussars, the correspondent
of the Pioneer newspaper with the force, who made himself useful
at critical moments . . ."

He did not hide his light under a bushel, but neither did he
exaggerate. Colonel Ian Hamilton records: "Churchill was out
all day, stalking the enemy snipers, or relieving some picket whose
position seemed to open an opportunity for bloodshed. At night
he wrote copiously."

The first days of the Indian campaign introduced a new element into Churchill's life—whiskey. He himself had begun in the
brandy-and-soda era. His father and model would have turned
away in disgust if anyone had offered him the new "smoky-tasting"

drink. At Sandhurst and Aldershot drunkenness was regarded as unworthy of the dignity of an officer. Of course they were not prohibitionists. Prohibitionists and drunkards alike were considered contemptible weaklings. And the drinking of whiskey was the first step on the downward path.

Hard days in the field in India changed all that. Whiskey did not taste of smoke at all now, but of encouragement. And courage was going to be needed. Churchill realized it as he put over his shoulder the lanyard of a fallen friend whose death he had seen the day before.

On the march to the Mamund country Churchill came under fire. The wild Mamunds, a tribe utterly pestilential in their cruelty, attacked the British forces. "If you want to see a fight," Sir Bindon Blood remarked to his young friend, "you may ride back and join Jeffrey's." Of course Churchill put spurs to his horse. He came up with the foremost advance guard of the Bengal Lancers. It was their task to clear the valley completely of the enemy. While all this was going on under a constant hail of bullets, the infantry pushed forward from the rear. They were to storm the mountainside, and to smoke out the rebel villages up above. Churchill turned over his pony to his boy, and scrambled up the cliffs with the infantry, sweating in the murderous Indian midday heat, not without worry because the Sandhurst teaching about "dispersion of forces" was still fresh in his mind, and pushed always further and further forward by his irrepressible delight in battle.

When they had mounted the slope the forest above came alive. An enemy rifle blazed behind every rock. The wild men rushed down from the trees, flinging themselves upon the Sikh infantry. Barbarian banners flapped in the faces of the intruders. Swords flashed through the air. From the mountain slopes in the background an army of apes, swinging from tree to tree, sprang at the English troops. No, those were not apes. Those were the Pathan swordsmen, their reserves now coming to the assault.

It was a hand-to-hand combat. Churchill, who as an officer of

ourse carried no gun, borrowed his Sikh boy's rifle. Methodically
e cleared the terrain around him. Ten, eleven, twelve bullets hit
he mark.

The hoarse bellowing of the Pathans made communication
among the English troops impossible. They broke up into small
groups. Churchill, turning around for a second, saw beside him a
ace streaming with blood, a man whose right eye had been cut
out by a barbaric knife. The wounded were the gravest worry. On
he Indian front, just as today on the German, it was better not
o leave them behind. It was a matter of honor with the enemy
o mutilate wounded Englishmen fearfully.

Consequently Churchill was trying to drag the wounded man
down the slope. His group withdrew. They had stumbled but a
ew steps downhill when twenty or thirty wild figures blocked their
retreat. The Sikh who was carrying the wounded man dropped,
shot through the head. His companion, the regimental adjutant,
was also felled. Four men struggled to carry him away. A knot of
wild men assaulted them. Their leader cut the dead officer across
he face with his sword—four, five times.

Now there was but one thing in Churchill's mind; he had been
fencing champion of his school. He would fight it out with the
Pathan chief, man to man. In a moment of strange calm that came
upon him amidst the hellish uproar he drew his long cavalry
sword. But the savage had already given way by twenty paces.
Then, from among his native warriors, he hurled a great stone
at Churchill. It missed.

The Sikhs had retreated. The young lieutenant stood alone
against the bestial horde. He thrust his sword back into the scab-
bard. Here only the revolver was of any use. At that each bullet
must find its man, and he must have opportunity to reload several
times. He had no chance whatever to get out alive.

He pulled the trigger—and the revolver balked. He squeezed a
second, a third time. Whether he was firing now he could not tell.
Pandemonium had broken loose. The long-haired Sikhs had returned to cut their lieutenant free. He borrowed a rifle again, and

this time he aimed straight, with an easy hand, although his breath was whistling and his heart beating wildly. He fired thirty or forty rounds, now at a range of from eighty to a hundred and twenty yards. There was no telling whether each bullet went home. But, by Jove, each one was meant to kill.

In his book *The Malakand Field Force*—unfortunately now long out of print—he describes this scene calmly and dispassionately. The book, published in two volumes, gives a complete description of the three years he served in India, almost all the time amid severe fighting.

He recounts the adventures of Mamund Valley, which was finally purged of the wild men. But every single village that had to be cleaned out cost the lives of two or three British officers and fifteen or twenty native soldiers. Military honor, even the young Churchill considered, is a cruel sport. Always in the thick of it himself, urged by a demonic pugnacity, he early became a pacifist by conviction. Nothing less than the life of his nation and the freedom of mankind could bring him voluntarily to say Yes to a war.

The second half of his Indian adventures took place on the celebrated Tirah expedition. Churchill was transferred to the 31st Punjab Infantry Regiment, which was so decimated by earlier battles that except for the Colonel there were only three white officers left alive. Even so it was unusual for a cavalry officer, and a celebrated polo champion at that, to get into the infantry. A few of his fellow-officers laughed. But Churchill paid no attention. He cared nothing for the finer distinctions of the brass hats. He thought the good soldier was the one who fought where help was needed. And so he served successively on three continents (after having tasted blood on a fourth, in the Western Hemisphere), in the following regiments: 4th Hussars, 31st Punjab Infantry, 21st Lancers, the South African Light Horse, the Oxfordshire Yeomanry, the 2d Grenadier Guards, the Royal Scots Fusiliers, and lastly the Oxfordshire Artillery.

Churchill remembered with pleasure his service with the dark kinned Punjabs. They were obviously glad to fight under a white officer, and when fighting they watched him carefully to see how things were going. As long as the officer was smiling, they were cheerful. At Tirah they grinned uninterruptedly, for Winston Churchill's smile never faded from his face, now burnt a dark red. He cheered his brown boys on through the rain of bullets.

Meanwhile, however, the gentlemen in his regular garrison at Bangalore decided he had had "furlough" enough, and summoned him back to his old regiment. He had now to do his regular routine duty, autumn maneuvers and all, popping off blank cartridges in sham fights while two thousand miles away the bullets among which he had been commanding his soldiers a fortnight before were still pattering.

There was but one authority before whom the generals of the Indian Army trembled—his beautiful Mamma in London. Here was one American mother who never dreamed of not letting her boy go to war. She personally besieged Lord Wolseley and Lord, later Field-Marshal, Roberts to bring her son back to the front.

Lord Roberts expressed his regrets in a polite letter: Winston had already been in the Malakand Field Force. Accordingly he had no moral right to join the Tirah Field Force. Others wanted their chance too.

Mother and son were deeply disappointed. But just at ebb-tide, then as always, Winston Churchill developed unexampled energy. He used his ten days of Christmas furlough to present himself before the Viceroy, Lord Elgin, at Calcutta. As if His Lordship had known that life would soon bring him into much closer contact with this young man, he granted the request, and arranged for a new assignment at the front. Churchill became adjutant to the brilliant commander Sir William Lockhart.

Nevertheless the feeling in India was not favorable to Churchill. His book, which had just appeared, had enjoyed too noisy a success. After all, it was the first success of his life. Though the reviewers did revel in the numerous typographical errors, they could not help feeling the force of the descriptions, of the dramatic presentation, and above all the shrewd, penetrating remarks and observations.

Perhaps the remarks were a shade too penetrating. It was not merely an account of military events. It was full of advice about all kinds of things. It discussed frontier policy, even conscription at home, and it lectured the government of India. Most of the remarks are definitely sane and wise. The reforms that Churchill proposed were in fact carried out to a great extent in the course of time. All in all, the future statesman and war lord announced himself quite plainly in the book.

To Colonel Blimp, however, it was the composition of a subaltern who patted Viceroys and Field-Marshals on the head. Especially the author's sympathy for the savages was sharply condemned. Why, had they not come close to butchering the man himself on countless occasions? And then this youngster talked of their innate conceptions of honor and their wholly understandable realism!

CHAPTER V

Twenty Minutes in the Soudan

KITCHENER remained irreconcilable. Young Churchill's reputation now was strangely double-edged. His readers were enthusiastic, his fellow-soldiers at Bangalore were proud of him. His commanders, beaming, slapped him on the back. But whenever a few intimates happened to be together, the mess buzzed with words like "medal-hunter" and "self-advertiser." Even in London the brass hats asked one another how it happened that this young second-lieutenant could manage to get furlough enough to be in every campaign. A couple of years' regular drill would do him no harm. Churchill had not, indeed, invented the strange duality of an officer who at the same time was a war correspondent; there were several of that type in the colonial theaters of war, but they were soon to be compelled by decree to choose between sword and pen. After all, it would never do for a young subaltern to dispense praise and blame to his superiors. What did he know of the higher strategy, anyway? The dilettante!

Dilettante was the one word capable of exciting Sir Herbert, later Lord, Kitchener. He forgot that he had made his own career sixteen years before by an arbitrary act that required an extension of furlough and the help of the press. Today he maintained the strictest discipline. When the Sirdar set out for the Soudan campaign, and of course an application for a commission in the campaign arrived from a certain sub-lieutenant at Bangalore, the reply was one syllable: no.

During the first World War Kitchener and Churchill sat together in the Cabinet, one as Secretary for War, the other as First Lord of the Admiralty. In the course of time a quite cordial rela-

tionship developed between the two. Or, more accurately, Kitchener surrendered to Winston Churchill's charm and enthusiasm.
Rather amused and a bit grouchy, he became reconciled to the
"dilettante."

Even as a young officer Churchill would not take no for an
answer. There was another furlough due—how on earth did he
do it?—and he made use of it to go to London. There lived his
oldest ally, his clever Mamma.

Once again Lady Randolph pulled all her silken strings. For
two months she lunched and dined her way through the entire
list of British generals. After all, they had been friends of her
late husband's. That would excuse an occasional torchlike American glance, which even the most intrepid warrior could not resist.

An accident came to her aid. The aged Lord Salisbury, for the
third time Prime Minister and omnipotent leader of the Conservatives—though the real power, Joe Chamberlain with the gold-
rimmed monocle in the marble mask, stood behind him—read
The Malakand Field Force. He invited the author to Downing
Street. Churchill was overjoyed. How could he know that one
day he would be master there himself, a mightier ruler than even
the great and wise Lord Salisbury? All he knew was that for
twenty minutes he would breathe the sacred air of the Cabinet,
in which the fate of Empire was decided.

The interview lasted far beyond twenty minutes. Half an hour
passed, and still the great man did not dismiss his youthful visitor.
When the stroke of the grandfather's clock warningly recalled the
frantic schedule of the day, Lord Salisbury settled back comfortably in his armchair again. Winston Churchill had no way of
knowing why the old gentleman was savoring the conversation in
such epicurean fashion. In reality Lord Salisbury was thinking
back to vanished days, the one special pleasure allotted to white
hair. Then he said with old-fashioned formality to the little lieutenant: "I hope you will allow me to say how much you remind
me of your father, with whom so many important days of my political life were lived." They were most unpleasant days. Never

had even an opponent involved the Salisbury Government in such critical situations as his own Chancellor of the Exchequer when he laid down his office. But memory gilds even bitterness. "If there is anything at any time that I can do which would be of assistance to you, pray do not fail to let me know!"

Churchill took a few days to assimilate this phrase. Then he turned to the Private Secretary of the Prime Minister, Sir Schomberg M'Donnell.

The next day a telegram from Lord Salisbury went off to the Sirdar. The following morning the answer was there: the Sirdar was sorry. He had all the officers he required, and if any vacancies occurred, there were others he would be bound to prefer before the young officer in question.

Finally drawing-room strategy proved more powerful than all Kitchener's military art. Lady St. Helier, a friend of Mamma's, spoke to Sir Evelyn Wood, the Adjutant-General in the War Office. At the moment Sir Evelyn was only an office general. But the stiff-necked independence of the Sirdar, "who, after all, is Commander in Field only of a very small part of the British Army," had long since got on the nerves of the office generals. The chance for a slight riposte must not be allowed to pass.

Of course the War Office could not force an officer into Kitchener's Egyptian Army. But what was the British contingent for, which was also leaving to join the Expeditionary Force?

"You have been attached as a supernumerary lieutenant to the 21st Lancers for the Soudan Campaign." Churchill got this letter forty-eight hours after Lady St. Helier's intervention. "It is understood that you will proceed at your own expense and that in the event of your being killed or wounded in the impending operations, or for any other reason, no charge of any kind will fall on the British Army funds."

To raise Churchill's spirits still further, the President of the Psychical Research Society begged him to get into communication if something unfortunate should occur.

More pleasant was the agreement with Oliver Borthwick, son

of the proprietor of the *Morning Post,* Colonel Blimp's own paper. Churchill received credentials as a correspondent, at fifteen pounds a column. His rate had tripled since India. When he reported six days later to the Regimental Headquarters at the Abassiyeh Barracks, there was but one worry in this best of all possible worlds: how would Kitchener take it?

The Sirdar simply shrugged when he heard of the War Office ruse. His thick skull was full of greater matters. The battle to annihilate the dervishes had already begun when Churchill arrived, just at the right moment.

The senior officers under whom he was put were not too friendly in their treatment of the uninvited guest. First he was left behind in Assuan to handle the surplus stores. Riding to camp one evening, he lost his way in the desert. For hours and hours he wandered about. His horse went lame. It reared, and assiduously kept its rider from falling asleep in the saddle. Then he began to be tortured by thirst. The night lay dark upon the desert. In its utter obscurity the lone man traveled in a circle. Not until the small hours did the stars rise. Eventually he could make out Orion, which points to the north. Gratefully he followed the faint light.

After two more hours he found the Nile—a spot where a few stunted palms grew. Horse and rider drank their fill. Then it was easier to go back into the desert. Somewhere he found a village. He wanted to inquire for his detachment. But the one word of Arabic he understood was baksheesh. The villagers who howled and danced around him received their tribute. He could get no information from them in return. Then with the point of his sword he drew on a mud wall a couple of crude figures of horsemen. Ah, now they understood him. In that direction, over there . . . no, there . . . wrong—there, there was where he would find his people.

At last by evening he reached the detachment. It was an advanced outpost. Some Lancers had just tracked down two dervish warriors in the bushes along the Nile. Churchill himself at once set out to hunt for enemies in the brush. His incredible good fortune never deserted him. Within an hour a long-bearded, half-naked wild man leapt from the scrub. Churchill's eager eye spotted him. He put spurs to his horse, snatched the cavalry saber from its sheath.

"Stop that nonsense!" the long-bearded, half-naked wild man shouted at him in elegant cockney. It was an English spy—painted or merely sunburned, there was no telling which.

The detachment laughed when Churchill came back from his adventure. He scarcely felt like laughing. A thoughtful Colonel put him in charge of the lame horses. The tragi-comic procession was led by two Lancers on donkey-back; then came the ailing horses, next the donkey boys, and last Lieutenant Churchill, the author of a famous book about the Indian war, and correspondent of the *Morning Post*. In this fashion they marched to the battle of Omdurman. "They want to break my heart, but I *will* write my book!" Churchill vowed to himself. He was too tough to be broken.

On the evening of August 15 the 21st Lancers crossed the left bank of the Nile at its confluence with the Atbara. In nine days' march they advanced to the camp north of the Shabluka Cataract. It was a perilous march through the desert. All precautions had to be strictly observed; the advance troops that Churchill was allowed to join after he had finally got rid of his sick horses might be in the midst of the enemy at any moment.

Truly? Where could the enemy be? Not a breath blew through the desert. Not the shadow of a grass-tuft appeared, let alone the shadow of a man. Probably the dervishes had retired. No doubt of it, they had crawled away somewhere into the impassable African interior. The road to the city of Omdurman, the dried-mud residence of the Caliph, would be a mere stroll. What a shame!

The flat-bottomed gunboats and the side-wheelers, with an endless line of sailboats laden with munitions and stores in tow, successfully forced the cataract. One of the gunboats was commanded by Junior Lieutenant, later Earl, Beatty. Churchill was—

shall we say delighted?—to see how freshly washed and ironed Comrade Beatty always looked in his white sailor uniform, while he himself was bathed in the sweat of his horse and the dust of the desert. This mild competition in dress did not prevent the two young officers from drinking each other's health of an evening in champagne, of which the gunboat's belly was full. Unfortunately they could not clink glasses. Lieutenant Beatty had to hurl the bottle overboard, where Lieutenant Churchill would catch it with monkey agility. Years later, when the one was First Lord and the other an admiral, in the midst of the first World War, the two were to recall this encounter.

This was to be another sort of war. The wars at the turn of the century were still a sporting pastime. No one so much as dreamed that he might fall. True, thirty or forty in every regiment bit the dust of the desert. They were simply unlucky. The more fortunate escaped with trifling scratches. Almost all of them fell on the Western Front fifteen years later, and only a few are left today, ready to die before the German tanks.

The German Army, incidentally, was represented by an observer in the Soudan campaign. The line of battle was drawn up on September 1st. Baron von Tiedemann, envoy of the Great General Staff in Berlin, monocle in eye, saber-cuts on cheek and all, could not choke back the remark: "This is the first of September. Our great day and now your great day: Sedan and Soudan!"

How despicable this comparison by the military tourist sounded —how arrogant! Sedan and Soudan! Germany's glory against a trifling success! But Lieutenant Churchill held himself in check. After all, the Germans generally were such charming people.

The fact that the Expeditionary Force had finally encountered the enemy, who was far from having crawled away into the desert sands, was reported to the Sirdar by none other than Churchill. With a little grin his commander singled him out for the job from among the officers of the advance guard.

Now that he was about to meet Kitchener face to face for the first time, Churchill was so excited that he began by leading his horse on foot for a quarter of a mile in order to gain time and compose himself. Then he set off at a trot, which immediately turned into a gallop. What was it they said of his father—"He galloped until he fell"?

Easy, horse, easy! A reconnaissance officer must not arrive breathless and excited. Lieutenant Churchill rode slowly toward the center of the infantry masses. Soon he caught sight of an imposing cavalcade following a bright red banner. The Union Jack flew by the side of the Egyptian flag. Kitchener was riding alone before his Headquarters Staff. His two standard-bearers marched immediately behind him. Then, at a respectful distance, came his entourage.

Easy, horse, easy! There, the horse had described a neat semicircle. The lieutenant came to a halt just in the rear of Omnipotence, saluting.

Kitchener looked at him. Not a muscle moved in the full, red face with its heavy mustache and impenetrable eyes. Of course he knew who stood before him. The Sirdar knew every officer in his army—and the only one he did not know was the one he knew best of all.

"Sir, I have come from the 21st Lancers with a report."

Kitchener did not devour him on the spot. The heavy head nodded faintly. He was ready to listen to the message.

Churchill blurted it out. Again and again he had prepared it on the way, lest he say a word too little or too much. One of the shortest speeches of his life, it was certainly the most difficult. The enemy were in sight, he reported, apparently in large numbers. Their main body lay about seven miles away from his own advance guard. Up to eleven o'clock they remained stationary, but five minutes later they advanced, and forty minutes before this moment they had still been in motion.

"How long do you think I have got?" asked Kitchener, who had gravely taken in every word. Was it possible that the Sirdar was consulting the pushing little lieutenant? War had no terrors left!

"You have got at least an hour, probably an hour and a half, sir," replied Churchill. That was his entire contribution to the strategy of Omdurman.

It was unintentionally misleading. For the dervishes had suddenly come to a halt, and spent the night standing, singing, praying. It was only at dawn on the following day, the historic second of September, 1898, that they attacked. By then Churchill was long since back at his outlying post.

And yet the famous cavalry charge of Omdurman, the next-to-last in history—the Canadians in the first World War executed the last—took about twenty minutes all told. For those twenty minutes Churchill saw red. He was the first officer in the rank.

Of course there was fighting and firing all day, from dawn until late at night. There is no space here to describe the celebrated battle of Omdurman, which has long belonged to military history. We must emphasize just one moment: the 21st Lancers were attacking; the great charge that each man had been dreaming of during the whole march from Cairo had come at last.

The howling dervishes flung themselves among the horses of the Lancers. Not ten yards away Churchill saw the first two enemies in his path. Odd, he noticed that they were dressed in blue. Both fired at him. Odd again, he noticed that he must have remained unhurt. He reached for his Mauser pistol; since his second shoulder injury he had not been very sure of himself with a saber. Knowing this, he had assiduously practised marksmanship during the entire expedition. Precaution is half of courage and the greater part of success.

A trooper behind him dropped from his horse. So one of the two bullets meant for Churchill must have hit him. With swift animal instinct his own pony bounded into a ditch to seek cover. But the ditch was occupied by dozens of dervishes. Churchill shot his way out. He bounded back upon the hard desert ground. A savage fell down before him. A dead man? No, the dead man was drawing his sword. Churchill flung the pony around out of reach of the sword, and at a range of about three yards he shot the man dead with two bullets. He was just settling himself in the saddle when another sword was flung out at him within arm's reach. The antagonists were so close that Churchill could simply clap the muzzle of his revolver to the enemy's head in shooting him down. Ten yards to the left an Arab horseman in bright-colored tunic and steel helmet popped up. Churchill blazed away. The horseman fled at a gallop.

A crowd of hostile riders had now collected forty or fifty yards to his left. Churchill thought he saw indistinctly a couple of brown Lancer uniforms in the turmoil. For that matter, he had straggled from his own troops. Congenital idiot! he cursed himself. What business had he to loiter in the midst of the enemy like this? At last he found his own detachment assembled two hundred yards away. The dervishes were in wild flight. Only one had remained behind. Suddenly he sprang up before the lieutenant, close enough to touch him. The Lancers were so bewildered by this unexpected sight that they clapped spurs to their horses. There was utter confusion. The Arab fell upon Churchill. How unpleasant, it flashed through the latter's head, to keep killing men so close. It was not even a yard's distance. Churchill fired. The Arab collapsed.

This small discomfort was soon overcome. "Did you enjoy yourself?" Churchill asked a sergeant.

After the triumph of Omdurman the Sirdar no longer needed the costly British cavalry. The 21st Lancers were sent home. Once again a war was over. But not for Churchill. He wrote his book about the Soudan campaign. And once again he sat in judgment upon the authorities. Once again he was the champion of the weak.

Why, he asked, was word allowed to circulate in the army that it was the Sirdar's wish to take as few prisoners as possible? Why had Kitchener had the grave of the Mahdi, the Mohammedan shrine, razed by fire from the gunboats? The head of the Mahdi was carried off as a trophy, and his body thrown into the Nile. No doubt the general had had his military reasons. The destruction of their holy place, which they had to watch helplessly, probably made it plain to the Arabs that resistance was useless. But even then, in his formative years, Churchill thought more as a statesman than as a tactician. Great Britain was the greatest Mohammedan state in the world. It was insane to provoke the most sacred feelings of countless millions of subjects. Furthermore it was unchivalrous, and this was what outraged the young lieutenant most deeply. "I shall not hesitate to declare," he wrote, "that to destroy what was holy and sacred with them was a wicked act, of which a true Christian, no less than a philosopher, must express his abhorrence."

This was not pleasant reading for the colonels and generals. They felt that this young officer was somehow not one of them. It was only later that he could prove how very much he was one of them. For the moment, as so often, despite all the recognition that fell to his lot he created a rather unfortunate impression. It was not cricket.

Was he to struggle with this profession all his life? Why, after all? There were no more expeditions left. He could never live on his pay as an officer. Nor did he want to use his mother any more. After all, he was already twenty-four. It was high time that he should take his place in the world. The two books he had published and the articles for the *Daily Telegraph* had cost him little trouble, and brought him in five times as much as three years' hard service in the Queen's uniform. The letters about Omdurman that he wrote in the *Morning Post,* though unsigned, brought him a fortune of three hundred pounds.

He would become a journalist. The *Allahabad Pioneer* had already made him a splendid offer: three pounds a week for a London letter.

Though, of course, there was still the polo tournament in India. That he must be in. He could not leave his old regiment in the lurch. Out of loyalty he went back to India for a few months more. But then he laid aside the red coat. He had had enough. War? Never again.

CHAPTER VI

First Failure

Of course they had heard in London of Winston Churchill's adventures in the Soudan. The thing that made him most popular was the incident of the Arab baby that he picked up at the capture of Omdurman. The brown dwarf was howling piteously. Evidently he was hungry. A good-natured Lancer tried to thrust a piece of sausage into his mouth. The baby with his five or six teeth was eating no sausage. "Of course not," said Lieutenant Churchill, who happened to be passing. "Biscuit soaked in water," he declared with positively maternal authority. He even had a few biscuit with him. The young ladies at home found him charming.

The young gentlemen found him remarkable. They were remarkable young gentlemen themselves: a group of Tory backbenchers who ranged themselves around Lord Hugh Cecil, son of the veteran Prime Minister. They received Churchill amiably into their circle. Later they were all to become his followers, and Lord Hugh was to be his first lieutenant in the struggle against the party machine. For the moment, however, Churchill could not feel quite at home among these suddenly made friends. They were all so much more highly polished. They had all passed their examinations at Oxford and Cambridge with distinction. And all had inherited traditional Conservative constituencies. You could never quite tell what they took seriously, and what they were making fun of. Slavery, for example, they defended as an eminently honorable institution. When Churchill raged against it in the name of the rights of man, the tranquil, worldly-wise Lord Hugh Cecil, who was already twenty-six, mildly said that they were not too much in earnest about slavery. They wanted to give their new friend a work-out, so that he should learn to argue.

Winston Churchill now saw plainly that he simply could not get on in life without the rhetorical learning of Oxford. The moment he got back from the Indian polo tournament he would matriculate. But alas, he learned that in order to do so he must pass entrance examinations, and, worst of all, learn Latin and Greek from the bottom up. When a man had wrestled for years with Cubans and Pathans and howling dervishes, he was too worn out to struggle with irregular verbs. And so he finally crossed Oxford off his agenda. The wound was never quite to heal.

He had now definitely decided to go into politics. At the end of November, barely two months after his return from the Soudan, he sought out the "Skipper," Mr. Middleton, the Chief Whip of the Conservatives, at St. Stephen's Chambers. Later he did not get along so well with party managers as on this first visit. Certainly Mr. Middleton would find him a constituency, and hoped to see his young friend soon in Parliament. Both the glorious memory of his great father and his record, which should be particularly popular with the working class, were excellent recommendations. There remained, however, the little matter of money. A candidate must not only pay his own expenses, he must devote some money to his constituency too. Some M.P.s contributed as much as a thousand pounds a year to the local charities, in exchange for the honor of holding the seat. Risky seats, of course, were considerably cheaper.

All at once young Churchill did not like the world he was trying to break into quite so well. But as he was asked to enter his name on the Speakers' list before he left the Central Offices of the Conservative Party, the sun shone again. He had not dreamed that there was a "Speaker-wanted" book. He had supposed that he would have to go to great trouble, perhaps putting Mamma to work again, in order to make a speech somewhere.

He made his platform debut at Bath before a gathering of the Primrose League, founded by his father. At least it was his official debut, since his rebel speech at the Empire Theatre was not on record. Of course he began with a profession of faith in the Tory Democracy that his father had brought into being. "England would gain far more from the rising tide of Tory Democracy than from the dried-up drainpipe of Radicalism." The sentence hit the mark. And indeed he had repeated it a hundred times before he dared mount the platform. The speech was a success. The *Morning Post* even devoted a short leader to the political initiation of their former war correspondent.

The first newspaper article that devoted serious, nay, prophetic, discussion to the new star in the British firmament did not appear until some months later. On the vessel that brought back Winston Churchill from the Indian polo tournament—he had faithfully done his duty, and shared again in the victory of his team—he met G. W. Stevens. This man was the ace reporter of the newly founded *Daily Mail*, which introduced a new style into English journalism. The sensation sheet came to birth. The old *Daily Telegraph*, which hitherto had served as printed food for the masses, took on positively Victorian respectability in comparison with the new product. In Mr. Harmsworth's *Daily Mail* the world was described in terms of people, not events alone, and the slogan was "Boom the Boomsters!"

G. W. Stevens, an old-timer in the newspaper world, could spot a boomster when he saw one. He had not altogether recovered from the impact of his encounter with Churchill when he told his boss back in London of this writing, adventuring soldier. "Write him up!" Mr. Harmsworth decided. So there appeared the famous article, "The Youngest Man in Europe," the first biography of Winston Churchill.

It said:

"He is the eldest son of Lord Randolph Churchill, and his mother is an American. Lord Randolph was not so precocious as he was popularly supposed to be, but they begin early in America. From his father he derives the hereditary aptitude for affairs, the grand style of entering upon them. But that inheritance alone would not give him his grip and facility at twenty-three. With us hereditary statesmen and party leaders ripen later. From his American strain he adds to this a keenness, a shrewdness, a half-cynical personal ambition, a natural aptitude for advertisement, and, happily, a sense of humor. . . . He was born a demagogue, and he happens to know it. At dinner he talks and talks, and you can hardly tell where he leaves off quoting his one idol, Macaulay, and begins with his other, Winston Churchill.

"At the present moment he happens to be a soldier. He may or may not possess the qualities that make a great general, but that question is of no sort of importance. In any case they will never be developed, for, if they exist, they are overshadowed by qualities which make him, almost at will, a great popular leader, a great journalist, or the founder of a great advertising business. What he will become, who can say? At the rate he goes, there will hardly be room for him in Parliament at thirty or in England at forty."

As a matter of fact Churchill was just thirty when he completed his shift from the Conservatives to the Liberals, and at forty he was a member of the Inner War Cabinet in the first World War.

In the summer of 1899 he was invited to call on Mr. Robert Ashcroft, Conservative member in the House of Commons for Oldham, Lancashire. Oldham was a two-member constituency, and Mr. Ashcroft was looking for a partner for the coming by-election. "I know," he said, "that young people often do not have as much money as older ones . . ." and with this the agreement was concluded.

As it happened, Mr. Ashcroft died a few weeks later. But as it was known in the constituency, which had held him in great respect for years, that he had fixed on Mr. Churchill for his running-mate, the candidature passed almost automatically to the latter. As a partner he was given Mr. James Mawdsley, the secretary of the Operative Spinners' Association. Mr. Mawdsley was a typical Tory labor man of the old days. His own party, the Conservatives, he argued, were not good for much either. But the Liberals were rogues and swindlers. As things were, Oldham had better go for the Tories.

Oldham was a notoriously fickle constituency. The "Skipper" in the Conservative Central Office congratulated Churchill on his candidacy with the remark that the Government of Lord Salisbury was not particularly popular at the time among the workmen of Lancashire. Better to lose both seats at the by-election, and recapture Oldham in time for the next General Election. At the clubs people were not too well pleased that Lord Randolph's son had joined forces with a labor representative, a notorious socialist, even if a Blue. But Churchill was enthusiastic. He was always enthusiastic when he was starting into a fight.

When he contested Oldham for the first time he had only a very limited idea of the fights that were to fill his parliamentary life from now on. But he settled into the hard work of electioneering with astonishing speed. Those were the days when the candidates drove from house to house in a landau and pair. First they stopped at the doors of the local magnates, then presented themselves to the committees, the Council and the executive. Then they learned by heart all the figures upon their political home: its industrial interests, its character, its likes and dislikes had to become part of the contestant's second nature. He must strike precisely the right local note in his election address, shake the hands of the local gentlemen of the press, appear at the Town Hall on nomination day, and smile amiably at the opposing candidate: "The weather is very cold . . . very hot, I meant to say . . . for this time of the year, isn't it? By the way, if there is anything I can do for your convenience, pray don't forget to let me know!"

The opposing candidates for the Liberals were Mr. Emmott, an Oldham grandee whose family had operated many thousands of spindles in the neighborhood for generations, and Mr. Walter Runciman, with whom Churchill was to come into conflict all the rest of his life. When the later Lord Runciman had the chief share in the betrayal of Czechoslovakia, the clash was to be deadly.

Messrs. Emmott and Runciman did indeed plead the cause of the little man, rebelling against the Conservative regime that had already lasted too long; but both were well-to-do representatives

of industrial capital. The "Socialist and the Scion," as the ill
matched pair, the labor man Mawdsley and the heir of the Dukes
of Marlborough, soon began to be called, did uphold the ruling
order of society. But only with difficulty could they raise among
themselves the five hundred pounds that their campaign swal
lowed up.

The campaign started off at a brisk pace. Labor in Lancashire—
the constituency was entirely a working-class district—was prosper
ous but tough. It was still quite well off. It was still producing the
textiles for India, Ireland, Japan. Unfortunately it was also pro
ducing the machines with which India, Ireland, Japan, would
soon shamefully undercut their own products. Nevertheless they
took no particular delight in tax increases. Now it happened that
the Government supporting Churchill was just planning the Cleri
cal Tithe Bill, soon rechristened the Clerical Dole Bill by the
Opposition, to assure the clergy a minimum livelihood.

The by-election in Oldham provided the first opportunity to
argue this proposal before the people. By-elections were always a
dangerous experiment. Cranks and fanatics gathered from all over
the country to let off steam. Oldham enjoyed some wonderful
rowdy meetings. On the first occasion the "Scion" was a little
startled at the unaccustomed tone of things. But soon he plunged
head first into the stream. Even today, when he has a moment
free for his memories, Winston Churchill recalls that the rowdy
meetings during the fifteen or sixteen contests he has fought
through were the best recreation he ever had. They gave him
his elixir of life: excitement. You don't have to make the same
old speech. Whereas a long sagacious argument makes the audi
ence yawn, a good answer at a turbulent meeting makes friends
by the dozen, even sometimes of the enemy. You must simply take
care never to let the smile leave your face. You must remain casual
and quite easy, as if you were talking to a single friend in some
peaceful place. If an adversary in the audience comes too close
you may throw off your coat like a flash, but in that case it is a

CHURCHILL AS A NEWSPAPER CORRESPONDENT
1898

good idea to whisper to your party friends at the back of the platform, "Hold me back! Hold me back!"

Unquestionably Churchill allowed his party associates to hold him back from supporting the Clerical Tithe Bill. The temper of the gathering of thrifty small people to whom he was speaking at the moment was obviously against the new expense. His friends on the platform murmured: "Don't you antagonize 'em!" And so Churchill let go the reform that his own party had proposed.

Hearing of this incident the following morning, Mr. Arthur Balfour, who was just in the process of taking the venerable Lord Salisbury's place at the head of the Conservative Party, said with a gentle, dangerous smile: "I thought he was a young man of promise. But he seems to be a young man of promises."

The phrase stuck, and in the middle of the first World War Mr. Balfour was still refusing to give Churchill a seat in a reconstructed coalition Cabinet.

Naturally his Liberal opponent made the best use of the handle that Churchill in his youthful insouciance had given them. "Do you want to vote for a Government whose own candidates do not stand behind its measures?"

Churchill had learned his first political lesson: a Party man must stand for many things he considers wrong or—as in this case —irrelevant. It did nothing to endear the Party system to him.

Polling Day approached. From early morning on the candidates circulated and meandered among the polling-booths and committee-rooms. One more despairing smile here and a beseeching handshake there. By nine o'clock all was over. Churchill was defeated by 1300 votes. His socialist running-mate was thirty votes behind him. Odd, but the first sign of encouragement after the defeat came from Mr. Balfour, of all people. Politics at that time was still a gentlemanly sport. A friendly note bridged even a personal disappointment. "I was very sorry to hear of your ill-success," Mr. Balfour wrote on July 10, 1899, "as I had greatly hoped to see you speedily in the House where your father and I fought many a good battle side by side in days gone by . . . Never mind, it will all come all right and this small reverse will have no permanent ill effect upon your political fortunes."

The great Joe Chamberlain, whom Churchill met two weeks later at the house of Lady Jeune, did not waste a word on the mishap. Cool and highly polished as the man looked, as if he had never had a worry in the world, he had worked his way up far too painfully, and reached the top by much too close a margin, to be upset by an early failure of a friend.

Deep in animated conversation the two, imperialist and beginner, cruised in a launch along the Thames. Chamberlain talked of nothing but Great Britain. The man who is building a world empire has no second interest. And for that matter, the moment was far too serious. The negotiations with President Kruger down in South Africa were not getting forward. Tensely the whole world watched London: Would the English strike?

The great Chamberlain was at once an activist and a realist. "It is no use blowing the trumpet for the charge and then looking round to find nobody following!" he said. Just then his glance, which usually seemed to hide in unconcern behind the gold-rimmed monocle, fell upon the boyish face opposite. Here was a young officer who would follow when the trumpet blew for the charge.

The two shook hands. Neither knew that this handshake was the beginning of a relationship whose stress and intensity would one day throw the whole Empire into turmoil.

CHAPTER VII

Captured

PRESIDENT KRUGER had missed the bus. At the outbreak of war Chamberlain was convinced of it. It was Chamberlain père, and the war was the Boer War—but still the similarity with our own days is positively uncanny.

General Sir Redvers Buller was, it is true, sent to South Africa with a British Expeditionary Force. Chamberlain believed that he might well come too late. Sir George White, who was already down yonder with sixteen thousand men, might have settled the whole thing before the troops from home even had a chance to come under fire. Smiling superciliously, the Olympian expounded this theory to young Churchill while the two were rattling in a hansom cab from Chamberlain's house at Prince's Garden to his desk at the Colonial Office.

Churchill had come to take his leave, and probably also for a few introductions to take along. Obviously he was already on his way to South Africa. The Boer ultimatum had been known in London for less than an hour when he put in his pocket a contract with Mr. Borthwick, proprietor of the *Morning Post*. The young correspondent was to get two hundred and fifty pounds a month—a record for the time—with four months' guarantee even if the Boers collapsed in four days; all expenses paid; and full discretion as to movements and opinions. For Churchill it was a victory before the battle.

For England there was to be a long period of battles without victories. Chamberlain could not conceive of it. He was sure the war would be quick and painless. In reply to an objection from Churchill he admitted that Mafeking might perhaps be besieged.

"But if they cannot hold out for a few weeks, what is one to expect?" He pulled luxuriously at a black cigar. Young Churchill, even then a celebrated connoisseur of cigars, could not quite enjoy the weed that day.

"Of course I have to base myself on the War Office opinion," Chamberlain added somewhat more cautiously. But he had full confidence in the War Office. To say nothing of the leader of the Expedition, General Sir Redvers Buller.

The War Office at that time was the result of three generations of economy and disdain. The best-functioning of all the departments was the Military Intelligence, which was pretty well independent, even being housed in its own building. Its chief, Sir John Ardagh, sent General Buller a two-volume work that was later submitted to Parliament, a comprehensive survey of the excellently defended Boer Republics. The report referred to the large quantities of munitions that the Boers had obtained from Holland and particularly from Germany. It called attention to the new form of heavy Maxim, firing one-inch shells soon to obtain a sanguinary fame as "pompoms." It came to the conclusion that the South African war would require at least two hundred thousand men.

General Buller sent the two-volume work back to the Intelligence an hour after receiving it. With it he sent the message, Thank you, he knows everything about South Africa.

Sir Redvers Buller committed one blunder after another, and stumbled from one disaster to the next. Still the confidence of the Government and of the country in him remained unshaken. Under Lord Rosebery's rule he had once shown liberal tendencies. As this was unusual in a general, he was considered an independent thinker and a strategical genius.

Though the phrase was not yet invented, everyone in England was sure that it would be a lightning war. According to the best estimates it would last three months and cost ten million pounds. In actual fact the Boer War lasted three years, and devoured two hundred million pounds.

Churchill never forgot this lesson. Twenty years later he implored his country: "Never, never, never believe any war will be smooth and easy, or that anyone who embarks on the strange voyage can measure the tides and hurricanes he will encounter. The statesman who yields to war fever must realise that once the signal is given, he is no longer the master of policy but the slave of unforeseeable and uncontrollable events. Antiquated War Offices, weak, incompetent or arrogant commanders, untrustworthy allies, hostile neutrals, malignant fortune, ugly surprises, awful miscalculations—all take their seats at the Council Board on the morrow of a declaration of war."

A farewell dinner united forty gentlemen in high good spirits at the Carlton Hotel. Churchill could not quite understand the universal jollity. Still, he was always impressed anew by the sovereign independence of London society. The host was Sir Ernest Cassel, the Jewish banker who had begun as an errand-boy in the City. The Prince of Wales was among the guests.

On October 11, precisely at the hour when the Boer ultimatum expired, the *Dunottar Castle* put to sea with the commander of the Expeditionary Force, Sir Redvers Buller, his entire staff, and the correspondent of the *Morning Post*. During the whole voyage Churchill suffered the tortures of the damned from seasickness.

Even worse than seasickness was the uncertainty about what might be happening in South Africa while the *Dunottar Castle* was at sea without news. Certainly the armies must already have established contact. Finally, close to the African coast, she met a tramp steamer. The crew, some twenty ragged and tattered figures, held up a blackboard on her deck so that the passengers of the English vessel could read it: *Boers defeated.*

Churchill timidly suggested that they should stop the tramp, ask for details, and perhaps even get hold of a Cape Town paper.

The mule of English officialdom balked. Possibly there might be a claim for damages against the Government if they were to stop a foreign vessel. Besides, Sir Redvers Buller was not at all uneasy for news, although it might be useful if he could have a general view of the situation when he landed in Cape Town. "It is the weakness of youth to be impatient," the General decided in reply to Churchill's suggestion. Anyway, as he gave the young man plainly to understand, the habit of questioning superior officers was unfortunate even for a war correspondent, particularly if the latter had but recently worn the red tunic himself.

It was a mere trifling incident, but one that was to be repeated for decades in every possible form. In the holy war for England's destiny, to which Winston Churchill devoted himself first by temperament and natural inclination, later from the consciousness of his mission, he was to spend the greater part of his energies fighting the inadequacy, the apathy, the bloodlessness that ruled England.

The *Dunottar Castle* came in on October 31. That day General White suffered a disastrous defeat in the vicinity of Ladysmith, the British stronghold, and had to withdraw his troops into the city. It was to be encircled almost immediately. Churchill of course was determined to get into the fighting in time. By a local train he sped at about ten miles an hour to East London, the end of the line. There he took ship for Durban. It was a wretched little coasting steamer of about a hundred and fifty tons burthen, and she rocked like a nut-shell in the fearful Antarctic gale that she sailed into. Seasickness was not the word. Churchill was practically in his death agonies.

At Eastcourt, whither the railroad brought him from Durban —the last station not yet occupied by the Boers on the road to Ladysmith—he found no sympathy for his suffering, but merely a grinning face. Leopold Amery, the correspondent of the *Times* who received him here, now felt revenged for his plunge into the Harrow pool.

Even Eastcourt was under enemy fire. Ten, twelve thousand Boer horsemen occupied the terrain around the little British garrison. Ten or twelve Hussars daily swarmed into the field to spy out the enemy's movements. On the fourteenth of November the commanding general had a novel idea: he would send out an armored train for perhaps fifteen miles, or however far he could get, along the stretch where traffic had been stopped, to reconnoiter the terrain. Captain Haldane was put in command. So many accidents happened, however, that the real commander would be the civilian Churchill.

The disaster was inevitable. An armored train of six trucks, three before the engine, three behind, might indeed seem to the eyes of the time an extremely formidable weapon. But as a matter of fact the enemy had merely to blow up a bridge or even simply to tear up the tracks to block the monster's retreat, and the train would be immobile, helplessly at the mercy of any attack.

And this was exactly what happened after the armored train, manned by a company of Dublin Fusiliers and a company of Durban Light Infantry, had passed Chieveley station, fourteen miles from Eastcourt. The Boers lay in wait for the train. Suddenly it was deluged with the pompom shells of whose existence Sir Redvers Buller had been unwilling to learn. The engineer speeded up. The train roared along at forty miles an hour. Suddenly there was a tremendous shock. Captain Haldane, Churchill, the soldiers all rubbed broken heads, bouncing around on the floor of the truck. The engineer had hit a curve at his tremendous pace; the train was derailed.

The engine, thank God, was still on the rails. The front truck was somewhere to one side. The next two blocked the track. The three attached behind were unharmed.

In the rain of Boer bullets a splinter hit the engineer. He, a civilian, could not see why he should expose himself to bombshells for his pitiful wages. He was about to make off. In that case of course the train was lost. The infantry might hold off the attack for an hour, perhaps for two. Not more.

Churchill grabbed the engineer by the shoulders: "Man!" he shouted. "Lucky dog! You have got off with a scratch! Didn't you know a man can never be wounded twice on the same day?"

The engineer was reassured. Very well, he would stay and try to push the two front trucks, which blocked the tracks, out of the way with his engine.

Meanwhile the two companies of infantry kept the superior enemy force at a distance from their trucks. A few men had to get out in the midst of the pompom fire because Churchill, who of course resolutely stayed outside, needed their shoulders to push the trucks one last bit out of the way. The Major of the Durban Light Infantry was the first to leave cover and jump from the train. Nine volunteers followed. As a matter of course they took orders from the civilian, who was a born leader. Churchill knew he must keep his men's spirits up. He cheered them on with the exhortation: "That will make excellent copy for my paper!"

The difficulties of putting a half-derailed train back into service under enemy fire were beyond description. Churchill was Figaro-ci, Figaro-là. He was everywhere at once. His revolver belt got in his way as he worked. He carelessly flung the weapon away. But Providence must have noticed that little motion.

Everybody had to lend a hand in pushing the train back the first few yards. Naturally they ceased firing for the moment. The Boer horsemen did not let the opportunity escape them. They swarmed up at a gallop. But the engine was just starting to move. Churchill shouted to the engineer to take the wounded, forty tattered and bleeding soldiers, back across the bridge, and to wait beyond the Blue Krantz river for the Dublin Fusiliers, who would be covering the retreat meanwhile. There was not a second to be lost. The shells hit the engine crash upon crash. The locomotive panted; the train started to move. Churchill jumped off into the rain of bullets. Of course he would stay with the Fusiliers. But his companions were now two hundred yards away, and two Boer fighters seemed to grow out of the ground directly in front of him. Slowly, with true Dutch calm, they aimed their rifles at him. Churchill jumped into the ditch for cover. Then a horseman galloped furiously up, a tall dark figure, holding a rifle in his hand.

Churchill reached for his revolver-belt. So far, as correspondent and civilian, he had kept strictly out of the fighting. But his neck was at stake now. And now too he had time to look around and hunt for his companions at a distance. Not a man in sight. The infantry under Captain Haldane were already captured. Finally Winston Churchill raised his hands. It was the most painful moment of his life.

"Come on!" said the horseman. And he brought his captive back to his own column. Two or three hundred horsemen received the young Englishman. They had bearded faces, brand-new muskets, excellent horses. They were sheltering from the steaming tropical downpour under umbrellas.

Churchill's capture on the fifteenth of November, 1899, had an epilogue. Six years later, when he was Under Secretary in the Colonial Office, a group of South African statesmen came to him to seek a loan for their devastated country. He agreed with pleasure. He had the pleasantest of personal memories of the Boer War.

For that matter, his fellow-soldiers too remembered Churchill's feat of heroism. One of them wrote to his mother: "If it had not been for Churchill, not one of us would have escaped." And the Inspector of the Natal Government Railway, Mr. J. Campbell, wrote to the General Manager of the Railway on the very evening of Churchill's capture: "The railwaymen who accompanied the armored train this morning ask me to convey to you their admiration for the courage displayed by Mr. Winston Churchill, to whose efforts, backed up by those of the driver, Wagner, the fact is due that the armored engine and tender were brought successfully out, and that it became possible to bring the wounded in here. The whole of our men are loud in their praise of Mr. Churchill, who, I regret to say, is a prisoner. I respectfully ask you to convey their admiration to a brave man."

Churchill told his South African visitors with amusement how a Boer rider had once fetched him out of a ditch and taken him prisoner. General Botha, the leader of the delegation, listened attentively. Then he asked: "Do you recognize me?" Churchill shook his head. "I was the horseman," said the general, who of course looked like a different man in his evening dress.

When Louis Botha became Prime Minister of South Africa, and relations between the Dominion and the Mother country became increasingly close, Churchill was altogether delighted that he had once been careless enough to drop his revolver. Indeed the two statesmen became the best of friends. In 1913 Botha, coming back from a stay at the German baths, called on Winston Churchill, then First Lord of the Admiralty. "Mind you are ready," he warned his former prisoner after a cordial handshake. "Do not trust those people in Germany. They are very dangerous. They mean mischief. I hear things you would not hear. Mind you have all your ships ready. I can feel that there is danger in the air. I am going to be ready, too. When they attack you, I am going to attack German South West Africa and clear them out once and for all. I will be there to do my duty when the time comes. But you, with the Navy, mind you are not caught by surprise."

The honest general from the African bush felt obliged to give this emphatic warning because even shortly before the outbreak of the first world war Churchill was considered an especially warm friend of Germany. And it was quite true that he had urged conciliation again and again. But though Botha did not know it, and Kaiser Wilhelm did not know it, and nobody knew it, he had had his fleet ready for war since 1911.

CHAPTER VIII

Escape

EVER since the prison warden of Ventnor, the brother-in-law of his nurse Mrs. Everest, told the child his sad and grisly prison stories, Winston Churchill has had a sort of claustrophobia.

Churchill now was a bird in a cage. If there was any condition that he was simply physically unable to bear, it was captivity. It was worse than seasickness. True, the British officers among whom the war correspondent was thrust, despite his vehement protests, were kept under honorable arrest in the buildings of the State Model Schools at Pretoria. But even so the confinement was intolerable. Senseless disputes broke out between the most intimate friends—what prisoners of war call barb-wire psychosis. There was but one thought, one subject of conversation, one obsession—out!

Sixty British officers, among them Captain Haldane of the armored train, were guarded by forty "Zarps"—South African Republican Police. Being elderly, and no longer fit for service at the front, the Zarps were by now rather easy-going. On this Churchill, Haldane, and Lieutenant Brockie based their plan. From a window in the lavatory it was easy to climb down outside the walls. Of course they would probably run straight into the arms of the sentries who kept guard over the east side of the building at intervals of about fifteen feet. Churchill had noticed that these backwoods warriors would often talk together when the nights were long and lonely. He had only to find the right moment, while they were absorbed in their gossip.

On December 11 the three conspirators made their first abortive attempt at escape. It did not work. The risk that the guard would look up, and shoot without stopping to ask questions, seemed too great. But it was only for twenty-four hours that it seemed too great. By then Churchill had determined to run any risk. He would lead the way, slipping through the tiny window of the lavatory, and swinging down from the roof. Then he would hide in the garden of the villa across the way, which was full of bushes, and await his two companions, who would follow at once.

Lieutenant Brockie had dug up somewhere a compass and a few provisions. He also spoke Dutch and Kaffir. They would need it all. The Portuguese frontier was about three hundred miles away.

Late on the night of December 12 Churchill stood at the narrow opening of the window. His heart was beating a tattoo. The nearest two sentries were standing down below, as stiff as wax figures, staring ahead. Suddenly one of them faced sharply about, and walked toward his companion. The two voices rose in monotonous conversation.

Twice Churchill pulled himself up to the loophole. Both times his courage deserted him. On the third attempt there was no more question and no calculation. Better right into the bullets than back into the cell. Once more the fugitive pulled himself up. He forced his way through the loophole. His waistcoat caught on the ornamental metal-work at the top. In the moment he needed to release himself he could see one of the sentries lighting a cigarette. The man was standing so near that Churchill could make out the lines on his palms in the light of the match. Then he let himself down the wall. A leap, and he was hidden in the shrubbery of the neighboring garden.

At that moment a Boer civilian, evidently the owner of the villa, came out of the house. He took a couple of steps toward the bush where Churchill was hiding. Then, halting, he gazed into space. His dog came further. The animal's luminous, live-coal eyes stared straight into the fugitive's face. Chance or fate? The dog did not bark. It returned in answer to a whistle from its master. Other people, obviously guests, walked through the garden. Churchill could not leave his hiding-place. Besides, he had to wait for his two companions.

Suddenly a voice came from the prison. "All up!" A burst of laughter followed, and the noise of two occupants obviously having a royal good time. Churchill listened tensely. The jolly, noisy conversation was interspersed with Latin fragments. A few words of English and a few words of hog-latin, shrouded in constant laughter, yielded this sentence: "They cannot get out. The sentry suspects. It's all up. Can you get back again?"

The Portuguese frontier was far away. Except for a few bars of chocolate he had no provisions. He did not speak the language of the country. They were sure to discover his flight by morning roll-call at latest, and to harry him all through the city, and all through the country if he should get out of Pretoria.

"I shall go alone!" Churchill replied to the laughing voices.

And now begins one of the greatest escape stories ever told. Winston Churchill has told it dozens, probably hundreds of times on lecture tours all over England and the United States. He has described it in books and magazine articles. He has relived the story of those days for years.

Today it sounds like a dream. Perhaps even then it was a waking dream. With somnambulistic certainty he found his way through the unknown streets of Pretoria, which were menacingly populous even at night—precisely in the right direction, always toward the south. Orion, his companion of the Nile, may have guided him. After half an hour's wandering he struck a railroad. Which way to Portuguese Delagoa, to eastward? So far as he could judge, the tracks led north. Perhaps the rails made a curve at just this point. He would follow them. It was still cool. Winston Churchill breathed deep of the air. He had a sense of freedom whose bliss could not be described. Fool's paradise! Within an hour they would have him.

He began to calculate methodically. Naturally he could not cover the three hundred miles on foot. He must steal a ride. Perfectly simple—he would jump aboard the next train. But that in turn was not so simple, no matter how carefully calculated. After two hours on foot he saw the lights of a little railway station. That meant there would be people near by. That meant he must go around, stooping deep in the ditch, and lie in wait two hundred yards beyond the station. By the time the train, which would undoubtedly stop at the little station, arrived at this point it would not be difficult for him to jump aboard. Winston Churchill was a close figurer, even in the middle of an adventure.

He did it. Just how he did it he could not tell afterward. He vaguely remembered seeing yellow lights flash out. In the glare of the locomotive the sharp silhouette of the engine stood out black against the night sky. The rumble of the train turned to a roar as it charged up. The cars were ungainly steel masses. Churchill leaped at a car. His hands sought something to cling to. They slipped off. He tried again. Again his hands flapped helplessly in the air. The third time they found some sort of fastening. And in the middle of a carload of sacks covered with thick coal dust the exhausted youth fell asleep. It was to be hoped that he was sleeping in the right direction, not back into the middle of the land of the Boers.

The morning sun shone straight into his eyes. It rose in the east. He was travelling eastward, in the right direction. But he could no longer trust to the train. At sometime during the day there would undoubtedly be an inspection. The sacks were so soft and the African soil would be so hard! Nevertheless, forward! He leaped from the rattling train, fell into the ditch, turned both ankles, laughed, dragged himself to a brook, took a drink. He thought things over.

It was now four o'clock in the morning. He must wait until evening before he could take another train. He had therefore to stay hidden for at least fourteen hours. Would they find him meanwhile? He could not help laughing again. Not a soul could know where he was. He had not the faintest idea himself. But he was hungry. And he must be sparing of his chocolate. He

could not afford but one bar at most for today. Who could tell
when another decent meal would come his way?

By noon the heat was so oppressive that he collapsed under the
small grove of trees that he had chosen for his refuge. He was too
weak and exhausted to get further. So a vulture seemed to think.
With flapping wings the amiable creature circled about its presumptive victim. The monster knew it would be having a square
meal shortly. By tomorrow at latest.

Suddenly the vulture flew off. Human beings were near by.
Boer farmers, heavily armed, with their Kaffirs. Men were more
dangerous than vultures. Winston Churchill prayed: Lord, let
them miss seeing me!

His companions in Bangalore, who did not quite believe in
the Lord, were idiots. The Boer farmers overlooked the lonely
man.

All day Churchill stared at the railroad line. Two or three trains
had passed. After dusk he would jump aboard another. But after
dusk there were no more trains. Probably railway traffic was halted
for the night, he reflected. It soon turned out that he was right.
It was a war measure that extended to this part of the country.

And so he began footing it again, hungry and worn out as he
was. After hours' walking he came to another little station where
three freight trains were sleeping. Should he trust one of them?
Impossible! Who could tell where the trains might go tomorrow? Suppose he looked at the labels on the trucks or the mer-
chandise. He crept closer. Then he heard the roaring, howling
laughter of some Kaffirs. Of course he could go no closer to the
station. After all, he would be running straight into certain arrest.
But neither could he walk on. It was still at least a hundred and
fifty miles to the frontier. If he could no longer depend even on
the trains, the jig was up.

Lights were burning a few hundred paces beyond the little railway station. Probably it was a Kaffir kraal. Churchill came to a
decision. The Kaffirs, so pitilessly exploited by the Boers, could
not possibly be faithful to their masters. Even if they knew

nothing of Great Britain, which was coming to free them, they could understand the comforting crackle of a British banknote. Churchill had twenty pounds in his pocket. With the equivalent of a hundred dollars a man is not altogether lost. He dragged himself toward the lights with his last strength.

Indeed it must have been a dream. No such miracles happen by day. When he knocked at the next house the door opened a crack, after some minutes, and a voice asked in perfect English, "Who is this?"

He had run into the only house for thirty miles around where they would not have betrayed him—the house of Mr. John Howard, manager of the Transvaal Collieries, a Britisher.

What he had taken for a Negro kraal was in fact a village of miners, which Mr. Howard directed. Out of consideration for his English origin—and for a suitable present made to the local Field-Cornet of the Boers—they had not drafted him to fight against the British invaders. At the moment neither of the two men facing each other through the half-open door knew who the other was.

"I am a burgher." Churchill began the tale that he had thought up in a flash. "I have had an accident. I was on my way to join my commando at Komati Poort. I have fallen off the train. I have been unconscious for hours. I think I have dislocated my shoulder."

"Come in!" said the householder.

Inside he looked at the intruder more closely. "Just a minute," he growled, leaving his unexpected guest alone. When he came back into the room he brought a cold leg of mutton with him. "Help yourself, Mr. Churchill," he grinned. "Of course you are the man they are looking for. I have just been reading your description. And the Field-Cornet has already been asking about you. Naturally I am suspect as a Britisher. All the English houses in the republic are being searched for you. Do you want to see?"

Sure enough, there was the warrant:

A PRISONER IN THE BOER WAR

An old photograph showing Winston Churchill (right) before his dramatic escape

"Twenty-five pounds REWARD is offered by the Sub-Commission of the Fifth Division, on behalf of the special constable of the said Division, to anyone who brings the escaped prisoner of war CHURCHILL dead or alive to this office. For the Sub-Commission of the Fifth Division, (signed) Lodk. de Haas, Sec."

Another paper from those days, also promising twenty-five pounds' reward to the captor, describes the fugitive more carefully, if less flatteringly:

"An Englishman of indifferent build walking with a forward stoop, pale appearance, red-brownish hair, small and hardly noticeable moustache, talks through his nose and cannot pronounce the letter S properly."

Mr. Howard made a worried face. Did he not dare to assist in the flight of a criminal for whom a warrant was out?

No, that was not it. It was worse. He was afraid of his Dutch cook. "She keeps spying on me. Tomorrow she will be asking what became of the leg of mutton." (Churchill had meanwhile devoured it down to the last scrap.) "You can't possibly stay here. We'll hide you in the coal mines. You can sleep in the office today. During the day I'll keep the Kaffirs away from you. I'll tell them the office is bewitched."

The following evening three more Britishers arrived whom Mr. Howard had drummed up in the neighborhood. Two were Scotch colliers, the third, Mr. Dewsnap, came, of all places, straight from Oldham. "It's a scandal that they let you be beaten," he greeted the half-dead Churchill with a firm handshake. "Well, just wait. Next time you'll be elected in triumph. I'll take care of that!"

"You don't say?" Winston Churchill was himself again.

Now he had merely to stay hidden a few days in a half-flooded mine. By day he read a book that Mr. Howard had picked out and brought to him as suitable reading—Stevenson's *Kidnapped*. By night he fought off the rats. Sometimes he was even so tired that he paid no attention to these four-legged companions of his imprisonment.

On the evening of December 18 Mr. Howard paid a visit to the mine. "The Field-Cornet was just with me," he grinned, "to bring me the good news that you were captured at Waterval Boven yesterday. Now they won't be looking for you quite so hard. This is the moment to get out of the trap—before they realize their mistake."

Next morning a train left for Delagoa Bay in Portuguese territory with a consignment of wool. The shipper was an amiable Dutch merchant, Mynheer Burgener. He had no objection to an English lieutenant's being packed into one of the wool bales.

After an endless journey eastward through the Transvaal the wool and Churchill arrived in Delagoa Bay—and freedom. The car in which the fugitive lay hidden had not been examined at the frontier. The customs inspection had taken place at the point of departure, and the car was sent off in an armor of barbed wire so that nothing should be smuggled into it en route.

The nearest British consul was at Lourenço Marques. The fugitive went to call. "Sorry," said the secretary, "the Consul is very busy."

"Just tell him Mr. Churchill of the *Morning Post* is calling."

The Consul came close to falling over backward as he welcomed the visitor.

Lourenço Marques was a hotbed of Boers and Boer sympathizers. They tried to kidnap Churchill. Their most publicized prisoner of war was not going to get away from them so simply as all that.

Better, then, to take the next vessel for Durban. A fig for seasickness, thought Churchill, who had gone through worse things than that.

The American hospital ship *Maine* lay in harbor at Durban. An American lady was in figurative command on the bridge— Lady Randolph Churchill. With the help of friends in her native land she had outfitted the hospital ship, and put it at the service of the wounded in the Boer War. Accompanying her was John Churchill, Winston's younger and much-beloved brother, who was in the expedition, and had received a slight injury.

Reunion on the *Maine*. But not yet homeward. Winston had still a small account in Pretoria to settle. Once more he joined the campaign. As a reward for his adventures the sleepy General Buller once more bestowed the old lieutenant's uniform on him. But Churchill did not keep it on long. Disguising himself as a civilian he rode a bicycle through the middle of the city of Johannesburg, the enemy general headquarters, still held by the Boers, with a message to Lord Roberts, on the other side, from his old friend Ian Hamilton, whose troop he had joined.

Then he was entangled in another dozen fights—wherever there was hot work. Once he got lost again in the midst of the enemy. A Lancashire Hussar told him to mount behind on his own horse, which presently was shot from under its two riders. Churchill tried to console the man from Lancashire: "After all, you saved my life by taking me along."

"Who cares for you?" replied the lad, with tears in his eyes. "It's my horse I'm grieving for." The Hussar was Trooper Roberts, who received the Distinguished Conduct Medal for his valor on this occasion.

And now the little account in Pretoria was due at last. With the Boers in full retreat, two young English officers stormed the city quite alone. They had not even their boys with them. One was the Duke of Marlborough, the other was his cousin Winston.

Winston found his way to the State Model Schools like a flash. It had been much harder in the other direction.

The sentries lowered their rifles as the two Englishmen galloped up.

"Captain Haldane!" yelled Churchill, although his mother on board the *Maine* had just been telling him that he really *must* learn to mend his manners. "Captain Haldane! You're free! You're all free!"

The prisoners had been expecting this day. One of them had even patched together a Union Jack out of colored rags. It waved now over Winston Churchill's head.

CHAPTER IX

Magic Lantern

Was it Field-Marshal Lord Roberts or Lieutenant Winston Churchill who conquered South Africa? asked a London newspaper as the fame of the young hero spread like wildfire over the old country. It was one of those malicious questions that English mediocrity has always in readiness for English genius. Churchill was to be obliged to get used to it. It was always to be the same. Perhaps Fate, which had spoiled him so, was at the same time a trifle jealous. Just before the outbreak of the present war it was to be the same old story, and this time his personal misfortune would be a national tragedy: just as in the days of his glorious return from South Africa the people would cheer him, but the political power machine would stand him off until zero hour. The reserve in official regions grew chillier as the waves of popular enthusiasm carried him higher. Among his own kind the idol of the nation was solitary. No one loved the much-beloved.

After his adventures in the Boer War Winston Churchill was the most petted young man in England. The army was full of his deeds of arms. Newspaper readers at home knew him as the most important of all the war correspondents, who scooped all his colleagues. But precisely this successful journalism was the source of constant friction. Until the day when he brought Hamilton's message Lord Roberts had simply not seen young Churchill, although the Field-Marshal had been an intimate friend of his father's, to whom he had owed his appointment to the command of the Indian Army years before. Nevertheless Lord Roberts allowed the assignment of the *Morning Post's* correspondent to his staff only late and reluctantly, and personally never recognized it. He had a double reason for his unfriendly reserve. In the first place Kitchener was not yet reconciled with the author of the fault-finding book about the Soudan campaign, and Lord Roberts did not want to give a rebuff to his Chief of Staff. In the second place Churchill severely criticized the speech of a Church of England army chaplain in a dispatch to his paper. "A ridiculous discourse on the peculiar and unconvincing tactics by which the Israelites were said to have procured the downfall of the walls of Jericho," Churchill called this sermon, which was delivered the evening before the battle of Vaal Krantz, at a time when the assembled troops were especially apt to receive the consolations of religion. "As I listened to these foolish sentences, I wondered whether Rome would again seize the opportunity which Canterbury disdained."

Naturally such an opinion seemed more than severe. The *Morning Post* did indeed publish it, but the paper clearly dissociated itself from its correspondent by a leader in the same issue. There was a storm of indignation in Anglican church circles. To Lord Roberts this merely made the matter worse. In the first place, as a sincere churchman, he was hurt by Churchill's attack. And then he resented the reaction of the "civilian." He was man enough to maintain order even in the Military Chaplain's Department. One morning Churchill crossed his path in the marketplace of Bloemfontein. The lieutenant saluted. Of course the Field-Marshal knew perfectly well who the young officer was—among other things he was an intimate friend of General Ian Hamilton's and other gentlemen high in the Staff. But Lord Roberts merely replied with a casual gesture, and went on without summoning Churchill to speak to him. According to the etiquette of those days, at once more formal and friendlier, it was an execution.

When Churchill joined General French's cavalry division toward the end of the South African campaign, he was not much better off. The senior officers simply could not stomach this hybrid combination of subaltern and war correspondent. They would tolerate no criticism, whether approving or hostile, from a young man whose business it was to stand rigidly at attention while he received their orders. In addition there were personal motives involved. Colonel Brabazon, now a general, was fighting a private feud with General French throughout the war. "Brab" had been in it as early as Afghanistan, in 1878, and in Suakim in 1884 he had held an important command. At Suakim French had been a mere subaltern. Now he was the general in command, and knew best about everything. He had no patience with old Brabazon and his young friend. And so it happened that while Winston Churchill kept seeing General French he was never able to speak to him.

Churchill bore no grudges. This was a characteristic that fundamentally distinguished his expansive nature from that of introverts and wiseacres. Stubborn he is, defiant if need be, but never opinionated. No man on earth has such good reason today to say, I told you so. He never says it. He is not conceited about his infallible instinct, which in later years has grown into a gift of prophecy. The other fellow has a right to his point of view too. And to his ties, limitations, even to his prejudices. Churchill puts a pacific ending to his account of every conflict in his battle-filled life as he looks back on it now. He allows adversaries a right to their standpoint. He allows even Neville Chamberlain, who kept him out of power for years during which the country was desperately demanding Churchill, to go on existing by his side, if only in the shade. He magnanimously allows the old man the position of leader of the Conservative Party that he himself has declined. Churchill wields the sharpest blade in England. But he draws it for the holy cause of tolerance.

Even in his reports from South Africa he showed an almost unyouthful feeling for tolerance. True, he advocated the continuance of the war to a successful termination. But it was not "bind your helmet tighter after victory." After victory, help the fallen to rise! His severest criticism was directed at his own countrymen, at their passivity, at their muddling through. "There is plenty of room here for a quarter of a million men," he wrote

in March, 1900. "Are the gentlemen of England fox-hunting? The
individual Boer is worth from three to five regular soldiers. The
only way of treating them is either to get men equal in character
and intelligence, or, failing the individual, huge masses of troops.
It is strange that soldiers in the field should have more tolerant
views than those prevailing at home. But beware of driving men
to desperation! We desire a speedy peace, and the last thing we
want is that this war should enter on a guerrilla phase."

On March 24 he telegraphed from Ladysmith, where he had
just distinguished himself in battle, to London: "I earnestly hope
and urge that a generous policy be followed. The wise and right
course is to beat down all who resist, even to the last man, but
not to withhold forgiveness and even friendship from any who
wish to surrender. The Dutch farmers who have joined the enemy
are traitors only in the legal sense. That they obeyed the natural
instinct of their blood to join the men of their own race, though
no justification, is an excuse."

This did not have a pleasing sound to a country still stirred up
by a war that they had all begun by regarding as a mere stroll.
It sounded least pleasant in British Natal, which had had to suffer so much from the war. The Natal press published furious
attacks on Churchill. The only man who understood him was
Sir Alfred Milner, the High Commissioner. While out hunting
he said to his young friend Churchill: "I thought they would be
upset, especially in Natal, by your message. Of course all these
people have got to live together. They must forgive and forget
and make a common country. But now passions are running too
high. I understand your feelings, but it does no good to express
them now."

Churchill on his side could understand this. With all his revolutionary impulses he had a deep respect for the statesmanship
whose last great figures survived from the Victorian Era. He was
a Victorian rebel himself. Naturally he would be a candidate on
the Tory platform when he came home.

On July 7, 1900, Winston Churchill took off the uniform. But this time it was definite, thought Great Britain's future Supreme War Lord. Leaving Cape Town, he arrived thirteen days later in Southampton. He spent those days and the greater part of the night apart from his fellow-travellers, in the quietest corner of the after deck, bent over the railing. In a voice of thunder he urged the waves to vote Conservative, and he drowned out the summer storms as he fulminated across the broad ocean, telling why he was for an energetic but humane conclusion to the Boer War. He was preparing for his election campaign. During these early years he still learned by heart every word to be spoken in public. No one in the auditorium ever noticed. When he had once perspired over each relative sentence he gave the impression of being a genius at improvisation. Here was the same histrionic talent he had shown in the school performance at Brighton.

He was in great haste to get to Oldham. New elections were already announced. He must proclaim his candidacy at once. His mother delayed him momentarily in London first. To young Churchill's astonishment it appeared that even mothers have a private life. The private life of the widowed Lady Randolph was named Mr. George Cornwallis-West. The two were now about to marry. Marry? The thought flitted through the head of the bride's son. Well, at least Mamma would take things easy for a little while. She too had been eternally in a hurry; it was a family characteristic. Churchill congratulated, assisted, even blushed on the suitable occasion, and plunged back into the tumult of Oldham.

When last year's defeated candidate marched into Oldham with a procession of ten landaus, the streets of the little city were packed with enthusiastic operatives and mill-girls. "God bless Churchill, England's noblest hero," a banner hung across the main street greeted him. "See the Conquering Hero Comes," the band played over and over again. In honor of the hero of the Boer War they played it oftener than "God Save the King!" Indeed Oldham had every reason to be proud of capturing Churchill for the contest. Eleven constituencies had offered themselves to him. Nevertheless he remained faithful to the notoriously fickle Oldham. "Because he is our adopted son," said the constituents in a pub of an evening. "Because I want to wipe out my black eye!" Churchill explained his own constancy.

The Lancashire anthem now was:

> Then there is Winston Churchill,
> And all I want to say—
> He is the greatest and the latest
> Correspondent of the day.

This ditty made the rounds of all the music-halls, it was sung at meetings, it rang out like a chorale at the Theatre Royal (yes, there was one in Oldham) when the candidate presented himself to his constituents. With all the enthusiasm that those constituents felt, Oldham was still a hot spot. Beyond doubt the majority of the working population were in the Liberal and Radical camp. On the other hand a wave of war enthusiasm was passing over the country. These were khaki elections, of the kind that was to be repeated after the first World War, and obviously the one to profit by this general temper was the Conservative Party. "Every seat lost to the Government is a seat gained to the Boers," was the slogan. The great Chamberlain had coined it. He was now at the height of his popularity and power. It was an unexampled distinction when he himself came to Oldham to speak for Churchill.

"The first time I came here to sell them screws," he smiled between tight lips as his young friend received him at the station. The great man looked like a well-groomed statue. His sharply chiseled face was motionless, rigid as a mask; his carefully waved hair slightly graying. The right eye, behind the monocle, was wide open, the left half closed; it had seen too much. His complexion was still rosy. That was what happened when a man got shaved three times a day. Of course he wore the black suit of the era, with silk lapels, white waistcoat, fat gold watch-chain across it, a pearl in the heavy black silk cravat with its white stripes, an orchid in the buttonhole. It seemed incredible that this man had struggled up from the very bottom as a tradesman and as a politician. It was incredible that he had once been the leader of the Radicals, the people's mayor of Birmingham, the darling of the slums. At the age of forty this hard-hitting business man had saved up a hundred and twenty thousand pounds, so that he could retire from his firm of Chamberlain & Nettlefold. At the same time, as local boss, he had parked, paved, assized, marketed, gassed and watered his city. From then on he belonged not to himself and the neighborhood, but to the Empire.

It was a transformation that reflected the blossoming-out of England. Outwardly it was astounding. Inwardly—remember, this was 1900—all was unchanged. The monocle and the orchid had not altered good old Joe. The Theatre Royal, where he was about to speak, was crowded with enthusiasts. In front of the building, however, a hostile Radical crowd had gathered that greeted Chamberlain and Churchill in their carriage with jeers and boos.

Churchill, rather dismayed, turned to the great man. How disagreeable to have involved him in such a situation! But Chamberlain's pink complexion had turned to a darker red, and there was a broad smile on his face. He took positively physical pleasure in the spectacle. He loved the roar of the crowd. He could feel that they were excited at seeing the great arch-enemy eye to eye. Somehow even they were under his spell. And he never feared English democracy. He received noise and catcalls with a friendly smile.

Then the great Chamberlain spoke to the meeting. He had prepared for his address with careful notes. He spoke in a low voice, forcefully, but with self-possession. Once he made a mistake in some figure. At once the hecklers were upon him. "Excuse me," he corrected himself. "Of course one should never be unfair . . ." At this the whole house applauded.

Churchill could not yet equal this perfection on the platform. One of his important backers interrupted him at some point. "I disagree with you," Churchill retorted. That would cost some dozens of votes. But even as a young man, Churchill followed the inner voice.

He grew swiftly accustomed to public speaking. The campaign lasted six weeks. In that time he made more than a hundred and ten speeches. He seldom forgot to work in his South African adventures. Once he mentioned the name of the estimable Mr. Dewsnap, the Oldham engineer who had helped him escape the Boers. "His wife's in the gallery," shouted a voice in the audience. Rather embarrassed, Mrs. Dewsnap got up and showed herself to the crowd. Churchill bowed to her from the platform. A storm of enthusiasm swept the Imperial Theatre. Now there was no further doubt of his election.

Oldham still remained Radical. Churchill's team partner, a certain Mr. C. B. Crisp, was defeated by his Liberal opponent. But of course even Liberals and Radicals voted for their hero. Mr. Walter Runciman, who had beaten him a year before, found that this time luck had deserted him. When the votes had been counted Winston Churchill strode through a tumult of cheers and exultations to the Conservative Club. He had won the race. From now on the House of Commons was to be his real home.

Overnight his election made him one of the most popular after-dinner speakers in the country. The great Chamberlain invited him to his own constituency of Birmingham for two addresses. London telegraphed to him. But just as he was on his way to the London meeting, a message reached him from Mr. Balfour, who had coined the phrase "a young man of promises." Now Balfour needed him for his own support at Manchester. There the Conservatives were holding a monster meeting with five or six thousand in attendance. The whole hall came to its feet, and gave the young man an ovation when he appeared in the midst of the demonstration. From now on he was never to speak to less than thousands. In the Midlands every house where he was announced to speak was jammed full. After three weeks of triumphs and successes he enjoyed his highest distinction: the great Chamberlain invited him to a bottle of 1834 port.

At the same time his two books about the Boer War appeared
in rapid succession; both were immediate best-sellers. This was
very important. For Churchill realized he was embarking on a
career that would devour him whole, and yet would never bring
him in a penny. But first he must make some money for a few
months. He started out on his lecture tour. With the help of a
magic lantern, the predecessor of our movie machine, he told
attentive audiences about his adventures in the Boer War, particularly his escape from Pretoria.

The greatest names in England took the chair when the young
hero spoke. Lord Wolseley led off. Sir Arthur Conan Doyle, the
father of Sherlock Holmes, was second. Lord Londonderry, the
Marquess of Ava, the Duke of Marlborough put themselves at
his disposal. He spoke every evening, and every evening meant
at least a hundred pounds. Liverpool was the most eager. Here
his lecture at the Philadelphia Hall brought him three hundred
pounds. In November, having visited but half of the United
Kingdom, he was able to deposit forty-five hundred pounds at
the bank.

Of course there was also opposition from the Radicals, who
would have none of the Boer War and its hero. This opposition
increased to the point of ugly personal attacks. He had violated
his parole, broken his word, when he broke out of the jail at
Pretoria, said some people. Why had he not looked after his captive companions better? buzzed others. Of course there was not
a word of truth in the parole story. He had never promised that
he would not try to escape. And as far as the "treason" to his companions went, they themselves wrote indignant letters to their
belated champions. They repudiated such slander.

Toward the close of the year Churchill went to America to
give his lecture on this side. Major Pond, the well-known lecture
agent, had engaged him. He announced his star with the poster:
"Winston Churchill, twenty-six years old, author of six books,
hero of four wars, Member of Parliament, forthcoming Prime
Minister of England." It was a very true prophecy, but young

Churchill was horrified when he read it. He insisted that the poster be withdrawn.

He had rough sailing in America. Mark Twain did introduce him most cordially at his New York debut, but the audience was planted full of Irishmen, who staged an anti-British demonstration. In Chicago the Irish made the lecture almost impossible. Still Churchill managed to handle them. When they burst out in demonstrations for the Boers, he took the wind out of their sails: "You are quite right, gentlemen. The Boers were brave and chivalrous opponents. If I were a Boer, I would certainly have fought against England." Nevertheless he did not quite understand why his American audiences, whose manners, language, appearance and behavior were so like those of the English at home, should sometimes display such hostile sentiments.

Mark Twain, who was no Irishman and had no axe to grind, explained the American standpoint to him. The Boer War, he said in substance, was an imperialist campaign.

"My country right or wrong," replied Churchill.

"But only when the poor country is fighting for her life," replied Mark Twain. Finally the white-haired American philosopher and humorist ended the debate by writing in one of his books for Churchill the dedication: "To do good, is noble. To teach others to do good, is noble—and no trouble."

At Boston, indeed, the audience spoke enthusiastically for Anglo-American friendship. An enthusiastic demonstration showed Churchill whose side the warm heart of the cool New Englanders was beating on. And in Canada, where the American lecture tour ended, the subaltern of the Boer War was made a national hero.

CHAPTER X

Youthful Vagaries

THE fever rose in the evening hours. By day the House had been occupied with strictly impersonal debate. It was customary in those days to discuss even the most trifling bill seriously for three days, to weigh pros and cons, to measure arguments. The papers filled many pages with verbatim parliamentary reports. The voters read every line and every word. It was the great age of parliamentarianism. Only the late hours, from nine-thirty P.M. to midnight, did spirits grow warm. The Leader of the Opposition focused all criticism in a sharp frontal attack. The Chancellor of the Exchequer, who was also Leader of the House, replied with the united strength of the majority. But numbers alone were not decisive. It was the power of conviction that counted, not the number of votes. If the Opposition sounded more convincing it was a very serious matter for the Government.

Since time immemorial the head of the Government had been Lord Salisbury, who embodied all the dignity and wisdom of the century that had just ended. The second in command, Chancellor and Leader of the House, the spokesman in debate, was Mr. Arthur Balfour, the coming man. But of course Joe Chamberlain, monocle in eye, orchid in buttonhole, dominated the Government.

Opposite, and below the gangway, as though to emphasize his opposition still more, sat a young Welsh solicitor in a shabby, rumpled suit. The smile he turned on Joe Chamberlain's splendor had not a trace of friendliness. Even the monocle, he thought would not cure the great man of short-sightedness. And orchid raising was far less important than the potato crop, for which

s usual, nothing had been done. Unperturbed, Chamberlain
miled back. To him the House of Commons was still the world's
oremost club, and political differences made no hard feelings.
On the contrary, if Mr. Lloyd George wished to speak, Mr. Chamberlain would listen with marked attention.

Certainly Mr. Lloyd George wished to speak. His followers,
few savage Radicals, a handful of undisciplined Welshmen, and
ighty Irish Nationalists who hated the House in which they sat,
were waiting only for the initial moment to cheer the leader of
he coming revolution. He mercilessly attacked the Boer War
nd England's accursed imperialism as well.

In the debate over the Boer War he presented an extremely
ame amendment. But when he got up from his seat on the third
bench, proceeding at once to a fierce attack, he would not move
is own amendment. He preferred to speak a few plain words.

The youngest member of the House felt a little uncomfort-
ble at this proclamation. Winston Churchill was to make his
maiden speech today. He had prepared a polished address tear-
ng the Opposition's amendment to pieces. *Oleum et opera per-
idi*—I have wasted oil and trouble—a sentence from Harrow came
o him, one of the few Latin quotations he remembered. For-
unately he had prepared and learned by heart a half-dozen
peeches, in order to be prepared for all emergencies.

Only four days before, on January 23, 1901, Churchill had
owed his way into the House and thus into history. The whole
House smiled encouragingly as the young man bowed to the
peaker. At that time he looked almost boyish, although he was
wenty-six years old, and the most-advertised youth of the age.
till his milky face, with the rather refractory reddish hair, the
estless eyes, the flickering lips, did not seem to fit into the
ong black silk-lapeled coat and high-buttoned vest; and his neck
was evidently unaccustomed to the wing collar with the short
ravat that he was now stuffed into. At his parliamentary debut
Winston Churchill really looked like a belated candidate for con-
rmation. A certain youthful spirit of contradiction was expected

of him. No doubt he would take his place below the gangway
perhaps in the seat of his father, who had always been a rebel. But
after taking his oath the new member for Oldham modestly with
drew to a seat behind the Government bench, as befitted a simple
back-bencher.

The older members, who spent their lives on those benches
and formed one big family among themselves, were faintly
touched and a little amused to see this image of his father
Winston had indisputably inherited the habits and even the
mannerisms of Lord Randolph. Like him he was in the habit of
throwing up his head—it had the same square forehead and the
same large eyes—and laughing loudly. Winston's hands too were
in constant motion, either tearing up pieces of paper or travel
ing uneasily over his chest and resting on his heart as if to soothe
pain. His voice was Lord Randolph's voice—resounding, with a
slight but menacing tinge of hardness. He crossed the lobbies with
the same quick pace, and he, like Lord Randolph, kept playing
with his hat as if swinging a cane. How deep the son's resem
blance to the father went was something that the elder members
would yet learn to their horror.

It was late evening, the hour to settle all scores, and Mr. Lloyd
George was tearing to shreds the conduct of the Boer War and
what he described as the inhumanity of the British troops
Churchill himself had attacked certain excesses. He had always
pleaded for honorable treatment of the Boers, and characterized
them as chivalrous foes. He had always thought farm-burning a
hateful folly. He had protested against the execution of General
Scheepers, and had played some part behind the scenes in avert
ing the execution of Commander Kruitzinger. He constantly ad
vocated finishing the war with generosity, and then making haste
to return to the paths of peace, retrenchment and reform. He
was not ashamed to use this slogan, which had originated with
the Liberal leader Gladstone. It had been constantly in Lord Ran
dolph's mouth.

But he would not tamely submit to the attacks on the army—

not yet. He got up after Lloyd George had amiably closed by saying: "I will curtail my remarks, as I am sure the House wishes to hear a new member," and riposted at once: "Instead of making his violent speech without moving his moderate amendment, he had better have moved his moderate amendment without making his violent speech."

The first round of applause rang out. Churchill's eyes twinkled gratefully toward his neighbor Mr. Bowes. The latter had put him up to this thrust. Then he went on with his speech. There was no denying it, the man who was to develop into the greatest orator in the English tongue stammered pitifully in his maiden speech. He was too excited. The entire house was listening to him with tense interest. That merely made matters worse. Gradually he forced himself to be calm. He fired off his well-prepared ammunition broadside after broadside. "His flowers of rhetoric are hothouse plants," an older colleague who understood his trade remarked later. But the broadsides hit home. Just one miscarried. "The Boers who are fighting in the field—and if I were a Boer I hope I should be fighting in the field . . ." he was saying.

Just then Chamberlain settled the monocle more firmly in his eye, and murmured a few words to his neighbor. The neighbor, Mr. George Wyndham, revealed later that the great man had said: "That's the way to throw away seats!" A conflict was in the making.

The eighty Irish members, who were of course pro-Boer and anti-British, kept interrupting Churchill. Nobody took this seriously. The Irishmen did not take themselves seriously. They interrupted the speaker chiefly for the sake of the argument. They took pleasure even in his arguments, and they laughed at Churchill's jokes at their expense. When he declared that he was for the continuation of the war, which on the whole was being conducted with unusual humanity and generosity, and that he asked for a full guarantee of the Boers' property and religion, and an assurance of equal rights and a promise of representative institutions, even the Irish applauded, perhaps a shade ironically.

Masters of verbal duelling themselves, they wanted to fight according to the rules. Their interruptions were intended to stimulate, not to discourage, the speaker. "Last but by no means least," Churchill wound up, "the British army would most readily accord to a brave foe all the honors of war."

The speech was a complete success. Some of the experts, of course, could tell that it had been learned by heart. But the industry and earnestness of the work impressed everyone. The great Chamberlain congratulated him; so did Herbert Asquith, the Liberal leader; Sir Robert Reid; and, most warmly of all, Mr. Broderick, the Secretary for War. He felt that his new assistant in Parliament was worth a division to him. Churchill was especially welcome as the son of Lord Randolph. Mr. Broderick had been Under Secretary for War when Churchill senior had chucked his career after a conflict with the War Office. Mr. Broderick had always felt that he was involved in, if not guilty of, Lord Randolph's tragic fall. Risen now to head of the War Office, he could work all the better with the son of his old adversary.

Churchill was so exhausted by his first cavalry charge in Parliament that he had to be plied with restoratives at the bar. Lloyd George happened to be standing there. A colleague formally introduced the two.

"Judging from your sentiments you are standing against the light!" murmured the unpressed Welsh Radical, who obviously had a mortgage on light.

"You take a singularly detached view of the British Empire!" retorted Churchill, the jingo.

Then the two clinked glasses, and fifteen years later they saved the Empire together.

Perhaps this first success went a little to the head of the parliamentarian in the making. A few days after his maiden speech he joined again in the Boer-War debate, pleading for a full account of the operations. "I have in many cases myself supplied the only report given to the country on some important matter," he said, referring to the correspondence in the *Morning Post*. "I feel keenly the responsibility which has thus been placed upon me, and I think it is time for the War Office and the Government to relieve me of some of it."

Whereupon Herbert Asquith spoke of "that burden of responsibility that at present weighs so heavily on the honorable member's shoulders." With this little touch of irony the Leader of the Liberals found the weak place in Churchill's heart. The Benjamin of Parliament was burning to shoulder some of the responsibility. A reorganization of the Government was due almost immediately. The aged Lord Salisbury was obliged at last to lay aside the burden of office. And Mr. Arthur Balfour, the presumptive Premier, must, indeed he must, find some minor Cabinet job for the hero from Pretoria, the Member for Oldham.

An opportunity to enter the limelight again occurred within a few weeks. It was the ticklish case of General Colville, who had just been appointed Brigade Commander at Gibraltar. Only after the appointment was made did the Government discover that the General had committed some minor military blunder in South Africa about a year before. They immediately relieved him of his new command. Naturally the affair was a splendid opportunity for the Opposition to create a disturbance. The Liberals constituted themselves champions of General Colville's persecuted innocence, pursued with positively Old-Testament vindictiveness by the War Office.

Churchill sprang into the breach. Here he was on his own ground. Perhaps, having been a subaltern himself but a few months before, he was attracted by the chance to sit in judgment upon generals, who had always made his life so difficult. But like David he was a wise, a just judge. He spoke softly for he did not as yet feel quite at ease in his place, a little hastily and with nervous gestures. Sometimes he bent forward; in his embarrassment he would lean on the front bench. But there was sound sense in his remarks. Nay, more, he successfully pulled off the priceless parliamentary feat of reconciling Government and Opposition both to what he said. "War is a game containing a large element

of chance," he said, with the authority of a fighter on three continents so far. "Defeat and victory are not necessarily an accurate
measure of capacity." His strong sense of justice and his eye for
both sides of the medal, a gift that was later to distinguish him
quite particularly from the great masses, found early expression
here. For the purposes of the moment, however, it was more
important that the attacks of the Liberal speakers, Harcourt, Asquith, Morley, and Sir Edward Grey—the first team had been
brought into play across the House—were repulsed, and that with
a shrewdness recognized by both sides. Beyond doubt young
Churchill had got his Government out of an unpleasant situation. Mr. George Wyndham, the Irish Secretary, who sat beside
Joe Chamberlain, later reported that the great man had murmured something like approbation and agreement.

But the harmony evaporated before it could really develop to
the full. Churchill was not yet fated for peace and quiet. More
than ever he stood under the shadow of his father, who had never
found rest on his short journey through life. He was scarcely in
Parliament before he conjured up the memory of the beloved
dead. He and the young aristocrats he had met in London during
his furlough from India, who of course all had inherited constituencies, founded a club that invited a guest of distinction
to dinner once a week. They even invited Lord Salisbury. The
Prime Minister asked to be excused, but invited the young gentlemen to be his guests in Arlington Street. Standing on the pavement after an evening of the statesman's wisdom, Lord Percy,
one of the group, said to Churchill: "I wonder how it feels to
have been Prime Minister for twenty years and just be about to
die."

The young gentlemen were rebels and skeptics. Lord Percy
went even further: he was a well-bred herald of doom. Walking
with Churchill one autumn evening at Dunrobin, he declared
that Armageddon was at hand.

Armageddon? Churchill knew the word only from the Bible.
What could it mean in this kindly world?

The world would not be kindly much longer, declared Lord
Percy. The skeptic in him cloaked a religious visionary. During
the night stroll with his friend he poured out his heart. Lord
Percy was unshakably convinced that twelve apostles had been
sent to warn mankind. But no one had heard their voice, and
as the last of the apostles had died at the same moment with
Queen Victoria, no new warning would come. With clairvoyant
certainty Lord Percy predicted an era of fearful wars and unmeas-
ured terror.

It was odd, but just at that moment, quite without apparent
relevance, Churchill was reminded of a good-looking, seemingly
innocent yet alarmingly strange young man who happened to
be staying at Dunrobin, and with whom he had sometimes played
billiards. He was the German Crown Prince.

The Thursday dinner of the aristocratic back-benchers was not
too popular with the Conservative Party. In an atrocious pun,
elder members called them the "Hooligans" because Lord Hugh
Cecil was their uncrowned leader. In addition to Winston
Churchill and Lord Percy, Mr. Ian Malcolm and Mr. Arthur
Stanley were also members. They were all scions of the greatest
families in the realm. In reality, people said, they were a group
of unreliable young people whose real object was none other
than to revive Lord Randolph Churchill's Tory Democracy.
Churchill flung himself with fiery zeal into the struggle for his
father's heritage.

Lord Randolph, who was Chancellor of the Exchequer at
thirty-seven after a brilliant period in the India Office, and
held the Conservative Party machine in his clutches as Leader
in the House of Commons, had shown new roads and new visions
to Toryism. Historically considered his weakness, and in fact
the cause of his fall, was his lack of restraint. Lord Salisbury,
almost sixty at the time, had treated the other and much younger
man as his equal throughout. But Lord Randolph wanted to be
a dictator. The ridiculous trifle of a few thousand pounds in the
Army Estimates, which he considered too large, was what he

took for an excuse, as we have seen, to exercise a pressure that was bound to lead to political suicide. The Tories were done with him. He could never have felt personally at ease in the Liberal Party, with which he had intellectually so much in common. Westminster and Whitehall were both full of his intimate friends, but he fitted into no political combination.

And now his son was walking in his footsteps, as like him as his own ghost. He too began to grouse about the Party almost before he was dry behind the ears. In April of 1902 the case of Mr. Cartwright came before Parliament. He had served a one-year prison sentence in South Africa for publishing a defeatist article in the midst of the Boer War. Now the War Office refused to let him into England. The radical defenders of human rights noisily took Mr. Cartwright's part. "It is undesirable to increase the number of persons in England who disseminate anti-British propaganda," replied the Secretary for War. He was quite right about this, and Winston Churchill today would be the first to say such a thing. But in those days he saw red if the War Office so much as opened its mouth. As the spokesman of the precociously world-weary "Hooligans," who made a joke of politics, he supported the hateful criticisms of the Radicals.

It was Thursday, and this time the great Chamberlain was the guest of the dinner party. "I am dining in very bad company," he began jokingly. Was the great man really joking? When the "Hooligans" objected that in the Cartwright case the Government had behaved ineptly and arrogantly, he replied out of his wealth of experience: "What is the use of supporting your own Government only when it is right? Just in a case like this you should have come to our aid!" But discipline was not yet part of young Churchill's flesh and blood. Perhaps they had tried to pound too much discipline into him at Harrow and in the 4th Hussars. He was indeed carried away by Joe Chamberlain's irresistible personality, which flashed at dinner with all its old splendor, but when the guest of honor took his leave with the words: "I will give you a priceless secret, young gentlemen. Tariffs! They are the politics of the future, and of the near future!", he pricked up his ears suspiciously. Tariffs. He had never really looked into the word. But it had an ill sound in his ears. It sounded like reaction of deepest dye. He would remember it. Not as Chamberlain meant it—"Study them closely and make yourself masters of them!" No, it roused his distrust. Tariffs! For twenty years that word would howl in his ears. It was to fix a great part of his destiny.

The first collision, however, was over the question of the Army Budget. The same spring when Joe Chamberlain dropped his dark hints about tariffs, Mr. Broderick presented his Army Estimates, by which six new army corps were to be organized, three of them always ready for service abroad. It was an attempt, modest in its actual demands but grandiose in conception, to make England army-conscious, to overcome that suicidal softness whose consequences we witness today. The failure of this first educational attempt was due largely to the resistance of the young M.P., Winston Churchill. He has worked all his life to make good this youthful sin. Nevertheless there is something of classic irony in the story—and in his life's history.

Churchill had only to see Mr. Broderick, his father's old adversary, stand up, and he would make demands similar to those that had wrecked Lord Randolph. At once Winston Churchill was on his feet, delivering a fiery anti-militarist speech that echoed throughout the Kingdom: "The House cannot view without grave apprehension the continual growth of purely military expenditure. The House desires to postpone the final decision on future military policy until calmer times."

It was the voice of Lord Randolph speaking from the grave. The *Times* of London, although itself opposing the bill, remarked: "Mr. Winston Churchill repeats again the most disastrous mistakes of his father's career. His amendment is a very mischievous and wrong-headed proposal." The Conservative leaders joined with the *Times*. When Churchill spoke again, they displayed open hostility. Were they to witness again Lord

Randolph's pride and fall? Were they to tolerate the pushful-
ness, the conceited insubordination of this youthful subaltern-
lecturer-politician-journalist-writer and ne'er-do-well? He was far
too ambitious; that was the trouble with him. They had to listen
resentfully to such words as these: "It is a great mistake to spend
thirty millions a year on the army. Many less soldiers than provided for by the new scheme should be kept ready for service
abroad. One corps is enough to fight savages, and six are not
enough to fight Europeans. Of course we must win victory in
South Africa. No price is too high for an early and victorious
peace. Then, however, in peace-time this expenditure must be
cut down. I refer to the half-forgotten episode of my father's
fall. Then the government triumphed, the Chancellor of the
Exchequer went down forever, and with him, as it now seems,
there fell also the cause of retrenchment and economy, so that the
very memory thereof seems to have perished, and the words themselves have a curiously old-fashioned ring about them!"

To the elder members it sounded like irony when the baby of
the House conjured up the good old days. But neither the elder
members nor Winston Churchill himself understood the deeper
irony. That irony was in the fact that the sudden arch-pacifist
was of course a born fighter, and even though it was now a white
banner fluttering ahead of him, he followed it at the same gallop
that had swept him forward in the cavalry charge of Omdurman.
Even when he attacked the army he could speak only in military
metaphors: "I am glad that the House has allowed me to lift
again the tattered flag of retrenchment and economy—the tattered
flag I found lying on a stricken field." Is that the language of a
pacifist, or of a swashbuckler from the Hussars? Basically it was
the fighting son, raising the shield of his fallen father on high in
the midst of the battle. "This cause I have inherited—a cause for
which the late Lord Randolph Churchill made the greatest sacrifice of any Minister of modern times." At the same time he saw
visions of the war of the future. "Now when mighty populations
are impelled on each other, each individual embittered and in-

flamed, when the resources of science and civilization sweep away everything that might mitigate their fury, an European war can only end in the ruin of the vanquished and the scarcely less fatal commercial dislocations and exhaustion of the conquerors. The wars of people will be more terrible than the wars of kings."

Prophetic words for the spring of 1901! None of his contemporaries spoke them. The junior Member for Oldham, aged twenty-seven, was a generation ahead of his world. He was the first to raise the question of the fate of modern man, which is now befalling us. But he could not find the right answer then. Beginning in the noonday of his life he ceased to do anything except give the right answer—defense of civilization! As a grim young warrior, however, he galloped down a blind alley. "The honor and security of the British Empire do not depend, and can never depend, on the British Army. The Admiralty is the only office strong enough to ensure the British Empire. We shall make a fatal bargain if we allow the moral force which this country so long has exerted, to become diminished or perhaps even destroyed for the sake of the costly, trumpery, dangerous military playthings on which the Secretary for War has set his heart."

The Liberals rolled this speech luxuriously across their tongues. No matter what the result of the division in the House, the Conservative majority was evidently split; the Liberals were bound to profit. In such terms did peaceful parliamentary democracy think when the foundations of national existence were at stake. The Liberals gave Churchill every sort of encouragement. Massingham, their journalistic spokesman, wrote: "The author of this speech will be Prime Minister—Liberal Prime Minister of England—I hope."

The Conservatives of course were horrified. "Wilful mutiny!" was their reply, and they shouted at the rebel, "Please go!" With all their indignation they remained gentlemen, not forgetting to say please. Mr. Broderick, the Secretary for War, whom Churchill had so intemperately attacked, replied with dignity and understanding: "Those of us who disagree with the Honorable Member for Oldham can only hope that the time will come when his judgment will grow up to his ability, when he will look back with regret to the day on which he came down to the House to preach Imperialism without being able to bear the burden of Imperialism. We hope for the day when the hereditary qualities of eloquence and courage he possesses may be tempered also by discarding the hereditary desire to run Imperialism on the cheap."

Lord Stanley, then Financial Secretary to the War Office, put his finger plainly on the sore spot. "Churchill's speech," he said, "is a quixotic attempt, which we must all admire, to take up again the cry of his distinguished father, and to try to assist what is a fallen cause and bring it back to life." Lord Stanley today is Lord Derby, England's grand old man, one of the strongest single influences in the realm. Immediately after the catastrophe of Munich he strained every nerve to put Winston Churchill in command of the Government before it was too late.

At an early division Churchill was the only Conservative member to vote against Broderick's Army Reform Scheme. It did not trouble him in the least that he was isolated in his Party. The country, he felt, was with him. English thrift and the easy-going ways of a fundamentally unmilitary nation were his natural allies. Even when he was wrong Churchill spoke from the heart of his people. The *Times,* which has always suffered from spasms of appeasement, printed a series of articles against the Army Reform Scheme, even if by no means with Churchill's arguments. The anonymous author, as it later appeared, was Leopold Amery, Churchill's Harrow schoolmate and lifelong faithful follower. When the Thunderer of Fleet Street puts on a troubled expression, it is never a good sign for the fate of a proposal bill. As a matter of fact the Army Reform Scheme was pushed off into committees, and ignominiously buried in some sub-committee after two years. England had again missed an opportunity to awake. A little back-bencher had got his way. Mr. Broderick, the loser, was transferred at the next change of Cabinet to the considerably less controversial India Office. And so Lord Randolph was avenged at last.

In those rushing days of battle Winston Churchill aged years in weeks. By the autumn of 1901, a few months after the fight for Army Reform began, no one would have taken him for the baby of the House. On October 2, 1901, the American journalist Julian Ralph, a disinterested onlooker, wrote in the *Daily Mail*:

> "Already Mr. Churchill's head is carried with a droop that comes to those who read and study hard. He drops his head forward as if it were heavy. That is what you see in one moment— a pose prophetic of what is too likely to fasten itself upon him before he reaches middle age."

The "Hooligans" went with their fellow. He controlled at first seventeen, then twenty-four back-benchers. They were now called the "Malcolmtents" after their zealous member Mr., later Sir, Ian Malcolm. They were not men to scorn strong language, and they cheered Churchill when he spoke in an address at Oldham in January, 1903, of "the phantom army, this total, costly, ghastly failure, this humbug and shame." Of course the taxpayers applauded as well.

Winston Churchill grew popular with astonishing speed, even if in a disastrous way. His anti-militaristic speeches goaded the country to a frenzy. In them he used one of the shabbier tricks of pacific propaganda. What a shame to waste the money! was the burden of the song. "I regard it as a grave mistake in Imperial policy to spend thirty millions a year on the army," he declared on March 12, 1901. "I hold that the continued increase in army expenditure cannot be viewed by supporters of the Government without the greatest alarm and apprehension, and by members who represent working-class constituencies without extreme dislike." Quite obviously the representative of the workingmen's district of Oldham was concerned primarily with vote-getting. In the second place he had to go on revenging his father upon Mr. Broderick. "If the capacity of a War Minister may be measured in any way by the amount of money he can claim from his colleagues for military purposes," he continued in the same speech, "the right honorable gentleman will certainly go down in history as the greatest War Minister this country ever had."

Could he not see that the vital interests of the nation were at stake? Yes, on the contrary, even in his earliest days Churchill had grasped the problem of the British Empire's existence more clearly than any other man of his peaceable, self-satisfied, carefree and unsuspecting time. Now, almost forty years later, his address before the Cambridge University Carlton Club on June 1, 1901, has a sound of somber prophecy: "Our position is one of great freedom, wealth and power. But it is also very insecure. We are an artificial country. We do not grow enough food to keep ourselves alive. We have an enormous industrial population crowded together in great cities, far removed from the natural agricultural life of man, and dependent for their daily bread entirely on the condition of trade. The food we eat, the clothes we wear, indeed our very existence depends on our power to hold our own in colonial and foreign markets. If we are undersold or outmatched or arbitrarily excluded, we perish. A vast number of working people who now get their living in England would have to migrate to the new centres of production. We should think as a nation of the world. I think that a melancholic possibility, but it is a possibility we must face."

Despite his clear realization of an inherent structural emergency that only national self-sacrifice could overcome, Churchill continued his campaign against national defense. In his twenty-fifth, twenty-sixth, twenty-seventh years he provided a classic example of the inner struggle between the politician and the statesman. Psychologically considered this may be a very interesting period in his development; from the historical standpoint he undoubtedly had, in his formative years, a disastrous share in English self-deception. He did not hesitate to describe the Army Reform, on February 13, 1903, as "The Great English Fraud." "You are spending too much money on your army," he shouted at the Government, to whose majority he himself still belonged, at least in

name. "You don't get value for the money you spend, and it is
all humbug to pretend you do. The professional soldier is an
artificial luxury, very expensive to keep, withdrawn both from
the industrial and family life of the nation. Consequently we
should have as few of him as possible. Mr. Broderick's policy is
to have a large army of 150,000 regimented soldiers in England
and, regardless of the cost, to organize it in army corps on the
German model . . . I do not believe that the increase (in men
and costs) is necessary, sensible or honest. The money . . . would
have been better devoted to the reduction of debt or taxation."

A few days later, on the 23rd of February, he observed with
satisfaction that the Army Scheme was not yet carried out, although two years had already passed since its introduction.

The promising young insurrectionary found it was much more
fun to attack the Government than to support it. In the House
he was still sitting among the ministerialists, but his applause came
more and more from the Opposition. Nor could it be denied that
the intellectuals opposite attracted him personally more strongly
than the traditionalists in his own ranks. Brilliant speakers like
Lloyd George, contradictory figures like Morley, peculiar minds
like Asquith and Sir Edward Grey, attracted him and seemed to
have much more in common with him than the well-bred Conservative mediocrities.

No one was such a perfect embodiment of conservatism as Mr.
Arthur Balfour. Nor was anyone so mistrustful of the erratic
"young man of promises." When he succeeded Lord Salisbury
according to program he did not even offer Churchill a junior
post in his Cabinet. That wound hurt. Deep in his heart Churchill
had counted on having a chance to show his abilities in the administration. Mr. Balfour simply overlooked the fact that he had no
other young man of such stature in his ranks. He noticed only
that the young man was always breaking ranks.

Remarkably enough it was the great Chamberlain who re-
proved this oversight. He said to Margot Asquith, the later Lady
Oxford: "Winston is the cleverest of all the young men. The mis-

take Arthur made was to let him go." Nevertheless it was Chamberlain again who had to give the sign for the final parting. The sign was the word Tariff.

This was the king of all the old Imperialist's ideas. At first he was quite alone in urging it, alone even in his own party. In the middle of May he made his celebrated speech at his own inherited Birmingham, where he could tell his people anything. Free Trade within the Empire! was his new watchword. The accent was on *within the Empire,* not on *Free Trade.* Imperial Preference which came into being many years later at Ottawa, was made into a platform. On the same day Prime Minister Balfour spoke on the opposite side. The Conservative Party was split.

Winston Churchill caught fire from the flames that were consuming the Party. "I wonder, Sir," he asked in a public address, "what will happen to this country if the Fair Trade issue is boldly raised by some responsible person of eminence and authority?" In rushing to oppose the Tariff Reform with all his might and all his fighting spirit, he maintained that he was also fighting for the tradition of the country and the soul of the Conservative Party. "This new fiscal policy means a change not only in the historic English parties, but in the conditions of our public life. The old Conservative Party with its religious convictions and constitutional principles will disappear and a new party will arise—like perhaps the Republican Party in the U. S. A.—rigid, materialist and secular, whose opinions will turn on tariffs and will cause the lobbies to be crowded with the touts of protected industries."

As we can see, it was not so much the economic results of protectionism that he feared. Churchill's deepest feeling was injured —his sense of political romance. He did not want the House to be degraded into mere representation of interests. He began to ask himself whether the Liberal intellectuals did not express the spirit of England better than the Conservative traditionalists. He pursued the great Chamberlain to his fastness of Birmingham. "Joe or Winnie?" was the question he propounded there.

In the reshuffle of the Cabinet that resulted from the Conservative split, the great Chamberlain retired. But it was only a tactical maneuver. His eldest son Austen, whom the great man had long groomed to become his successor, inherited the Chancellorship of the Exchequer. The protectionist course thus continued to be followed, although the Prime Minister, Mr. Balfour, declared himself neutral in the dispute.

A few weeks later the Duke of Devonshire, another Conservative Free-Trader, resigned his seat. In his farewell message he advised the Conservative electors at the by-elections in Dulwich and Lewisham to abstain from voting rather than support their own party's candidate. Churchill went one step further, and wished complete success to the Liberal candidate at the Ludlow by-election. His letter said: "The time has now come when the Free-Traders of all parties should form one line of battle against a common foe." Once again the libertarian was speaking the language of a hussar officer. He could not do otherwise.

The climax came when he ended his speech at Halifax with the words: "Thank God for the Liberal Party!"

At this the Conservative Association of Oldham resolved that Mr. Churchill had forfeited its confidence; he no longer had its support.

Naturally Churchill picked up the gauntlet. He moved to a seat below the gangway in token of his rebellion. When the Liberals in the House hatefully attacked the Government on account of the policy of Chinese coolie labor in South Africa, Churchill endorsed these attacks. He was still sitting on the Government side, but the system had no severer critic. And the Conservatives hated no man more bitterly. When Churchill asked for the floor on some trifling question of the order of the day, Mr. Balfour walked out without a word. Two hundred and fifty of his adherents followed him. A few turned at the door to get hasty interjections off their chests.

By the next day, however, it had been only a universal thirst for tea that had suddenly broken out. In letters to the *Times* a long series of parliamentarians declared they had been so weary from the preceding discussions that they had suddenly, simultaneously and absolutely had to refresh themselves. After Sir John Gort, a veteran member with forty years of Parliament behind him, had expressed his dissatisfaction at "the most marked discourtesy to Churchill," the members evidently regretted the unexampled breach of all the laws of courtesy to which the heat of the moment had led them.

Churchill had no regrets. "I have passed formally from the position of an independent supporter to the position of a declared opponent of the present Government," he declared.

Did this young man know what he was saying? Why, he was committing political suicide, just like his father! He was frivolously cutting off his own career. For a scion of the Duke of Marlborough there could be no career outside the Conservative Party. All his friends and kinsmen stood there. Thence all power came. He who was against the Tories was against centuries of England.

The House was stunned to silence. Some hundreds of estate-owners, substantial business men, and pensioned colonels no longer recognized their world. Applause came from only one seat. Serenely, not discourteously loud, but with casual, haughty distinctness young Lord Hugh Cecil was clapping his well-groomed hands.

In an incendiary speech a week later Churchill demanded a larger share for labor in English politics. No one could have recognized the future arch-enemy of socialism in these words: "When one considers how vast the Labor interest is, how vital, how human, it will surely be admitted that the influence of Labor on the course of legislation is ludicrously small. Its rest with . . ." but here he stuck. He tried again: "It rests with . . . with . . . with those . . ." He dropped back into his seat. He was barely able to murmur: "I thank the members for having listened to me." And now the members knew that Lord Randolph was not only resurrected but dead again.

Actually it was not so much the impact of this fateful moment that had confounded him as the fact that he was speaking for the first time without notes or outline. In this adventure his nerves had run away with him. The attempt was a failure. He was to repeat it gloriously. You couldn't keep Winston Churchill down. The day after his breakdown he received an invitation from the Liberal Association of North West Manchester to stand as their next candidate.

Now, in the middle of May, he made a speech that according to present notions would be called outright bolshevist. "We want a government that will think a little more about the toilers at the bottom of the mine and a little less about the fluctuations of the share market in London. We want a government which, instead of looking mainly abroad, will look mainly, if not, I think, entirely at home. We want a government and a policy which will think the condition of a slum in an English city is not less worthy of the attention of statesmen and of Parliament than the jungle of Somaliland. We know very well what to expect from a great Leader of a Protectionist party—a party of great vested interests: corruption at home, aggression to cover it up abroad, the trickery of tariff juggles, the tyranny of a party machine, sentiment by the bucketful, patriotism by the Imperial pint, the open hand at the public exchequer, the open door at the public house, dear food for the million, cheap labor for the millionaire. That is the policy of Birmingham, and we are going to erect against that the policy of Manchester . . ."

On May 31, 1903, he went to the House, had a drink at the bar to raise his courage before he entered the chamber, and walked to his seat below the gangway. He stared fixedly at the opposite side. He bowed to the Speaker, faced sharply about, and strode stiffly to an empty seat beside Lloyd George. The rumpled Welsh solicitor, the gadfly of the House, half rose to shake hands in welcome with the new convert.

CHAPTER XI

On the Far Shore

SAVROLA, the hero of his romantic autobiography, had now successfully concluded his revolution. When Churchill moved to Mount Street, Mayfair, he furnished his new quarters exactly according to the pattern he had drawn in his early novel. Here were the three rooms of Savrola's quarters—study, bedroom and bathroom. There stood Savrola's immense desk, a desk, incidentally, that Churchill has remained true to. He took it with him in all his ministerial wanderings; today it adorns the Prime Minister's quarters at No. 10. The flat in Mount Street was filled with remembrances of his father: his cartoons from *Punch* and *Vanity Fair* hung on the walls, and the large carved oak chair presented to Lord Randolph by the City of Manchester was drawn up before the table, on which stood a large brass inkstand, another legacy from Lord Randolph.

A cartoon of the lobby of the House, prominently displaying Lord Randolph, hung above the desk, and next to it a photograph of Lady Randolph; pictures of Disraeli and Grandmother, the Duchess of Marlborough; an engraving of the Duke playing chess; old prints of the first Duke of Marlborough, the great soldier, and of cavalry fights; and a picture of the mare Abbesse de Jouarre, his father's world-famous race-horse. Between the windows hung pictures of personal friends. All three rooms, even the bathroom, were crammed with books.

Winston Churchill was an omnivorous reader. Going to work now to write his father's biography, he devoured thousands of letters and documents. The work was a success. *The Life of Lord Randolph Churchill* was one of the biggest hits in English biographical literature. True, it was paid for with a good share of the author's health. Churchill looked prematurely overworked. The healthy red color vanished from his face, his eyes lost their brilliance, his figure began to spread out. The nervous gestures now became ever more frequent, the shoulders stooped unmistakably, the expression was careworn. His friends were fully convinced that the tragedy of the father would be repeated with the son. Winston too would be an old man at forty, and in the grave at forty-five.

Without question Winston Churchill was going through his first serious crisis. After all, his departure from the hereditary Conservative Party was a leap in the dark. He had lost more than the support of his friend and kinsman the Duke of Marlborough and the influence of his well-to-do family. He had lost his natural stay. And yet he felt that he was altogether in the right; that made matters still worse. Fundamentally he had not been greatly outraged by Mr. Broderick's Army Scheme, not even by the tariff reform. Why, indeed? The Tories themselves had finally abandoned their "militaristic" plans, and so far as protectionism was concerned, the new Prime Minister, Mr. Balfour, was icily cool toward it. Under the mantle of immediate political questions it was something else. It was the turmoil of youth.

"Young men can wait!" said the Conservative tradition. But Winston Churchill would wait no longer. Why should youth be handicapped? Why had Mr. Balfour passed him over in forming the Cabinet? Why did not the Conservatives make the slightest attempt to turn his rising opposition into enthusiasm for the common cause by giving him a small share of the responsibility? How could they expect barrack-yard discipline from a young man so individual, so colorful and so successful?

The Tory Party would undoubtedly have been better off if it had held on to Winston Churchill. It would then have possessed the magnetic personality so sadly lacking in its ranks during the bitter years from 1906 to 1914. Mr. Balfour, unwilling to tolerate opposition in his ranks at any price, even at the risk of losing the singular brilliance and courage of the most promising among the back-benchers, exacted a heavy price from his own party.

In later years Churchill took the most magnanimous of revenges. He spoke of Arthur Balfour throughout his life with warmth and respect—perhaps partly also owing to an uneasy conscience because his natural first reaction to being passed over was hatred and attack. Arthur James Balfour was one of those who always ride the crest. He never knew any such money worries as those that constantly pursued Churchill. He lived at his Scottish palace and his mansion in Carlton House Terrace on his inherited wealth, comfortably enough so that he never had to earn a penny, temperately enough so that he left some part of his inheritance behind him. Only those who know politics from inside can realize how kind Fate is to a politician who is remote from money. A lifelong bachelor, and thus never involved in family crises, Balfour was what Churchill later called "a lay priest, seeking a secular goal." With cool solemnity he observed the eternal march of events, his interest rather scientific than personal, undismayed even by death, which after all was but a metamorphosis, leaving behind at best a few moments of so-called immortality. When he was taken to the front as Secretary for War during the first World War, he glanced curiously through his spectacles at the shells that whizzed around his head. Arthur, later Lord, Balfour was ageless. "At eighty as at twenty," Ramsay MacDonald once said of him, "his interest in life, thoughts and affairs was equally keen." Looking back from late in life Churchill called him "the most perfect of men. He was the best-mannered man I ever met—easy, courteous, patient, considerate, in every society and with great and small alike."

True, Churchill was a long time in winning his way to this realization. When he left the Conservative Party in the midst of its grave tariff-reform crisis, he mocked Balfour, the man of the middle way, the apparently undecided, persevering but noiseless Prime Minister with the words: "Queens, of course, never resign." In that fashion he tried to work off his surrender of his traditional circle, his innate ideas and instincts, his hope of attaining the party leadership some day.

By nature converts are always extremists. Winston Churchill was now the spearhead of every attack against the dying Conservative majority. He was more radical than the most zealous radicals. His language went to the limit of parliamentary freedom, and sometimes a step beyond. "The two rival sections of the Tory Party are fighting like dogs worrying a bone!" was one of his similes. Mr. Balfour remained in power for some time yet. He showed his tactical genius in an almost desperate situation. Although what was the use? The forthcoming General Election was bound to be a landslide, and the Conservatives would simply be swept away.

The election contests began under the most favorable auspices. The country was fed up with Conservative rule. Voters wanted something new. There was nothing newer than Winston Churchill. Not yet thirty-two—this was 1906—he was the leading figure among the Liberals. His opposing candidate was Mr. Joynson-Hicks, a temperance lecturer and great churchman, later Home Secretary and a cabinet colleague of Churchill's. Mr. Joynson-Hicks was famous as a speaker. But Churchill spoke more colorfully, and in person was incomparably more interesting. The extraordinary success of the recently published biography of Lord Randolph contributed in no small measure to the personal interest shown him by Manchester, a city very proud of its intellectual standing. North West Manchester was happy to be represented by a successful author. The Jewish element, very strong in the city, was enthusiastically for Winston Churchill. The rich and influential Jews of Manchester awaited Chamberlain's tariff reform with ill-concealed suspicion. They were tired of Balfour's rule, feared the Government's Aliens Bill, and gratefully understood the sympathetic references to Zionism that Churchill interwove in his speeches. Mr. Joynson-Hicks, on the contrary, declined to speak before a Jewish gathering on Sunday. "Never as long as I am your candidate or your member will I go electioneering on Sunday."

There was not a trace of anti-semitism in this rigid sabbatarian attitude. But at an all-Jewish meeting the patriarch Nathan Laski, the head of the leading Jewish family in the community, declared nevertheless: "Any Jew who votes against Winston Churchill is a traitor to the common cause."

Churchill fought the election chiefly on the fiscal issue. Naturally he still talked his soldier's language. "Did you spend fifteen millions on your marvelous Ship Canal to have its mouth blocked with the sandbags of obstructive tariffs?" He defended himself against the reproach of treason to the Party that his adversaries naturally brought up, by saying: "Some men change their party for the sake of their principles—some change their principles for the sake of their party! . . . Yes, I was a Tory, heart and soul with the party, but I did not know then how the Tory Party had treated Lord Randolph Churchill. I had not seen his papers then." Whether or not this sounded quite credible, a reference to his successful literary masterpiece never failed of its effect in Manchester.

His meetings were overcrowded. Once the floor of the hall in which he was speaking broke down under the weight of the crowd. "Let justice be done, even though the floor falls in!" Churchill shouted. The resulting laughter prevented a panic.

After a meeting at the Coal Exchange his admirers were bruised and hurt in their rush to see him departing. A man in the crowd got a bloody nose. He shouted: "I am proud to give my blood for Winston!"

They pursued him into the Turkish bath of the Midland Hotel. Winston not only fascinated the crowd, he electrified it.

On the morning of Election Day Manchester was represented by nine Conservatives. By evening, when the votes were counted, the city had sent nine Liberals and Radicals to the House. Churchill himself won by a majority of 1241, a triumph in those days of limited votes. "It is a grand slam in doubled no trumps," were the words of Mr. Charles Hands, correspondent of the *Daily*

Mail, a Conservative and anti-Churchill paper, that evening at the victory celebrations in the Midland Hotel.

"You would have thought I was walking on clouds, I was standing on thrones," wrote Lord James of Hereford in his letter of congratulation. He also described the scene at Sandringham, and how King Edward was overcome by the result of the election.

It was an overpowering event all over the country. The Conservative Party lay in fragments. All its leaders except Joe and Austen Chamberlain had been defeated. Even Mr. Balfour, who had held his seat since 1885, was turned out. London, the Tory stronghold, returned 53 Labor and Liberals against 19 Conservatives. The new House had a majority of 377 Liberals and Radicals and 53 Labor against 132 Conservatives and 25 Liberal-Unionists. The solid block of 83 Irish Nationalists was of course opposed to both groups, and to the United Kingdom as well. It was generally called "a mad House." Sir Henry Campbell-Bannerman formed the first Liberal Government since the dim prehistoric ages of Lord Rosebery. Churchill, not yet thirty-two, received his first state post as Under Secretary for Colonies. Thus began the twenty years (with but a few months' interruption) of his activity in the Government. He got on splendidly with his chief, the Secretary for Colonies, Lord Elgin, whom he had known as Viceroy of India, where he himself had been a famous polo-player in the Anglo-Indian Army. Their system of working together was based primarily on the fact that His Lordship was confined to the House of Lords, while Churchill, in the Commons, ran the real politics of the department. He now began to concern himself with two problems that were among the crucial questions of the Empire: the Indian question and the Irish wound.

The moment he took office he proved himself an enthusiastic and painstaking administrator. Probably he felt obliged to show the Conservatives what a worker they had lost. The first thing to be put in order was the Transvaal Constitution. His Prime Minister entrusted this honorable task to him with the words: "You have done the fighting, you shall have the prize." Churchill came to an agreement on every point with a Boer delegation that included General Botha, the horseman who had once captured him. Then he introduced the official proposal with a speech in which he unfolded for the first time a picture of the world that he was to defend all his life long, infinitely beyond the confines of Africa. The speech went far beyond the immediate occasion. It ended with the words: "If the near future should unfold to our eyes a tranquil, prosperous, consolidated Afrikander nation under the protecting aegis of the British crown, then, I say, the good as well as the evil will not be confined to South Africa. Then, I say, the cause of the poor and the weak all over the world will have been sustained, and everywhere small people will have more room to breathe, and everywhere great empires will be encouraged by our example to step forward—it needs only one step—into the sunshine of a more gentle and more generous age."

Now that he was one of the called and chosen in the Government he mixed a little water with his radical wine. When his own companions in arms began to harass him about "Chinese slave labor" in South Africa, he replied: "The contract under which coolies are employed may not be a desirable contract and not a healthy contract, but it cannot, in the view of His Majesty's Government, be classified as slavery in the extreme acceptance of the word without some risk of terminological inexactitude."

The phrase "terminological inexactitude" remained alive. Friend and enemy alike held it up with a smile against the young Liberal statesman who was already talking like Gladstone the Olympian.

But when a Radical faddist asked him about the fate of a couple of dangerous Kaffir criminals who had been picked up as a catch-word by even more dangerous English humanitarian simpletons, Churchill answered impassively: "I have every reason to believe that the execution of these men was carried out this morning."

"Bloodthirsty murderer!" the faddist screamed at him. A few weeks before, Churchill would have spoken so himself.

CHAPTER XII

Women—and The Woman

THE All-Highest, on his white charger, surrounded by kings and princes, rode into the city at the head of his squadron of cuirassiers. The cuirassiers wore his own white uniform with the eagle-crested helmets. Old men were drawn up in lines all along the streets. They carried old-fashioned top hats, and each one wore the Iron Cross on his black Sunday best. These were the veterans of yesterday, cheering the heroes of tomorrow as Wilhelm II, Emperor of Germany, King of Prussia, opened the army maneuvers at Breslau. The foreign guests, personally selected and invited by the All-Highest, watched the majestic spectacle with admiration, and some of them perhaps also with some dismay. The young Englishman, the milk-faced boy among the notables, felt his soldier's heart leap up. True, he would have taken no pleasure in such parades at home. He would have calculated the cost in terms of tax rates. He would have nodded excited approval when his friend and mentor Lloyd George compared all this colorful pomp with the starvation in the mines whence came the coal and the voters. If one-tenth of this spectacle had taken place in England, he would probably have been talking again about the "Great English Fraud."

But here, for a few hot days of 1906, Winston Churchill was released from the tutelage of Lloyd George, the tyranny of ill-paid and undernourished voters, the duties of a successful politician. Sandhurst rose before his gaze, the red and white uniforms of the Indian Army, the cavalry charge of Omdurman. You had to go to Germany in order to be a man among men again.

The Germans made his stay very pleasant. His Majesty's personal guests were quartered at The Golden Goose, a comfortably old-fashioned hotel with far too large rooms. For their amusement —and instruction—they had shown them an entire army corps, and a complete mobilized division at war strength. They also got some idea of German industriousness. There was no time for sleep. The full-dress banquets lasted until midnight every evening. The All-Highest presided in person. If he was detained on the field of maneuvers, the Empress, a stately, pompous lady, did the honors in his place. The guests had to get up again at three in the morning to catch the special train that would take them to the battlefield. There they spent twelve hours in the saddle, roving about. They could inspect everything. The German Army had no secret weapons.

The Emperor, who frequently engaged Churchill in conversation, casually asked him whether he had looked at the new giant field gun. When he said that he had not, the All-Highest motioned to his adjutant. "Show our friend the gun. Let him see it by all means!" The adjutant was rather taken aback, but of course carried out the order. The artillery commander was even more astonished. An express reference by the adjutant to the will of the All-Highest was necessary to overcome his hesitation.

The adjutant and the commander were dunderheads both. The All-Highest knew perfectly well that Churchill was no artillery expert, and that a glance at the giant gun would tell him nothing more than the Intelligence Departments in Paris and London already knew.

In the grand parade fifty thousand men of all three branches goose-stepped past the Emperor and the galaxy of kings and princes that surrounded him. The infantry, Churchill noticed, swept along in waves like the billows of the Atlantic Ocean. Such waves Britannia did not rule. At home the parade of a single division or of one cavalry brigade at Aldershot was great event enough. It was just as well; he was fully reconciled to the fact. His native islands had been free from invasion for over nine hundred years. Surely they would remain untouched another thousand. Germany,

on the other hand, had to defend her borders. As if reading his
guest's thoughts, Wilhelm II motioned to Churchill. He did not
send the adjutant. He was fond of displaying his right arm in
sweeping gestures. (The left was crippled.) "What do you think
of this beautiful Silesia?" asked the monarch in his facile English. "Marvelous country, isn't it? Well worth fighting for!" He
laughed, because the beauty of a country was naturally in its military importance. "And well fought over. These fields are ankle-
deep in blood." This was a particularly excellent joke. The All-
Highest smiled, and the entire court, including a few minor German kings, whinnied. Once again the right arm went up in a
pompous gesture. "There is the town of Liegnitz, where Frederick
the Great fought his battle. Down there is the Katzbach stream,
where we beat the French in our war of Liberation, in 1813."
Here he turned his easy grin upon a gentleman to his left. This
was the French Military Attaché. His face was expressionless.
Churchill's capacity for putting himself in another's place was by
no means needed to imagine what was going on behind the officer's mask.

The infantry passed by in close ranks, tightly set, in endless
new waves. It was a terrifying spectacle. But the memory of
Omdurman flashed through Churchill's head. There eleven thousand dervishes attacked in much less dense formation, he thought,
and we shot them down quite easily at ranges far greater than
those being shown now on every side. What contempt the Germans displayed for their own men! Churchill was not the only
one to notice that the infantry here was being marched like cattle
to the slaughter. A German princess in an officer's uniform, riding at the head of her regiment—she was the Possessor of a Regiment, a German honorary title—called to him with royal unconcern: "What folly! It is madness. The generals should all be
dismissed!"

In the grand finale the All-Highest in person led a cavalry
attack of thirty or forty squadrons against a long line of field guns
right into the center of the enemy position. If it had been the

real thing, of course not a single horseman would have come out alive. In the maneuvers, however, the umpire dutifully declared that His Majesty had stormed and annihilated the batteries. The conquered artillery commander bowed no less dutifully. "After all, those are the Emperor's guns. Why shouldn't he capture them?" Only the suppressed smile with which he spoke struck Churchill.

After the "Cease firing" signal Wilhelm II on his general's hillock graciously engaged his guests in conversation. He showed a lively interest in England. Of course he did answer most of the questions himself. There was no doubt that he liked to hear himself talk. In the evening he could enjoy life. At the banquet that he gave to the dignitaries of the Province of Silesia, three hundred notables and city fathers puffed like peacocks and at the same time humbly groveling, he talked for an hour about the transformation of this blessed century. What a change from Jena, the battle of German annihilation, in 1806, to this today, Breslau in 1906! Never again should Germany go down!

Churchill was definitely an admirer of the Germans. Bursting with manhood himself, he could understand the virility of a nation that had arrived late, but not too late, at the dividing-up of the world. Why should not this mighty people, second to no nation in hard work, hard thinking, organization, business, science and philosophy, fight for its "place in the sun"? Why should Germany's expanding industries never stand on German-owned oil, tin, copper, rubber? Were they to be confined without show of resistance to Europe, where no two nations combined together could overcome them? Why was the old gray sea-wolf England or tiring France privileged to enjoy the dominance of the oceans and to build up and expand a splendid colonial empire? Holland was thriving upon her rich East Indies, and even little Belgium ruled the vast Congo; but Germany was barred from the Western Hemisphere by the Monroe Doctrine, from North Africa by an Anglo-French agreement, from China and the East by the international concert.

No one understood the German urge to world power better than the youthful Under Secretary for Colonies, as he stood there among the cuirassiers and veterans of an underprivileged giant. Must this urge lead to war? Churchill doubted it. With his almost visionary knowledge of humankind, admirably deep even then, he soon formed a picture of his host. The Kaiser did not want war. This master of sixty castles, owner of hundreds of uniforms, the abjectly worshipped All-Highest in a circle where titanic defiance and crawling servility were so strangely mingled, wanted to seem Himself like Napoleon without having to fight his battles. If you at the summit of a volcano, the least you can do is to smoke—so Churchill put it afterward. And if a war should come, it would be possible only because the machine had slipped from its master's hand.

Of course the Kaiser was spoiled by the slavish entourage in which he spent his life. But what mortal man would not become a megalomaniac if he were deified day in and day out as "the world's most glorious prince"? Wilhelm II was an extremely mortal man. His undeniable cleverness and versatility, to quote Churchill's later judgment again, his personal grace and vivacity only aggravated his dangers by concealing his inadequacy. He could stamp and snort, or nod and smile with much histrionic art; but underneath all this posing and its trappings was a very ordinary, vain, yet on the whole well-meaning man, hoping to pass himself off as a second Frederick the Great.

The All-Highest talked graciously and with much condescension to his English guest. He asked Churchill to tell him about the struggle in South Africa, and discussed with him the Church in the Army. He did not even mention his Uncle Edward. This too was tactful. For secretly he felt a strange and mischievous mixture of rivalry and contempt for his uncle. He, Wilhelm II, not Edward VII, wanted to be the first English gentleman. Secretly he admired English life, styles and customs. Edward, he told himself, had not been true to type even as Prince of Wales. Only recently the Emperor had asked an English visitor: "Where is your King now?" To the rejoinder, "At Windsor, Sir!" he replied: "Ah, I thought he was boating with his grocer!"—a clumsy, ill-judged allusion to the royal friendship with Sir Thomas Lipton.

But Kaiser Wilhelm's conversation with Churchill was troubled by no flaw in the harmony. When Churchill returned from Breslau, back to the Lloyd Georges and the human rights of the coalminers, he had filled his lungs with fresh air amid the splendor, pomp and fanfares.

In May of 1907 King Edward appointed him Privy Councillor. All Windsor was shocked when Churchill appeared on the day of his elevation in a cutaway instead of in the prescribed tail-coat. Must he even drag his revolutionary manners into Court? The King was the only gentleman at Windsor who overlooked this offense against etiquette. After the official audience he detained Churchill, which was a special mark of favor. The two men talked about Churchill's books.

In Parliament, meanwhile, the most divine peace reigned. The Liberal majority was fighting its way slowly forward, carefully advancing step by step upon its newly conquered ground. No one knew better than Sir Henry Campbell-Bannerman that his own front was thick with radicals, pacifists, and faddists, and that he must beware of the fruits of his own success. The Tories were still laboring under the after-effects of their shattering defeat. It was like a shot in the arm when a new member suddenly arose among them, raising their tattered banner once more in a sensational maiden speech. This new member was "F. E." as he was soon abbreviated all over the country—Frederick Edwin Smith, later the First Earl of Birkenhead.

F. E. was born in very humble circumstances to a family of miners in the West Riding of Yorkshire. His father had served as a private soldier on the Indian North Western Frontier, and had got his discharge at twenty-one as a Sergeant-Major. Returning home, he earned his way through the University—a positively fantastic achievement in Victorian England—was called to the

Bar, and died at forty-three, just on the threshold of a promising legal and political career. F. E., the son, was sixteen at the time. With the help of an uncle and a fellowship he made his way through Oxford, was called to the Bar in his turn in 1889, and was earning six thousand pounds a year by 1904. Brilliant, aggressive and extremely likeable, he had just one aversion. He did not want to know Winston Churchill at any price. He despised the traitor to his Party the more since he himself in his youth had looked up reverently to Lord Randolph's Tory Democracy. The son, he felt, had shamefully squandered a great legacy through frivolous unrestraint.

One day in the bar of the House a personal encounter was unavoidable. The two stormy petrels, Winston the Liberal and F. E. the Conservative, ran straight into each other's arms. All the spectators of this memorable scene awaited a collision of planets. Instead it became, from the first moment, the strangest friendship in English politics. In public, indeed, the two still opposed each other for long years, sometimes very sharply. In private life they became inseparable companions. They stuck together as if each had bewitched the other until the Earl of Birkenhead's death. Winston Churchill never found a better companion.

In the late autumn of 1907 he took a trip to the African colonies, partly in his official capacity, partly as a correspondent for the *Strand* magazine. The assignment was more than welcome. The adventure attracted him, and also, undeniably, the fee. The greater part of the money he had earned by his lecture tours and the biography of his father was already consumed.

When Winston Churchill went traveling, of course there were great doings. He shot a white rhinoceros, and also, somewhere between Mombasa and Nairobi, a few lions. He argued about politics with white and black men. He traveled by horse, motorcar, bicycle, steamer—on the Victoria Nyanza; he watched native dancers, fearlessly visited Entebbe, the disease-stricken capital of Uganda. He crossed the Lake by boat, marched three days through the jungle, went three more days by canoe along the river, then five more days' march from the other bank, and finally one day in a steam launch to Albert Nyanza. His Majesty's Under Secretary ate and slept in shelters of bamboo, thatched with elephant-grass, covered with a mosquito netting. Once he disturbed an army of marching ants, and was beaten off by the ants with the loss of his walking-stick. On the way home he visited Khartoum, and was delighted to see how the dervish camp had developed in ten years into a modern city. His valet fell ill and died at Khartoum, and the rest of the trip was spoiled for Churchill.

Coming home, he encountered death a second time. In April of 1908 Sir Henry Campbell-Bannerman died. Herbert Henry Asquith, hitherto Chancellor of the Exchequer, took his place.

Asquith was the last in the line of the British statesmen-philosophers. Scholarship, politics, philosophy, law, religion—all were his spheres. He was one of those who still regarded men and situations from the vantage-point of settled standards and sure convictions. Anything that failed to fit his neat formulas was not exactly hostile or strange to him, but neither was it altogether pleasing. "His massive finality stands forth, for good or ill," as Churchill was to put it one day.

An adverse fate made Asquith fight on the wrong front. When he came to power, all the stolid Conservative forces of England were rallied against him. He was obliged to use himself up in a furious fight for Irish Home Rule against the House of Lords—in battles where Churchill was always the standard-bearer—whereas in his heart of hearts he himself was of a conservative nature, so conservative that as a matter of principle he would not use the typewriter, for instance, or the telephone. He was a great patriot who stood firm for King and Country as Leader of the Opposition and as Prime Minister alike, in the Boer War and in the first World War, during the General Strike and in the Irish crisis when it sharpened into civil war. He was progressive owing basically to tradition. He was patriotic because that was a matter of course, even in the company of the pacifists and appeasers whom he led. He had to keep secret from his own circle the elaborate defense preparations that the recognition of the German peril forced upon him. If things had been managed according to his own clear, sometimes rather rigid, legalistic mind, he would not have been battling with the House of Lords while the shadows loomed on the horizon. But as it was, he shrugged his shoulders resignedly with the catch-phrase that he coined, and that perhaps expresses England more profoundly than any other: "Wait and see!"

Mr. Asquith appointed Churchill President of the Board of Trade in his newly formed Cabinet. At that time a change of portfolio still required a by-election. Two years after the Liberal landslide this was no mere trifling adventure. By 1906 the pendulum had undoubtedly swung too far to the left. All over the country the Tories were rising again.

"I am still young enough to enjoy a fight!" Churchill laughed as he prepared for battle. But then women crossed his path, and for the first time the hero of three continents forgot to laugh.

Manchester was the home of the Pankhursts, and the memory of those three ladies, Mrs. Pankhurst and her daughters Christabel and Sylvia, still occasionally startles Churchill from sleep, not merely twenty-two years but a world later. The Pankhurst ladies led the newly started Suffragist Movement, for which Churchill at first had a certain sympathy, as he did for everything that was new and absurdly behaved. But a certain sympathy was not enough for the modern Amazons. They wanted the franchise—and the candidate's legally binding promise that he would get it from the Prime Minister. The idea that the traditionalist Mr. Asquith would yield to the demands of the Suffragettes was a naive one. But the hatred that made a legion of frustrated English women into hyenas was directed not so much against Asquith, who was a well-known admirer of female beauty. It burst upon Winston Churchill. Here was a he-man who stirred their deepest subconscious emotions. Probably he was so virile that his mere appearance on the platform, head held high, laughing teeth between full lips, chin upthrust, provoked the battle of the sexes. The battle of the sexes has always involved a good many small misapprehensions. Among the most painful was the fact that they considered Winston Churchill a misogynist. Legions of would-be girl friends, some gray-haired, some thin as rails, plump mothers and shopgirls, hungering not for bread alone, all flung themselves upon the enemy.

At the Free Trade Hall in Manchester Miss Christabel Pankhurst had to be forcefully requested to leave the hall after throwing the meeting into pandemonium. The idea! Winston Churchill allowed unprotected women to be beaten? He should not open his mouth again. When he started to speak the following evening a shrill voice interrupted him: "What about the women?" Another lady was shown out. But now they grew up in every nook and cranny like mushrooms. "When are you going to give the women the vote?" they would interrupt him just as he was talking of Free Trade or Tax Reform. It was a well-organized conspiracy to keep the candidate mute. "Traitor!" female voices rang out in chorus. "The devil in trousers!" was the label they pinned on him.

Mr. Joynson-Hicks, afterward Lord Brentford, the churchman and sabbatarian, was the one who profited by this women's revolution. On April 24, 1908, he was elected by 5,517 votes against 4,988 votes for Churchill. "It's the women who have done this!" screamed one of the female warriors when the result was announced. She rushed alarmingly close to her victim. "Get away, woman!" Churchill bellowed back.

The Town Hall is five or six minutes away from the Manchester Reform Club. A raging mob of Suffragettes accompanied him. When he entered the Reform Club, they held out a telegram to him. The Liberals of Dundee offered him their seat, which was just becoming free since Mr. Edmund Robertson, the then Member, was about to be promoted to the House of Lords. Dundee was one of the safest Liberal seats in the country. It had belonged to the Party since 1832. Here the Suffragettes would shout themselves hoarse in vain.

Still, they tried. A procession of women started off from Manchester for Dundee. At their head went "La Bell Maloney," an extremely pretty Miss Maloney who owed her nickname to the fact that she constantly agitated a dinner bell to keep Candidate Churchill from talking. In this she did not succeed at Dundee. The burgesses of Dundee were seriously interested in their candidate, who turned his brisk campaign toward the Right, uttering a warning against the socialism-in-the-making that was now rampant. On polling-day La Bell Maloney drove defiantly through the city, constantly ringing her bell out of the cab window. At the station she took the train back to Manchester.

The grimmest opponent Churchill had to fight was an outsider, Mr. Scrimgeour, who was later one of the strangest figures in Parliament. Mr. Scrimgeour headed a small group of Christian Socialists. He was a fanatical teetotaler, determined at any price to dry up Dundee, which at that time enjoyed the reputation of "the drunkenest city in Scotland." He lived a life of extreme self-denial, and spent fifteen years entirely on the work of conversion in each house and each family in Dundee. Churchill naturally was like a red rag to Mr. Scrimgeour. With the best will in the world nobody could have taken him for a teetotaler. As a matter of fact he was quite cheerfully addicted to the moderate use of wine. When he criss-crossed the United States on a lecture tour in 1931, during prohibition, one of the conditions of his contract was that the agent must provide a bottle of champagne every evening. Churchill believed in the motto, In vino veritas. Mr. Scrimgeour believed that Hell awaited the jolly toper. And indeed at his first attempt he successfully contrived to raise three or four hundred followers of his own persuasion.

Churchill was elected in triumph, with 7,000 votes against the combined opposition, which drew 4,000. Now he could be appointed to his new Government post.

Even this election did not go off entirely without feminine

intervention. The white-haired Countess of Airlie was the strongest single influence in Dundee, and this influence was completely at Churchill's disposal. The Countess had a daughter, Lady Blanche Hozier, widow of the late Colonel H. M. Hozier, K.C.B., and from this marriage in turn sprang the Honourable Clementine Hozier, who became Mrs. Winston Churchill in September, 1908, a few months after the battle of Dundee.

The London matchmakers had already seen Winnie in repeated romantic entanglements, once with a famous American actress. It was all empty talk. As a matter of fact he was living at the time with his younger brother John in a modest apartment in Bruton Street, Piccadilly. Brother John, a young man of the world, was fond of dinner-parties and dances. Brother Winston was too serious for them. Again he copied his home-made model, Savrola. "Savrola did not dance. There were some amusements which his philosophy taught him to despise."

Still, the sight of Clementine did seem to take from philosophy some of its importance. Just as in the case of his parents, it was love at first sight, and the happiest marriage in the world resulted.

Winston Churchill's marriage took place at St. Margaret's, Westminster. Lord Hugh Cecil, the leader of the "Hooligans," was best man. All London celebrated. Gifts came from the King and Queen. From friends came twenty-five candlesticks, twenty-one inkstands, fifteen vases, twenty bowls, fourteen trays, ten cigarette cases, not forgetting eight sets of salt cellars. The bridegroom seems to have been in a less solemn mood than anyone else. To this day the rumor stubbornly persists that he appeared at his wedding in brown shoes.

The young couple spent the first days of their honeymoon in Blenheim Palace. Then they went by way of Paris to Lago Maggiore, moved into their first apartment in a house in Queen Anne's Gate, and finally settled down in Eccleston Square, Victoria.

The wedding was the greatest adventure in Churchill's life up to that point. The two young people had entered into a marriage without money. The youthful statesman no longer had time for the literary and journalistic work that had helped out at critical moments hitherto. He was entirely dependent on his salary as a Minister—an extremely uncertain and almost always inadequate source of income in any parliamentary democracy. But Churchill did not worry too much about it. His marriage provided him with a stimulus unknown thus far, and he drew strength and inspiration from his life together with the woman whom he continues to love to this very day. He ends his own story of his early life with the simple statement: "In September 1908 I married, and I lived happily ever afterwards." The greatest speaker in the English tongue could find no words to express the inexpressible. Happiness is mute.

CHAPTER XIII

The Children of Anak

FOR the second time the German regiments were marching past the guest from England. Wilhelm II had quite evidently taken a liking to Winston Churchill. He had invited him again to the Imperial maneuvers, this time at the Bavarian city of Würzburg. Wave after wave of valiant manhood poured across the parade ground. Thousands of strong horses dragged cannon and great howitzers up the ridges and along the roads. At a bugle blast a hundred thousand heels clicked. At another a hundred thousand marching boots moved. Again the Emperor, towering on his foaming white horse, the points of his moustache rising heavenward, reviewed the parade. Once again the hussar officer whose foot had slipped to the left could feel the enchantment of this military splendor with the full force of kinship.

The maneuvers at Würzburg showed a great change in German military tactics. The infantry formation was modernized and adapted to actual war conditions. The artillery was dotted wherever convenience dictated. The cavalry were hardly visible; one saw them only on distant flanks. Machine-guns, the new weapon, were spotted everywhere. This time it looked not merely like a parade, but like a serious matter. The atmosphere was tense—and not in Würzburg alone. The controversies between the Germans and the British Admiralty were sharp. England and France had gradually drawn closer together. The Young Turkish revolution had set the Balkans aflame. Two ranking Turkish generals, Mahmoud Shevket Pasha, the newly installed Minister of War, and Enver Pasha, the leader of the Young Turks, were Wilhelm II's especially preferred guests at Würzburg.

Churchill quickly became friendly with Enver Pasha, then a fine-looking young officer, the hero of his nation. He showed a desire to discuss the problems of the Bagdad railway, which the Germans were just building, with the English minister. Churchill's department was particularly concerned with this question, which was provoking general uneasiness in London. And so Churchill gladly welcomed the opportunity when Enver Pasha loitered with him a little during a ride at maneuvers, and began to talk about the distressing railway with which Berlin hoped to fasten itself in the East. The conversation can hardly have been to German liking. The horse of the Imperial Equerry who was always assigned to guests of distinction apparently got out of control. The equerry could not master it. Four times it brought its rider into the immediate neighborhood of the two foreigners, deep in conversation. Each time the equerry excused himself for his intrusion. Churchill and Enver Pasha smiled understandingly. The following morning Churchill inquired who the maladroit equerry was. One of the best horsemen in the German cavalry, he was told.

The three years that followed passed in the same frantic haste that was now the pace of Churchill's life. They were filled to the brim with events that rocked all England. In retrospect, indeed, they were petty events—wars between frogs and mice that ended in fruitless victories. Nevertheless those three years when nothing of any consequence happened were the years of Winston Churchill's life most laden with fate. In the period from his thirty-fifth to his thirty-seventh year he went through the momentous transformation by which the man vanished and the voice was raised. He sank deep in his fall from grace; purged of his sins, he rose to the heights on which at last, today, he stands alone.

He came back from Würzburg so deeply impressed that in August of 1908 he fiercely attacked Lord Cromer for his "alarmist warnings of coming dangers from Germany." In a letter to the chairman of his party organization at Dundee he exposed what he called the four cardinal errors current in naval circles. "The fourth and most fundamental error," he wrote, "is that any profound antagonism exists between England and Germany." Although it did not appertain to his office as President of the Board of Trade, he waged a vigorous campaign against the Naval Estimates of his fellow Cabinet member Mr. McKenna, the First Lord of the Admiralty, who in the spring of 1909 demanded the building of six dreadnoughts on account of the rapid expansion of the German fleet. This demand was popular throughout the country. "We want eight and we won't wait!" speaking choruses chanted. As a matter of fact England was in the process of losing the naval supremacy that was the basis of her existence. In 1905 Great Britain planned four battleships, and Germany two. In 1906 the British program was reduced to three, the German increased to three. In 1907 the English Government contented itself with two, while the Germans laid the keels of four battleships. The Liberal Government in London played into the hands of pan-Germanism in Berlin. "They are an over-civilized and pacifist society," grinned Admiral von Tirpitz. "That's quite all right with us. Let the virile race advance to the place of the effete."

Churchill was highly thought of in Berlin. Not without reason, they considered him and Lloyd George, the Chancellor of the Exchequer, the leading exponents of decadent English pacifism. Sir Edward Grey, Foreign Secretary, and the two Service Ministers, McKenna and Haldane, were the representatives of Liberal Imperialism in the Cabinet. Prime Minister Asquith remained neutral between the two groups of his colleagues.

Measured in the terms of our time the combination of Churchill and Lloyd George embodied all the elements of both the recent Front Populaire in France, which abolished work and sabotaged defense, and the English appeasers of Munich. The mother country, so it seemed, was but an empty word to them. For what they called social progress, i.e., speculation on popular pressure-groups, no price was too dear, though the nation pay it with its very existence in the end. But it must be admitted that this comparison is only outwardly justified, and then only for a very short time.

Fundamentally Winston Churchill was made of different stuff from the gentlemen of the Cliveden set and the agitators of the Palais Bourbon. Even during the time of his aberrations it is more just to compare his and Lloyd George's self-styled progressive policy with the work of Woodrow Wilson and Franklin Delano Roosevelt.

Messrs. Churchill and Lloyd George, then, proclaimed that four battleships would be enough. Perhaps in the narrow sense they were right—in relation to the deep trend of destiny they were absolutely wrong. But destiny had to knock at the door much louder before these gentlemen would awake. Incidentally Churchill, who had a more delicate ear and came from another world than the Welsh rabble-rouser, was the first to awake.

He could not be accused of being deaf. For the moment he heard with only one ear. Beyond doubt he accomplished much by the progressive legislation that he sponsored. No previous President of the Board of Trade had ever carried out such far-reaching reforms in such rapid succession. He introduced the Miners' Hours Bill, the Licensing Bill, the Small Holdings Bill, the Old Age Pensions Bill, the Education Bill. In September he established the first court of industrial conciliation. The Labor Exchanges against unemployment represented a tremendous forward step, if a costly one. Although this whole period, more than thirty years past, seems almost antediluvian to us today, it is nevertheless memorable as the first manifestation of a spirit that later took shape in the New Deal.

New Dealers even then were unpopular in influential circles. The English have special, painless methods for disposing of unpopular politicians. Early in 1909 the office of Viceroy of India was offered to Churchill. For a man of thirty-five that would be an honor without parallel—the dream palace at New Delhi, white elephants, the Imperial tent at the polo matches. The Anglo-Indian press, however, was indignant. It had no use for a New Dealer. "An irreparable blow to British prestige in India . . ." they wrote, and *"Men* are wanted in India . . ." Churchill himself had no use for the honor that was planned for him. He wanted to stay in politics. He was already utterly enslaved. He sat in his office from daybreak until late at night. He looked prematurely aged and weary. On one occasion he was so tired that he fell asleep in a corner of the House. That day he wore a pink silk shirt with his flannel suit. The following morning he read in the papers that he had entered the House for a division in pink pajamas. England believed it. This New Dealer was capable of anything.

Lloyd George introduced his first budget. England had expected almost anything from the debut of the new Chancellor of the Exchequer. But the figures that were laid before the country took away the breath even of those who had expected the worst. The estimates were called "The crazy budget" by friend and foe alike. One side said it in fury, the other with the same pride that once made the Dutch noblemen call themselves "Geuzen," beggars. Of course the House of Commons with its overwhelming Left majority passed the budget. It followed Lloyd George by 379 to 149 votes. The House of Lords, however, rejected it by 350 to 75. And now Churchill went over to the counter-attack.

He carried his campaign against the upper House all over England. In vitriolic speeches (published as a book by Hodder & Stoughton of London in December, 1909, under the title of *The People's Rights*) he slashed at their Lordships. Seldom had anyone attacked the House of Lords so fanatically as the heir of the Dukes of Marlborough. "The House of Lords has disdainfully swept out of existence the work of session after session. It is a lingering relic of a feudal order. The House of Lords has invaded the prerogatives of the Crown and the rights of the Commons. The British monarchy has no interests divergent from those of the British people, but the House of Lords is refusing supplies to the Crown. It claims to tinker, tamper and meddle with every kind of legislation. The people's account with the Lords is a long and heavy one. The House of Lords is responsible to no one. It represents no one. The Lords' plan is: 'Heads I win, tails you don't get paid!' "

The attacks were directed not only against the Lords, but equally fiercely against Capital. Although Churchill had spoken in his last election campaign of the misleading doctrines of socialism, now no labor agitator outdid him in fulminating against monopoly, which he declared an "unsocial form of wealth." In the future, the President of the Board of Trade promised, the tax-collector would not ask, "What have you got?" but "How did you get it?"

If a man shout in the forest, echo answers. He was now, even more than Lloyd George, the best-hated man in English Conservative circles. That hatred was to have after-effects when the problems and questions of 1909 were long forgotten. As a matter of fact this period of his life explains the widespread suspicion that pursued Churchill more or less loudly until the outbreak of the present war. The punctilious English could not understand that a man who had left his predestined path was battling so grimly simply because he was fighting his own shadow. For that matter, Mr. Churchill himself would hardly agree with this interpretation even now. In his memoirs he still upholds his struggle against the Lords. He spoke of "the violent inroads of the House of Lords on popular government, which by the end of 1908 had reduced the immense Liberal majority to virtual impotence, from which condition they were rescued by the Lloyd George budget of 1909. The rejection of this measure by the Lords was a constitutional outrage."

The middle-class press was the most furious in its assaults on Churchill. Of course these attacks did not scare him. Under the slogan, "The people or the Lords?" he went into the General Election of 1910, confident that the platform can always beat the press.

The women could make it most unpleasant on the platform. Once again the Suffragettes rushed at him wherever they could lay hold of him. It was no longer politics, but simple hysteria, capable of none but a clinical explanation.

At Bristol a Suffragette gave him three whistling cuts with a riding-whip. Churchill contented himself with twisting the whip out of the excited lady's hand, and putting it in his pocket. At Southport his meeting had to be put under police protection. Even so, three girls crawled into the ventilator in the ceiling, and kept bellowing for "Votes for women!" When he took the train, a few Suffragettes chained themselves to the railings, saying that they would stay there until they received the vote. "A man might just as well chain himself to the railings of St. Thomas' Hospital and say that he wouldn't move until he had had a baby!" was Churchill's good-natured answer. The situation became more serious, however, when a male adherent of the Suffragette movement attacked him. Now he could not go out without a bodyguard. Even little Diana, only three months old, had to be guarded in her perambulator by detectives. A plot to kidnap the baby had come to light.

In order, quite openly, to provoke his Conservative opponent still further, when the nation was called to the polls, Churchill picked a fellow-candidate from the ranks of the Trades Unions, Mr. Wilkie, a ship's carpenter by profession. Mr. Scrimgeour, the teetotaler and Christian Socialist, who of course stood for Dundee again, spoke of a sacrilegious combination. Still he won only a few dozen votes more than his three hundred of the previous election. Dundee remained true to Churchill.

Throughout the country, however, the elections did not turn out happily for the Liberal Government. The people mistrusted an attempt to play them off against the Lords. The Liberals returned with a bare majority—there were now 275 of them against 274 Conservatives; they had lost over a hundred seats. The working capacity of the new House depended on forty Labor deputies and the eighty Irish Nationalists.

The Government needed a firm hand now to weather the storm. And so Churchill went up a step in the administration.

He became Home Secretary. The House of Lords, which before the election had combated the great majority, yielded to the much smaller one that now returned to the Commons. The Lords realized that under the unusually difficult circumstances then prevailing their continued resistance must lead to a crisis in the affairs of the State. Not wishing to be the grave-diggers of England, they preferred to commit political suicide themselves. In April, 1910, they passed the once-rejected budget. Since that precedent the House of Lords has led but a shadow existence in the British constitution. When the Parliament Bill, which definitely rendered the Upper House powerless, was voted in 1911, Churchill wound up the debate with words, "The time has come when outworn controversies of the Victorian period should be honorably settled." He did not yet realize that he himself was to live on as the last figure of the Victorian period. He considered himself a resolute progressive. His first measure in the Home Office was an extensive prison reform. It was undoubtedly owing to a remnant of his own claustrophobia in his youth that he now introduced lectures and concerts in the prisons. Oddly enough, even this provoked the Suffragettes, whose advance guard saw themselves cheated of their martyr's crown if they should be jailed.

By the testimony of the Civil Service Churchill was in general an uncommonly hard-working and efficient departmental official. The rigor of his administration was none too welcome to some of his associates. He showed little feeling for the niceties of the service etiquette. But both in the Home Office and in Scotland Yard his conduct won unmitigated praise.

His carriage now was stiffer. His face, still persuasive and still lighting up occasionally, began to show the first wrinkles of responsibility, rising steeply between nose and corner of the mouth. His hair was receding. Only one tiny upturned curl of forelock still indicated the youthful revolutionary. Winston Churchill was at the turning-point of his embattled existence. Instead of a fighting-cock, he slowly grew into a warrior of the Lord.

He had not yet quite overcome his little weakness for Germany.

He spent his first leave from the Home Office on a Mediterranean cruise aboard his friend Baron de Forest's yacht *Honor*. At Constantinople he met Marschall Baron Biberstein, the German diplomat. Germany was just proclaiming her *Drang nach dem Osten,* and the famous Berlin-Bagdad line was haunting all the German newspaper editorials. It was the expression of naked pan-Germanism. The Bagdad railway, just then under construction, was to symbolize and assure the supremacy of the Kaiser in the East.

Could not England and Germany exercise joint rights over the Bagdad railway? Churchill suggested pacifically.

"After one has made a bed, one does not care to turn out of it to make room for another," replied Baron Biberstein.

"One might, however, share it as man and wife." There was no getting Churchill away from appeasement.

F. E. was also a guest aboard the yacht *Honor*. The rude refusal given to his friend by the German ambassador set him to thinking. In the light of the Mediterranean moon the two discussed the world situation, which was becoming ever graver. At home too conditions had reached an intolerable state of stress. Parliament, without a real majority, was barely capable of functioning. The Irish troubles grew constantly more threatening. A strong coalition of both great parties was the necessity of the hour. Unfortunately it went no further than the conversation under the Mediterranean moon. Neither the Liberals nor the Conservatives were ready to bury the hatchet.

To learn its lessons Democracy needs more time than the nation still had left. To Churchill, however, these talks with his friend and opponent were a cause for reflection. Perhaps he had gone too far into the lowlands of party politics. Perhaps after all the Union Jack was more important than the considerably bespotted white banner of pacifism.

To Churchill, of course, reflection meant action. When he went home the first labor troubles were blazing up, to keep England's breath bated till the outbreak of the first war. Contrary to all expectations, in contradiction to his record of the preceding years,

he took the part not of the trouble-makers, but of orderly government. No doubt he did take a prominent part in the peace negotiations with the rebellious masses. But when the dockers struck
he called out troops in South Wales, and in the railway strike he
once more summoned the military to maintain communications.

At that time London was overrun with international anarchists,
chiefly Russian Nihilists. Ostensibly the comrades were merely
taking refuge from the police of the Tsar. In reality they constituted a dangerous criminal element that lived on assault and rob-
bery, and made Whitechapel in particular unsafe. When the
public read, on the morning of December 17, 1910, that a
policeman had been shot in a house at Houndsditch, the name
of Peter the Painter was on every tongue. Peter the Painter was
a Russian Nihilist from Lettland, one of those human beasts who
were later to devour and ravage the Russian people in the days
of the Bolshevik overturn. In the meantime he was roaming the
underworld of London, stealing, robbing, and heading a gang of
Russian fellow-criminals.

At about ten o'clock on the morning of January 3, 1911,
Churchill was summoned from his bath. The Home Office calling.
Absolutely immediate. At the telephone the dripping Minister
was told: "The Anarchists who murdered the policeman have
been surrounded at 100, Sidney Street, and are firing at the police
with automatic pistols. They have shot one man and appear to
have plenty of ammunition. Authority is requested to send for
troops to arrest or kill them."

Churchill was at the Home Office within twenty minutes, and
in Houndsditch half an hour later. Probably His Majesty's Minister should have exercised a little more restraint instead of departing personally for the scene of a crime. But the Home Secretary
had been a rough rider only a few years before, and traces were
still in his blood. The excited crowd that had gathered in Houndsditch did not give Churchill in his astrakhan and top hat a particularly friendly reception. In the first place astrakhan and top
hats are seldom worn in the East End, and in the second place the

Liberal Government had just rejected drastic laws restricting the immigration of aliens. " 'Oo let 'em in?" was the rude question of the mob that greeted him.

For once Churchill was left without an answer. At that second a shot was fired, a second, a third; a regular fusillade started off, right in London in broad daylight. Such a thing had not happened within living memory. The street was of course closed off. Churchill walked straight into the rain of bullets. A press photographer snapped his picture as he ventured forward while his companions cautiously sought refuge in an entry. It was another "Winnie show."

The situation was somehow embarrassing. On the one hand of course the Minister was not supposed to interfere personally in a police action, and on the other hand in his presence nothing could be done without his personal authority. For the first time since he had heard the whistle of bullets Churchill felt something like homesickness for his quiet desk. Still he could not simply get back into his car and go home in the middle of the fight.

The police were reinforced by a detachment of Scots Guardsmen. Plans were hastily made to storm from several directions at once the house where the murderers had barricaded themselves. This of course would cost some lives. Groups entering from different sides would be bound to fire at one another. Churchill had an idea. Why should not the Scots Guards and the policemen detailed for the action take shelter behind sign-boards? In feverish haste the signs were taken down from the grocery stores and laundries of the neighborhood.

Meanwhile, however, the besieged house in Sidney Street had burst into flames. Still the Anarchists did not surrender. Story by story they came down, still maintaining their fire. The brick walls of the neighboring houses and the pavement bore countless bullet marks. Just as the flames were reaching their highest, a marvelous English jurisdictional conflict broke out. The fire department had arrived, and the brigade officer wanted to go to work. The police inspector forbade the firemen to enter the zone of automatic-revolver fire. But there was not a word about auto-matic-revolver fire in the regulations of the London Fire Brigade. On the contrary, these provided unequivocally that a fire breaking out was to be extinguished at once. The police inspector and the brigade officer were almost at each other's throats before Churchill issued his pronouncement. In his capacity of Home Secretary he temporarily suspended the regulations. Very well, growled the officer, we'll hear of it in Parliament. He was a decent fellow, almost ready to give his life to risk his life.

So were all the mad Englishmen who were standing around there. For several minutes the Anarchists had not fired a shot. At any moment the police expected to see them rushing out of the house, pistols in hand, screened behind a last wild rain of bullets. Churchill knew there was not a moment to be lost. He nodded to a detective inspector. The honest fellow needed not a word of explanation. He walked quickly to the door of 100 Sidney Street, and kicked it open. Churchill went with him in a few great strides. A police sergeant with a double-barrelled shotgun joined the group.

The house was ablaze. There were two corpses in the ruins. One had been felled by police bullets, the other evidently suffocated by the smoke. The two were later identified as Fritz Svaars and Jacob Vogel. Both were members of Peter the Painter's gang. The boss was not involved in the affair; he had made off in time, and got away to Russia.

London cheered its courageous Minister. But Arthur Balfour got up in the House to ask the "young man of promises": "We are concerned to observe photographs in the illustrated news-papers of the Home Secretary in the danger-zone. I understand what the photographer was doing, but why the Home Secretary?"

For the second time in his life—the last time to date—Churchill was left without an answer. He had no wish now for conflict with the leader of the Conservatives. Such sensational incidents as the one just behind him were losing their meaning for him. He no longer took himself so seriously. The air he was breathing now weighed heavily on his chest. His instinct awakened. Occupying himself furiously with departmental worries in the Home Office, he could feel the world being plunged into worries of a quite different nature. Had he been led astray by the German Imperial pomp at Würzburg? Must he do penance? Was some guilt his to atone for? While England still gazed listlessly at the sky, Churchill could see the flash of the lightning.

The panther leap of Agadir snatched from him with painful sharpness the illusions of years. On July 1, 1911, Kaiser Wilhelm sent his warship *Panther* to the Moroccan port of Agadir. The Mannesmann brothers, the German heavy industrialists, had complained that the French Government of Morocco was making difficulties for them. And so the All-Highest drew the flashing sword he had so often rattled. Again it was only saber-rattling. But this time the world no longer ignored the discordant jangle. Even Lloyd George realized his blindness. The leader-to-be of Great Britain in the first World War gave a sign of what was to come in a historic address at the Mansion House: "Peace at the price of humiliation would be intolerable for a great country like ours to endure!" he thundered, shaking his lion's mane.

Churchill did not thunder. Already half bald, he had no mane to shake. But he functioned. Through a chance conversation at a garden party for members of Parliament he learned that the magazines where the naval supplies of cordite were stored were under his, the Home Secretary's, jurisdiction. They were guarded only by a small force of unarmed policemen. He addressed himself at once to an elderly officer temporarily in charge of the Admiralty, requesting him to dispatch sailors to the magazine. The old armchair soldier refused the request, referring to some dusty regulation. Churchill went to Mr. Haldane, Secretary for War, and demanded soldiers. Haldane gave him what he wanted.

In his own domain Churchill made feverish preparations for war. He began by signing a warrant permitting the opening of spy correspondence. This did indeed violate the privacy of correspondence, a thing unheard of in peace-time, but the measure allowed the British Intelligence Service to make such complete acquaintance with the German spy ring that the latter could be rounded up down to the last man at the outbreak of war. Since that success Churchill has continued to be interested in espionage, which until then had never been mentioned in polite English society.

At night he studied the secret plans for defense. Asquith summoned a secret meeting of the Committee for National Defense that Mr. Balfour had formed after Parliament had adjourned in August, and for the first time Churchill was admitted to the circle. Only now was he one of the initiates. He learned how far the negotiations between Foreign Secretary Sir Edward Grey and the French Government had already progressed. Until then Asquith had not informed the "super-pacifists" of his own government about the negotiations.

The military authorities were of the opinion that in case of war Germany would make rapid progress during the first week. During the second week, however, France would be strong enough for a counter-offensive. Between the ninth and thirteenth days the German offensive would be broken, and the French advance would begin. Much too optimistic! said Churchill, the dilettante. During the second week the French would still be too weak to halt the German advance. On the twentieth day, he predicted, the French Army would be in full retreat from the Meuse to Paris. The Germans would be fully extended, occupied with their sea flank, bound to meet the slow-striking Russian Army in the rear. Not until the fortieth day of fighting would the French be able to hit back.

Churchill recorded his thoughts in a memorandum, the first of a long series of documents with which he was to harass his fellow Cabinet members throughout the war. General, later Sir Henry, Wilson, speaking for the General Staff, emphatically rejected the "silly memorandum." He disposed of it as an "utterly amateur legend." As a matter of fact there is not one document in the archives of the first World War that predicts the actual events with such visionary acuteness. Three years later, when it came to a trial, the French were in full retreat on the twenty-first day. The Battle of the Marne began on the forty-first or forty-second day.

Mr. Asquith was deeply impressed by the fiery zeal of his young colleague. In October, 1911, he invited him to a secret rendezvous "somewhere in Scotland." The two gentlemen played golf, and talked about the weather. On the way home from the links the Prime Minister suddenly asked: "Did you ever hear the word *Weltraumpolitik?*"

"I am not so good in German," Churchill confessed rather shamefacedly. As a matter of fact the Teutonic gutturals have always caused him insuperable difficulties. "I am afraid I am not going to learn German until the Kaiser invades this island with his troops," he had just joked at some party. It sounded like an excellent witticism.

So Mr. Asquith explained to him what *Weltraumpolitik* meant. Fundamentally it was the same thing that the Nazis today call *Lebensraum,* living-space: the dominance of the master race. The Prime Minister had a wealth of documents to prove beyond question that Germany was planning to attack. Probably the Reich would strike at England first, before overpowering France. "We have only the navy," he said. "It is our only hope."

Churchill jumped. Why, this old gentleman with his smooth-shaven rosy face beneath the carefully brushed and parted white hair knew that England was on the brink of the abyss—and he played golf all day? And the navy went on rusting in peace!

Quiet, but sure of his man, Asquith asked: "Would you like to go to the Admiralty?"

"Indeed I would," replied Churchill equally quietly.

The moment was too great for words.

There was no use in talking at length about the difficulties. Just in passing Asquith happened to mention that he had already asked the then First Lord, Mr. McKenna, to exchange his office for the less important one of Home Secretary, and that McKenna had nodded acquiescence without further questions.

The fading light of evening disclosed in the far distance the silhouette of a battleship steaming slowly out of the Firth of Forth. My ship, it suddenly flashed through Churchill's head. The talent entrusted to me! My mission!

And from that day until this very moment he has never had a thought except for the fulfilment of his mission. Worldly ambition has fallen away from him. The flames of vanity have no more warmth. What was it he had once called Mr. Balfour—a lay-priest with a secular goal? Now he himself was a monk—a belligerent, bibulous, learned monk it is true, devoted to beauty in all its forms, but a God-fearing crusader nevertheless.

Returning to his guest-room, Churchill found a Bible on his bedside table. On any other day this would have been chance, and not an uncommon chance. Now it was Fate. He opened the book at random. It was the ninth chapter of Deuteronomy. He read: "Hear, O Israel, thou art to pass over Jordan this day, to go in to possess nations greater and mightier than thyself, cities great and fenced up to heaven."

He could not help thinking of Würzburg, a city great and fenced up to heaven. The self-styled All-Highest was riding at the head of his white cuirassiers. What? Was that in Breslau? The infantry formations were modernized and adapted to actual war conditions. At a trumpet blast a hundred thousand heels clicked. At another a hundred thousand marching boots moved. Wave after wave of valiant manhood poured across the parade ground. Such were the Germans—towering in the splendor of their Imperial faith, and delving down in their profound, cold, patient, ruthless speculations. Thousands of strong horses were dragging cannon and great howitzers up the ridges and along the roads. They were a nation full of thoroughness and all that their triumph in science implied. The British, on the contrary, were a peace-loving, inoffensive, little-prepared people. England's mission was nothing but good sense and fair play.

"A people great and tall, the children of the Anakims, whom thou knowest, and of whom thou hast heard say, Who can stand before the children of Anak!

"Understand therefore this day, that the Lord thy God is he which goeth over before thee; as a consuming fire he shall destroy them, and he shall bring them down before thy face; so shalt thou drive them out, and destroy them quickly, as the Lord hath said unto thee.

"Speak not thou in thine heart, after that the Lord thy God hath cast them out before thee, saying, For my righteousness the Lord hath brought me in to possess this land: but for the wickedness of these nations the Lord doth drive them out before thee.

"Not for thy righteousness, or for the uprightness of thine heart dost thou go to possess their land: but for the wickedness of these nations the Lord thy God doth drive them out from before thee, and that he may perform the word which the Lord sware unto thy fathers, Abraham, Isaac, and Jacob."

The candle on the bedside table guttered out. Churchill's vanity died with it. From that Scottish couch a missionary was to arise on the morrow. Meanwhile the Emperor of the Anakims rode through the narrow room on a foaming white horse. He did not affright the sleeper. For the last time Winston Churchill enjoyed a long rest. For the first time he knew blessed sleep.

PART II

The Voice

CHAPTER XIV

Full Speed Ahead

BERLIN rubbed its hands, and the British pacifists were delighted. Winston Churchill was their best bet. This perennial advocate of economy in the Services, the outspoken opponent of McKenna's demands for a modest increase in battleship-building, the man who had coined phrases like "No real antagonism exists between England and Germany," and who spoke of the cardinal error in naval circles as seeing the Reich as a potential enemy—why, was he not the answer to the prayer of all anti-Imperialists, domestic and foreign? If, in the words of the Order in Council, this man should now be "responsible to Crown and Parliament for all the business of the Admiralty," the rapidly growing German fleet would certainly have easy sailing.

The shameless joy with which England's enemies welcomed Winston Churchill was but one more spur to him to summon all his powers. At thirty-seven he was already thoroughly weary of honors, of offices, of success. To the man who grows beyond himself there are but two real stimuli: personal danger and creative work. He was to enjoy both in full measure now that he set out "to put the fleet into a state of instant and constant readiness for war in case we are attacked by Germany." The first dangers, and perhaps the worst, to which Churchill exposed himself and his mission as First Lord were of a personal nature. His new broom swept clean and bare the antiquated Admiralty that he found on his arrival. In the process unfortunately a very valuable man had to go overboard—Sir Arthur Wilson, the First Sea Lord. "Old 'Ard Art," as he was known throughout the navy, was a pure, spotless, unselfish character, unfortunately obsessed with old-fashioned strategical ideas. He was absolutely without ambition; everything to him was duty, which one did as well as one could without ever expecting or even accepting a reward. This spirit he had propagated in the navy, where he was greatly beloved. His fall raised almost an outburst of insurrection among the senior officers. As had been Churchill's fate all his life, so now he was received as an outsider, a dilettante and trouble-maker. Only Sir Arthur himself kept aloof from the clamor. When Prince Louis of Battenberg replaced him, he took leave of Churchill on friendly, if cool terms. He refused a peerage.

On November 16 the new First Lord established a new Board of Admiralty. He passed over the four or five most important senior Admirals. Instead he made Rear Admiral Beatty, his old friend from Omdurman, and the youngest flag officer, disliked by the entire navy for what they called his "push" and for his recent refusal of an appointment in the much-coveted Atlantic Fleet, his Naval Secretary. Rear Admiral Beatty, who was later in command of the battle cruisers at Jutland, was full of modern ideas. He became Churchill's closest associate.

Everywhere young officers were being promoted to the most responsible jobs. Automatic promotion ceased. Jellicoe attained the rank of second-in-command of the Fleet in home waters. His promotion aroused the liveliest disapproval among his ranking colleagues. But Jellicoe had been nursed by Fisher.

Here appears the most fantastic figure among the many great, remarkable and unforgettable men who have crossed Churchill's path. The two had met for the first time four years before. In 1907 Winston Churchill encountered John Arbuthnot Lord Fisher on a holiday at Biarritz. At that time Lord Fisher was First Sea Lord, and exactly twice as old as Churchill. Despite this difference in ages and despite the fact that Lord Fisher was generally honored as "the father of the navy," while Churchill was still called a parliamentary rabble-rouser, the two men struck sparks like flint and steel at their first meeting. The young Under Secretary for Colonies was a firebrand, the old admiral an inextinguishable

THE FIRST LORD OF THE ADMIRALTY ON THE "REVENGE"

volcano. His creations ranged from the introduction of the submarine—originally called "Fisher's toy"—to the "all-big-gun ship,"
the common education scheme, the water-tube boiler, the scrap-
ping of great numbers of ships having little fighting power, the
naval programs of 1908 and 1909, and the advance to the 13.5-inch
gun.

Like every man possessed by an idea, of course Lord Fisher had
provoked violent opposition. The dynamic little Admiral seems
to have had little patience with opposing opinion and argument.
Unhesitatingly he fired admirals and captains who did not agree
with his slogan, "Ruthless, relentless, remorseless!" And while the
pensioned gentlemen were eating their hearts out "on the beach,"
Fisher still pursued them with horrible oaths and imprecations.
"May their wives be widows," he used to curse his opponents.
"May their children be fatherless, and their homes a dunghill!"

The same volcanic qualities, found in the young man with
whom he was strolling on the beach at Biarritz, seem to have
attracted Fisher irresistibly. The letters that he wrote to Churchill
after their first encounter invariably began with "Beloved Winston . . ." and ended with such assurances as "Yours till hell
freezes . . ." or "Yours until the charcoal sprouts . . ." Hell froze
and the charcoal sprouted in 1915, when the conflict over the
Dardanelles put a tragic end to one of the most fantastic, dramatic and exciting of masculine friendships. But in 1911, when
Churchill went to the Admiralty, his most urgent business was
to visit Fisher at his home, Reigate Priory.

The Admiral was then seventy-one years old, and had been
pensioned off for a year in accordance with the Service age regulations. He was not immediately willing to receive Churchill,
because he wanted to keep faith with McKenna, Winston's predecessor in office. Only when he had assured himself that Churchill
himself was innocent of the exchange with McKenna, and had
made no attempt to get the First Lordship of Admiralty, did the
doors of Reigate Priory open. Then, indeed, they flew open wide.

Churchill came with his seven-point program in his head. In

the first place new War Plans for the Fleet must be worked out, since the old ones had been exclusively based on the principle of close blockade. In the second place a new organization of the Fleet was necessary to increase its instantly-ready strength. Third, there were measures to be considered against surprise attack; fourth, the formation of a Naval War Staff; fifth, coöperation with the army; sixth, increase of gun-power in ships of all classes; seventh, personal changes in the high command and on the Board of the Admiralty.

With fiery zeal Fisher plunged into the discussion. Particularly the shift from blockade strategy to the technique of aggression stirred his martial spirit. "We must fight on the blue water, no longer bottle the enemy up in their home waters," he announced. "We must dig them out like rats from their holes!" he said of the German vessels. About the personal changes, however, he said nothing. Not that he was uninterested. Quite the contrary. The old sea-dog was waiting, trembling in every nerve, for the question: "Do you want to come back and help me?" But Churchill did not ask that question—not until the hour of decision struck, three years later. He was having trouble enough of his own, and more than enough, with his staff. The old despot's return to active service must have kindled all the fires of hell. The "band of brothers" tradition that Nelson had bequeathed to the Fleet would have been irreparably destroyed by the revival of the old feuds and antipathies. Fisher reforms without Fisher methods were Churchill's shrewd solution.

John Arbuthnot Lord Fisher understood the unspoken words, though they froze his wild, untamed, warrior heart. After discussing, reforming, criticizing, modernizing the navy with fiery zeal for three days, the two rode back to London together. The journey took an hour. The conversation halted. Would Churchill say the word? Waterloo Station, all change! Churchill was mute. With a cool, formal bow Fisher took leave of his old friend and the dream of a second youth.

Of friends and of dreams you can take leave. Not of the navy.

Fisher was scarcely at his hotel before he sat down and wrote the
first of an infinitely long series of letters to the First Lord of the
Admiralty. He had forgotten to mention during their three days'
discussion . . . The stream of letters flowed uninterrupted. They
were regularly eight to ten closely written pages, over three thousand pages altogether, each letter fastened with a little pearl pin
or a scrap of silk ribbon, and containing every sort of news and
counsel, from blustering reproach to supreme inspiration. Only
about himself the old man wrote not a word.

To complete the changes in the navy discreetly Churchill would
have needed fifteen years; he agreed with Fisher about that. As a
matter of fact they probably had about a year and a half; this also
they both realized. And under no circumstances must the secrecy
of the preparations suffer. The Liberal Government now knew
that war with Germany was inevitable. Each week the courier's
pouch from Berlin convinced them anew. So long as the faintest
chance yet remained of showing Berlin the hopelessness of pan-
German adventures the British nation must not know how serious
the situation was. The public displeasure would definitely bar
the door to conciliation. This attitude on the part of Mr. Asquith,
actively supported by his Chancellor, Lloyd George, was certainly
in the interest of European peace. It was certainly not in the interest of the British nation, which had not been taken into its Government's confidence, and was neither intellectually nor morally
prepared when it turned out that the scarcely possible hope of
sanity at Berlin was impossible. For the first time England was
going through the disastrous process of appeasement.

Churchill at the Admiralty was the one worst hindered by the
necessity for caution and secrecy, by the impossibility of appealing
for popular support of his work, on which the existence of the
Empire depended. Within his department he strained every re-
source. He ordained a state of constant readiness for war. By his
order one of the Sea Lords, each in turn, must sleep in the Admiralty building so as to be on hand in case of need. The maga-

zines were now guarded by heavy-armed soldiers. But he could scarcely talk of these measures even to his chief.

The Right Honorable Herbert Henry Asquith was of so highly moral a disposition that he felt extremely ill at ease in the role of conspirator that was forced upon him. Besides, he insisted with puritan severity on keeping business and pleasure apart. With him the court was open or closed. When Mr. Asquith and his wife and elder daughter were guests aboard the Admiralty yacht *Enchantress* during the parliamentary recess of 1911, he enchanted the whole party with his knowledge of the world and his social talents. Baedeker himself could not have known the Mediterranean, the Adriatic, and the Aegean, where the *Enchantress* was cruising, better than he. At parlor games he was the unchallenged master. No one could write down in a five-minute period more generals beginning with L or poets beginning with T. He basked in the sunshine and read Greek. He even fashioned impeccable Greek verses in complicated meter, and recast in terser form classical inscriptions that displeased him, Churchill, suffering once again from the lack of a university education, could not help much here. He would probably have been of some use in decoding the cipher telegrams that Asquith received every day from Downing Street. Even in those days he was the only one who could read the secret signs of the times. But Mr. Asquith tolerated no help, and imparted no confidences. He was the boss.

Nor did the Prime Minister really approve of the wild passion with which Churchill flung himself upon his new "hobby." The thing that may have seemed so to Mr. Asquith was in reality the weapon of the future, just then in its infancy—the air arm. It is perfectly just and correct to describe Winston Churchill as the founder of the English air arm. He may have performed more conspicuous achievements at the Admiralty, but none of such momentous significance. Once again it was his feeling for things to come that drove him on.

With the exception of the year 1916 Churchill was responsible for the creation and development of the Royal Air Service during the first eleven years of its existence: from 1911 to 1915 as First Lord, from July, 1917, to the end of the war as Minister of Munitions in charge of the manufacture and supply of all aircraft needed for the war, and from 1919 to 1921 as both Air Minister and Secretary for War.

In 1911, when he took over the Admiralty, the Royal Navy had about half a dozen airplanes, and perhaps the same number of pilots. Everything else had to be invented—even some of the words, such as "seaplane."

From the very beginning he had a definite feeling that a new arm was coming to birth here, destined some day to supersede the old branches on water and on land. And so from the day he took office he was resolved to develop and extend the naval air service by every means in his power. A small group of adventurous young officers under the leadership of Commander Sampson were the pioneers in naval flying. Naturally Churchill could not share in their work without exact knowledge of it. Early in 1912 he took his first ride in a seaplane, piloted by Commander Spenser Grey. It was a thrilling and stirring experience. In those days every flight was a gamble with life and death. Once the First Lord invited a young officer to fly with him in a three-seater machine. The young man accepted. When they returned safe and sound, he did admit having spent the morning making his will. And that officer proved in the World War that he was no coward; he won the Victoria Cross under circumstances of extraordinary bravery.

Churchill flew as an example and an encouragement to his young officers. At least so he said in defending himself to his fellow Cabinet members, who were not enthusiastic. But as a matter of fact the thrill of danger was what counted. He admitted this himself in later years. Indeed there was no lack of dangerous thrills. True, death passed by this man with his charmed life, but his companions felt the icy hand. One day Churchill took a prolonged flight in a seaplane of a new and experimental type. Immediately afterward—he had just gone aboard the Admiralty yacht *Enchantress*—he learned that the machine had nose-dived into the sea with three officers, all of whom were killed. Again a few weeks later he had agreed to take a flight in a dual-control machine. He invited two friends, both officers, to join him. A suddenly-arranged conference forced him to excuse himself. He was still sitting at the green table when a note was passed to him: The machine, having flown perfectly for hours, had suddenly plunged and smashed to pieces, gravely injuring both of Churchill's friends.

Had he had enough? Nothing of the sort! He continued to court the winged death through all the years of the airplane's development; and though today he no longer sits at the controls of a machine, the airplane is still his natural means of travel. He needed some distraction in the great game.

The game grew ever more perilous. The German armament race went on at a frantic pace. Berlin had plunged most wildly of all into the enlargement of the Imperial Navy. Dark clouds hung on the horizon in England. The Irish disease infected the Kingdom. Only an operation could cure it; but an operation might be fatal.

The Government's leading spokesman in the Irish question was Winston Churchill. This had really nothing to do with his office. Nevertheless it was on the navy's account that he now leapt into the breach again. His administration of the Admiralty was under attack from several quarters. The anti-militarists, of whom he had until recently been one, distrusted his sudden naval enthusiasm. The Conservatives were still unwilling to entrust the fleet to him. His own staff and the naval officer's corps felt injured by his reforms. The highest authority in all questions of defense was Lord Kitchener, a national saint in his own lifetime. True, he had never meddled in maritime affairs, but that was not altogether sufficient explanation for his refusal even to meet the newly appointed First Lord. Quite evidently his resentment toward the "dilettante" subaltern-journalist of the Soudan campaign was still alive. Such were the odds that Winston Churchill had to fight against—it has always been so throughout his entire career. He took up the fight because he was convinced of his mission. The children of Anak now had no more resolute opponent. He was no quitter. He even fought on another front in order to hold his own position in the rear. He had to make himself so indispensable to the Government as Irish mediator that he could keep his Admiralty. And so that he could get his heavy naval appropriations. They were to bring tears to the eyes of his own Liberal majority when he presented them the following spring.

Three problems were pressing him at once: the naval rivalry with Germany; the Home Rule fight; and, not least, the vitriolic controversy about woman suffrage that still disturbed his public and private life. There was one thought behind all his struggles: England must be strong. For the rest of his life he has had no other thought.

Financial worries, for instance, he would not take seriously, although they became more and more urgent. For a year he could not occupy his official residence simply because he could not raise the money to move. Not till Sir Edward Grey took his house in Eccleston Square off his hands could he settle in at the Admiralty. This official residence has remained his favorite dwelling. Even when he had to move to No. 10 Downing Street in the present war, he was months in taking leave of the familiar apartments. His son Randolph, who was born in that year of 1911, was a blessing, but still the future of a completely penniless boy created one more problem. Yet he did not let such problems trouble him. Winston Churchill was no longer his own man.

Outwardly he was little changed. He still looked youthful, but his hair was retreating alarmingly. He was even rather more careful of his clothes. Morning and evening he was shaved and rosy. He was at pains to keep some of the stoop out of his shoulders. This naturally made him look considerably broader than he had a few years before, but not yet fat. At the same time he took great pleasure in his meals. His dinner parties were soon famous, for he was a celebrated gourmet. Years afterward, at the wedding banquet of his son Randolph, who was marrying the Honorable Pamela Digby, he formulated his culinary philosophy. Between ice-cream and champagne he expressed his paternal emotion in the words: "After all, eat we must, anyway!"

We must drink heavy red wines, too, and smoke the famous black cigars. "My ideal of a good dinner," he declared, "is first to have good food, then to discuss good food, and after this good food has been elaborately discussed, to discuss a good topic—with myself as chief conversationalist."

He became a famous host on the Admiralty yacht. He was soon called "the enchanter on the *Enchantress*." Everyone vied for the honor of drinking his wines and smoking his cigars, but even more for the privilege of listening to his conversations. In conversation he was rash and audacious, whereas in public speeches, particularly in Parliament, he considered each word six times before uttering it for the official record. His small talk, on the contrary, was extremely uncensored. His retorts were sometimes sharp. For a short time he wore a moustache, which led a suffragette lady to remark: "I like your moustache as little as your politics."

"Don't worry," replied Churchill, "you won't come in contact with either."

His intimate friends were afraid he was not himself. Sometimes in the midst of an animated discussion he would fall silent, and stare into space as if wholly absent. Of course this did not happen often. It was probably not a sign of hidden melancholy, but rather simply an expression of his special capacity for thinking ahead. Mr. Asquith was still busy with Greek verses while Churchill was hearing the Irish curses that awaited the two on their return.

And yet neither Asquith nor Churchill deserved anything of Ireland but gratitude and appreciation. Mr. Asquith had fought for the Irish cause with dignity and resolution through many years. The Irish did not make the struggle easy for him. They kept letting him feel that his nominal Liberal majority depended on their eighty votes in the House. They refused to Ulster the right of self-determination that they so fanatically claimed for themselves.

It cost Churchill much struggle with himself to intervene as an honest broker in the Irish negotiations. To a man of his chivalrous views it did not at first seem altogether easy for a Minister of His Majesty to receive members of a revolutionary group whose members at home had, as a deliberate method of warfare, cruelly assaulted, ambushed and murdered humble agents of the Crown, engaged in the faithful exercise of their duties. No doubt the Irish rebels called themselves soldiers and formed an army. But they wore no uniforms, no marks of identification, and conformed in no respect to the laws and customs of war. But Churchill was not merely a hussar officer from Sandhurst and Aldershot. Above all he was a just man, one who always looked for the other side. He understood that the Irish assassins were acting out of fanaticism, quite selflessly so far as they themselves were concerned, and that each of them was hazarding his life. He recognized also that in the main they were supported by the sentiment of their fellow-countrymen. And finally he realized that the Irish wound must be healed. For almost forty years the Irish Nationalists had poisoned the parliamentary life of England. They made and broke governments with their eighty-odd votes, swaying the fortunes of both parties. This must be stopped. The concessions that each London government had made since 1903 had never quite kept pace with the constant new demands. After his change of front in foreign politics Winston Churchill became an appeaser at almost any price, in order to solve the crucial problems of the Empire at home.

He received the two Irish spokesmen, Mr. Griffith and Michael Collins. Only very gradually did personal relations grow out of the political negotiations. Griffith was that rare type, a silent Irishman, suspicious and hesitant about thawing out. He was also a great student of European history and politics. Michael Collins had had little formal education. He was the favorite of his country's extreme parties. But he had native wit, political sense, and personal devotion. The greater his difficulties with his associates, the higher stood his prestige and influence. (To anticipate the outcome: after long years of negotiation, in which Lord Birkenhead took a prominent part on the English side, he signed the Irish Treaty; to F. E.'s remark, "I may have signed my political death-warrant tonight!" Collins replied, "I may have signed my actual death-warrant." But he had no fear of death, his close neighbor of many years, threatened as he was by fellow-fighters, whose methods he knew so well, accused of treason and perjury by some of his own confederates, the target of a dozen murder conspiracies. "I expect," he said to Churchill, as the end was drawing near, "that I shall soon be killed. It will be a help. My death will do more to make peace than I could do by living." Soon afterward he was shot from ambush.)

Returning to the pre-war scene: on the English side Churchill was decried as a traitor and renegade for thus energetically taking the part of the Irish settlement, which certainly was a grave blow to the homogeneity of the British Isles. Well-bred Conservatives did not indeed shoot from ambush, like the assassins of the I.R.A. But when Churchill came back early in 1912 from Belfast, where he had made himself anything but popular with the Ulstermen, a Conservative protest meeting was held at, of all places, Blenheim Palace, his own birthplace; the speaker cried with uplifted hand: "That is the man whose father coined the glorious phrase, Ulster will fight and Ulster will be right!" A fierce uproar of indignation shook the paternal house of the prodigal son.

Churchill had no time to reply. He knew the full significance of the Irish conflict. But he felt that the full significance of domestic questions, even the most burning and painful ones, was as nothing beside the dark menace that rose over the German Ocean. Once again his clairvoyant foresight was ahead of his time. When he came back from Belfast somebody in the Glasgow shipyards on the Clyde handed him the Kaiser's speech announcing large increases in Germany's naval forces. Churchill did not wait

until he was back in London to reply. He never even considered
securing the approval of Cabinet or Prime Minister. Right on
the spot in Glasgow he made a speech in which he pointed out
to Wilhelm II that the navy was to England a necessity, to Germany a luxury. It is existence for us, it is expansion for them, he
declared.

The speech was a bombshell to London as well as to Berlin.
His colleagues in London were dismayed—how could Winnie
speak so sharply just when Haldane, the Secretary for War, was
on a mission of conciliation to the Kaiser? Certainly the speech
was bound to destroy Haldane's work. In Berlin people took up
the catchword "luxury." At a sign from above the entire German
press began to talk of "Our luxury fleet, which we shall indulge
in now, more than ever."

When Haldane returned he reported that Churchill's speech
had had a very good effect, and had come just at the right moment to show the German negotiators that England too could
be in earnest.

The Glasgow speech had another epilogue—and a very pleasant
one. Lord Kitchener made an opportunity to shake hands with
the fighting First Lord. The two men stood face to face again
for the first time since Omdurman. It cannot be asserted that
there was an immediate sentimental reconciliation. In fact Kitchener seemed rather amused at the master of the Admiralty, who
had been his irreverent critic at twenty-four. But at any rate a
working association developed between the two, which bore good
fruit in the hour of supreme need.

The Glasgow speech lost Churchill his whole reputation as a
pacifist and appeaser. A few weeks later he tried to restore it.
In the Commons he rose to suggest declaring a naval holiday
for the coming year, 1913. That he wanted to give the Germans
one last chance to show some will to reconciliation, if they had
any.

Admiral Tirpitz did not even deign to reply. The Germans
had backed the wrong horse when they counted on Churchill,

and they were, as they proved on a later occasion, bad losers. Kaiser Wilhelm would never again invite to maneuvers and put up at the Golden Goose the English friend who had been ungrateful enough to warn his country of the ambush. First the Conservatives had branded Churchill as a "renegade"; now the German press spread what it called his questionable reputation throughout the world.

Acts were his reply to slander. His first important measure was the shift of the navy from coal to oil fuel. The ships' cruising radius was thus considerably increased. Oil was the navy's new lifeblood. Churchill could become positively lyrical in talking of oil. A quarter-century later the second World War, waged more with oil than with bullets, proved him overwhelmingly in the right. Incidentally Lord Fisher agreed with him. The old admiral stopped sulking in his tent at Reigate Priory to take the chairmanship of the Oil Fuel Commission, which was formed after the Government took control of the Anglo-Persian Oil Company. At the same time Churchill secretly replaced the 13.5-inch guns with 15-inch guns in building the five new dreadnoughts. It was a breath-taking gamble. Grandfather Jerome, the American race-track king, would have enjoyed it. In the navy they called the new giant the "hush-and-push gun." If they had shaken apart the ships they were built into, the whole blame would have fallen on the First Lord. His entire career would have been wrecked, and worse still, the fleet would have been jeopardized at the very outbreak of the war. Churchill—literally —stuck to his guns, and the experiment succeeded. "We acted without ever making a trial gun. We trusted entirely to the British naval science in marine artillery," he said later. As a matter of fact the superior firing power of the new dreadnoughts considerably strengthened British naval supremacy in its hour of trial.

For 1913 Churchill's watchword was that all the forces of the navy must be assembled in readiness for a supreme effort in the following twelve months. In his Naval Estimates, presented in March, he demanded the building of a fast division of battleships—the Queen Elizabeth class—with 15-inch guns, sailing twenty-five knots. But now the Opposition in the House went wild. This time it was the Conservatives who wanted to defend the taxpayer against the nation. It was a role that suited the Tories extremely ill, even though it offered tempting parliamentary possibilities. With a shrug of the shoulders Mr. Bonar Law, the new leader of the Tories, turned to the First Lord: "That inconvenience is time's revenge for your own obstructionist tactics in 1905." He was thinking of Broderick's army reform.

"Inconvenience?" Churchill replied. The country was in danger of its life, and the Leader of the Opposition enjoyed the "inconvenience" of a member of the Government? "I have had the privilege of listening to a very interesting and amusing debate," Churchill went on. "The delay that occurred this afternoon proved my point. I mean the difficulty under which the strongest naval power lies in being ready to meet at its average moment the attack of the next strongest naval power at its selected moment." Democracy was blind and deaf. But Churchill was not talking about the decay of democracy. He merely called the spectacle a very interesting and amusing debate.

Mr. Bonar Law felt no sympathy. He was mortally insulted by an incident that had occurred a few days before in the Home Rule debate. In defending Ulster's rights he had said: "Ulster would almost rather be subject to a foreign nation than to Nationalist Ireland." Whereupon Churchill leaped on him: "What? You want to secede to Germany?" Of course this was a gross exaggeration that slipped out in the heat of battle. Parliament, it became ever plainer, was unequal to the nation's crisis of nerves.

At the Lord Mayor of London's banquet early in November, 1913, Churchill spoke the prophetic words: "The needs of the national safety demand also the best possible measures for aerial defense." Once again he spoke a quarter-century too soon. Not a soul cared for aerial defense. Count Zeppelin was a German ec-

centric, and a jolly good fellow besides with his bushy white
moustaches.

The radicals and pacifists were aroused. Mr. F. W. Hirst, the
editor of the *Economist,* denounced Churchill's speech as "naval
and aerial bombast." At the National Liberal Federation the
president, Sir John Brunner, bemoaned "Churchill's falling off
from his old way." And Lloyd George, knowing very well which
side a politician's bread is buttered on, fell upon his friend and
fellow Cabinet Minister from the rear with a sensational interview in the *Daily Chronicle* of New Year's Day, 1914. He urged
a reduction of armaments in view of both the need for economy
and the increasingly better relations with Germany. So that his
readers should make no mistake about whom he meant, he referred to Lord Randolph's glorious fight for economy and retrenchment. It was a personal thrust at Winston, whom nothing
could hurt more deeply than any accusation of betraying his
father's memory. When he had to forsake even the beloved
shadow in order to save England, Churchill was truly alone.

Lloyd George's attack encouraged the pacifists in the Government camp to demand of the Prime Minister Churchill's dismissal. Mr. Asquith, however, if sometimes weak, was always a gentleman. He sent away the radical deputation with a definite re-
minder that the Cabinet as a whole was responsible for the policy
of the Admiralty.

Of course the public heard of these conflicts, and took the
sedate interest that the defense of the country required from a
nation of cricket-players, but no one understood the fundamental
emergency. All London laughed when the *Punch* of January 14,
1914, printed a cartoon showing Churchill in sailor's uniform
holding a life-sized roll marked "Naval Estimates" on his arm
like a sweetheart, while a chorus of Tories, in the form of light-
skirted ballet girls, sang the popular song: "You made me love
you, I didn't want to do it!" It was a gay light-skirted time, that
winter of early 1914.

Churchill joined in the general gaiety. Early in March he

handed to a small group of Cabinet ministers whom he himself called the "Invasion Committee" five short memoranda. He called them "imaginative exercises couched in a half-serious vein, but designed to disturb complacency." One of these memoranda was called "The Timetable of a Nightmare," another, "A Bolt from the Grey." His colleagues in the Cabinet did not quite know what to make of these horror pictures, which prophesied in the dying horse-and-buggy age what we today call Blitzkrieg, and a German invasion of the British Isles as well. Was it prophecy, or a premature April Fools' joke?

Probably Churchill was so horrified by his own vision that he dared express it only with the excuse of a humorous whim. He proved that it was meant in deadly earnest a few days later, when he brought in the Naval Estimates, up to that time the largest in English history. He demanded fifty-one and a half million pounds, and backed up a figure that seemed fantastic in those days with the words: "Unless our navy's strength were solidly, amply and unswervingly maintained, the Government could not feel that they were doing their duty to this country."

A terrible uproar in the Liberal party's Left wing answered him. His own criticism of the comparatively modest McKenna estimates was held up against him by embittered party associates. The Conservative Opposition even raised a suspicion that the whole business of naval armament was only a smoke-screen behind which the Government was extending its Irish policy. Defenders of the native soil were already arming in Ulster. Churchill dispatched a squadron of battleships to the island of Aran, and the Firth of Clyde, "where they would be in proximity to the coasts of Ireland in case of serious disorders occurring." The *Times* took him sharply to task: "Does Mr. Churchill expect and hope that purely precautionary measures to look after stores will lead to fighting and bloodshed?" The worst of it was that these lines in the old Thunderer were written by Leopold Amery, his lifelong friend. "A hellish suggestion!" Churchill replied. He had to apologize for this unparliamentary expression. Personally, indeed, he was to hear far worse things. Admiral Lord Charles Beresford made a violently personal speech against Churchill in the House. "The First Lord was a terrible failure in the army!" he shouted. Asked for proof, the gallant and honorable member was forced to fall back on "hearsay."

No man was more deeply entrenched in the struggle for Ireland, but at the same time none saw more plainly that the fate of the Empire was now at stake, no longer the Constitution or the loss of a rebellious province. He introduced the Second Home Rule Bill, partly because he realized that the Irish must have their freedom, partly because the Government he belonged to depended on the Irish vote in the Westminster Parliament. He did not want to give up Ulster, but the Ulstermen's open preparations for civil war irritated him. He realized that only this rebellious patriotic defiance could save Belfast from the dictatorship of Dublin. It is the grace that is in him, and at the same time his disaster, that it is given to him always to see both sides.

All the same, while Germany was sharpening her sword he had no patience with rebels, patriotic or not. "Ulster will not fight," he said, "but if she does—well, there are worse things than bloodshed!" Hundreds of faces of opposing members glared at him, startled, passionately excited, distorted with hatred. Then Winston Churchill laughed. His laughter was confident, victorious, full of trust in God and belief in England: "We know that at a touch of external difference or menace all these fierce internal controversies would disappear for the time being."

In the summer of 1914 he dispensed with the usual naval maneuvers. Instead, the very moment Sir Edward Grey had confided to him that the world struggle was imminent, he tested the plans for full-fledged mobilization. The navy passed in review before His Majesty the King on July 18, 1914. Seventy thousand officers and men in two hundred ships steaming fifteen knots passed the saluting point in the course of six hours. The press was asked to publish no details of the maneuvers, but simply to emphasize the power of the Fleet and the spirit of the crews.

On the following Thursday there was a Cabinet meeting. It was devoted almost exclusively to the Irish troubles. At the moment when the session came to an end a messenger arrived from the Foreign Office, bringing word to Sir Edward Grey. Sir Edward skimmed the paper, and mutely handed it to the Prime Minister. In a quiet, firm voice Asquith read out to his colleagues the terms of the Austrian ultimatum to Serbia. The curtain was going up on tragedy.

Winston Churchill could scarcely wait to get back from the Cabinet meeting to his office at the Admiralty. To give Germany one last warning, he instantly published a communiqué: "Orders have been given to the First Fleet, which is concentrated at Portland, not to disperse for maneuver leave for the present. All vessels of the Second Fleet are remaining at their home positions."

On July 27 he warned the commanders that hostilities might begin at any moment. Two days later he dispatched a warning telegram: the Fleet was to sail secretly in the darkness to its war stations, lest it be bottled up in the Channel or exposed to a surprise attack.

Even during those feverish hours this order was a stroke of daring. Would not the Opposition think it the excuse for a new thrust? F. E. listened around among the Conservatives. He was able to reassure his friend: no, the Conservative Opposition was perfectly loyal. But the Liberal Government had one last attack of jitters. On August 1 it vetoed Churchill's plan to call out the naval reserves immediately. But learning that Germany had declared war on Russia, the First Lord simply acted over the veto. On the evening after the Cabinet meeting he summoned the reserves. The total force of the navy was now mobilized. They waited, watch in hand, for the order that was bound to come. On Tuesday, August 4, at eleven P.M. there went out to the British Navy the General Order: "Commence hostilities at once against Germany." Five minutes after eleven the vessels were already on their way.

Happy ending?

There was no happy ending. Ten months later Churchill was busy cleaning out his desk drawers at the Admiralty to make way for his successor. He was a broken man, despairing of life. And then the door opened and the great Kitchener came in with an embarrassed smile on his tanned face. He cleared his throat, hunting for words that would not come easily. He shook hands with Churchill, and said: "There is one thing they cannot take away from you; the Fleet was ready!"

CHAPTER XV

The Tragedy of the Dardanelles

TEARS streamed down Winston Churchill's face as Mr. Asquith announced to Parliament: "Great Britain is at war." Three years of fighting in the darkness were ended now. The wear and tear on the nerves was killing. The first shot rang out as a relief.

At the same time the task was growing to monstrous proportions. The First Lord stood at the helm of the ship of state. Beyond question his office was the most important among the Service Departments. The navy alone could win the war. Even the immense responsibility of directing the navy in war did not use up Churchill's boundless, dynamic energy, bursting all restraint. He was not yet quite forty years old. The hot blood pulsed through his veins. No, this man was not born to look on. He had not prepared himself in Cuba and India, in the Soudan and South Africa for a war that he would wage from the desk. He really wanted to be in it from the first day, in the front rank.

A sense of responsibility held him back. The decisive battles would be fought for the soul, the will, the morale of his own nation. This realization is the basis of Churchill's statesmanship today.

The English, constitutional pacifists that they were, had no idea what the score was, nor how high the stakes. The war had begun, but private life must not be interfered with. Churchill had demanded immediate conscription. But the Liberal Government could not make up its mind without great difficulty to take this step. Old John Morley, Lord President of the Council, had already resigned to prove his love of peace at any price. Sir John Simon followed him into self-imposed banishment. He too did not want any share of the blame for conscription. Churchill alone pressed the issue. Even in the first few days of the conflict he was considered the leader of the war party in the Cabinet. This was a very ticklish position. He had no personal following in the House. The Radicals opposed him for advocating rapid conscription. The Tories were still nursing their grudge against him. The accusation of dilettantism began to be circulated again. The Conservative *Morning Post* spoke of the "amateur Commander-in-Chief of the navy." The people, indeed, as against the professional politicians, stuck by him. The immense popularity he had won by his successful mobilization of the navy kept him in office.

The German bombardment of Antwerp began on September 28, 1914. Four days later the Belgian Government sent its S. O. S. to London. A night conference of the British war lords took place at Kitchener's house. The Field-Marshal himself set the tone: "You must personally dash to Antwerp," he said to Churchill. "Explain to Broqueville that he must hold out with the help of the Royal Naval Division another four days, until British reinforcements come." Thus began the adventure of Antwerp. It was doubly memorable, in the first place because it was laid on Churchill's shoulders all the rest of his life, in the second place because it reads today like a dress rehearsal for the Norwegian tragedy with which Mr. Chamberlain's inglorious rule ended and the lightning war began.

It was not by accident that Kitchener chose Churchill. He counted on the brilliance, the dash and the persuasion of the young Minister—qualities whose effect upon the frantic Belgian Government was absolutely necessary in that hour of stress. Nor did Churchill disappoint the Field-Marshal. The American journalist, E. Alexander Powell, in *Fighting in Flanders*, described his arrival at Antwerp as follows:

> "At one o'clock that afternoon a big drab-colored touring car filled with British naval officers drove down the Place de Mer, took the turn into the Marché-aux-Souliers on two wheels, and drew up in front of the hotel. Before the car had fairly come to

a stop the door was thrown open and out jumped a smooth-faced, sandy-haired, stoop-shouldered, youthful looking man in undress Trinity House uniform. As he charged into the jammed lobby he flung his arms out in a nervous characteristic gesture, as though pushing his way through a crowd. It was a most spectacular entrance, and reminded me for all the world of a scene in a melodrama, where the hero dashes up bareheaded on a foam-flecked horse, and saves the heroine, or the old homestead, or the family fortune, as the case may be."

Churchill had more to rescue than a melodramatic heroine or the family fortune. Probably the neutral observer did not quite realize it was a matter of saving Antwerp and stopping the German advance. Nevertheless this description, drawn without inner understanding though it is, probably presents an outwardly true picture. Here was the great gesture that once led Mr. Asquith to speak of "my youthful and picturesque colleague"—and here was a shrewdness perfectly capable of judging the optical, perhaps even histrionic effect of his appearance on an audience that needed to be given fresh spirit. Churchill fought for his mission with all the weapons of his personality, not with the sword alone.

But his joy in sword-play was no longer to be restrained. The First Lord personally put himself at the head of the Royal Naval Division. General Ian Hamilton said: "Churchill handles them as if he were Napoleon and they the Old Guard. He flings them right into the enemy's open jaws!" The Royal Naval Division showed themselves brilliant swordsmen. None of them while he lived would yield up a foot of ground. Unfortunately they were poor shots. They had not even rifles enough for each man, and most of those they had were obsolete. Of their 8000 men, only 2000 were fully-trained Marines. The others were quarter-trained, ill-equipped reservists, mostly well-educated men who quickly earned the title of "the suicide squad."

Churchill had promised the Belgian Government that Rawlinson would come himself with from thirty to forty thousand men. He made the promise in good faith; his official instructions were to deliver that message. The prospect of Rawlinson, and the arrival of the Naval Division, which was regarded as simply an advance guard, cheered the Belgian Government as well as the hard-pressed Belgian soldiers. Churchill's personal optimism and persuasiveness, his leadership in the field, his rising above himself in the moment of emergency—all this achieved excellent results. The Belgian Army fought on for four or five days more, which meant that nine-tenths of their troups could join the British Expeditionary Corps at Nieuport, and were thus spared to continue the war to the very end.

After the first two days of fighting Churchill was so grimly absorbed in the struggle that he cabled Asquith a request for his release from the Admiralty. He preferred to take over the entire Antwerp force of 130,000 men, including the Belgians, and remain in the fighting till the end. Asquith showed the cable to Kitchener and Haig. Both had the highest opinion of the military abilities possessed by the heir of the Marlboroughs. Kitchener at once offered to promote Churchill to the rank of Lieutenant-General. But Mr. Asquith decided that he was too important at the center of war to take over any mere glorious side-show. By telegraph he refused Churchill's resignation.

Rawlinson did not come to his relief. Probably the auxiliary force of thirty or forty thousand men that had been promised existed only on paper. Churchill and the Belgian Army were ordered to retreat. The Royal Naval Division proved itself in the catastrophe brought upon it by irresponsible ill-equipment and unreliable armchair strategy. It lost between 800 and 900 prisoners, 138 wounded, 50 dead, and 7 fallen officers.

"An eccentric expedition!" was the judgment of the experts. "A pitiful waste of brave men's lives!" Churchill heard when he was back in London. It was the day that Antwerp fell. That same day his daughter Sarah was born.

The "eccentric expedition" was the last occasion when Churchill gave his temperament free rein. Temperament, he realized, was not statesmanlike—at least not always. It was a bitter lesson that he taught himself. He learned the difficult art of re-opening his clenched fist, even when the fingers grew tense of their own accord. "I ought never to have gone to Antwerp," he conceded later. "I ought to have remained in London and endeavoured to force the Cabinet and Lord Kitchener to take more effective action than they did, while I all the time sat in my position of great authority with all the precautions which shield great authority from rough mischance. Instead, I passed four or five vivid days amid the shells, excitement and tragedy of the defense of Antwerp. Luckily my resignation from the Admiralty was not accepted, for I should only have been involved in the command of a situation which locally at any rate had already been rendered hopeless by the general course of the war. In all great business very large errors are excused or even unperceived, but in definite and local matters small mistakes are punished out of all proportion. Those who are charged with the direction of supreme affairs must sit on the mountain-tops of control; they must never descend into the valleys of direct physical and personal action."

At the end of October Louis, Prince of Battenberg, retired on account of popular misgivings about his German parentage. The post of First Sea Lord was free again. Churchill hastened to offer it to Lord Fisher, who was now seventy-four years old and more passionately inflamed with youthful vitality than ever. Beyond question Lord Fisher was the foremost naval brain of England and of the world. His devotion to the navy was an obsession. His admiration for Churchill bordered on idolatry. The two men went to work together as if two generations of England were reaching out the hand of fellowship. The first German U-boats had just appeared. There was no denying that they had sunk the *Aboukir*, the *Hogue*, the *Cressy*, on the Dutch coast, with a loss of fourteen hundred officers and ratings, and this on the day after Lord Fisher had declared he would dig them out like rats from their holes. The danger demanded radical defense and thoroughly effective measures.

Unfortunately the harmony of Lord Fisher's and Churchill's

coöperation soon proved superficial. They were too much alike to get along. Both were headstrong and brilliantly unbalanced.

Churchill was displeased with the overcaution shown by some of the admirals of his own choice. Above all there was Jellicoe, who felt sure the Germans had naval reserves that the British Intelligence Service did not dream of. Such suspicions annoyed Churchill. He was at once patron and admirer of the Intelligence Service. He was annoyed even more by the chatter about the "outsider," which followed him like a curse. Admiral Sir Reginald Bacon once went so far as to say: "In an executive command in the field Mr. Churchill would in all probability have earned undying fame. But temperamentally he was unsuited to fill the post of a civilian head of a mighty technical department in war-time."

Growing a shade sharper each time, Churchill observed: "A series of absurd conventions became established in the public mind. First and most monstrous was that the generals and admirals were more competent to deal with the broad issues of the war than the abler men in other spheres of life."

The conflict became serious—Churchill's everlasting conflict with the expert—when Lord Fisher complained that his chief was constantly intermeddling in his work. It was the first rift in the friendship to reach the public.

Gallipoli brought the parting. Gallipoli was the tragedy of Churchill's life. The case of Antwerp was merely a feeble prelude.

Both Churchill and Fisher were convinced that the stalemate in the west must be broken if the Allies were to win the war within a reasonable time. Just to kill Germans on the Western Front, which was Kitchener's idea, would bring about no prompt decision. Germany must be attacked on the flank. In this the navy would have the most important share. It must either force the Dardanelles or break through in the Baltic. Lord Fisher was for trying the Baltic. The Germans, he believed, would soon have completed the Kaiser Wilhelm Canal to the point where the British Navy could use it when the German Atlantic Fleet was put out of action. Churchill expected a much more smashing success through the opening of the Black Sea. It would be possible to supply the Russians with Allied ammunition, bring the campaigns in Mesopotamia and Palestine to a victorious conclusion, knock out Turkey and Austria, and attack Germany in her undefended rear. The slaughter that had to be counted on would still be smaller than if they had to go on for years killing Germans on the Western Front.

His arguments convinced Mr. Asquith. Lloyd George too was all for the "war through the back door," though action in Salonika seemed more promising to him. In general London was hopeful. Downing Street believed that the Turks would put on as poor a show in the Dardanelles as they had just done along the Suez Canal. Initial successes increased these hopes. When the *Queen Elizabeth*, Churchill's special pride, with her new monster 15-inch guns, helped to destroy nearly all the outer defenses of the Straits on February 15, 1915, and the Fleet could consequently penetrate for six miles, it seemed as if the game were won. The Turks, London believed, only put up a resistance at all because they were in terror of the German cruisers *Goeben* and *Breslau*. Everybody was cheerful. Churchill, perhaps one of the chief originators of the Dardanelles action, certainly its most enthusiastic promoter, its best salesman at home, saw the war already won.

Only Lord Fisher, restless and uneasy, fidgeted about at the sessions of the War Council. He spoke only when spoken to, and even then confined himself to snappish, monosyllabic answers. He had a personal score to settle. He resented the dominant position of Lord Kitchener in the Council.

Certainly the Marshal was not an agreeable colleague. He was gravely overworked, and not particularly enthusiastic about the whole Gallipoli affair, because as a soldier grown gray in honor he still clung to the old tradition of killing as many Germans as possible in fair fight. He had no use for war through the back door. Yet although he could not put his heart into it, he could never quite let anyone else have his say, either. He would not tolerate interference—and yet the glorious Sirdar, looked at in daylight, was nothing but a commissioned officer, to whom he, Lord Fisher of Kilverstone, was fully equal in rank. But the worst of it was that Fisher saw his own department, his beloved navy, misrepresented. Churchill was wrong. Through the back door, yes. But the real back door was open in the Baltic.

While the war for Gallipoli was being waged in the London offices even more bitterly than in the Straits themselves, Churchill had a conversation one day with Admiral Murrey Sueter, head of the Naval Air Service. The following day they included Admiral Bacon in the discussion, and finally Colonel Swinton was brought in. They talked about Hannibal and Leonardo da Vinci, of all things, and also to some extent about the striking success of the Naval Division's armored cars in Belgium. These successes depended on the same principle on which Hannibal so successfully used his elephants. Centuries later Leonardo da Vinci had also foreseen it: a machine that would cut through the enemy lines like butter. Admiral Sueter proposed some kind of steamroller that would rush through the German trenches; Colonel Swinton laid down definite proposals before the Committee of Imperial Defense.

The Committee could not quite see what to do with these suggestions. Obviously they were just another of "Winston's follies." So the whole thing was simply turned over to the Admiralty. Churchill at the time was in bed with a severe attack of fever. On the 20th of February, 1915, the Landships Committee was formed in his bedroom, with Sir Tennyson d'Eyncourt, Chief Constructor of the Admiralty, as chairman. The Committee seemed to stray into speculation. And so Churchill, with swift decision, resolved early in March that work on the monstrous new weapon should begin without more ado. He ordered eighteen "landships" at a price of £70,000. Not a penny had been previously sanctioned. The Treasury would roll its eyes when the bill came in. The landships were not yet finished when Churchill had to give up the Admiralty, a few months later. His successor, Mr. Arthur Balfour, canceled the orders for these crazy contraptions. He allowed one sample to go through. When the sample was finished, it was named "Big Willie." In early February of 1916 it made its debut in the park of Hatfield, Lord Cecil's home, before the King and Mr. Lloyd George. Lloyd George was enthusiastic over the new weapon; His Majesty seemed skeptical.

Big Willie moved slowly and creakingly, only two miles an hour on fairly hard ground, although it was motored with a hundred and five horsepower. But it embodied the caterpillar tractor—and the rest was merely a matter of construction and evolution. Obviously the Admiralty had had an excellent new idea. On February 12 the War Office placed an order for forty of these new monsters. It was a secret weapon and had to be built in strictest privacy. As a blind, the meaningless name "tank" was adopted.

Shortly afterward, the order was increased to one hundred and fifty. The Machine Gun Force began to be trained to fight as a "heavy section" with the new weapon. Although Churchill, now dismissed from his post, pleaded desperately against revealing "Big Willie" to the Germans until many hundreds of similar machines were ready for use, the War Office used 49 tanks for the first time in the battle of Thiepval on September 15, 1916.

The German Army was stunned. So were the British lines. An airman sent home a message: "A tank is walking up the High Street of Flers, with the British Army cheering behind." The war correspondent of the *Times* found his aesthetic sense offended. He cabled about "a huge shapeless bulk resembling nothing else that was ever seen on earth." It was not until a year later, at Cambrai—by then Churchill was already Minister of Munitions— that the Allies made full use of tanks. It was a decisive weapon in the military outcome of the World War. Ludendorff attributed the necessity of asking for an armistice to "enemy tanks in unexpectedly large numbers."

Certainly Churchill is not the inventor of the tank. But without his incomparable instinct, his ruthless decisiveness, his acuteness and his unique power of "pushing things over," Hannibal's elephants and Leonardo's ideas would never have awakened to new life. Without the bad luck that so constantly pursued Winston, fortune's darling, the matter would not have been so fearfully slow and awkward in developing. The suspicion and delay of the Government offices and incredibly half-hearted maladroitness with which England used the inspiration named Churchill nearly spoiled the idea. But since after all there was evidently some British god to protect the English from their own inadequacy, Winston Churchill could take leave of the Admiralty when the time came, with the consciousness that he had made one more decisive contribution.

The time was soon to come. On March 16 Sir Sackville Carden was replaced as Commander-in-Chief in the Dardanelles by Sir John Robeck. Sir John had orders from the First Lord to push on. The Admiralty had expressly authorized the order. Forty-eight hours after taking over his command Sir John delivered the blow. It rebounded. On Monday, "Anzac Day," the troops had indeed gained a foothold, but nothing more. The battleships *Irresistible*, *Ocean* and the French *Bouvet* were sunk, and the *Inflexible* and *Gaulois* were out of action. The combined fleet suffered a complete repulse. No new action could be undertaken. The danger of mines was too extreme.

This defeat was a fearful personal blow to Churchill. Everyone made him responsible for the adventure and the ensuing failure. But, quickly pulling himself together, he denied that the failure must necessarily be final. It was a legitimate war gamble, he insisted, and the lack of cohesive effort at home could be made good if an energetic command could be brought into being; Constantinople could still be taken. He showed the inflexibility that has remained his watchword ever since: in disaster—defiance. But Kitchener had now had enough. His attention was concentrated wholly on the good old Western Front. In his dislike of the Dardanelles he even became somewhat more friendly to Lord Fisher. The latter made use of the new intimacy with his rival to deliver an ultimatum: "Either the *Queen Elizabeth* or I leave tonight."

No one wanted to lose the old firebrand. They knew that with all his crotchetiness he was irreplaceable. And so Churchill, First Lord of the Admiralty, had to sit by helplessly while his pride, his very own ship, was sent off. It was a stroke of luck in misfortune, another typically Churchill episode. A fortnight later the dummy of the *Queen Elizabeth* was torpedoed.

Admiral Fisher made use of the favoring wind to sail on to a new success. He forced upon Churchill a working agreement by which he, the First Sea Lord, had the disposal of the Fleet. In this fratricidal struggle Churchill took his revenge with one of his increasingly celebrated smooth-tongued memoranda, in which he evasively but unmistakably made clear the inherent right of the First Lord to dispose of the navy. The moment Fisher learned of this memorandum he handed in his resignation. Mr. Asquith, however, probably smiling in secret at the duel of the two stiff-necked friends, replied with an official communication: "Lord Fisher, in the King's name I order you to remain at your post!"

When seized by the sword-knot, the old sea-dog could not say no. But he was in despair at having to watch his personal fleet, the creation of his mind, ruined by an amateur, squandered, sacrificed to the damned Dardanelles. In this suffering there was but one refuge—religion. The Admiral spent the entire day in Westminster Abbey, where his heathen-sounding prayers rose up to the Christian God. He never appeared in the office at all. The First Sea Lord was on strike. He hid in his own house; the curtains were drawn over the windows all day. As he was still in the King's service, he signed the most important documents, but when he had to go to his desk he refused to use the passage through the Admiralty Office. He was afraid that some chance might throw him together with Churchill. And Churchill he would not see again at any price. He sent him a somber letter of farewell: "You are bent on forcing the Dardanelles, and nothing will turn you from it—nothing. I know you too well!"

Those were three fateful days. On May 15 Churchill had his decisive struggle with Lord Fisher. On the 16th the German Atlantic Fleet ventured from its hiding-place. But it crawled away again before the Grand Fleet could bring it to bay. It was only a reconnaissance at full strength; the British Navy saw itself cheated again of the liberating battle that Churchill and Fisher both were so eagerly awaiting. On the 17th Churchill brought the list of the new Board of Admiralty before the House of Commons. "The tamed list?" asked the leader of the Conservatives, Mr. Bonar Law, with unusual cheerfulness. His cheer had its reason. He had just agreed upon a Coalition Government with Mr. Asquith, who was impelled to consent through the disclosure of the munitions crisis. Churchill had not learned of this until then. This was the fulfilment of a demand he had been making for months. From the very day war broke out he had been insisting that the Conservatives, who were weaker than the Liberals by only two votes, should be admitted to a national emergency Cabinet. He had not known, indeed, that he was talking himself out of a job. For the Conservatives would have nothing to do with the renegade. They used Lord Fisher's sit-down strike to prove Churchill's "dilettantism." He must go from the Admiralty.

But he would not go. Gallipoli had not been quite given up. His mission was not yet fulfilled. The war was going on. The voice called. In desperate self-abnegation Churchill wrote a letter to Mr. Bonar Law. He would wrench the matter of Lord Fisher back into joint. An intimate personal friend, Lord Beaverbrook, the newspaper king, who came from Canada—and who is Minister of Aircraft Production in Churchill's Cabinet today—pled for him among the Conservatives, one of whose hopes he himself was. Bonar Law replied that the decision was irrevocable. Churchill must go. Mr. Arthur Balfour, who was more dependable than the "young man of promises," moved into the Admiralty.

Was Lord Fisher avenged? On May 19 Mr. Asquith had a letter from him: "If the following six conditions are agreed to, I can guaranty the successful termination of the war and the total abolition of the submarine menace." Point 1 was: "That Mr. Winston Churchill is not in the Cabinet to be always circumventing me.

Nor will I serve under Mr. Balfour." The other five points also established his unlimited personal naval dictatorship.

Mr. Asquith allowed three days to go by. Evidently he spent them in speculation upon the inscrutable nature of man and the bitterness of a second youth in the eighth decade of a man's life. Then he replied simply: "Dear Lord Fisher: I am commanded by the King to accept your tendered resignation of the Office of First Sea Lord of the Admiralty. Yours faithfully H. H. Asquith."

Churchill received a nominal Government position, the Chancellery of the Duchy of Lancaster. He was to remain a member of the War Council. But he must no longer have any direct influence on its policy. "Four thousand pounds a year for doing nothing!" he commented. This self-mockery was really self-deception— and one not fated to be successful. Outwardly Churchill endured his lot with a smile. In his heart, of course, his political career was not the point at all. His tragedy was that he had to watch, and this from a ringside seat, while others ruined his work. As a member of the War Council he was still informed of the most intimate secrets, but as Chancellor of the Duchy of Lancaster he had no vote in the Council. He was condemned to passivity while the storm raged over England, and all hands were feverishly occupied on deck.

"The change from the intense executive activities of each day's work at the Admiralty to the narrowly measured duties of a councillor left me gasping," he recalled. "Like a sea-beast fished up from the depths, or a diver too suddenly hoisted, my veins threatened to burst from the pressure. I had great anxiety, and no means of relieving it. I had vehement convictions and small powers to give effect to them. I had to watch the unhappy casting-away of great opportunities, and the feeble execution of plans which I had launched and in which I heartily believed. I had long hours of utterly unwanted leisure in which to contemplate the frightful unfolding of the war."

Those long hours of utterly unwanted leisure were undoubtedly the most dismal ones of his life. And yet out of them grew salvation, spiritual and intellectual equilibrium, which at some moments he had feared he would lose. He found refuge in painting.

Till his fortieth year Churchill had never had palette and brush in his hand. His native artistry had been expressed only in speech and writing. Even there he could not develop himself to the full. What he wrote was history; what he said, politics. He was a prisoner of his own career. Now his career was suddenly broken off. Now an insurmountable dam was halting the stream of his life. And so this stream broke an outlet for itself in another direction, perhaps its original course. One Sunday afternoon in the country Churchill, who was a fond father, watched his children playing with their box of paints. The following morning he bought a complete outfit for painting in oils.

Like one who was walking forbidden paths Churchill slunk off secretly into the park. There he stood with a palette reflecting many colors, the brush that he knew not what to do with weighing heavy in his hand. The worst part of a thing, as he knew from many other occasions, is the beginning. He gazed into the sky. The sky, conversely, looked down blue and white at him. Blue and white . . . that was the beginning. Bashfully Churchill painted a blue and white spot on the canvas, up near the top. The man who only yesterday had been the dynamo of the Empire was so timid in the face of the mystery that he was daring to profane, art, that he ventured only to paint a very tiny spot, no bigger than a bean.

At this moment the angel of God came to his assistance. The angel was announced by the sound of a powerful motor car that stopped behind him with a screech. The angel descended from the car. It was Lady Lavery, the wife of the celebrated painter Sir John Lavery, an artist of standing herself. "Painting?" she exclaimed. "But what are you hesitating about? Let me have a brush —the big one." And Lady Lavery went after the canvas. The earth did not open, the heavens were not darkened, the canvas did not burst into a thousand fragments. It worked; it really worked. At this Churchill took the little brush, and assaulted the canvas with a furious cavalry charge, strongly reminiscent of Omdurman.

He has not become a modern master, but he is a painter of considerable maturity, distinguished by a strong color sense; his landscapes were soon sought after by dealers and galleries. The Long Gallery at Sutton Place featured his pictures. "Charles Marin" interested the art critics, and sometimes earned an extremely welcome few thousand francs.

Painting restored his inner balance. He spoke only hesitantly, almost shyly of his newest love. He sounded as if he would excuse himself: "It is a delightful amusement to myself and at any rate not violently harmful to man or beast. There is no subject on which I feel more humble or yet at the same time more natural. It is something to occupy your leisure, to divert your mind from the daily round, to illuminate your holidays. It would be a sad pity to shuffle or scramble along through one's playtime with golf and bridge, pottering, loitering, shifting from one heel to the other, wondering what on earth to do, when all the while, if you only knew, there is close at hand a wonderful new world of art and craft, a sunlit garden gleaming with light and color of which you have the key in your waistcoat pocket. We may content ourselves with a joy-ride in a paint-box. For this audacity is the only ticket . . . I must say I like bright colors," he explained with a little more of the personal touch. "I rejoice with the brilliant ones, and am genuinely sorry for the poor browns. When I get to heaven I mean to spend a considerable portion of my first million years in painting, and so get to the bottom of the subject. Painting is a complete distraction. I know of nothing which, without exhausting the body, more entirely absorbs the mind. When I have had to stand on parade for half an hour at a time, or even, I regret to say, in church, I have always felt that the erect position is not natural to man, has only been painfully acquired, and is only with fatigue and difficulty maintained. But no one who is fond of painting finds the slightest inconvenience in standing to paint for three or four hours at a time."

Perhaps he went a little far in his new obsession. For it is not true that the erect position is unnatural to man. It is, in fact, the only thing that counts. When the Prime Minister formed a war committee of five, Churchill was excluded from the new inner circle. Thereupon, still holding his head high, he wrote to Mr. Asquith: "I am an officer, and I place myself unreservedly at the disposal of the military authorities, observing that my regiment is in France."

He stood up in Parliament for the last time. Perhaps it would be the last time in his life. The House indulgently awaited the defense of the man guilty of the disaster of the Dardanelles. The members would not be vindictive with one of their own going under fire. They would clap politely, perhaps even put in an occasional subdued "Hear! Hear!" if he pleaded mitigating circumstances. They would give him some final consolation.

But it was Winston Churchill who consoled Parliament, who yanked it up to its full height again amid the deepest depression of the war's reverses. The speech with which he took leave of the House was one of the greatest in his oratorical career. It sounded prophetic then; it might have been delivered in 1940:

"There is no reason to be disheartened about the progress of the war. We are passing through a bad time now, and it will probably be worse before it is better. But that it will be better, if we only endure and persevere, I have no doubt whatever. The old wars were decided by their episodes rather than by their tendencies. In this war the tendencies are far more important than the episodes. Without winning any sensational victory we may win this war. It is not necessary in order to win the war to push the German lines back over all the territory absorbed, or to pierce them. While the German lines extend far beyond their own frontiers and while her flag flies over great capitals and subjected provinces, while all the circumstances of military success attend her armies, Germany may be defeated more fatally in the second and third years of this war than if the Allies had entered Berlin in the first. Some of these small states are hypnotised by Germany's military pomp and precision. They see the glitter, they see the episode. But what they do not see or realize is the capacity of the ancient and mighty nations against whom Germany is warring to endure adversity, to put up with disappointment and mismanagement, to renew their strength, to toil on with boundless suffering to the achievement of the greatest cause for which men ever fought."

A storm of enthusiasm swept the House off its feet. It was the voice of England that had spoken.

Mr. Asquith leaned over to his neighbor on the Government bench: "A wise councillor, a brilliant colleague, a faithful friend!"

And even the leader of the Conservatives, who had just rejected Churchill, Mr. Bonar Law, could not help admitting: "He may have the defects of his qualities. As his qualities are large, the shadow they throw is pretty large also, but I say deliberately that in mental power and vital force he is one of the foremost men of our country."

Churchill was no longer listening to what they whispered after him. He took leave of his wife, who had not a second to spare herself, because she was busy every day at a canteen for munition workers in the north of London where she was feeding some hundreds of hungry mouths. He was on his way to the front. Fundamentally that was his predestination.

A month after he had gone off to the trenches the Gallipoli front was evacuated. Turkey triumphed, Bulgaria joined the Central Powers, Russia crashed, the Allied armies suffered severe losses, a whole army was marooned in Salonika.

The argument about the blame went on for years. Those most enraged were the Australians, who had made terrible sacrifices. The official Australian War History says: "Through Churchill's excess of imagination, a layman's ignorance of artillery, and the fatal power of young enthusiasm to convince the older and slower brains the campaign began and failed."

Churchill absolutely assumed the responsibility for the beginning of the campaign. Its failure, however, he ascribed to domestic indecision, lack of resolution in the War Council, the disastrous reluctance to follow things up, the half-heartedness in London. He sticks to it that the attack on Gallipoli was "the right, the logical, the natural thing." The hesitating ones should have followed through to the end.

Today the conflict is history. Sir Maurice Hankey, Secretary to the War Cabinet, put an end to it in his passionless, impartial report. This report completely exculpates Churchill. There is, indeed, no doubt left in the historian's mind that Churchill had produced a perfect strategic scheme which unfortunately was frustrated by indecision and half-heartedness in London.

CHAPTER XVI

While the Bullets Whistle

THE leave-boat was landing at Boulogne. Leave-boat, of course, is an English understatement. In actual fact it brought the men back from their leave to face the trenches again, and the German death.

"Major Churchill! Major Churchill!" The port landing-officer approached the lonely traveler who leaned over the railing, staring at the tormented French soil. "We have orders for you to go to the Commander-in-Chief at once; there is a car here from G.H.Q."

That meeting with Sir John French was a remarkable one. The two had met for the first time in South Africa, eternities ago—was it really but thirteen years? At that time the celebrated cavalry general had quite simply looked the other way when the ill-famed subaltern gave him a smart salute. Later they had become friends. In the autumn of 1908 Churchill had witnessed the cavalry maneuvers that Sir John was commanding in Wiltshire. Through his adjutant the latter hesitantly invited His Majesty's Cabinet Minister to a meeting. For the first fifteen minutes it was an interview between potentates of equal rank. Churchill, with his strong majority in the House and his assured tenure of office, was regarded even then as the man who one day must surely become Prime Minister. Sir John was generally recognized to be the leading fighting commander in the event of war. But within half an hour titles, dignities and importance were forgotten. Two fanatical horsemen had found each other. Two patriots had formed an alliance.

The connection between the two had deepened swiftly during the years of crisis. When Sir John French was promoted in 1912 to be Chief of the Imperial General Staff, a period of work in close association began. Both men's eyes were on Germany. Each had his own personal experience with Kaiser Wilhelm. The All-Highest had invited Sir John to his maneuvers in 1913, and had said to him afterward in his amiable way: "You have seen how long my sword is; you may find it is just as sharp." Sir John French could not reply until after his return to London. Then his first call was at the Admiralty, to discuss with the First Lord plans for the shipment to France of an expeditionary force, if and when . . .

In mid-July of 1914 the two visited the great shipyards on the Tyne. A young Scottish laird, Sir Archibald Sinclair, a fanatical admirer of Churchill's ever since, and his colleague in the present War Cabinet, took them to the first trials of a circular airplane on which he had spent a great deal of money. French's hour struck a fortnight later.

At home they were not altogether pleased with his conduct of the war. The great Kitchener was growling, but of course he always growled. Sure enough, the French Army under General Lanrezac fell back before the German attack in the severe battles of Charleroi and Mons: the British forces, which had given an excellent account of themselves at Mons, had to join in the retreat toward Paris if they were not to be cut off, encircled and destroyed.

In the London Cabinet Churchill made desperate efforts to present the situation in its true light. He tried to smooth out the disagreements between French and Kitchener. He warned against the costly policy of "killing Germans" that the forthright, soldierly Kitchener considered imperative. Churchill raised a warning voice against the autumn offensive of 1915. For the first time he acquired the nickname that was to cast a deep shadow upon his later years: Cassandra. The will-power of Joffre, the outlook of the French General Staff, the complacency of London prevailed. During the second half of September the French lost a quarter of a million men, the British Expeditionary Force in proportion. Sir John French was made the scapegoat.

His position was already shaken beyond repair when he received Major Churchill of the Oxfordshire Yeomanry at the Château of Blondecq, his headquarters at the time. He held out both hands in greeting, as if his guest were not an inferior officer—as a matter of fact Churchill, who had always kept his position in the Yeomanry, was one of the oldest majors in the British Army—but still the First Lord who had successfully brought the troops to the Continent. "What would you like to do, Winston?"

"Whatever I am told."

The conversation halted. Two shadows gazed at each other. One had ruled Britannia's waves yesterday; tomorrow the other would be writing memoirs of his days as a lieutenant. Neither of the two hard, steely faces showed a flicker. Churchill's face was broad, sharply chiseled; his chin jutted slightly. His eyes, as always, roamed the distance. Sir John, so much the older of the two, kept his gaze slightly downcast. His shoulders too were sagging a little. But his bushy white cavalry moustache was twirled downward with all the elegance that the rules prescribed. Thus, as if they were sitting on top of the world, the two had their pictures taken on horseback while they were out for a little ride before dinner. They were absorbed in army gossip.

The following morning Sir John French said, rather abruptly, it seemed, "My power is no longer what it was. I am, as it were, riding at single anchor. But it still counts for something. Will you take a brigade?"

Of course Churchill would be proud to do so. But before he could undertake any such responsibility he must learn at first hand the special conditions of trench warfare. He would go back to school again at forty-one. The Guards was the best school of all. Lord Cavan, Commander of the Guards Division, thought so too when he was summoned to the Château of Blondecq. A couple of days later he took Churchill with him to the front, and introduced him to the Colonel of the Grenadier battalion that the ex-First-

Lord was to join as a major under instruction previous to higher appointment.

Salutes, smiles, clicking of heels greeted him. But when Lord Cavan got into his car the attitude of his new companions suddenly changed. Politicians were not welcome in the army, Liberal politicians least of all. "I am afraid we have to cut down your kit rather, Major." This was his welcome from the regimental adjutant. "We have found a servant for you, who is carrying a spare pair of socks and your shaving gear. We have had to leave the rest behind."

Churchill was used to sharper opposition than this. "Quite right!" he nodded. "I am sure I will be very comfortable." His fellow-soldiers were not so sure.

The headquarters of the battalion were established in a pulverized ruin called Ebenezer Farm. The house had been shelled down to the ground. Its ruins still barely offered a little shelter from enemy fire, but none of the jerries would suspect that it could yet serve for human habitation. A small sandbag structure behind the ruined walls was the Colonel's headquarters. Here the officers ate—tinned food and strong tea with condensed milk. Nevertheless these frugal meals were very formally conducted. There was no talk except when the Colonel set the tone. He confined himself to curt, military-sounding statements. During the first evening Churchill learned an art that he had found very difficult during the first forty years: the art of silence.

Where did he want to sleep? He had the choice of a signal office at the Battalion Headquarters or a dugout two hundred yards away. Those two hundred yards were a perilous stroll. You could not even strike a match on the way in order to get through the rubble of the ruins in the pitch-black night. Jerry would fire without warning. On closer inspection the dugout proved to be a pit four feet deep, containing about one foot of water. This shelter was guaranteed to give you "trench feet," the prevalent disease at the front. As bullets whistled unceasingly about their heads, Churchill very formally thanked the regimental adjutant for being so kind as to bring him here. If he was offered the choice, however, he would prefer the signal office. The Adjutant said nothing. He had gradually become accustomed to risking his life on the most unnecessary errands.

Forty-eight hours later he was silent no longer. In two ice-cold days and nights the entire staff of officers of the 6th Royal Scots Fusiliers thawed. Even the Colonel became talkative. Though he talked only of the economy and discipline of his battalion, he did not weary of encouraging his new officer: "Always ask me anything you want to know . . . It is my duty to give you all information," he added in a growl. But that was only a strategic retreat. Even the Colonel could not escape Churchill's irresistible charm.

From the first it was made plain to him that nothing counted at the front but rank, subordination and personal courage. For a man to have been a Cabinet Minister, particularly in a Liberal Government, was against him, if anything. It would do a politician no harm to be put in his place. The fact that Churchill had been in the cavalry, and was among the most-decorated young officers of the colonial wars, was something none of the gentlemen knew. When they found it out—not from him, but through a chance guest from another front—their behavior changed with astonishing speed. No doubt brother Churchill had strayed from the paths of righteousness, but the half-civilian's precision, his discipline, his bravery were satisfactorily explained when people learned about his beginnings. When Churchill asked his Colonel for permission to sleep out with the soldiers in the trenches instead of at the Battalion Headquarters, he was definitely established. By way of official explanation he said that he would come to know life at the extreme front more quickly this way. Of course everyone was sure that as a matter of fact he was on fire with heroism. In reality the point was that liquor was served at the soldiers' simple dinner, whereas there was strict abstinence in the officers' mess. And Churchill could not stand the strong tea with condensed milk.

The Colonel now took him on the rounds on which he personally visited the most advanced outposts, once by day and once by night. Together they tramped through mud and snow. More often than not a rain of bullets received them. "They are all high!" said Churchill optimistically.

"I hope so!" was the Colonel's only reply.

Death now lay constantly in wait. How Churchill kept escaping it will be talked about as long as there are Scots Fusiliers. One of the most famous of the regiment's stories concerns an event which took place a bare week after his arrival at the front. It is still told wherever soldiers are talking about fate or chance or God or just good luck.

Churchill was sitting in his little sandbagged shelter, writing a couple of letters home. Jerry's usual morning chatter was already finished, so that a quiet afternoon was to be expected. An orderly presented himself at the entrance to the shelter. "The Corps Commander wishes to see Major Churchill at four o'clock at Merville. A car will be waiting at the Rouge Croix crossroads at 3:15."

Now it was highly unusual for a commanding general to summon an officer from the firing-line. In great wonderment Churchill set off through the rain-plowed, snow-decked forest to the rendezvous. The car did not come. After an hour's wait a staff officer appeared on foot. "There was a mistake about sending the car for you. It went to the wrong place, and now it is too late for you to see the General. You can rejoin your unit."

"Why did the General want to see me?"

"Oh, it was nothing in particular. Just to have a talk with you as he was coming up this way."

Churchill cursed silently. Just to have a talk the General had to send him chasing all that damned way through the woods! He tramped back, feeling peevish.

His sergeant received him with a salute: "We have had to shift your kit to another dugout, sir. Five minutes after you left a whizzbang came in through the roof and blew everything up."

But Death was not to be shaken off so easily as that. It was ever-present, but to speak of it at the front was not good manners. The only man who violated this rule of etiquette was Sir John French himself. Churchill called on him the day the aged soldier was to lay down his command, and he accompanied his chief in the car on his farewell round among the corps commanders. He was a heart-broken man. His being created Lord French of Ypres was no consolation. He would rather have lost his life than his command.

Sir John did not fear death. In a moment of profound emotion he spoke of death as a release. Dying was not hard. You had only to raise your head a little above the parapet. If a bullet came over, the only thing that happened was that you could no longer remain in communication with your friends and companions. You would continue to look on from up above, only unfortunately the wishes and ideas that went through your shattered head could no longer be communicated to earth. Then some day you would lose interest in earthly things. A new light would break out, and everything would be all right again.

On December 15 Churchill was promoted to the rank of colonel, at the same time taking over the command of the 6th Royal Scot Fusiliers. With this the harmony that had hitherto existed around him was suddenly destroyed. The battalion had worshipped its grouchy old colonel, who was now being relieved. It did not understand the meaning of the change. Did dark political influences play their part? When Churchill had his young friend Sir Archibald Sinclair transferred from the 2d Life Guards as his second in command, the worst fears seemed justified. All the battalion's officers were exceptionally young; one alone among them was a regular Sandhurst graduate of 1914. Everyone knew the new man was a fanatical political follower of Churchill's; what was he doing here? Probably it was some new machination of Asquith, the armchair warrior. The battalion did not like Mr. Asquith or his creatures. The whole front was against the Prime Minister. He seemed to them too soft.

The battalion was wrong. These were no machinations of the

Prime Minister. Churchill liked Asquith's conduct of the war as little as they did. The previous November he had written another of his dreaded memoranda. It was called *Variants of the Offensive,* and dealt with new means of attack. Among other things it gave an exact explanation of the importance and use of the new tank arm. A copy of the memorandum went to the Commander-in-Chief, another to the Committee of Imperial Defense in London. There, however, it seemed to fail of its effect. Nothing further was heard from Mr. Asquith.

Galley proofs of the highly secret document went back to Churchill at the front for correction early in February of 1916. That was the only reaction from London. But thereby hangs a tale. There was, of course, a rule against taking secret documents to the front line. The Germans were scarcely a thousand yards away, and you could depend on jerry to begin by going through the pockets of any British officer who might fall in no man's land. Besides, part of the civil population had remained in the village of Ploegsteert, where the 6th Fusiliers were now quartered. The British Intelligence Service had called the front officers' attention to the fact that undoubtedly there were German spies among this civilian population.

Variants of the Offensive, then, had no business here. And as a matter of fact one day the document that contained the secret of the tank was gone. The farmhouse where Churchill was billeted became the target of a fearful German cannonade. There was no question but that jerry had found out who was the enemy Colonel at this particular part of the front. Churchill himself knew definitely that he was a marked man. "I am just as well-known and as popular with the Germans as Tirpitz is with us," he smiled. Nor did he lose his smile when the heavy howitzer shells crashed into the farmhouse. "War is a game that must be played with a smiling face," he said. Still, he sought cover in a back room. After a cannonade of an hour and a half "Plugstreet"—that was how the English pronounced it—was a heap of ruins. There were just two brick walls between Churchill and Sir Archibald Sinclair on the one side and devastation on the other. Then the German howitzers fell silent.

Churchill returned to the heap of ruins that had once been a farmhouse. The room where he had been sitting was now a pile of smoking fragments. His desk was not to be recognized. And *Variants of the Offensive,* which had been lying on the desk—for God's sake, where was the document?

Somebody must have taken it away while the house stood empty during the artillery fire. The paper bore large and plain the words "This document is the property of His Majesty's Government." The first glance must have been enough to make it evident that these pages would be worth thousands of francs to the German Intelligence officer.

Churchill went through a fearful searching of conscience. How could he have parted for a single instant from this irreplaceable paper? He rent his bosom—literally.

In his breast pocket he found the document for which he had been vainly hunting for three days. Of course he never had parted from it for a moment. Unconsciously he had thrust it into his pocket as he left the room.

The soldiers worshipped their Colonel, whereas the officers at first were extremely chilly. And indeed he had a strange way of introducing himself as a commander. He summoned his officers one after another to his room, shook hands with them, and then, leaning back in his chair, scrutinized them from head to foot with unusual interest, but without a word. Then he would explain that he had certain little peculiarities. For instance he did not want people to answer "Yes, sir!" or "No, sir!" but simply "Sir!" There were others that he did not explain. For instance he never confessed why he wore a blue French helmet instead of the regulation cap. It had rather a comic-opera look. The battalion doctor, indeed, who subscribed to *Punch* at home, knew that Churchill was always a little peculiar about his headgear.

Churchill reformed the battalion with a new broom of iron. He polished it to a high degree of resplendence. The prisoners were guarded now not by a far-from-sober-looking old military policeman, but by a smart tall soldier with fixed bayonet. The Regimental Sergeant-Major, who as if by a miracle now polished his own buttons until they shone like stars, barked at soldiers and prisoners in most authoritarian fashion, while the Colonel nodded his agreement.

On one of the first mornings Colonel Churchill assembled his Scottish captains. "War is declared, gentlemen," he began, "on the lice!" A scientific lecture followed that took even the medical man's breath away. Good heavens, what the Colonel knew about the *pulex Europaeus*—its origin, growth, habitat, its importance in wars, ancient and modern. He asked the doctor to form a committee for the utter extermination of the louse, and to make suggestions looking toward that end. The committee worked wonders. Within three or four days the louse was abolished on that section of the front. Word of the "liceless" battalion spread throughout the entire army. The Colonel acquired a new honorary title. His men called him deloused Churchill.

In endless conversations with Sir Archibald, Churchill said he wished the Imperial Committee for Defense would do as good a job. He did not confine his political speeches to his friend and second-in-command. Anyone who liked could listen to Winston Churchill reforming the World War from Plugstreet. All the company commanders were his personal guests at dinner. The traditions of the *Enchantress* were gloriously upheld. The host always managed to provide for the table. The officers' mess was no longer dry.

His hospitality went further. All the officers might use the bathtub that Churchill had dug up somewhere. Watts, the batman, sighed heavily because he had to carry hot water with infinite pains for each bath, but the village beauties were enthusiastic over all this masculine hygiene. "Evidemment," they said, "puisqu'il est votre ministre . . ." They greeted him as "Seigneur," with a countrified curtsy, and a seductive smile on their thin, undernourished faces.

The story of the hospitable bathtub gave rise to the wildest surmises among the men. The Fusiliers were largely lowland Scots, many of them miners from the Ayrshire coal-fields. A man who took a bath every day, and even invited his fellow-officers to share with him, must be a duke at least. "The Duke of Churchill has taken over our command," one of the lads proudly wrote home. Others described him to their families as Viscount, Earl, Sir in their letters. During the first few weeks the battalion mail actually told of nothing else.

The result was a flood of letters from the families to Churchill. He was asked for requests for leave or discharge, for increased pay or higher pensions; he was requested to replace lost birth certificates or return an erring husband who was supposed to have strayed from the path of duty with some mademoiselle. Churchill carefully answered every letter. He was the father of his troops.

He proved that he really was, one day when his mount crossed the path of a marching detachment. The men happened to be singing the battalion favorite, whose refrain was as follows:

"I'll paint you and you'll paint me,
We'll both paint together—oh
Won't we have a hell of a time
Painting one another, oh!"

Now the verb painting can be replaced ad lib., and the Scots Fusiliers had an infinite variety of verbs in their vocabulary. The Colonel's sudden appearance, however, stifled the loveliest verbs in their throats. At this he shouted to them: "What the hell! Sing on!" And now they were really his, body and soul. They sang merrily on. It was still not *Tipperary*, but at any rate:

"Marching, marching, marching!
Always jolly well marching. . . ."

Churchill laughed. He went on laughing when he heard a fusilier requesting his too-haughty corporal to perform certain notoriously impossible physical feats or to proceed to a certain nonexistent destination.

In the service, indeed, he could not take a joke. He insisted on his soldiers' carrying the bayonet again though it was gradually going out of fashion. Thousands of colored booklets, which were not to be taken into the trenches, and consequently were lying round in every dugout, taught the art of bayonet fighting. It was an exceedingly disagreeable art, used in raiding enemy trenches, when the most casualties occurred. Churchill personally looked out for each wounded man, particularly in raids, which he always led himself. He discussed each individual wound to his men with the doctor, and took care that the victim should be looked after as well as possible. He assigned bodyguards to his officers on their patrols. It was not much protection, but better than nothing. In return he demanded increased precision of them, even in their reports. "A blind shell is to be referred to as such, not as a dud!" he said, reading company reports.

So far as that went, he preferred reading his pocket Shakespeare to reports. His intellectual activity was in no way interfered with by the simpler life at the front. Amid the hail of bullets he discussed the most intimate events in the House of Commons with Sir Archibald. Of course he was homesick for the House, his real home; but he took care not to show it. With grim pride he slaved to make his troops into a model battalion.

To physical fear he was a total stranger. He denied that it had anything to do with heroism. He laughed when people talked of danger, and pointed out that he led a charmed life. Very shortly after his occupancy of the farm in Plugstreet a shell fell through the roof, nearly blotting out Churchill, and wounding his adjutant, MacDavid. Churchill bandaged his adjutant's injured thumb himself, but refused to transfer his quarters to a safer place. Instead he asked his own artillery to answer jerry with a few vigorous rounds. He had to bargain and haggle for each round, for ten, for twenty. His own artillery command back there could not see why somebody should want to start a battle. There was neither an offensive of their own planned, nor an enemy one expected. But of course Churchill got his way. His own artillery fired, the enemy replied. The shells roared, hissed, rumbled and bellowed through the air. "Do you like war?" Churchill asked one of his soldiers. He was still the same young man who had asked the sergeant after the charge of Omdurman: "Did you enjoy it?"

But there was more to it than joy in battle. Churchill realized that the offensive spirit must be kept up at least in his sector. If it gradually died out, the loss would be irreparable. In the present war the French Army in the Maginot Line was shattered by such a loss.

Churchill's fellow-officers found some of his ideas rather far-fetched—"recherché" as the strategical handbook put it. Sometimes they seemed too subtle for every day's practical test of fighting. But every one of his orders, they admitted, was a startling innovation. Even when he simply ordered "work," which meant trench-building and -improving or the building of new parapets, traverses and parades, the idea of keeping the front from going to sleep was always behind it.

Churchill's success in dealing with the rank and file was remarkable. He personally explained to every single sentry what his duties were. But there was never the least condescension or hauteur about him when he talked to his Scottish lads. After all, every one of them might be a voter some day. For every one he selected positions giving the maximum of shelter, and at the same time making possible a perfect outlook. Often he would walk up the fire-steps, encouraging the boys by showing what a small chance there was of being hit. He acted as a supreme, but never a superior commander. Just one thing he would not tolerate under any circumstances—sleeping at the post. When that occurred, the Colonel could be extremely unpleasant.

In other respects he was known far and wide as the pleasantest of all commanders. His headquarters became the Mecca of every officer for fifty miles around who began to feel like enjoying a warm dinner and a long black cigar. A couple of neighboring Canadian generals, in particular, made regular appearances. Churchill had an especially warm spot in his heart for the Canadians. From some Canadian scoutmasters among his guests he learned how to carry out efficient night patrols. His fellow-officers shook their heads in secret. "Those Canadians ate and slept all day," a company commander reported later, "emerged and came down to drink towards evening. When darkness had fallen, they showed how to climb over the parapet and the wire, lie on their bellies in a dip in no man's land, and back to their bat-like existence in the most comfortable dugout on the line." That the Colonel himself must crawl around with them was something that the honest company commander could not get into his head.

There were also exalted visitors. General Seely was a regular guest. He sang and played at the battalion concerts that Churchill had introduced. General Tudor, General Officer in Command of the Divisional Artillery, made frequent appearances. Famous airmen came. They were forever astonished at Churchill's minute knowledge of their own art. One February day Lord Curzon suddenly turned up. Wearing a shocking soft cap, and equipped as unmilitarily as possible, his Lordship scrambled around with the Colonel in the front-line trenches. Those were unforgettable hours for Churchill. A breath of Westminster reached the trenches, where he had built himself a fool's paradise. He did not say he wanted to go back. On the contrary, he shook his head vigorously in reply to a hint from Curzon.

He grew daily more foolhardy. The next time that he was called on by two generals, whose names shall be forgotten, he fed them an excellent meal, and then suggested: "I am sure you'd like to see my trenches, General." A heavy bombardment was going on at the time. But of course the exalted personage had to agree. "And you would like to come too?" Churchill asked the second potentate. The three slunk along the ground. They could not go by way of communications now; it was too dangerous. They forced their way through the trenches. When they arrived in the front line, the soldiers burst out laughing. It was too funny to see the two old gentlemen with the Colonel tearing their well-cut breeches on the barbed wire, and wallowing in mud.

"But this is very dangerous," said one of the generals. The other nodded his silver head gravely.

"Indeed, this is a most dangerous war." Churchill nodded his agreement.

One day they brought a prisoner before him. Churchill embraced him. F. E., of all people—how did he get here in handcuffs, with a detective on each side? F. E., the later Lord Birkenhead, was working at headquarters as a military state's attorney. He held a colonel's rank, but wore civilian dress. He followed up the more important cases of espionage. They had taken him for a spy himself because he was roaming about the front without passport or identification. He had not been able to resist the temptation of looking up his friend Winston.

And now Winston Churchill could not resist the temptation that beset him in every word of the conversation with F. E. Magically the House rose before him. A division was no longer a number of regiments, but the decision about bills, power over Parliament, the goal of all striving. It was March, and the Naval Estimates would come up for discussion in a few days. Was he again to argue them only with the faithful Archibald in the dugout? Churchill took a short furlough, and went to London to take part in the debate on his own subject. It occurred to him that during his younger soldiering years all his important decisions had come during furloughs in London. The Colonel was a young subaltern again.

Once again the House greeted him as a hero. In an astute and inspiring speech he gave warning of the revival of submarine warfare. The best means of defense, he suggested, was to recall Lord Fisher as First Sea Lord. "There was a time when I did not think I could have brought myself to say it. But I have been away for some months, and my mind is now clear." When you live on terms of intimacy with Death, petty human conflicts are forgotten. That was more or less what he thought. The one who understood him best was Lloyd George, who listened to his speech with extreme interest. It seldom happened that Lloyd George let other people talk, let alone listened to them. But these were notes that his acute ear could understand. England needed that voice. When he formed his own Government—he smiled amiably at Mr. Asquith—he would not let Churchill escape him.

Another man was smiling too. Lord Fisher was sitting in the gallery. He savored comfortably the words that his last love, his last enemy was hurling out into the hall on his behalf. Yet words no longer meant anything. Lord Fisher was past seventy-five now. He no longer had any idea of exchanging his regular seat in Westminster Abbey, where he was spending his last days, for a desk at the Admiralty. In the midst of the World War he had made his own private peace with the world. Now, reconciled, he was only waiting for his summons to join Nelson's great host.

Immediately after his speech Churchill went back to the front. He did not want to fall under the spell of politics again. There were great doings at his modest officers' mess. Every night there was talking, drinking and music until dawn. He had brought along a gramophone, which ground out familiar tunes: *Dear Old Dublin, Chinatown, Chalk Farm to Camberwell Green.* Oddly, Churchill never joined in the refrain. He spoke of Kitchener, who was "a good old cup of tea," and of Lord Fisher, "the type of man that is needed to win the war." He did not speak of Mr. Asquith. Like all the front soldiers, Colonel Churchill considered the Prime Minister inadequate. Yet Churchill the Minister owed him much. Shall we put on another record?

As the days passed it became increasingly difficult to fill the gaps in the Scottish regiments. The gay soldier life at the front devoured immense numbers of lives daily. Troop units had to be merged. Churchill's 6th Battalion was united with the 7th (Service) Battalion of the same regiment. Churchill was the junior colonel. He had to give up his command.

Everything was topsy-turvy again in London. It was beyond question that Mr. Asquith could no longer cope with the task, which grew daily more difficult. It was not Churchill's delight in politics that called him back now. It was the voice of England, wanting the colonel-without-a-command back in the center of events, not in some glorious side-show. Had he not learned the lesson of Antwerp? Had he not done his best already to find a suitable hero's death? He was condemned to live. For the next quarter-century more desperately than ever before, England needed vigor, energy, drive. England needed Winston Churchill.

He yielded to a torrent of demands for his return. He would take his place in the driver's seat again. He gave a farewell dinner to his fellow-officers in a restaurant across from the Gare de Bethune. They expected a thumping good speech from him. But he said just one sentence: "I am grateful for the opportunity to have found out that the young Scot is the most formidable fighting animal."

He took care of the rest with actions. After the war he personally made sure that each of his fellow-officers and soldiers found a job. He had made enemies all his life—but not in his old battalion.

CHAPTER XVII

The Yanks Are Coming

ANYONE who came back from the trenches remained a marked
man. The shadows of his fallen Scots Fusiliers accompanied
Churchill through the carpeted halls and the soundproofed walls
of Westminster. The battalions had had to be merged in his own
regiment, the losses were so terrible—half the men had been killed.
Things were not very different anywhere along the front. The
battle of the Somme was a butchery. Government and public at
home, however, believed it a most successful encounter, particularly in view of the alleged disastrous enemy losses. Here Churchill
set himself his new task. It was senseless, he recognized, just to
control a minute portion of the fighting line. He must find himself another responsible position in the direction of affairs. The
old hands in which the fate of the Empire had rested were trembling terribly now. He would demand a more vigorous prosecu-
tion of the war, but at the same time would utter a warning
against the strategy of adventures and catastrophes.

With this warning he got into politics again. He wrote a secret
memorandum on the battle of the Somme, which his friend Lord
Birkenhead passed around in Government circles. This memorandum contradicted important statements from General Headquarters about the battle. Once again a Churchill document was written with clairvoyant accuracy. It contained exact data on the then
unknown and disputed numbers of enemy forces, casualties, proportion of losses. The military authorities dismissed Churchill's
statements as "amateur guesswork." Sir Douglas Haig, the new
Commander-in-Chief, wired from the Somme: "There is sufficient
evidence to place beyond doubt that the enemy losses have been

considerably higher than those of the Allies." Churchill, on the other hand, estimated the proportion of the German losses to the British at 1:2.23. The official German figures did not become known until after the war. As a matter of fact German losses in comparison to the British stood in the relation of 1.2:2.7. British Headquarters estimated the total German losses as "no less than 130,000 men." Churchill maintained in his memorandum: "They were 65,000 at most." As a matter of fact the Germans on the Somme lost 60,000 men. Churchill estimated the number of German divisions taking part at fourteen or fifteen. There were actually sixteen. He took a vigorous stand against further dissipation of manpower. Headquarters finally declined to continue the discussion. Churchill did not take it amiss. He had long since outgrown his private feuds; they had no further importance. He knew the British Expeditionary Force would have to pay in blood and sorrow for the lack of cannon and explosives. He admired the Olympian calm that Sir Douglas Haig managed to preserve with his front crumbling under the greatest German assaults, with his own army collapsing in the mud and blood of Paaschendaele, with an ally always exacting and frequently irregular. But he stuck to his theories. After the war Churchill's memorandum was used at Sandhurst as an example of how the deductive process can be used in military calculation.

Of course this discussion took place in deep secrecy. Churchill's first public speech after his return to the House dealt with his favorite subject, military aviation. The demand for a separate Air Ministry was here made for the first time. Britannia must rule the clouds as well as the waves. If she did not, Britannia one day would find herself done for. Most of the members felt that their gallant and honorable friend's ideas were getting rather high-flying again. But Lloyd George listened with tense interest. His dynamic energy, which hitherto had found outlet in radical reforms, was just in the process of turning in an imperialist direction.

The public too became interested. A newspaper syndicate

offered Churchill a contract for twelve articles about the war at five hundred pounds apiece. Mr. Balfour, the First Lord, gave him another literary task. Would Churchill write an appreciation of the battle of Jutland for the foreign press? Precisely because he was known as a critic of the existing administration and the Admiralty a description from his pen must carry especial weight. Of course Churchill agreed. His main work, however, was an exhaustive document for the newly appointed Committee of Enquiry into the Dardanelles Campaign, in which he presented his case. Until he was morally acquitted by this supreme authority there was no hope of his returning to the bosom of the Government.

But even as an outsider without rank or dignity his prestige swiftly rose. He was the center of resistance in London; everyone could feel that. Those who understood it best were the boys at the front. Since his service in Flanders he had been one of their own. M. Paul Painlevé, then French Minister for War, invited him to visit the French front. In Paris Churchill met Marshal Foch for the first time.

Foch was at the lowest point of his career. As Joffre's fighting lieutenant he was made responsible for the dreadful losses on the Somme. His triumphs on the Marne and the Yser were overshadowed by his unlucky offensive in Artois during the spring of 1915. He had had to give up his command, and now held the post of "military adviser" in a humble office near the Invalides. But he did not seem in the least downhearted. As if he were still setting in motion armies, and not merely ideas, he explained his conception of the conduct of the war to his English visitor in a swift flow of words underlined by pantomimic gestures that would sometimes have seemed comic if they had not been so compelling. The two shook hands. They were to remain friends.

But what did such personal successes mean? Nothing, less than nothing. Winston Churchill wanted to capture Berlin, not Marshal Foch's heart. While he was riding high again on the waves of popularity, he suffered severe attacks of depression at lonely moments. He had to watch the German thrust advancing more and more alarmingly. He saw his beloved isles exposed to the horror of unrestricted submarine warfare, which the Kaiser had let his admirals talk him into on February 1, 1917. Tirpitz and Pohl explained to their All-Highest that with the hundred submarines they had ready they could sink 600,000 tons of British shipping a month, and that these losses must necessarily bring the English arch-enemy to her knees in five months. Of course that would force the Americans into the war. "But the Americans can neither swim nor fly," said Vice-Chancellor Helfferich, in high good humor.

Inactivity, or at least lack of responsibility, under such circumstances drove Churchill to the verge of a nervous breakdown. Again there was just one safety valve—painting. He found a thoroughly military approach to art. "In all battles two things are usually required of the Commander-in-Chief," he declared. "To make a good plan for his army, and, secondly, to keep a strong reserve. Both these are also obligatory upon the painter. To make a plan, thorough reconnaissance of the country where the battle is to be fought is needed. Its fields, its mountains, its rivers, its bridges, its trees, its flowers, its atmosphere—all require and repay attentive observation from a special point of view . . . But in order to make his plan, the General must not only reconnoitre his battleground, he must also study the achievements of the great Captains of the past. He must bring the observations he has collected in the field into comparison with the treatment of similar incidents by famous chiefs. Then the galleries of Europe take on a new—and to me at least a severely practical—interest . . . But it is in the use and withholding of their reserves that the great commanders have generally excelled. After all, when once the last reserve has been thrown in, the commander's part is played. If that does not win the battle, he has nothing else to give . . . In painting, the reserves consist in Proportion and Relation. And it is here that the art of the painter marches along the road which is traversed by all the greatest harmonies in thought . . ."

Praise God, he did not have to content himself too long with painting as a substitute for warfare. In December, 1916, Lloyd George finally formed his new Government, the Cabinet to win the war. He was deeply impressed by Churchill's doctrines of "active defense," by the theory of wasting no more lives simply on "killing Germans," but of exterminating the U-boat instead, and waiting for American help. Churchill understood at once the decisive importance of America's entry into the war. He was not to be led astray by the then popular catchwords—that the U. S. A. had no army, that her soldiers would take years of training, that it would be impossible to equip and supply them with munitions across an ocean. Provided that the British Navy could handle the German U-boats there was no danger. And even if the American Expeditionary Force had to be used for some time mainly as reserves, those reserves would decide the struggle. It was just the same as in painting.

He delivered a stirring speech to that effect at a secret session of Parliament in May, 1917. The House was convinced. Churchill, "a member without responsibility, if with some inside knowledge," as he half-ironically described himself, now snatched the reins that had dragged so disastrously long upon the ground. Although the enquiry into the Dardanelles affair was not yet finished, and although the Conservatives were still grumbling, Lloyd George offered his friend the Ministry of Munitions on the 16th of July, 1917. Those weeks after the speech passed before Lord Northcliffe's firm resistance to Churchill—whom he had really discovered when he had boosted him many years before in his *Daily Mail* as "The Youngest Man in Europe"—could be overcome. Northcliffe was in America just then. The Earl of Birkenhead, the ever-faithful F. E., gradually eliminated personal resistance among the Tories. He could not, however, prevent the National Union of Conservative Associations, as well as a few influential Conservative Members, from protesting. But Mr. Bonar Law returned a very stiff answer to his own Party's deputation. Sir Edward Carson and General Smuts, the South African Prime Minister in the present war, used their influence toward Churchill's appointment. After twenty months of bitter exile word spread through the House: "Winnie is back."

The voters of Dundee had to agree first. Every change of Cabinet required a by-election. Mr. Scrimgeour, the local teetotaler and Sunday preacher, took no notice of the domestic truce that ruled during the war. He learned that Churchill had even partaken of an occasional glass of whiskey at the front. Instantly he announced his own candidacy. But Dundee simply laughed him aside. Churchill was reelected in triumph.

His ensuing tenure of office at the Ministry of Munitions was probably the happiest time of his life. He was in the midst of battle, his native element, and yet every moment he was filled with the realization that this battle could no longer be lost. The intervention of the United States electrified him, and from him the sparks leaped over to the men, masses, councils, even to the government bureaus with which he came in contact.

The Americans had taken their time. They had hesitated until the fighters for freedom in the Old World were almost bled white. But now that they were there, no tyranny could resist their impact, their determination, the strength that their conviction gave them. Churchill was immensely proud of being American on his mother's side. And indeed his half-American descent, the fact that he had one foot in each camp, was an important factor in inducing Lloyd George to give him the office whose duty it was to maintain the closest contact with the new ally.

It was very characteristic of Churchill's sense of Americanism that he immediately organized his own ministry on the American plan. Many of His Majesty's most faithful—and somewhat gouty—civil servants vanished, and business men took their place. Churchill reorganized the staff of 12,000 officials and fifty principal departments that he found in his Ministry when he took it over into ten large units, the heads of which were directly responsible to him. The units were known by letters. D stood for design, G for guns, F for finance, P for projectiles, X for explosives, and so forth. Churchill governed as Prime Minister among the unit-chiefs forming his private Cabinet. "Instead of struggling through the jungle on foot I rode comfortably on an elephant." This was his picturesque description of his business arrangements.

Lloyd George was happy to have found his new associate. Churchill's inventive grasp of the machinery of the war as well as his immense industry and drive were unparalleled. His imagination and enthusiasm now had full scope. No longer must he squander almost all his gifts to overcome petty opposition. The time was far behind when he had had to wrestle for £70,000 for his first tanks. He now demanded thousands of these monsters, which had so successfully withstood their baptism of fire. He wrote a new memorandum urging the War Cabinet, in typical Churchill phrase, "To organize mechanical development upon the principle: somebody must stop the tiger!" Oddly enough the only objection came from his own Admiralty. Mr. Eric Geddes, then First Lord, demanded the lion's share of the steel production for the navy, to balance the large steel output for the tanks.

The whole island was an arsenal working for the Minister of Munitions. But the demands of the fighting forces increased constantly. Their requirements were imperative and apparently insatiable. Four factors limited the output: tonnage, steel, skilled labor, dollars—in that order. The shipping stringency was acute; tonnage therefore remained the controlling factor in production. The production of steel was doubled. But the dependence for iron ore upon the north coast of Spain was a handicap. How to find a sufficient number of dollars was a problem.

Many another good man's breath would have come quicker under the burden of these worries. To Churchill each new task was another encouragement. What was this? He must also provide for the demands of the Allies? All the better. The Italians had fired away almost all their ammunition at Caporetto, where they had got such a dreadful beating? Never fear, Churchill would take care of new supplies! Better and more naturally than other people he understood the significance of the steel war, of supplies, machinery, inventions. To him these were no lifeless objects; they were living values, almost friends.

Now came his greatest job: the United States Government entrusted him with the immense commission of equipping its growing army in France. That was an order he had been waiting for. He could feel in every nerve that this was his very own personal mission now waiting for fulfilment. Without America's entrance the war at best must have ended at a stalemate, in complete European exhaustion. Now that America was making the great, the supreme sacrifice, the mere threat, "The Yanks are coming!" was enough to bring about the complete collapse of enemy morale at the front and of the spirit in the German hinterland. In vain Ludendorff ran his race against time. He meant to force a victory before the Americans were able to fight. But the Americans were being poured across the Atlantic. Then they were absorbed into the French and English armies to complete their training.

Churchill's peculiar sympathy with the American mind, his fame on the American continent made him one of the few Englishmen who could arouse the New World. By the end of the year the Americans hoped to have in France forty-eight divisions—six armies—each requiring 12,000 guns. Of this their own country was able to furnish but 600 heavy guns and howitzers. So Churchill accepted a contract for $500,000,000 to supply the whole requirements of the American Army in medium artillery, without profit or loss on either side. It was a gentleman's agreement, and it worked perfectly. Anglo-American cordiality had reached its peak. Never before or since was the intimacy of the Anglo-Saxon sister nations so firmly grounded. Although it was years later before Churchill actually met his opposite number in America, Mr. Bernard Baruch, they were bound by a firm friendship even across three thousand miles of ocean, clinging as they did to the same ideals with the same devotion.

His work brought Churchill in contact with all the war lords of his day. His particularly trusted adviser was General Lipsett of the Third Canadian Division. For a time he commuted across the Channel. In the morning he would be at his desk in White-hall, at noon he would take a plane, and two hours later he would be at the French château near Verchocq where Headquarters was. He flew over the lines regularly. He would personally see important skirmishes through to the end.

Usually he flew in old, worn-out machines, since the new models were needed for service. This was bound to lead to accidents. On one occasion he had bad luck twice in the same day. He took off from General Headquarters to keep an appointment in London. Five miles beyond the French coast a valve broke, and the plane had to come down. It was a gray afternoon, with not a ship near. The old plane had no "bathing suit," as inflatable air-jackets were then called. Churchill wondered whether he could swim in his thick clothes and heavy boots, or whether he should hastily throw everything away. He wondered for perhaps half a minute—half an eternity in that situation. Then the old engine began to cough and sputter again; the pilot, a young officer gravely wounded at Gallipoli and on the Somme, yanked the plane around, and after ten endless minutes reached Gris Nez, the point of land on the French side of the Channel. They barely managed to reach the aerodrome of Marquise, where a large number of English and American planes were standing ready.

Following his old principle that a man is never hit twice on the same day, Churchill and his pilot started off across the Channel for a second time, with one hour of daylight left. Churchill was wrong. Head winds held up the plane, another old crate, and the engine was pulling poorly. It took forty minutes to cross the Channel. Scarcely was English soil under their feet before another *pop* in the engine drove them to a forced landing. The pilot came down neatly between two tall elms.

Churchill used to sleep in his office at the Ministry of Munitions. The night of March 27, 1918, Mr. Lloyd George had him fetched out of bed. A week before, March 21, the Germans had broken through the Allied front. Every second now might be a matter of destiny.

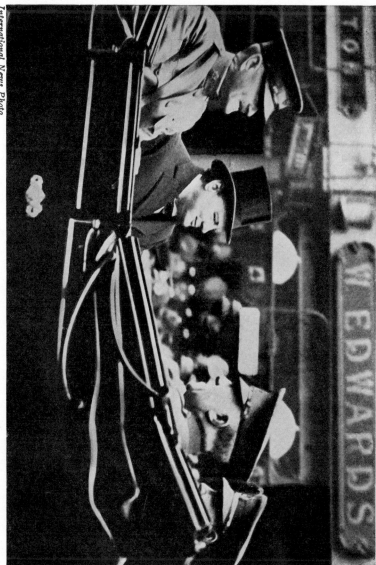

International News Photo

CHURCHILL WITH GENERAL PERSHING DURING WORLD WAR I

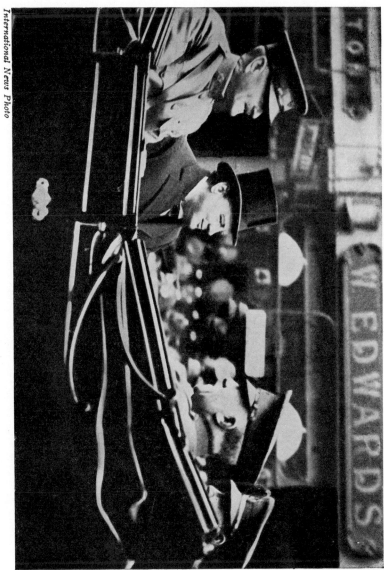

International News Photo

CHURCHILL WITH GENERAL PERSHING DURING WORLD WAR I

Lloyd George was in bed himself, but his night light was burning. The Prime Minister was buried under a heap of reports and documents. "Go to France," he said without preamble. "I can't make out what the French are doing. Unless they make a great effort to stop the German inrush, the Germans will break through between us to the sea. See Foch. See Clemenceau. Find out for yourself whether they are making a really big move or not."

At eleven o'clock in the morning Churchill started off on a destroyer across the Channel, with the Duke of Westminster as his sole companion. On his way to Paris he called briefly on General Headquarters at Montreuil, to get a more detailed explanation of the situation. In Paris he was amazed by the funereal quiet he found. While the armies at the front, barely a few miles away, were grappling in a life-and-death clutch—the remains of the Fifth Army already streaming back toward Amiens, the Third Army desperately engaged, every English soldier who could bear a rifle rushed forward to stop the German advance—there was a total absence of excitement and bustle in the Paris offices.

"The Commander-in-Chief!" Churchill demanded.

"The Commander-in-Chief is taking his afternoon ride. So sorry, sir!"

The Chief of Staff, however, pointed out on the map to the English visitors the few French divisions that had actually come into action. At that moment a telegram arrived: *The Germans have occupied Montdidier*. With inimitable calm the Chief of Staff took a few puffs of his cigarette. He shrugged his shoulders, the famous French gesture: "No doubt they are doing their best."

At midnight Churchill retired in the Hotel Ritz. No rest was to be his. In the gray of morning he called on General Sackville-West, the head of the British Military Mission, and demanded to see Clemenceau personally. The Tiger's answer came at noon: "Not only shall Mr. Winston Churchill see everything, but I will take him myself tomorrow to the battle, and we will visit all the commanders of corps and armies engaged."

The Tiger appeared the following morning, punctual to the

second, with a suite of five military motor cars, and greeted his guest in his fluent English: "I am delighted, my dear Mr. Wilson" —evidently he had other things on his mind—"Churchill, that you have come. We shall show you everything. We shall see Foch, the Corps Commanders, we shall also go and see the illustrious Haig and Rawlinson as well. Whatever is known, whatever I learn, you shall see as well."

It was March 30, 1918. That day remained in Churchill's mind, unforgettable forever. It was the day with Clemenceau.

After a bare two hours the cars stopped before the Town Hall of Beauvais. Foch, just appointed Generalissimo of the Allied forces, awaited the guests in a room in the second story. Three or four of his General-Staff officers were with him. A lean little man, a typical cavalryman, first attracted Churchill's attention. His sunken cheeks and a forehead much too high framed a pair of coldly gleaming eyes that surveyed the English guest coolly.

"I didn't get his name," Churchill said to the French Minister of Munitions, Loucheur, who was doing the honors as his equal in rank.

"Weygand. Maxime Weygand."

The doors were elaborately locked. A dozen men gathered around the table. A map about two yards square hung on the wall. It showed the portion of the front affected by the German break-through. Seizing a long pencil as one would draw a dagger, Marshal Foch began to explain. He spoke so fast and, it seemed to Churchill with his rather scanty French, so erratically that the latter had considerable trouble in following his explanation. But the iron logic of Foch's bubbling, whirling French, with its gestures of passionate emphasis, soon impressed itself upon him: "The Germans broke through the 22d. First stage of the invasion. Oho, how tremendous! 23d: deuxième journée d'invasion. Another enormous stride. The 24th: Quatrième journée . . . Oho!" Foch suddenly ejaculated. "Oho! Oho!" he repeated. Here, on the fourth day, then, something must have changed. And with a precision that brooked no contradiction he finished: "Yesterday, dernière journée d'invasion. The last day . . ."

At this Clemenceau broke ranks: "My General, allow me to embrace you."

Before the astonished eyes of Mr. Winston Churchill, who was unused to such outbursts of feeling, the two great men of France were in each other's arms. They did not in the least mind the fact that they had always quarreled before, and would probably be clashing furiously tomorrow.

Lunch was taken at Rawlinson's mess. Within a few minutes Haig appeared. He brought good news. Jack Seely with the Canadian Cavalry Brigade had just stormed the Bois de Moreuil. It was the memorable last cavalry charge in the history of war. Omdurman flashed through Churchill's head. How far back it all was! How old he had grown!

"And now," the Tiger cried, "we will pass the river and see the battle!"

Rawlinson shook his head uneasily. "We are not at all sure of the situation beyond the river. It is extremely uncertain."

"Good," was all Clemenceau said. "We will re-establish it. You come with me, Mr. Winston Churchill."

Churchill did not have to be asked twice. He even took the lead when they reached the British lines along the river. The Bois de Moreuil, still soaked in the blood of the cavalry charge, was just ahead of them. Shells were bursting with monotonous horror a hundred yards away. Churchill and Clemenceau were in the highest spirits. "Irresponsible as school boys on a holiday," Churchill recalled later. The French Staff Officers, however, showed increasing signs of concern for the safety of their beloved old man. But of course no one dared ask him to retire. Finally Churchill had to undertake the delicate task. At that moment a shell burst just in front of them. Churchill was too much taken aback to repeat his old question of Omdurman: "Did you enjoy it?" But Clemenceau, giving him a long look, said: "What a delicious moment!"

General, later Marshal, Pétain received his Prime Minister with the utmost ceremony in the French Headquarters train on the siding of the Beauvais railway station. He had been French Commander-in-Chief himself until his defeats had compelled him to accept Foch's overlordship. If he nursed a grudge, at any rate he never showed it. Nevertheless Churchill's impression of him was: "A skilful, frigid, scientific soldier, who often disagreed with Foch." Pétain described the events he expected for the next four days. There was none of Marshal Foch's demoniacal possession, none of his excited "Ohos" and great triumphant gestures. Pétain concluded his cautiously calculated résumé with the words: "If the front holds where it is, we shall be just in time with rebuilding the roads. If it recedes, we shall have to begin all over again."

Churchill was a little exhausted after seventeen hours at the front. Clemenceau, on the other hand, showed no fatigue at all. He withdrew with a good-natured smile, saying: "Tomorrow I must work. But Pétain has arranged for you to be received wherever you wish to go. There will always be dinner for you in his train."

Churchill did not avail himself of this kind invitation.

CHAPTER XVIII

Moscow Dress Rehearsal

THE war of 1918 was to be the war of tanks. Foch and Haig had finally been won over to Churchill's weapon once it had proved itself so splendidly before Amiens. Amiens had given a fore-taste of the lightning war. In a "noise barrage" created by low-flying airplanes, 600 tanks (324 of them weighing over 30 tons) emerged from clouds of artificial fog, and cut through the enemy lines. The result of four days' fighting was 22,000 prisoners and 400 captured guns. It was a decisive victory for the Allied arms. Foch was now convinced that final victory would be won in the spring of 1919, and peace concluded the following autumn. As a matter of fact the German collapse came six months earlier.

After the victory of Amiens Churchill could take a few days' leave. Of course when he wanted to get a moment's rest he flew to the front. He called on General Rawlinson, and congratulated him on his triumph. From Château Verchocq he sent another memorandum—that was how his nights of leave were spent—to the Prime Minister. Again he urged pushing the tank arm. "I suggest training up to 100,000 the personnel of the Tank Corps. The tank men are killed and wounded in considerable numbers, whereas the tank recovers very quickly from its wounds and hardly ever dies beyond recovery." He even dreamed of tanks.

The strike of the munition workers that broke out at home brought him back in haste to London. This was the form that the nervous breakdown of an exhausted nation took. Churchill, the most sensitive among the leaders, the man with the ever-alert instinct, had a feeling that this was not a mere movement for wages, but that the people's will to resist once was at stake. England was in a breathtaking finish, and more than a neck ahead. Could the horse be allowed to collapse just short of the finish line? Once more Churchill yanked up the reins. Receiving a delegation from the striking workers in his munition factories, he presented them with an ultimatum: "Work, or go to fight at the front." Thus far munition workers had been exempt from service at the front. Under pressure of this threat they yielded. The strike collapsed. The last hurdle was taken.

Churchill's unpopularity among the defeatists, indeed, rose to the boiling point. "A traitor to the workers!" was the very mildest of the abuse that was shouted at him. The Left now hated him more passionately than even the Tories had hated the "traitor to the Party." But he went unperturbed upon his way. He had to bear it in silence for a few weeks. Then all the bells were ringing.

Winston Churchill, his wife at his side, rode through Whitehall in an open carriage, among cheering crowds that had just been cursing and imprecating him. When they turned the corner into Downing Street, Lloyd George was waiting for them. Without a word the two men shook hands. Thus they celebrated victory. Thus they celebrated peace.

Few men went through the first World War at such high tension. What had it not meant to Winston Churchill? The feverish preparation at the Admiralty that was almost a conspiracy; the Hussar assault on Antwerp; the racing hope of Gallipoli and the subsequent tragic disappointment; the fearful duel with Lord Fisher, his fatherly friend; then the depression, almost the weariness of life, that took possession of the ex-Minister; the brief, wild joy of fighting in the trenches; the return to power that had to be fought so fiercely for; the parting with Asquith; the demoniac devotion to the tank and the air arm; the countless bitter disputes called diplomatic conversations with weary, exhausted, hopeless leaders; then the elation over America's entry, the twenty-four-hour day in the munitions ministry, the dread of setbacks that came close to catastrophe, the jubilation over momen-

tary successes, finally the struggle with the workers that meant
turning away from so much of his own past.

It was indeed a superhuman strain. A man can go once through
heaven and hell—not twice. Never another war! That vow was
the final note of the victorious jubilation all over the civilized
world. Churchill raised his right hand as he took that vow. He
was the first to demand that the blockade of Germany be given
up at once, even before peace was signed, and that food ships be
sent to Hamburg. When Foch called on him at his office in London, insisting that the British Army of occupation in Cologne
should be replaced by a French one, he proposed: "Don't you
think that you could let us all come home?" The old Marshal
said nothing. He must simply put in safety the peace of his country, won with his last atom of vitality, and then find rest. Unlike
Churchill, he had not half a life ahead of him.

The Khaki Elections in December, 1918, backed up Churchill
with renewed authority in the reorganized Lloyd George Cabinet. They went off in triumph. Only the inevitable Mr. Scrimgeour, the Prohibitionist, once more was not to be prevented
from raising his head. In celebrating victory it was generally
overlooked that he had after all reached four or five thousand
votes from the three hundred with which he had begun his first,
unsuccessful candidacy. Churchill did not campaign against him
at all. This disdain must have wounded Mr. Scrimgeour specially deeply. "My day will come!" he barked as Churchill took
the train for London.

There two offices at once were awaiting him—the War Office
and the Air Ministry. The usual Conservative displeasure was
manifested again. In his youth he had been a medal-snatcher,
they grumbled. Now he seemed to be a portfolio-collector. Captain Wedgwood Benn, M.P., organized a noisy protest. General
Seely, Under Secretary for Air, demonstratively resigned. It was
no use. It might be highly unusual for a Minister to manage two
service departments at once, but after all, Winston Churchill was
a highly unusual Minister.

Above all he had now to carry out demobilization, a formidable organizational task. Four or five million soldiers had to be put back into private industry. Some hundreds of thousands were still under arms. In February, 1919, Churchill warned employers to hold places open for those who were still in Germany. At about the same time he created a new army system providing garrisons for the entire Empire. The most difficult legacy that he found at the War Office was the agreement—heartily approved of by the War Cabinet—by his predecessor, Lord Milner, to help the White Russian generals against the Bolsheviks. At first Churchill did not approach this inherited task with any particular enthusiasm. The profound English war-weariness would stand no more adventures. He himself was in a let's-all-shake-hands mood. He knew his soldiers. They had enough laurels to do them for some time. Bread and jobs were what they wanted.

Lukewarm as he was, he shifted the matter to the Supreme Council, which decided in the spring of 1919 with the consent of President Wilson that the support of Admiral Koltchak and General Denikin should continue, since the two had promised to establish a democratic Constituent Assembly in Moscow after their victory.

The negotiations with the Supreme Council brought Churchill frequently to Paris again. The hairbreadth escapes that had repeatedly ended his aeronautical attempts during the war did not in the least deter him now from using planes again and again. He confessed that he had not developed a proper "air-sense" at all. But he regarded it as the duty of the Air Minister to set a good example. His critics talked of histrionics. Just as he had shown his soldiers in the trenches by his own example that not every bullet found its mark, so now he set his officers a model of an intrepid flier. He was constantly getting involved in accidents. Surely few living men (with the possible exception of stunt fliers) have crashed as often as Winston Churchill, the man with the charmed life.

After the war Colonel Jack Scott, a famous ace at thirty-eight, was his personal pilot. The two usually flew a dual-control machine, with Churchill at the controls and Scott supervising. One particularly foggy and cloudy morning when they were starting back for London from Buck aerodrome they had to climb to 15,000 feet to get above the cloud-banks. In these airy altitudes they lost their way. Colonel Scott took the controls. With extraordinary skill he went down to 300 feet. But here they got into a driving rainstorm, and still the ground was invisible. They must be somewhere between Paris and Amiens, over a wooded, hilly region extremely dangerous for low flying. Still they did not see ground until they had gone down to 100 feet. Now they could orient themselves. They got to the Channel, crossed it in a raging storm, and reached Lympne Aerodrome on the other side after four hours of most unpleasant flying. Ordinarily that stretch required forty minutes.

Churchill and Scott, undismayed, continued their flight toward London after refueling at Lympne. On the way a blaze broke out in the motor. Colonel Scott again had to go down a thousand feet, this time in a power dive, while he extinguished the fire. A few seconds more, and the plane would have gone up in flames. When they felt solid ground under their feet with a sigh of relief, it was not Churchill this time, but his pilot, who asked with a grin: "Did you enjoy it?"

A few weeks later an Avro biplane nosed over in a starting crash, and made a complete turnover. Unnecessary to remark that Churchill was in it; still more unnecessary to observe that nothing happened to him, although the machine was completely smashed. That same summer, 1919, he was in the air with Colonel Scott again when one of the usually fatal sideslip accidents, the commonest of all, sent the machine helplessly earthward. "This is very much like death!" Churchill had time to reflect. Then he began picking up the pieces of himself. He got off with a few abrasions. Jackie Scott, indeed, lay senseless and bleeding on the ground. He recovered, thank God—and then came the Churchill touch; the faithful pilot did not simply recover. He had been crippled in the war; now, the operation that he had to undergo after his accident with Winston had the additional effect of straightening his injured leg. It was double good luck in misfortune.

The Big Five in Paris had decided to support the White Russian counter-revolution. Churchill was entrusted with the execution of an action he was not responsible for. But there is no denying that once the decision was made he was all on fire to carry it out. In the Dardanelles affair *he* had had an idea, and the execution had failed, particularly in the person of Kitchener, who went back on his undertaking to send the 29th Division to reinforce the army gathering in Egypt, and had delayed for nearly three weeks. The Russian matter must not be the reverse, with Churchill failing to carry out a plan entrusted to him. In association with the Chief of Staff, Sir Henry Wilson, he worked out a program to equip and arm the various White Armies from surplus war stores, and to help them with expert officers and instructors. He would not have been Winston Churchill if he had not grown in the process, and caught fire from his task. At the beginning of March the War Cabinet authorized him to make any necessary arrangements to evacuate marooned Allied troops in Archangel and Murmansk. He immediately raised 8,000 volunteers behind whose shield the worn-out fighters could be withdrawn. At the end of May the Supreme Council received Admiral Koltchak's binding promise that he would introduce democracy in Russia, and would not restore Tsarism. The Supreme Council thereupon decided to support the Admiral with munitions and food.

The delegates of the White Russians were strange figures. Their official spokesman was Lieutenant-General Golowin, who described himself as "the representative of the Russian Army." He arrived in London in the spring of 1919 with an introduction from Sazonov, the Tsarist Prime Minister, and to begin with was received at the Foreign Office by Sir Samuel Hoare. Thus began a series of negotiations whose secrets have never been en-

tirely revealed to this day. Thus, as we can see, Sir Samuel's
anti-Bolshevik record, which has occasionally brought that statesman (now British Ambassador at Madrid) painfully close to Hitler and Mussolini, goes back more than twenty years. Nevertheless we must of course be skeptical of this so-called "Hoare-
Churchill" action as described by Moscow.

According to that description Churchill saw Lieutenant-General Golowin on May 5, 1919, at 5:30, in the War Office, after
the latter had had a conversation with General Radcliff and
brought his pourparlers with Sir Samuel to a successful conclusion. Golowin was speaking for all the White Russian commanders; for Koltchak, for Denikin, and even for Yudenitch, who
was considered friendly to Germany. After an hour's conference
Churchill is supposed to have offered him 10,000 volunteers, who
would actively support Koltchak's left wing, 2,500 technicians
and specialists for Denikin, no armed assistance for Yudenitch.
The material aid was to amount to twenty-four million pounds.

Still according to the Bolshevik story, Lieutenant-General Golowin, returning home, wrote down from memory a record of the
conversation which a certain Dr. Elsox, a Communist doctor
from Archangel, later discovered in the secret archives of the
White Murmansk Government, and brought to Moscow. This
Dr. Elsox never makes any personal appearance. But a delegation of the British Labor Party to whom the alleged document
was given at the Kremlin made a political sensation of it at
home. In vain Sir Samuel Hoare issued an unequivocal statement denying the authenticity of the so-called document. The
report of the conversation, as he showed, had been forged in Moscow for obvious reasons.

Churchill says that Golowin had called on him on behalf of
Sazonov, the last Russian ally. The interview was "inaccurately
and untruthfully" recorded. He himself was under orders from
the War Cabinet, and played no part in the course of the events.

This was literally correct. Nevertheless the radicals, skilfully
using popular conceptions of the adventurous crusader, spread

the word: "Winston is gambling with gold and lives again!" Churchill, the comrades screamed, was not satisfied with one world war. He wanted to set the English boys on Russia, the Fatherland of the Proletariat. He was a professional war-monger.

Later developments have shown how grotesque this accusation was. British Laborites today are Churchill's staunchest supporters. They are compelled to eat the words with which they once abused him. But the name war-monger is hurled at him from every side. Defeatists, pacifists, Communists, Nazis and Fifth Columnists and all their advance guards, enemies at home and abroad, no matter when or in what garb they have appeared, all have held it up against him.

In all his metamorphoses Winston Churchill has remained at bottom a Victorian figure—the statesman of a cause that can develop only in peace, and flourish only in tranquillity. In wars and conflicts the thing that Churchill once called the "artificial state," that is, the Empire, a creation of harmony and compromise, can only come to harm. The honorable peace that he demanded for the Boers, the self-sacrificing compromise that he made with the Irish, the outstretched hand that he offered at once to fallen Germany after the first World War, all came from his native disposition more than from political calculation. Moreover, Churchill himself, with his personal taste, his joy in life, his strivings toward social reform, so oddly matched with his clinging to traditional forms of life, his love of beauty, his Epicurean gaiety, his pleasure in man, who to him remains the focus of all things— Churchill too could develop only in peace. The world that he so joyfully affirmed, with its spring and its autumn, with all the fun and all the duties, with its inexhaustible possibilities of joy and suffering—that world must remain free!

He would devote the period of his life's maturity to the struggle against the slave state, and if need be the rest of his days as well. He had struggled once with the German Empire for human rights, not for frontiers. But now, in 1919, he saw before him the world's enemy incarnate. Asiatic tyranny, based on the grossest form of materialism, must be averted by the British Empire, the champion of Christian civilization. If the Empire should fail to stem the deluge, Churchill saw the American nations as the last line of defense.

As far as the world's enemy was concerned, the Russian experiment proved to be only an intimation of the total barbarism that befell Germany. Twenty years later the world was to know better —Churchill, for that matter, some years before his contemporaries. But in 1919 he was fighting, though for the same cause, on the other front.

The task that had been given him simply because it was part of his department grew into a personal mission as he watched the savagery of the Bolshevik revolution of blood from close at hand. He openly advocated "the overthrow and destruction of the criminal regime of Bolshevism." He wrote and agitated against the red specter, whose shadow, spreading from Moscow, was sinking over the Empire in Europe and Asia. His bark was a little worse than his bite. In action he confined himself strictly to carrying out the decisions of the Supreme Council in Paris, and of his own government. All told, British assistance came to £46,000,-000. But Labor yelled: "Churchill has thrown a hundred and fifty millions into the maw of the White Russians!"

As a matter of fact the help that the Big Five decided to give was half-hearted and lukewarm. In a desperate attempt to get more and quicker support Koltchak appointed as his accredited agent to the Supreme Council the small, pale, wolf-eyed, noiseless Boris Savinkov. It was a strange alliance. Koltchak was an Admiral of the Imperial Navy; Savinkov was a Nihilist and lifelong professional conspirator. His name had a sanguinary sound far beyond Russian frontiers. In an autobiographical novel, *The Pale Horse,* he described in elaborate detail how he killed Grand Duke Serge and Von Plehve, the Tsar's dreaded Minister of Police.

When Churchill first received Koltchak's agent, he was expecting a figure out of his Sidney Street adventure. Instead he saw an unusually ceremonious, at once confidential and dignified man of indefinite age, with a face beautifully carved, though marked with a thousand creases and wrinkles until it looked like crumpled parchment. His gaze was calm, laden with dignity, nonchalance and an infinity of somber destiny. Boris Savinkov was a unique figure—a democratic terrorist. Under Tsarism he was one of the bloodiest conspirators; during Kerensky's abortive republic he made a final effort to stiffen the collapsing army against the German front. Under the Bolsheviks he advanced to the position of Public Enemy No. 1. He knew Churchill's weak spot, human freedom. "M. le Ministre," he began, "I know them well, Lenin and Trotsky. For years we worked hand in hand for the liberation of Russia. Now they have enslaved her worse than ever."

And indeed Savinkov was pursuing the Bolshevik bosses yet more implacably than he had hunted Grand Dukes and Police Ministers of the Little Father. They have replaced tyranny with slavery, he said. But the flame of freedom was burning in his blood. He was an admirer of Western Democracy, for which he worked with Asiatic methods.

Churchill introduced his guest to the Prime Minister at Chequers. But Mr. Lloyd George had already forgotten his own quasi-revolutionary beginnings. He had made his peace with the world; of course he had his own smooth arguments to back it up. Revolutions, like diseases, ran a regular course, he argued. In Russia the worst was already over. The Bolshevik leaders, confronted with the responsibilities of actual government, would quit their revolutionary theories, or they would quarrel among themselves and fall, so that others weaker or more moderate would succeed them; and by such successive convulsions a more tolerable regime would be established.

"Mr. Prime Minister," replied the learned bomb-thrower with old-fashioned courtesy, "you will permit me the honor of observing that after the fall of the Roman Empire there ensued the Dark Ages."

The shot missed its target. Even in his bumptious beginnings
Lloyd George had been only a rabble-rouser, not a real revolutionary. He had not the faintest notion of the secret of revolution.
And so it happened that later he failed also to grasp the ele-
mental force of Nazism, and rather less than crowned his brilliant
life's achievements with the blindness of preaching appeasement
with Hitler.

In 1919 he was against all anti-Bolshevik enterprises. He cherished the secret hope of converting Bolshevism into an ally of
the Empire. Mr. Lloyd George never knew that Lenin a few
years before had passed by the House in Westminster, and, point-
ing to the stronghold of democracy, had said to his companion:
"There is our real mortal enemy." Nor would he probably have
believed it. In those days Litvinov was the trusted confidential
adviser of the Foreign Office Russian Section, and the notorious
Comintern agent Rothstein was employed to interpret Russian
newspapers to the Foreign Press section of the War Office.

The head of the War Office was Churchill. Much as he wanted
to, he could not throw out Rothstein. But he was not so blind
as his Prime Minister. He knew that Lenin and Trotsky regarded
the British Empire as at once the strongest bulwark against and
the most fruitful field of agitation for world Bolshevism. He
knew the methods of underground propaganda. In May, 1919,
while he was supporting anti-Bolshevik action in Russia, he circulated among the commanding officers a secret document enquiring about the readiness of their troops to maintain communications in the event of a communistic general strike. The *Daily
Herald,* the Labor paper, noisily revealed the circular. "Admitted!" was Churchill's only answer.

Savinkov had to leave without getting any real help. He was
going to his doom. For four years more he waged his desperate
battle to stir up the civilized world against Bolshevism. He gradually began to realize that the civilized world was a sound sleeper.
Then Kamenev and Trotsky let him know there was a new position with great influence waiting for him at home. After a mock

trial and the ensuing acquittal he was to be one of the elements
of sanity who were destined to help Russia save herself. In response to this invitation Savinkov went back to Moscow in June,
1924. There he vanished into the cellars of the O.G.P.U. No one
knows whether he committed suicide or was liquidated. Everyone does know the fates that overtook Kamenev and Trotsky.

Mr. Asquith awoke from his torpor long enough to make a
sharp flank attack on Churchill's anti-Bolshevik policy. He called
General Denikin "a reactionary adventurer." Churchill replied:
"A man is called reactionary in Russia if he objects to having his
property stolen and his wife and children murdered. Denikin has
drawn off three-fourths of the Red Army, which otherwise would
have overrun the East of Europe."

Lloyd George in his Guildhall speech of November, 1919,
argued for the policy of "on the one hand, on the other hand,"
in which he was a master: "Britain is not unmindful of our obligations to the gallant men in Russia who helped us fight the
Germans, when the Bolshevik leaders were betraying the Allies
. . . but Lord Beaconsfield, remember, regarded a great, big,
colossal, growing Russia, rolling onwards like a glacier towards
Persia and the borders of Afghanistan and India, as the greatest
menace the British Empire could be confronted with. And that
is exactly what Denikin is fighting for."

The Bolsheviks immediately broadcast this speech all over Russia. It was like a knife in the back to Denikin.

Churchill was already too late when he depicted the Bolshevik
terror and Russian misery in his glowing speech of January 20 at
Sunderland. He wrote several articles on the "foul baboonery of
Bolshevism." He publicly expressed his hope that Germany would
join in the anti-Communist front, in which case he promised all
imaginable British help. He wanted to make use of the opportunity finally to liquidate the results of the war. But he was already too late to mobilize England for the anti-Bolshevik cause.
A question (probably prearranged) by the Left Liberal Sir Donald Maclean, M.P., gave the Prime Minister an opportunity to

dissociate himself vigorously from the attitude of his War Secretary. Meanwhile the White troops and counter-revolutionary government collapsed. They had no further outside help to hope for. The Kremlin even amused itself by making Churchill a member of the Order of the Red Flag "for services to the Communist cause." With Lloyd George Moscow made a trade treaty by which England formally recognized the Bolshevik Government—and thus gave it every opportunity to spread its propaganda through the Empire.

Churchill's anti-Bolshevik policy was defeated. Today it seems rather an anachronism, though all the elements of the Hitler-Stalin pact are to be observed in these old battles. Even then the Communist overlordship, which owed its seizure of power to German Imperialism—Lenin and Trotsky had been brought back to Russia by Ludendorff's High Command—was directed fundamentally against democracy and its bulwark, the British Empire. This fundamental position continued through periods without treaties and charged with conflict, and also through periods when treaties for trade and friendship existed.

Psychologically considered, Churchill was following his own straight line. No matter if he was being driven back now to the Right, if the Reds called him their arch-enemy, he was still faithful, just as he is today with Right Radicalism finding in him its last European adversary, to his basic element: the protection of culture, of human decency, of Christian faith. His fight against Moscow was only a dress rehearsal.

CHAPTER XIX

Successes and Reverses

On one of his visits to the Paris Peace Conference Churchill had an unforgettable experience: he met Lawrence of Arabia. The desert warrior was not particularly popular at that time. He ran up and down the boulevards in an Arab burnous, curved dagger in red belt. Of course this was a form of demonstration. Lawrence had parted from the world of traitorous palefaces who would defraud his Arabian friends of their victor's prize. He associated with entirely unsuitable company. At any time of day you could find him with Emir Feisal. Even at the cocktail hour, when a man belonged in the Ritz Bar or the Crillon, he preferred Arabian conspirators' cafés on Montparnasse. Whenever he did irrupt into the white world, it was always with some dire significance. Day after day he assaulted Clemenceau to wrest from him the freedom of Syria. It was odd, but the Tiger, who kept English and American Ministers waiting, and had no time for the head of his own Cabinet, was always at home to Mr. Lawrence. He had a deep, an almost mystic feeling for the East. And, as he once growled through his teeth, he considered the convert who spoke for the Arabic world "a genius without example in our epoch." Of course this made no difference in his determination not to release Syria. France had not bled herself white in the trenches of Flanders to emerge from the war without her share of conquered territories.

Her English ally yielded to this determination. Lawrence did not yield. When his King received him in audience in order to give him the Commandership of the Bath and the Distinguished Service Order, he asked leave to decline the distinctions. He no longer had any use for English declarations.

The Excellencies assembled in Paris were indignant. Only Churchill invited Colonel Lawrence to lunch. And so they met for the first time. Before the hors d'œuvre was served, of course Churchill, as Secretary for War, had to reprove the affront that his guest had taken the liberty of putting upon the King. Lawrence, who had appeared for lunch in a simple sack suit, looking like any other brilliant, rather ineffectual Oxford boy, took these reproaches good-naturedly. He explained that he had had no other way of calling the attention of the country's highest authority to the fact that Great Britain's honor was at stake in the treatment of her Arab allies.

Churchill was a man-eater. Men whom he wanted for friends he simply would not let go. When he went over in the spring of 1921 to the Colonial Office, where he had begun his ministerial career sixteen years before as Under Secretary, he remembered his lunch with Lawrence. Now he could use the man.

When Churchill took it over the Colonial Office was the sore spot of the administration. A very bloody revolution in Iraq had just had to be suppressed, and upwards of 40,000 troops at a cost of £30,000,000 a year were required to maintain order. The strife between Jews and Arabs in Palestine threatened at any moment to become a violent outburst. The whole Middle East presented an alarming picture.

And so Churchill decided to organize a Middle Eastern Department in his office, chiefly to coördinate the various and contradictory interests in Iraq. Early in the spring he called a conference at Cairo, which later continued its sittings in Palestine. Half a dozen men from the India Office and others who had served in Iraq and Palestine during the war formed the nucleus. Churchill asked Lawrence to attend.

His associates could have been knocked over with a feather. Not that they did not appreciate Lawrence's genius. But after all, the fellow was a hermit, an outsider, a man who had never been able to submit to administrative discipline. "Wilt thou bridle the wild ass of the desert?" said one of the conferees.

But when Lawrence accepted the invitation, greatly astonishing most of them, and reported for work, he proved to be by no means a trouble-maker, but on the contrary a thoroughly coöperative and extremely helpful ally, patient and ready to work with others in perfect harmony. He seized this opportunity to redeem at least a measure of the promises he had made to the Arab in England's name. For that cause, sacred to him, he even squeezed himself into the restrictions of civil service. Of course it was only a brief episode in his meteoric career. With the organization of the Middle East largely accomplished, Churchill offered him a Governorship or some other one of the Colonial Service's high prizes. Lawrence replied with his cryptic smile: "All you will see of me is a small cloud of dust on the horizon."

The Conference submitted three main proposals to the Government: first, to repair the injury done to the Arabs and to the House of the Sherifs of Mecca by putting Emir Feisal on the throne of Iraq as king, and by entrusting Emir Abdullah with the government of Trans-Jordania. Second, to remove practically all troops from Iraq and give over its defense to the Royal Air Force. Third, to adjust the immediate difficulties between the Jews and Arabs in Palestine.

All three proposals aroused a storm of resentment. The French regarded Emir Feisal as a defeated rebel. The British War Office predicted uproar and carnage after the removal of the troops. Jews and Arabs alike seemed disinclined to release their conflicting monopolies on Palestine.

Nevertheless the proposals were put through. The French became reconciled to Emir Feisal. The release of the British Army from Iraq proved to be a blessing. Instead of the thirty million pounds its maintenance had cost, its successor, the Air Force, cost but four million. The lives of countless soldiers were saved, and still order was completely maintained in the country. Rule from the clouds, always a favorite idea of Churchill's, seemed to prove itself splendidly. The first peace negotiations began in Palestine.

In his memoirs, *The Seven Pillars of Wisdom,* Lawrence writes of this episode:

> "Churchill in a few weeks made straight all the tangle, finding solutions, fulfilling, I think, our promises in letter and spirit, where humanly possible, without sacrificing any interests of the Empire or of the people concerned."

Churchill now seemed to be at the zenith of his success. In war and peace he had proved himself a great administrator—a quality that the English appreciate. His private life was extremely happy. He devoted himself so passionately to his cause that there was simply no room for personal crises. He had overcome physical handicaps from childhood by constantly doing everything that the doctors had forbidden him—fencing, riding, polo, flying. Now, indeed, he did have to give up his favorite sport, polo. The ponies could not quite carry him. This was the result of the good cooking at the family's new home in Sussex Square, on the north side of Hyde Park. Mrs. Churchill took an interest in the kitchen herself. Her husband assisted. He was not only a great statesman; in his spare time he was also a great chef. For that matter Mrs. Churchill was interested in everything, even in politics. She canvassed for her husband at election time, accompanying him on the platform. She was his constant inspiration. He was her constant worry: he smoked too much.

Now Churchill had been told all his life that he should not smoke. Even his father had advised him: "Why begin? If you want to have an eye that is true, and a hand that does not quiver, if you want never to ask yourself a question as you rise at a fence, don't smoke." This paternal instruction, it is true, Lord Randolph smiled through the thick blue smoke of his cigarette, and he lighted a new one in the middle of the sentence. Winston took his father's example more to heart than his words. And when his wife occasionally called his attention to the fact that he was steadily poisoning himself with his fat black cigars, he replied that smoking had saved his life. If he had not once turned back at the front to get the forgotten matchbox from his dugout, he would have walked straight into a shell that burst a hundred yards in front.

Life slipped peacefully along. Churchill rode the crest of the wave. Suddenly there was a shock: Mamma died. Down to her last hour Lady Randolph (later Mrs. George Cornwallis-West) remained her son's trusted friend and adviser. She heard every one of his parliamentary addresses from the Distinguished Visitors' Gallery of the House. Her own intellectual and political interests never flagged. As editor of the *Anglo-Saxon Review* she took an active part herself in the intellectual and social life of her times. Among the contributors to her review—unparalleled success!—were a number of crowned heads. She arranged Shakespeare festivals. She was a celebrated hostess whose guests included Queen Alexandra and King Edward VII, but also George Bernard Shaw, whom, many people have said, she actually parlor-broke. But above all she was proud of being the famous mother of a famous son. She cherished in a tin box the black robe that her husband had worn as Chancellor of the Exchequer. She had hoped to live to see Winston in that garment. It was not vouchsafed her. So she bequeathed the robe to him—and thirty thousand pounds, which remained from her marriage settlement.

Immediately afterward, incidentally, a distant relative, Lord Herbert Vane-Tempest, died, leaving Churchill an income of five thousand pounds a year and an old castle in Ireland. The castle was soon burned down in the Irish disturbances. The income made him financially independent.

In March of the eventful year of 1921—Churchill was at his conference in Cairo at that time—it seemed as if his father's robe would come into its own. Lloyd George reshuffled his Cabinet, and everyone knew the only person who could take the post of Chancellor of the Exchequer in the Government: the most successful member of many ministries, the most popular of England's statesmen, the glamor boy of the United Kingdom. Only the Conservative machine knew that the Party turncoat would

THE PRINCE OF WALES AND WINSTON CHURCHILL

The future Duke of Windsor with Britain's future war leader on the Polo
Field in 1921

never get the Chancellorship, which implied the leadership of the House and sure expectation of the Premiership. Lloyd George could not afford to lose the Conservatives. On the contrary, he must bind them more closely to the coalition. And so he gave the Chancellorship to Sir Robert Horne, the candidate presented by the Party.

England was stunned. Never had any bet been so sure as Churchill. Never had the prophets gone so far wrong. Who could solve the puzzle?

"A gentleman with a duster" offered an explanation. Behind this pseudonym there hid, for a long time successfully, the author Harold Begbie. In his *The Mirrors of Downing Street* he drew a portrait of Churchill which, although written without any special sympathy for its subject, still has an astonishing and sometimes a prophetic sound after all these years. The sketch has not completely caught Churchill. It has, in fact, reproduced many current misjudgments. But the essential element in his metamorphosis is drawn with astonishing accuracy.

> "With the exception of Lloyd George"—says the gentleman with the duster—"Mr. Churchill is the most interesting figure in the House. From the start of his career he was an element of great promise. Sometimes he disappointed his admirers, but he never destroyed their hopes. His intellectual gifts, his unique fighting qualities, also in politics, his boundless personal courage are singular. No man is more difficult to shout down. From his youth he fiercely loved England, war and politics. Politics, to him, are almost as exciting as war and quite as dangerous. In war you can only be killed once, but in politics many times.

> "He has many qualities of real greatness—but has he the unifying spirit of character? He has truly brilliant gifts, but you cannot quite depend on them. His love for danger runs away with his discretion. His passion for adventure makes him forget the importance of the goal. Mr. Churchill carries great guns, but his navigation is uncertain. His effect on men is one of interest and curiosity, not of admiration and loyalty. His power is the power of gifts, not of character. Men watch him, but do not follow him. He beguiles their reason, but never warms their emotions. You

may see in him the wonderful and lightning movements of the brain, but never the beating of a steadfast heart. His inconsistencies have brought him too often into inferior company. . . .

"All Mr. Churchill needs is the direction in his life of a great idea. He is a Saul on the way to Damascus. Let him swing clean away from that road of destruction, and he might well become Paul on his way to immortality. This is to say that to be saved from himself Mr. Churchill must be carried away by enthusiasm for some great ideal, an ideal so much greater than his own place in politics that he is willing to face death for its triumph, even the many deaths of political life. At present he is but playing with politics. Even in his most earnest moments he is 'in politics' as a man is 'in business.' But politics for Mr. Churchill, if they are to make him, if they are to fulfill his promise, must be a religion. They must have nothing to do with Mr. Churchill. They must have everything to do with the salvation of mankind. It is high time he hitched his waggon to a star."

The star, as we know, has risen—the black star of Hitler. What is ordinarily called politics has indeed become a religion to Churchill. He faces death with a smile, and not merely the many deaths of political life. And if ever a life was devoted solely to the salvation of mankind, it is Churchill's.

Harold Begbie's prophecy is amazing. His psychology is not quite so sure. By 1921 the wanton element that the author of *The Mirrors of Downing Street* condemned in Churchill had long since been overcome. True, it had had to be fought down. What escaped the critic is that Churchill at forty-seven was already through with straying on bypaths. General William Booth of the Salvation Army put it all much more simply. "You stand in need of conversion, Mr. Churchill," he said.

Events proved that England stood in grave need of conversion.

One single push was enough in 1921 to set the Conservative machine in motion, and halt the dynamo, the only one post-war England had. Mr. Churchill need not trouble to take his father's robe of State out of mothballs. He stayed in the Colonial Office.

All right, he would remain at his minor post, for no post was minor where Churchill was in charge. Once again he plunged head over heels into the most ticklish problems of the Empire. The Irish question had gradually become insoluble. The World War was scarcely over when it blazed up again. True, the coalition of the two parties in the House was strong enough to end the terror of the Irish Nationalists. No longer did they hold the balance, as they had done for so many years. But Churchill had finally come to realize that the Irish had better manage or mismanage their own country than the Empire. His own house in Sussex Square was the center of the consultations that finally led to the Irish Treaty, liquidating an almost century-old quarrel. The Irish had their independence; Ulster saved herself for England and the Empire.

So far as Churchill personally was concerned the peace had the effect of bringing him a bodyguard from Scotland Yard to protect him from assassination by Irish malcontents. For years Sergeant Thompson performed this duty. He became the shadow of his ward. While the latter painted landscapes the Sergeant (whose expenses, including the state salary, incidentally were paid by Churchill out of his own pocket) stood by the hour at a respectful distance. He watched the passers-by who disfigured the landscape more attentively than he did the beauties of nature. As this went on for many hours Sergeant Thompson had his own ideas about the eternal quality of art. When Churchill was in the House the honest Sergeant waited tirelessly before the entrance reserved for Cabinet members. In his chief's office he scrutinized the anteroom. Once, it is said, he even refused to let in Viscount Gort, the present Commander-in-Chief of the British Army. Gort had announced himself in a suspicious brogue.

The importance of these precautions was shown six months after the Irish Treaty was signed, when Field-Marshal Sir Henry Wilson was shot down in the streets of London by two Irish revolutionists. In a memorable speech in Parliament Churchill warned the Free State that it must discipline its people. "The ambiguous position of the so-called I.R.A., intermingled as it is with the Free State troops, is an affront to the Treaty. If such a state of things is not brought quickly to an end, we shall regard this treaty as having been formally violated."

He made another important speech about Palestine. Strong opposition to the national home for Jews was manifested in the press and Parliament. "On the portal of the new Jerusalem, do you want to inscribe: No Israelite need apply?" Churchill asked the House, which gave way, laughing.

That session was called the "Churchill session," so completely did his oratory dominate it. No, he would not be downed. Merely because the war was over, it did not mean he was worn out. Party intrigue did not bother him. His Conservative colleagues in the Cabinet stuck by him. When the disturbance among the Tories increased, they met for Sunday dinner on October 22, 1921, at his house. Lord Curzon came, Austen Chamberlain, the Earl of Birkenhead, Sir Laming Worthington, and also Lloyd George himself. Over dessert they resolved to hold together, come what might.

Tuesday Churchill announced to the country at a meeting in Bristol that all was in the best of order. There was absolutely no reason for a Government crisis. A few days later, the following Monday, he woke up in terrible pain. On Tuesday the pain became unbearable. At the same time came the news that a fierce diehard, an anti-coalition Tory, had won by a large majority in a by-election at Henport. Democracy was growing restless again; it was too long since the country had devoured a victim.

Wednesday Churchill was operated on for appendicitis. They carried him to the nursing home on a stretcher. Thursday Lord Curzon failed to appear at the Carleton Club. Obviously he had decided no longer to support Lloyd George. That meant the break-up of the coalition. Lloyd George resigned, dragging Churchill down in his fall. A fortnight before, the whole country had been talking of the Churchill session. Not a thing had happened since. Only the country's hero had fallen, for the inscrutable reasons that lead the people to devour its favorites.

CHAPTER XX

The Volcano Slumbers

THREE days after his operation Churchill was still barely able to talk. He had to force each word out several times with infinite striving before his secretary could understand. It was his letter to the voters of Dundee. Mrs. Churchill personally carried the message. With the help of a few friends she campaigned tirelessly for her husband in his constituency while he still lay on his sickbed. Even worse than the physical anguish was the political abstinence imposed upon him just at the moment when the country was going into a fateful election.

It was not the old country any more. The dreadful exertions of the war, loss of blood, and above all overstrained nerves, had completely exhausted England. As a matter of fact the British Isles never recovered from their exhaustion until the middle of this second war, when they were faced anew with the supreme test. The first time, their arms had triumphed by a frantic effort, but their will to power was broken. In the Khaki Elections of 1918 the joy of victory still drowned the anaemic whisperings. But three lean years had passed since then. The new bodies of voters that now fixed the destinies of the country were shot through with general discontent and ill-will. Women had been given the vote. Envy at home and complete lack of interest in the world, its progress and menaces, paralyzed the country.

The men who now came into power expressed perfectly the weakness and sleepiness of England's lost generation—the generation between the two wars. The Parties maintained contact with the voters by carefully avoiding waking up the masses from their pacifistic wish-dreams and their nightmares of the last war.

England was playing dead. The people were called on to make no decisions. Ease and comfort first!

The soporific method was splendidly effective. The British nation was spared Communist and Fascist upheavals against the existing order. Governments and public opinion met on a common level—the lowest in the proud history of Britain. Personal recriminations are therefore meaningless. Amid general approval the stage was set for Messrs. MacDonald, Baldwin and Neville Chamberlain to lead England down the road to suicide.

That was a march with which Winston Churchill could not keep step. From the first he was a dead weight, heavy with glorious memories that people wanted to forget as fast as possible, the embodiment of a coalition that had held the country together in a grip of iron during the emergency, but that was now supposed to give way to unchecked party rivalry, a man from the age of heroes in the beginning of the jazz era. His Victorian poise now seemed antediluvian. And in any case a superficial age could not understand his inner harmony; it saw only the outward signs of an extremist who fought with both Right and Left. People could not understand how the same passion might lead a man to fight the rear-guard action of both sides. The standardized opinion of the mass age that arose after the first World War as a reaction to mass suffering understood only what it read every day in the tabloids. About Mr. Churchill it had read chiefly in connection with Antwerp and Gallipoli.

"Antwerp! . . . Gallipoli! . . ." howled the mob when the candidate arrived in Dundee two days before the election. It was the twenty-first day after his operation. The doctor had merely shrugged his shoulders when Churchill insisted on leaving the nursing home. "Either with his shield or on it . . ." the learned medical man muttered resignedly.

Churchill had to be carried on to the platform in an invalid chair. His wound was still open. Red rowdies kept stopping him everywhere, abusing him blasphemously; only the patient's obviously desperate condition prevented them from laying hands on him. To the new category of voters, hitherto disfranchised for non-payment of rates, the man who had broken the munitions-workers' strike and preached the crusade against Bolshevism was the Devil incarnate.

The meeting itself went off in quite orderly fashion. It was a ticket meeting, held in the afternoon, and the man who had paid for his ticket wanted accordingly to hear what the Right Honorable Mr. Churchill had to say. Churchill did not mince words. Although he was standing as a Liberal candidate, he was also appealing for the Conservative vote (as a matter of fact the Conservatives of Dundee had always stood by him), to give warning of the Red torrent that threatened to flood the British Isles. In his mind the old conflicts between the traditional parties had lost their meaning. A man home from the World War did not think about Liberals and Conservatives. Unfortunately the Party leaders had not been at the front.

That evening the utterly weary and exhausted man had to speak again, in the Drill Hall. This time it was not a ticket meeting, but an assemblage of eight or nine thousand rough customers among whom his opponents heavily predominated. The hatred that Churchill felt welling up to him was positively bewildering. A favorite expression of his father's came into his head: "I never fear the British democracy." No, he did not fear it either. But for the first time it was somehow strange to him; that was even worse.

This was not the British democracy interrupting him at every word, shouting him down and bursting into hoots of laughter when the sick man made a helpless motion of defense. It was the Red mob.

The opposing candidates had put in an appearance: Mr. William Gallacher, today the only remaining Communist member of the Lower House, Mr. Morel, a renegade Liberal, who was now heading the Socialist ticket, and his team partner—none other than the God-fearing Prohibitionist Mr. Scrimgeour, the

newest devotee of Marxism. In a high, rasping voice Mr. Scrimgeour prayed God to annihilate the notorious toper Churchill.

Either his prayer was heard or else perseverance triumphed.
At the sixth attempt Mr. Scrimgeour, who had started out on
his dry crusade a few years before with three hundred votes, won
with 32,578 votes; his team partner, Morel, had 30,292. Churchill
was beaten with 20,466, and his Liberal mate Mr. MacDonald
(not to be confused with the Socialist leader) was only about 2,000
better off. Lastly the party Communists managed 5,906 for Comrade Gallacher. When it came to the customary vote of thanks
to the returning officer, Mr. Scrimgeour moved it instead to
Almighty God.

Labor had won all along the line. The Conservatives and the
Liberals both were done for in Dundee. The Tory machine, however, was unperturbed. It reckoned only in parliamentary arith-
metic. The majority throughout the country for the new Bonar
Law Government was sufficient. Churchill's absence was a blow
they could get over; he had always been rather too self-willed an
ally.

Churchill also did his figuring, but he was not satisfied with
merely adding up seats. In the Victory Election he had won by
15,000 votes in the same constituency that now rejected him by
over 10,000. Those 25,000 who had strayed over to Labor, he
calculated, were the fluctuating element of the British nation. It
had dark days before it.

Churchill was out of Parliament for the first time since 1900.
For all practical purposes this meant that he was out of politics.
For a man who had something to say, for a man who still saw
a tremendous task before him, this was a hard lot. But Churchill
did not mutiny against Fate. He had learned by then to take its
changes philosophically, even when they involved himself. When
the sick man was brought back to London in his invalid chair,
he merely shook his head slightly. Certainly 1922 had been the
most prosperous year he had had as a Minister in the House so

far. Iraq, Palestine, the Irish Treaty, nothing but successes. He had had an assured seat on the Government bench, a large following among both parties, and all the rest of it. And overnight, as he said later, no office, no seat, no Party, and no appendix.

The moment he was anything like able to travel, Churchill was shipped to Cannes, where he spent six months convalescing. He had a drab and dreary time. He did not deceive himself into thinking he had merely suffered a minor parliamentary accident; there was trouble ahead for his country. Among Conservatives and Liberals he had always remained an outsider, even when he was in power. But if the country went Red they would all be outsiders soon, and the outsiders would be in. Would that still be England? The question occurred to him while he was spending his mornings at the desk and his afternoons with the palette on the beach. His evenings, incidentally, he usually spent at the Casino, where he generally bet on red, "having a preference for the optimistic side of things," he said.

The rolling ball on the Casino table set him to thinking. He was now reaching the reflective age when, in Goethe's words, "All transitory things become a parable." Nothing was more transitory than the course of the ball on the roulette table. No, he did not trust in fortune. Man is not so constituted that he can seize good fortune. For that reason too he would not be downed by misfortune. All transitory things are but a parable.

As his hand gradually grew stronger, his pictures gained in intensity and color. On the palette, if not on the roulette table, he preferred not red but a dark, radiant blue. He did not care much for water colors. Oils, he said, are a medium that offers real power if you can find out how to use it. Then he added: "You can't do anything in this world of ours without power." Did he only mean oil paint? He defended it in a jingle:

> La peinture à l'huile
> Est bien difficile,
> Mais c'est beaucoup plus beau
> Que la peinture à l'eau.

Again and again he defended his painting, which his friends may have smiled at in secret. He defended it quite naively: "Just to paint is great fun. The colors are lovely to look at and delicious to squeeze out. Matching them, however crudely, with what you see is fascinating, and absolutely absorbing. Try it if you have not done so—before you die."

It was queer how the thought of death kept creeping near of its own accord in the midst of the gayest hours with brush and palette. No question of it, his mind was returning from the sun-drenched Côte d'Azure to the foggy island kingdom, which Churchill could feel dying away in beauty—in beauty, self-deception, and culpable weakness.

Churchill painted some of his loveliest pictures on the Riviera: Cap Ferrat, the race-course at Nice, daybreak near Marseilles, and others. But when he painted English summer landscapes at home, meadows in Sussex or an interior at Breccles, Norfolk, his hand was guided not by his sense of style alone, but by a sense of life.

Mornings he was in England, even when he was at his villa in Cannes. Between breakfast and lunch, pacing his room with swift steps, he dictated in ceaselessly onrushing periods, which no secretary could quite keep up with, his life work, *The World Crisis,* an account of the first World War and its origins. His own past rose before him. He was not yet quite fifty when the book came out, but already he was a classic in the realm of intellect, and an elder statesman, for whom the country had no further use, in politics. Now the story could be told. Churchill told it with great splendor of language, acuteness of thought, with minute care about his facts and respectful justice for his adversaries. Sir Arthur Conan Doyle, who had introduced him as a young lecturer on an English platform just after the Boer War, wrote when the book appeared: "I have long recognized that Winston Churchill has the finest prose style of any contemporary." J. L. Garvin, not always a friend of Churchill's, said in his *Observer:* "None in the line of English statesmen is more sure of a lasting place in literature. Churchill is one of the born organists of language. He is all color, vigor, personality. His feeling for mechanism, his sense of action, his incomparable gift of making technicalities lucid and familiar, are astounding. There is style, because there is a man." A writer in the *New York Times* put it very simply: "An aristocrat born and bred, Mr. Churchill is only interested in great persons, great issues, great events."

Let us quote one brief passage from the fat tome. It shows the whole power of the author's language and thought, and his farsightedness. Churchill describes what would happen if the British sea power were abruptly broken. "Open the sea-cocks and let our ships sink. In a few minutes, half an hour at most, the whole outlook of the world would be changed. The British Empire would dissolve like a dream, each isolated community struggling forward by itself, the central power of union broken, mighty provinces, whole Empires in themselves, drifting hopelessly out of control and falling a prey to others, and Europe after one mighty convulsion passing into the iron grip and rule of the Teuton and all that the Teutonic system meant. There would only be left far across the Atlantic unarmed, unready, and as yet uninstructed America to manage single-handed law and freedom among men."

All literary England realized that a man had risen here whose knowledge, insight, precision of thought and clarity of language lifted him high above all contemporary historians.

The first volume of *The World Crisis* appeared in April, 1923, the next on October 2. Churchill completed the work in 1927. A book carrying on with later events appeared under the title *The Aftermath*. The author received a hundred thousand dollars. Now at last he could realize his dream: he bought an English country house, and went, he hoped, into retirement.

In the spring of 1923 the family moved to Chartwell Manor, the beautiful old house three miles from the Kentish town of Westerham. It was Churchill's permanent home, his last abode, as he called it, for the "duration." Here Winston Churchill turned into the country squire whose picture became familiar to England and to all the world—the picture almost of John Bull himself.

He helped rebuild the house with his own hands. He was a perfect bricklayer in overalls, laying up his own walls. The red brick Elizabethan house was soon shining in new splendor. Churchill himself in old clothes worked out of doors, digging, building, sinking rock gardens—and all the time while he was working with his hands he was developing new ideas, thinking out new thoughts, probably fighting off old ones as well. He still could not forget the Dardanelles. He stood up to his knees in water, forcing a reluctant little stream to break through a miniature Dardanelles of his own planning. His house guests had to work too, quite regardless of the damage to their clothes. He said it would do their souls good. When he went to work felling trees with mighty blows, he recalled that this was Gladstone's preferred hobby, and doubtless the explanation of the great man's vigor in old age.

Everyone was touched by Churchill, who had found peace. Only the Guild of London Tailors protested against "the sartorial terrors" of a man who by rank was a born fashion leader. The Guild carried on a fierce campaign to reform him. Churchill was so popular in the country where his word meant nothing that the question of his clothing became a national problem. Sorrowfully the tailors' periodical recalled that even Lord Randolph had been a careless dresser, and in fact the first to enter the House in brown shoes. Winston was known to have appeared at his own wedding in "disreputable old boots." He had even been seen riding in Rotten Row in patent-leather boots with suède tops. When he had gone out walking as a young officer with his lovely Mamma and his sartorially impeccable brother, the trade paper observed that he had often been taken for the groom because of his untidiness.

On the other hand his careless dress won enthusiastic adherents. A man was summoned before a police court for breaking a restaurant window. "I was so eager to get back," he defended him-

CHURCHILL ENGAGED IN A FAVORITE HOBBY—BRICKLAYING

self, "to recover my fur-lined coat—it once belonged to Mr. Winston Churchill."

The second group of critics were the bricklayers. They were very much against allowing a non-union member to work at Chartwell Manor. Of course this was a mere malicious attack on the so-called "red-baiter." Churchill laughed. He filled out a card for the bricklayers' union, and applied for membership.

In sports he had to be careful now. The first attempt on a neighboring golf links was a failure. The shoulder he had injured in youth was inclined to balk. So he gave up golf, and tennis as well. Mrs. Churchill indeed remained an excellent tennis-player, and her husband is her most enthusiastic and expert spectator.

He was a model husband, a splendid father, and united to his younger brother Major Churchill by the closest of friendships. His children, indeed, were yet to cause him some worries. Diana married the young Conservative M.P. Lieutenant Sandys, who was almost court-martialed for a parliamentary question that ostensibly violated military secrets. However, the young officer came out of the affair with complete credit. Sarah, the second daughter, eloped to America with the comedian Vic Oliver. His son Randolph was defeated at the Liverpool elections, but received a seat in the autumn of 1940. Only Mary, the youngest, has as yet kept out of the headlines.

Calmly and harmoniously the days passed at Chartwell Manor. Churchill learned to go to bed betimes. To make up for it he was astir by six o'clock in the morning. The newspapers, correspondence, manuscripts and documents already awaited him, not to mention the cigars. He spent the greater part of the morning reading and dictating in bed. Then the day took its peaceful course.

The volcano slumbered while the sky darkened over England. The soft, balmy air of the island was electrically charged. Was that the rumble of distant thunder? No, it was only the voice of Winston Churchill, who broke away from his idyl only a few days after moving to Chartwell Manor—on May 4, 1923—and made a speech at the Connaught Rooms in London before the Aldwych Club:

"The destruction of the coalition has paved the way for socialist power. There are no longer great crucial questions separating Liberals from Conservatives. Yet Mr. Asquith regards any Liberal who cooperates with Conservatives as positively unclean, although without his own Conservative vote the good town of Paisley would have sent another Socialist up to Westminster. The only important thing, we are told, is for all orthodox Liberals to excommunicate Mr. Lloyd George with theological ferocity, and for the true Conservatives to ostracise Lord Birkenhead with classic ruthlessness . . . the quarreling parties assure the country that there is no danger of a Socialist Government, that it is a mere bogy or bugbear not worthy of serious attention."

So: now he had got that off his chest. The ridiculous party barriers that he had long since passed beyond were now pilloried before the country for what they were. They were calculated to destroy national unity, to play into the hands of the third front: the Reds, the defeatists and pacifists. Now he could trudge back to Chartwell Manor to lay bricks and write immortal prose.

"Ludicrous panic-mongering!" press and politicians shouted after him. "Never will there be a Socialist Cabinet in England!"

But less than a year passed before Mr. Ramsay MacDonald formed His Majesty's first Labor Government. The first of the three grave-diggers of England went to work. The march to Munich and the battle of France, smoothed in turn by Socialist, Liberal and Tory complacency, began.

CHAPTER XXI

Happy Ending?

In December, 1923, Mr. Stanley Baldwin followed his fellow-Conservative, Bonar Law, as Prime Minister. He was a well-meaning man on the whole, a manufacturer with classical inclinations, who liked to quote Latin tags. Two of his sayings have a certain curiosity value. "How could I tell the country that Germany was feverishly rearming without running the risk of losing the Conservative Party's majority?" This was one. Another was briefer: "Democracy must always limp two years behind dictatorship." Besides these two utterances, Mr. Baldwin was famous for his pipe.

He suddenly appealed to the country on the Protectionist issue. His very start showed the limitations of his ability. The country would have none of Protectionism. The voters flocked over to the Socialists, who did not indeed win a majority, but were helped into the saddle by Asquith's Liberal fragment. For the first time a Socialist was His Majesty's Prime Minister.

Churchill was not really interested in this election. He considered it the height of insanity. He could foresee its results. The moderate parties would break each other's heads again, and the Socialists alone would profit. Churchill was somewhere among the moderates. Nominally he still belonged to the Liberals. But he watched their Leftward trend with great anxiety. Besides, in the previous eight years of coalition government he had usually worked much more intimately with his Conservative Cabinet colleagues than with his own party allies. Nevertheless he could not leave the new attack of Protectionism unanswered. A great number of offers to stand reached Chartwell Manor, and he decided rather unwillingly to run as a Liberal Free Trader for West Leicester.

Lord Wodehouse and the ever-faithful Sir Archibald Sinclair were his assistants. But once again the most valuable help came from his own wife. Once more Mrs. Churchill stood on every platform where her husband was announced to speak. She carried a bunch of white heather with a ribbon: "From the Nurse and the Children." This picture of serene family life did not fail of its effect. Churchill now presented himself to the country as "daddy."

His opponents denounced him as a dangerous man. To his Conservative opponent, Captain Inston, he was still a traitor to the Party; to the Socialist, F. W. Pethick-Lawrence, simply a reactionary.

Mr. Pethick-Lawrence represented a new type that was soon to attain considerable influence in politics, and not in England alone—the white-collar Labor leader. For years he was one of the masculine leaders of the Suffragette movement. Now he was the Socialist intellectual economic expert, specializing in the capital levy. His very simple program was to make over the property of the richer neighbor to the poorer.

This answer to the social problem made a deep impression on the masses. Mr. Pethick-Lawrence was hope, Churchill the old Nick in person. He has always had a special talent for provoking his adversaries to the limit. When Mr. Pethick-Lawrence maintained in an argument: "The Labor Party is the only conscientious party!" he replied: "It certainly supplied the greatest number of conscientious objectors!"

The mob answered by bellowing "Antwerp!" and "Dardanelles!"

The better people in England, indeed, were already tired of these labels. A. P. Herbert of *Punch* came to Churchill's aid on his platform. "I am neither Liberal nor Free Trader," he declared. "I am just a veteran member of the Royal Naval Division in Gallipoli, and I want to defend Mr. Churchill's Dardanelles policy!" Then he related his story, which was, all told, a great compliment for Churchill. Next Churchill must speak for himself. But bands of rowdies prevented any of his speeches from being properly delivered. Hooligans climbed in on ladders through the windows of his meeting-places. Churchill had to stop speaking amid catcalls and insults. When he visited London, a man in the crowd spat at him. Another one put his arms through the window of Churchill's car. He tried to hit out, but Thompson, the bodyguard, warded off the blow. The would-be assailant simply told the police: "I don't like Mr. Churchill!"

Mr. Pethick-Lawrence was elected by 13,643 votes to 9,236 for Churchill. The Conservative candidate, Captain Inston, was left behind with 7,692. The dissension of the bourgeois parties brought its own retribution. It ruined national politics. Mr. Asquith, who could not understand that his time had long since gone by, devoted his last strength to keeping the Socialists in power. He could not forgive the Conservatives for not having accepted his leadership in the Coalition Cabinet of the war years. Now he swung the Liberal Party round to support the MacDonald minority. Churchill called this "a serious national misfortune." Personal respect for his old chief restrained his usual acidity of criticism. But he took a step whose plainness left nothing to be desired: twenty years after he had crossed the floor with the words: "Thank God that we have a Liberal Party!" he resigned from it. He called himself a "Constitutionalist." The name sounds like a makeshift. It has been a good deal smiled at. As a matter of fact it is a profession of faith. A constitution, even unwritten, is lasting. Churchill had grown beyond the restrictions of ephemeral matters. Progress, retrogression, Right and Left were problems of an inferior order, capable of solution by the laws of common sense and the demands of the time. The man who was rising from crusader to prophet cared only for what was lasting, essential, English. The constitution was still the best way of putting it. Once again a storm of indignation at Churchill's "inconsistency" raged through the land. From Liberal throats the storm sounded like a death-rattle. The great, historic party, it seemed, had fulfilled its destiny. If it was to be merely an appendage of the Socialists, it would soon vanish completely from the scene. Churchill's logic was compelling. But it was distorted by the last Liberal Party men into its opposite. They howled that Churchill had given the final kick to his own party (which in reality, always the Cassandra as he was, he had urgently warned against political suicide). The rats are leaving the sinking ship, they shouted after him.

The Conservatives rubbed their hands with glee. Liberal competition was now disposed of forever. Memories live a long time in England. Disraeli was now revenged on Gladstone, and Lord Salisbury on Lord Rosebery. That was a satisfaction, even if the direct heir of the quarrel, the next Prime Minister, was Ramsay MacDonald, conscientious objector and defeatist. The Conservative machine still had no use for Churchill. As long as twenty years before, they had realized that the traitor would also betray his new friends. Let him cherish no hope of returning now to the House of his fathers. The Party that was producing not Dizzys, not Lord Salisburys, but Baldwins, and a Neville Chamberlain instead of Joe, did not need Mr. Churchill. Let him make his own way as best he might.

Churchill put up a vigorous defense against the jeers and sneers from both sides. He quoted Emerson: "A foolish consistency is the hobgoblin of little minds, adored by little statesmen and philosophers and divines. Think what you think now in hard words, and tomorrow speak what tomorrow thinks in hard words again, though it contradict everything you said today."

To save the traditions of England, he had to turn away from the traditional parties. Democracy, given over to catchwords instead of being devoted to the idea, did not understand him. Churchill was among the best-known, even the most popular figures in public life. But the country did not quite understand him. His uncompromising, patriotic morality was not "cricket." Nine out of ten of his countrymen would grin when they heard his name (the tenth saw red because he was a Red himself); "but

. . ." they were sure to add, and then followed the verdict without appeal: he crosses party lines a bit too often. That's not my cup of tea. No, sir; I was born and bred a Tory (or a Liberal) . . . and then the spirit of Disraeli or Gladstone would be conjured up.

It was a hard road for a man to follow the inner voice instead of Mr. Asquith's resentful tactics or Mr. Baldwin's blundering nobility. The road grew ever rockier. Now Churchill's country did not trust him. That was bitter enough. Soon it would turn a deaf ear when he raised his voice to cry in the wilderness. How did he manage to maintain his healthy red complexion, his invariable smile, his joy in the beautiful things of life? Probably most people would have given way, shrugged their shoulders, gone to raising peonies. Not Churchill. He was under an inner compulsion. He had not fulfilled his mission yet. It grew ever more complicated. The signs of the times horrified him. German restlessness, Russian tyranny, the new castor-oil rule in Italy, did not appear to him as isolated phenomena. It was not yet a power puzzle for the world to solve. Germany was only drilling a hundred thousand men, though the Reichswehr had already built its first secret aerodromes in Russia. The Red Army was a civil-war rabble. The triumph of Fascism depended chiefly on gangs of pimps and pickpockets who beat up liberal professors and burned the crosses in churches. But it was a question of will. The terrorist nations *would*. England wanted peace and quiet. And so Churchill plunged again into the fray. And when he called, the best men of England stood at his back.

The by-election in the Abbey Division of Westminster, in February of 1924, was a struggle memorable in parliamentary history. For the first time the elite of society rose against the regimentation of parties. Volunteer electioneers offered themselves from all over the country for this man who was an outcast of the political machines, but England's only hope of capturing one of the most important and most stubbornly contested seats.

The heart of London beat in the Abbey Division. This little district is to England what Washington is to America. It includes the Houses of Parliament, Buckingham Palace, the seat of government, the principal clubs and theaters, St. James's Street, the Strand, Soho, Pimlico and Covent Garden. And dukes, Cabinet Ministers, and courtiers vote here. But here too vote the poor, and, in addition, the rowdies of Soho, and Pimlico. Every trade, profession and interest has its headquarters here. London's blood pulses through the great thoroughfares.

Of course this constituency was fiercely contested by all parties. The Conservatives were represented by the young, punctilious Captain Nicholson, whose chief importance was as the nephew of the recently dead Member from the district, General Nicholson. The radical Scott Ducker and the socialist Fenner Brockway wrestled for a majority from the slums. Churchill stood as an "independent and anti-Socialist" candidate, a liberal and free trader who wanted to join with conservatives to stop the march of Socialism.

He had no party behind him, no organization, and no time to build up anything of the sort. There was only a fortnight available for the fight. But those two weeks were enough to show a revolutionary awakening of all the patriots. Even after the first week Captain Guest, his campaign manager, was able to assure Churchill that he was excellently supported.

The support came above all from the camp of malcontent Conservatives. The best and most independent minds in the Kingdom were fed up with official sleepiness. Churchill attracted them like a magnet. Thirty Tory M.P.s exposed themselves to the wrath of their bosses and the danger of losing their own seats by speaking on Churchill's platform. Among them was Commander Locker-Lampson, M.P. for the Harmsworth Division of Birmingham, who is one of Churchill's inner circle today. His American-born wife designed and stuck up posters for Churchill. Also among them were Edmund Harmsworth, the son of his old adversary Lord Northcliffe, Sir Martin Conway, M.P. for the English Universities, Sir Philip Sassoon, M.P. for Hythe, an intimate friend of the King's, ranking officers from the House like

General Seely, who had been with him in the war, Admiral Sueter, Lord Darling, just retired from the High Court Bench, who admitted that he was campaigning for the first time in twenty-five years, the Duke of Marlborough, Sir Eric Geddes, Lord Ednam, and Lord Wargrave. The helpers of the previous election, Lord Wodehouse and Sir Archibald Sinclair, were again in the front rank.

It was a revolution of education and property. Such *grandes dames* as the Ladies Wodehouse, Blandford, and Bessborough, paraded through the ill-lit side lanes of Pimlico with Churchill's pictures. Even more effective than the picture of the candidate was the photograph of his baby daughter Mary, who smiled "Vote for Daddy!" from all the house-fronts.

It was not merely the educated and prosperous, however, who flocked around him. The chorus girls of Daly's Theatre sat up all night addressing envelopes and dispatching the election address, and would not take a penny for their work. Jockeys, prizefighters, actors and business men plunged into the fight for Churchill. Indeed the English sense of fair play was aroused, and that was what gave this election its particular character. They would no longer see their man kept down; they would not have him slandered any longer.

The London press was unanimously for Churchill, with the *Morning Post* the only exception. This was the official mouthpiece of the Conservative Party. And Churchill was still anathema to the official party. Obstinately the Whips threatened with instant exclusion every Party member who sided with the apostate of twenty years before. All they accomplished by this, however, was a gaping split in their own organization. The result was a battle of the generations. The old people stayed in line; they followed the banner of the youthful Captain Nicholson. The sons and daughters of venerable Tory dynasties, on the other hand, cheered Daddy Churchill, the most youthful of them all. Family bonds were torn asunder, brothers quarreled, friendships by the dozen were shattered.

The supreme leadership of the Party watched the struggle with
Olympian calm. Certainly Mr. Baldwin's heart was with Captain
Nicholson. But Mr. Baldwin was no fighter, as Adolf Hitler was
soon to learn. He wrapped himself in silence. And then a miracle
happened: Lord Balfour wrote a letter supporting Churchill's
candidacy. He had put many difficulties in the path of the "young
man of promises." He had pushed him out of the Admiralty,
which, as he privately admitted, might have been a mistake. He
had never properly supported him during the Coalition. But at
the same time he had learned to respect him. Lord Balfour now
was an ancient man, even though his friends did call him "ageless." Perhaps he was remembering decades long past when he
and Lord Randolph had led the House of Commons, and had
enjoyed musical evenings with Lady Randolph, above all Schu-
bert and Bach. He was a wise and a just man. His skill at balanc-
ing merits and duties was incomparable. So he wrote the letter
for Churchill. But it could be released only with Mr. Baldwin's
approval. His was the final responsibility for the Party.

Churchill's followers importuned Mr. Baldwin for his approval.
In vain. That letter, he believed, would split the Party. Finally
a compromise was wrung from him: Lord Balfour's letter might
be published if some Conservative voice spoke openly for Captain Nicholson.

This was very difficult. Even among the diehards nobody
wanted to swim against the stream.

And then the following morning an article appeared in the
Times in praise of Captain Nicholson, supporting "this brilliant
young man of the shadow cabinet, the ardent Protectionist." The
article was indeed tucked away in a corner of the paper, but no
one could deny that the *Times* spoke with an extremely conse-
quential Conservative voice.

Mr. Baldwin was sitting at breakfast, bent over a steaming bowl
of porridge, when Churchill's men burst into his house, waving
a dozen copies of the *Times.* "You are too late," he greeted his
noisy guests with a smile. "Half an hour ago I sent Winston Lord

Balfour's letter for publication." Later it turned out that the inconspicuous but decisive article had been written by good old
Leopold Amery.

Balfour's statement allowed the Conservative Government
members, Lord Birkenhead and Sir Austen Chamberlain, to
speak for Churchill against their party's candidate. This offensive
was a most effective diversion.

The fight on the Left front was carried on not with ruses, memories and refinements, but with bare fists. The Socialist crowd,
pouring out of Soho and Pimlico, assaulted Churchill's bodyguard with knuckles and knives. Oddly enough Scotland Yard
had no objection. Regrettable as the continual breach of the
peace was, still a considerable number of long-wanted underworld
figures from Soho made their appearance in this occasion. Some
of them even had the nerve to lead an anti-Churchill parade.
What the parade looked like can be guessed from the statement
of the stationmaster at Victoria Station: "A crowd of foreigners,
just arriving, happened to run into the Socialist procession. Bewildered, they believed the revolution had broken out, and returned by the next train to their own countries."

Even so, the final spurt in the contest began most promisingly.
As the last packet of votes was being carried up to the table,
somebody—just who it was later impossible to determine—told
Churchill: "You are in by a hundred!" Churchill was apparently unable to suppress a cry of triumph, and a loud cheer went
up from all sides. The crowds waiting outside took up the cheer.
The journalists rushed to the telephone booths. The whole world
knew that Churchill was in again—

—even before it turned out that the regular Party candidate had
beaten him by 43 votes. Captain Nicholson had 8,187 votes, Mr.
Churchill 8,144, Fenner Brockway 6,156, and the radical Liberal
Scott Ducker all of 291.

It was one of the finest moments in Churchill's life. Even years
later he rejoiced in the memory of a defeat that was in reality
a triumph, an awakening of England, a confirmation of his life's

principle that the man is stronger than the machine. After the petty success they had wrung from him, the Conservatives could no longer oppose his return to political life. No one cared to expose the creaking party machine to another such test.

All London honored the runner-up. The gallant Captain Nicholson marched into the House rather unnoticed, if in excellent order. Churchill had not felt the joy of battle so intensely since Omdurman. He knew he had fought for a good cause; in fact the interlude of this little by-election contained all the elements that were to fix his attitude from now on: the fight against plebeian radicalism, resistance to the feeble-mindedly powerful party machine, no more experiments of radical Governments, redoubled enthusiasm for Merry Old England. Against all tradition the better part of England followed him enthusiastically. Tomorrow it would be all England.

He wrote no more books now, painted no more landscapes. He did not even lay bricks. He actually reduced his hip measurement somewhat—a sign of his revived vitality. He accepted dozens of invitations to speak. At about that time he estimated that he had so far delivered six thousand speeches, more or less. But what he delivered to his listeners now was really more like sermons than speeches. Good-humored sermons, no doubt, not obscure and heavy stuff. His oratory rose to unparalleled heights. He galvanized the King's old-fashioned English. He appealed to common sense and unpretentious patriotism.

In Liverpool he urged all reasonable people to coöperate with the Conservatives in the interest of the country and of defeating Socialism. Mr. Baldwin gave him a friendly welcome. That was simple enough now. Even for the crucial question of protectionism an amicable formula could be found. Churchill remained what he had always been, a free trader, but with qualified acquiescence in the principle of imperial preference. With this a burden that he had borne for twenty years fell from his shoulders. The other questions made no more hard feelings. Churchill was the stoutest of the fighters against Bolshevism. He warned the Mac-

Donald Government against treading in the footsteps of its Red competitors. When the Government began considering a plan to abandon the building of a naval base at Singapore, long since approved, Churchill insisted on letting the nation decide.

It is notorious that Czechoslovakia was rather remote from the English. Singapore is closer to that nation of old salts and sea-dogs. The smell of ocean is in their nostrils. Mr. Mac-Donald was turned out; the Conservatives won an overwhelming success. Now they no longer needed Churchill and his "Constitutionalists." But Mr. Baldwin did not want to lose his tower of strength. He offered Churchill a sure seat in Epping, the same that he still represents. "Amid the glades of Epping," said Churchill, "I found a resting-place which will last me, I hope, as long as I am concerned with mundane affairs." He returned to the House as a full-fledged Conservative member. Baldwin made him Chancellor of the Exchequer. In this the old chess-player made a splendid move. His second master move was to be made against Churchill's intention—sweeping the King from the board.

In 1924 Churchill stepped into Lord Randolph's shoes. In the meantime he had held more Cabinet posts than any other living man. But it was only when he took the black robe of the Chancellor from the tin box where it had lain for forty-eight years that his goal was reached. Could his father look down and see him?

CHAPTER XXII

Credo

THE Treasury is England's Holy Grail. Worldly-wise priests guard the sanctuary. Poverty, unpretentiousness and anonymity are their three mighty weapons. Millions in gold, the chessman on the board, are moved with a sure hand. Not a breath of gold dust clings to those hands. They go to third-class restaurants for lunch, and get a new business suit every third year so that their sons can go to Public Schools and some day lunch in their turn at third-class restaurants. They smile as they read of the financial geniuses of the City, who do not get past the anterooms of the Treasury offices, and they remain taciturn when some new apostle arises to distribute this world's goods more justly. So far as the gentlemen of the Treasury are concerned, their job is to prepare the budget. Then England will be another year further on.

How would Winston Churchill, to whom the name of publicity-hound and self-advertiser still clung, and who radiated such a brilliant light all about, fit into these drab surroundings? To the general surprise he settled in very nicely. In a few weeks he mastered the difficult and unaccustomed secret language of the Treasury. This man who had always avoided doing the simplest sums was quickly at home in finance. His own bills had given him a headache all his life. Now he worked out a careful State budget. After joining in reparations discussions at Paris, he introduced his first budget.

It included a return to the gold standard. This measure has been much criticized. It was not his own idea, but followed the recommendations of expert committees set up under the previous administration. Nevertheless the sin of the gold standard long pursued him. Churchill had lost another Dardanelles.

In addition the budget imposed a duty on silk; death duties were increased; the McKenna duties on motor cars and pianos revived; and a small tax was put on imported hops. Both income tax and supertax were slightly reduced. Reaching this part of his report, the Chancellor duly apologized to the House before picking up a glass of wine.

The House applauded gaily, perhaps a bit enviously. Churchill smiled. His eyes sought the Distinguished Visitors' Gallery, where his wife, his eldest daughter Sarah, and his son Randolph were sitting.

In the ranks of the Labor Opposition there arose a lean figure in ill-fitting Sunday-go-to-meeting suit, and a voice creaked "Shame! Shame on you!" It was the Member from his old constituency of Dundee, Mr. Scrimgeour. The Prohibitionist protested in holy zeal against this spectacle—a Chancellor of the Exchequer indulging in wine in the midst of his budget speech!

Mr. Scrimgeour's own party associates had to quiet him. Then there arose from among them the hunchback Philip Snowden, who had been the first Socialist Chancellor of England under Mac-Donald's regime. Mr. Snowden, crippled by an accident in youth, a dwarfish man with a white mask of a face from which two excessively large eyes flashed blue fire, was one of the most feared Parliamentary warriors. "This is the worst rich man's budget of recent times!" His words whistled like a whip. "You have changed your views in taxing silk imports!"

Here was the same old argument again: you are changing your views, Mr. Churchill! You are a renegade, a traitor! All your life the chorus of revenge will pursue you!

Churchill replied: "There is nothing wrong in changing, if in the right direction."

"You are an authority on that!" the hunchback retorted.

A lady got up in the Distinguished Visitors' Gallery. She left as quietly as possible. She could not stand listening.

At this Churchill, fixing his adversary with his eye, said with the unshakable certainty of a man who has long since thought everything out for himself: "To improve is to change. To be perfect is to have changed often."

It was odd, but Philip Snowden said nothing, although a debater of his skill must have had many easy retorts at his command. Perhaps he had premonitions. He too was soon to change. When he entered the National Government he was to split from head to toe with a single gesture the Socialist-Labour Party, whose chief architect he had been for more than thirty years. Then England would have a second "arch-traitor.'

Lloyd George could not be silent. Churchill had grown beyond him. The budget must suffer for that. In the name of the Leftist Liberals he mercilessly attacked item after item. But Mr. Walter, later Lord Runciman, Churchill's successful election opponent years before, now defended the Chancellor with equal vehemence on behalf of the Rightist Liberals. Factional wrangling was all that remained of Gladstone's great legacy.

The social tensions, the sickness of the generation between wars, were expressed more and more sharply in debate. "It is to the common interest to make sure that there is not growing up a general habit of qualifying for unemployment insurance," Churchill said. With these words he put his finger on the sore point. Years before, when he was appealing for the votes of the Oldham textile workers, he would not have talked like this.

The Honorable Member for Dundee, Mr. Scrimgeour, did not miss the opportunity to point it out. He flew into screaming hysterics. Old Lansbury, the father of pacifism—the same who spent his last years in propaganda for subjugation to Hitler, the Leader—seconded him at the top of his lungs. Churchill could no longer make himself heard; the Opposition simply shouted him down. Finally Mr. Saklatvala, the Parsee Communist Member, got the floor. Of course nobody listened to his endless tirade. And so the House gradually quieted down. The coffee-colored Comrade was able to conclude with the proud words: "The Chancellor of the Exchequer having failed, it falls to me, a Communist revolutionary, to restore order."

This was the state of democracy, this the state of the parliamentary system in April of 1925, when Mr. Adolf Hitler, just released from his vacation (entitled "honorable arrest") at Landsberg, began to arm for the great offensive. In England they were breaking one another's heads over the silk tax. In Germany *Mein Kampf* was published.

Churchill was perhaps the only man, certainly the only world figure, who openly told where the cause of all confusion lay, the source of all dangers. His instinct, proved hitherto in his sure feeling for people and for the central point of a problem, brought him cosmic perception now that he had passed fifty. He saw that humanity was at the crossroads. "Mankind," as he put it, "has never been in this position before."

His minutely detailed office work at the Treasury left Churchill time to write three essays that should have stirred the world. Instead, only a small circle ever knew about them. The first, "Shall we all commit suicide?", appeared in 1925. This was the period that confused exhaustion with peace. "Let it not be thought for a moment that the danger of another explosion in Europe is past," Churchill warned. And with those words began his desperate, single-handed, fourteen-year struggle for England's soul and power of vision.

Today his own people is reverent, the whole civilized world astonished and admiring as they look back on the achievement of those fourteen bitter years when an aging man, born to gaiety, joyous life and comradeship, but banned by fate to the solitary heights of insight, was swimming against the current. Churchill was the only one who could read the signs of the times. Not only their outer appearance, but their deeper causes. Not only did he see through the figures on the world stage with his invariable penetration, he realized the dark forces that made little men into great lords. From about his fiftieth year onward Churchill, with three lives already behind him, passed for old-fashioned, remote from the times. It is only now, in his patriarchal years, which he carries with youthful vim, that they realize that he alone could solve the puzzles of the age.

In "Shall we all commit suicide?" he warns that "Russia will brood incessantly upon the wars of Peter the Great." Fourteen years later, after the signature of the Pact of Moscow, which opened the road to cheap and unhampered expansion for Bolshevism, Stalin claimed the laurels of the new Peter.

In the same essay Churchill called attention to "the soul of Germany, smouldering with dreams of a War of Liberation or Revenge." This was the time of Stresemann, of Franco-German rapprochement ("From one end of Germany to the other an intense hatred of France unites the whole nation," declares Churchill)—what the optimists expected to be the birth of a new Europe. Stresemann himself was a good European, and fought passionately for his faith. But Winston Churchill at Chartwell Manor understood the profoundest urges, the abysses of the German soul, better than Stresemann in the Chancellery at Berlin. Churchill knew—and put down in his essay—what was really going on under the German surface. It was science gone mad in the hands of demon-ridden masses.

"If science ran amuck," Churchill declared, "it must necessarily lead to the destruction of mankind." Not that he did not realize the blessings of science. No one understood better than he how infinitely its fruits have raised the living standard of the broad masses. But he feared its curse if it should get into the wrong hands. And he saw it in those hands. It sounds like a premonition of Hitler's much-publicized "secret devices" when Churchill talks about the war of electricity, of explosives—probably guided automatically in flying machines—of diseases.

In "Mass Effects in Modern Life," the second of these essays, he welcomes the age of mass production and social progress, but he questions its effects upon national character and psychology. Out of the age of mass production is born the mass age, which finds its expression in the Bolshevik social structure. And soon he was to realize that this is but a preliminary stage of the Nazi ant state.

Whither does the road lead out of the dilemma mankind is in? Churchill did not undertake to answer this last question. His is an analytical mind, not a speculative genius. He contents himself with examining this happy yet shocking progress—he is more clearly conscious than the young people of how swiftly the world is changing—and he opens wide the windows for a view of "Fifty Years Hence." This is the title of the third essay. Here he predicts a swifter change of conditions of life, owing to rapid scientific advancement, than those changes the world has already experienced. Nuclear energy, he foresees, will largely replace muscular energy; geography and climate will obey human orders. He has just seen *R. U. R.*, the Czech dramatist Karel Čapek's fantasy of robots, at a London theatre. The play had made a profound impression all over the world. It struck Churchill not as a mere fantasy, but as an immediate danger arising from the combination of science and agnosticism. A few years later the robot state had become a reality—in the heart of Europe.

Would Democracy be able to keep pace with the developing power of the robot state? Churchill is every inch the archetype of the nineteenth-century parliamentarian. Nevertheless he realizes with agonizing clarity that the parliaments of all the democratic states are a failure. They don't represent even a fraction of the strength and wisdom of the community, he declares, and their democratic governments drift along the lines of least resistance.

Opposed to this he saw the menacing creation of a new order of states whose power by far exceeded the intelligence of its human raw material, while the intelligence of this raw material exceeded its own nobility.

Here in a few vigorous strokes is the complete picture of the Nazi man and Nazi society that Churchill hears pounding on the door, demanding admittance and the overlordship of the world to boot. He knows we are too helpless, too disunited, too sordid to defend ourselves. Are we to become as they are?

By no means! No one feels the weakness of democracy more painfully than Churchill, but no one more passionately and unyieldingly defends the one sort of life in which a man can walk with his head erect. In those years long ago he uttered what a democracy fighting for its life, quite despairing of its survival, and already banished from the European Continent is gradually beginning to realize in its unspeakable agony, though still far from completely: Democracy is a function of morality, living with it and expiring without it.

"Mercy, Pity, Peace and Love!" is what Churchill demands if the world is not to perish.

He had gone upward from horseman to statesman, from fortune's darling to one who despised success. At fifty Winston Churchill was solely a warrior for mankind, for the Son of God.

CHAPTER XXIII

Elder Statesman

No man is a prophet in his own country. His cry for contemplation and self-searching echoed unheard. But when he presented his second budget, providing for a tax on betting, Winston Churchill's name was once again the battle-cry of the country. The Englishman's most sacred possession was at stake.

The Tories, the ones after all who would have to put the budget through the House, would much have preferred to evade the responsibility. It was a venerable institution that the Chancellor was now laying his heavy hand on. Was it sensible to have brought back to office and authority so incalculable a disturber of the peace? Why, tomorrow he would be introducing a cricket tax! He was always talking muddled stuff about the present turning-point in our world.

The Socialists noisily complained that Churchill was a reactionary exploiter trying to deprive the little man of his one pleasure. The last Liberals turned their backs when Churchill passed by their sadly shrunken benches. They were holier than he.

This time the parties really expressed the popular feeling. An inundation of protesting letters poured into the Treasury. A particularly large number of women wrote. They threatened simply to give up betting. And what would become of England then?

Churchill had a form reply prepared: "I am sure that though the revenues might lose on the fruits of your operations, they will gain by their increased usefulness in other directions." In general he grinned merrily at the hurricane he had raised. Apparently peace was not fated to be his. Not even peace with the spirits of the past. Lord Randolph would certainly have hated to see his famous mare, Abesse de Jouarre, taxed, and what Grandfather Jerome, the King of the American Turf, must have been thinking in his grave was better left unsaid. But when Churchill was Chancellor, he worked for just one boss, the tax-collector. Again one of "Winston's follies" was merely the expression of his absolute sense of duty.

The uproar over the tax on betting, which the Conservative majority duly passed, had not yet died down when the new earthquake shook England. The General Strike of 1926 broke out. Not since the first World War had the United Kingdom been so close to the abyss. The wage disputes in the mines, with which the trouble began, were more than a fight over working hours and rates of pay. Churchill realized that the whole structural weakness of England in the post-war period was here laid bare. The country's coal-mining was simply no longer profitable. The mine-owners were paying out so heavily that they could not maintain the pits. The Government had reached the limit of its capacity to subsidize if it was to keep the budget in balance. The workers, the more fortunate of them, got starvation wages. Most were without work. The famous British coal, the best in the world, found no buyers.

Churchill strained every nerve to bring the quarreling parties together. Tirelessly he played the part of the honest broker. It was a wearying experience; not since the Irish negotiations had he had so difficult a task. But all in vain. Socialistic influences exploited the distress of the mining districts to stir up all the workers in the country against the system. The first Labor Government had lasted but a short time before public displeasure at the polls turned it out. Perhaps this was the chance to reëstablish Socialism, this time without putting democratic methods of election to work.

For a little while the bulk of British labor followed the agitators. But the citizenry in general showed a starch in its backbone that had been painfully missing for years. Under Mr. Baldwin's leadership, resolute for once, the public was mobilized to keep factories and transport facilities going and to stave off anarchy. It was a question of will-power. Churchill was convinced that the first necessity was to keep the public informed, so as to maintain and strengthen its determination.

The newspapers were included in the General Strike, and had to cease publication. Only the *Times* put out a two-page emergency edition. So the Chancellor of the Exchequer took over an editor's desk. He produced the *British Gazette,* a fighting, crusading sheet; there has never been an official organ like it. Churchill himself chose, rejected, wrote the articles. Every line, from leader to the smallest note, was submitted to him. On its second day of publication the paper had a paid circulation of three million copies. Till a recent attempt in New York it was the first great modern newspaper able to subsist on circulation alone without advertising. Churchill was inordinately proud. He had always known that he was really born to be a journalist.

But of course it was too late now. After his strenuous exertions Churchill gradually began to feel that we all get old. When the General Strike collapsed he took a short vacation, and went to Rome. The Duce received the illustrious visitor. Whether the familiar operatic scene that Mussolini runs off like clockwork for all his visitors—the vast, empty studio where he receives; the high chair on which the great man sits, the low one where the guest must be seated; the tempestuous handshaking that tries to seem powerful and is merely frantic; and all the rest of it—made any special impression on Churchill is something that will never be known. He called himself "a critical admirer" of the Duce when he left the Palazzo Venezia. Of course the Reds at home concluded he had gone over to Fascism.

His holiday trip took him on to Egypt. Churchill spent a few weeks on quite different things, which he has always considered the best vacation. The weary man spent six hours a day painting the Pyramids, and another six reading the proofs of *The World Crisis,* Volumes Three and Four. Just so that he heard nothing more about the strike, and nothing about the tax on betting!

On the way back he could not resist an excursion to Monte Carlo. He had hardly entered the Casino before he ran into a prosperous acquaintance from London, a bookmaker. "You have ruined my business with that betting tax of yours!" The world had caught him again.

His 1927 budget raised him again to the summit of success. The acclaim that welcomed it was universal. Only a slight increase in the whiskey duty gave Mr. Scrimgeour, the Prohibitionist, a chance for one of his exhibitions. Not a soul in the House took it seriously, not even his own comrades. A high-pitched feminine voice did go up from one seat on the Conservative benches. The noble Lady Nancy Astor, Virginia-born, evidently wanted to transplant the dry laws of her old homeland to the new one. She fired a barrage of interjections at the Chancellor.

Churchill stood patiently under this fire. Then he returned it: "I have great regard and respect for the noble lady. But I do not think we are likely to learn much from the liquor legislation of the United States."

There was a storm of laughter in the House. Europe just then was flooded with true tales of Prohibition.

"Why not?" was all that Lady Astor could think of to reply. She obviously did not enjoy being worsted in debate. From now on she showed scant sympathy for Winston Churchill. He was well advised not to show his face at her hospitable country house, in later years the home of the Cliveden Set, the appeasers' headquarters.

Churchill's humorous allusion to the nonsense of Prohibition was of course no reflection on America. In that very year, 1927, he took occasion to refer to the common destiny of the English-speaking peoples, whose coöperation he expected to defend civilization. When the troubles in Shanghai reached their height, Churchill said: "I felt a strong feeling of sentiment when I saw in the newspapers yesterday that the Coldstream Guards and the U. S. Marines are standing there side by side. It looked to me as if, once again, the great unconquerable forces of progressive and scientific civilization were recognizing all they have in common and all they will have to face in common." At the same time he displayed the U. S. Distinguished Service Medal that had been presented to him by General Pershing. Churchill is the only Englishman to wear it.

It looked now as if Churchill would be Chancellor for life. Fate was being kind to him. The son was enjoying what had been withheld from the father. Even the Conservative rebel was once more acknowledged by the Party. In the summer of 1927 Mr. Baldwin addressed a mammoth meeting of the Primrose League at Albert Hall. The Prime Minister recalled his youthful appreciation when Lord Randolph Churchill, "the distinguished father of our principal speaker today, struck again that Disraelian note to which we then dedicated our lives."

Winston Churchill had to catch his breath for a moment before he started to speak. He was now delivering something like his eight-thousandth public address, and there were other achievements and successes to his credit, but this was the greatest evening of his life. Tory England and the beloved shade were reconciled. Peace descended upon the old warrior.

For two years more it was yet fated to be his: two years without storm and struggle, at least without visible disturbance on the surface. His management of the Treasury was, on the whole, unopposed. The parliamentary struggles of those days were mainly within the limits of the usual war between frogs and mice. Of course the ruling Tory Government was gradually wearing itself out in the process. Democratic peoples demand a change of cast on their political stage.

At the General Election of the year 1929 the specious domestic peace was shattered by the mildest, the softest-spoken gentleman in the country. Mr. Ramsay MacDonald staged a comeback. He won at the polls. He had long ceased to be the conscientious objector, the pacifist, the organizer of the dissatisfied and underprivileged who had built up the Socialist Labor Party with the help of Philip Snowden. Through forty years of public life Mac-

Donald had grown into tradition and the traditional atmosphere. The glamour of old England appealed to him irresistibly. With the naked eye you could not tell the good-looking, well-groomed old man, who was a Christian philosopher in the evening of his life, from a Tory.

But the Tory regime was done with only for the moment. Smiling peaceably, altogether reconciled with the world, Churchill stowed away his father's black robe again in the tin box where it had lain waiting so patiently for many years. Together with his Conservative colleagues in the Cabinet he resigned to make way for the new lords of Labor. He bore them no ill-will. For Mac-Donald he showed a great deal of human understanding, even liking. In a brilliant pen portrait he depicted the old Labor leader, "who has seen life at close quarters, although he would have liked to have viewed it from afar." He paid full personal tribute to the man, who remained all his life a rabble-rouser, yet was always hounded by the rabble. He understood that what Mac-Donald, ripened and matured with the years, wanted was simply tranquillity, the tranquillity of English parks, cultivated table conversation, recognized conventions, and he knew that Socialist agitators who have made their peace with the world are the best quasi-Tory Ministers.

Nevertheless Churchill never forgot for a moment that the time was too serious and the responsibility too great.

Downing Street was not a spot of tranquil retirement. No. 10 needed a vigorous, energetic, driving master. Churchill saw through the smoke-screen of apparent European peace. The self-preservation of the Empire was a question of will-power. In weak hands the reins must drag disastrously. But for his part he was weary of inner struggles. He must be sparing of his own strength. He might be needing it again.

Churchill noiselessly took his leave. No loud-voiced wrangles accompanied his retirement. There were no fanfares as the crusader sheathed his sword. Churchill simply took a vacation. He

THE CHURCHILLS ON THEIR VOYAGE TO AMERICA
Mr. and Mrs. Winston Churchill and daughter Diana

went to Canada to get his lungs full of fresh air and to paint the Rocky Mountains.

After twenty years in Liberal and Conservative Governments and in coalition Cabinets, after holding more state posts than any other man, he was now England's elder statesman. He had not retired from politics, but he was in the second line, no longer in the public view. The voters of Epping kept faith with him. His reëlection when Mr. Baldwin appealed again to the country was a personal tribute to Churchill, not a national matter.

For himself he cast up a gently melancholy balance, in another essay written for the *Strand*. It was, he concludes, a happy and vivid life, full of interest. But he would not like to live it again.

He was a wise man now. In addition he was the country squire of Chartwell Manor, and a man who lived in the past. He wrote the biography of his ancestor, the first Duke of Marlborough— and once again it was a masterpiece of English historiography. He drew himself up erect, leaning on the greatness of the old country. He had always been a progressive spirit, never a worshipper of the past. But the time that was now approaching was one he did not really fit into. He analyzed it with penetrating acuteness. The more clearly he saw the signs of the times, the less at ease he felt in this present period. "The exhaustion that resulted from the war," he recognized, "is not merely economic, but psychic, moral and mental." He needed another breath of fresh air. And so he crossed the Atlantic once more. He went to America on a lecture tour.

Churchill arrived in New York harbor aboard the *Europa* on December 11, 1931. Reporters crowded around him on the sundeck of the ship. He was amiable and ready with information for all his colleagues. The reporters took the word "colleagues" for one of the customary phrases with which great men pat them on the back. They were wrong. Whenever Churchill came in contact with newspaper men he felt that he had really missed his vocation. Of course he was cautious about what he said in a foreign country. "The crisis that afflicts us is not political. It is an economic condition." It is hard to pull the wool over the eyes of New York ship-news reporters. He spoke "with a twinkle in his eye," a gentleman from the *New York Times* remarked.

When he talked of Anglo-American coöperation his restraint altogether left him. "The coöperation of the two great English-speaking nations is the only hope to bring the world back to the pathway of peace and prosperity. There is one thing we can be sure of: wherever the pathway leads, we shall travel more securely if we do it together like good companions."

His first public lecture, on "The Destiny of the English-Speaking People," was set for December 14 in the Brooklyn Academy of Arts and Music. Churchill went to spend the preceding evening with Bernard M. Baruch. He got out of the car, crossed Fifth Avenue between 66th and 67th Streets, and was run down by a taxi. "It's my fault!" he managed to say.

Mario Contasino, hack-driver, 300 Yonkers Avenue, thus made his appearance in history. The tabloids printed his picture and his account of the accident. It agreed with Churchill's own statement. The latter insisted on taking all the blame. He was accustomed to English left-hand traffic, and consequently had walked blindly into the car, which was moving quite properly on the right. Why had he rushed across Fifth Avenue at such frantic speed? He shrugged his shoulders. Must he try to explain that all England called him "the old man in a hurry"?

At one o'clock in the morning Dr. Pickhardt issued the first bulletin at the Lenox Hill Hospital: the patient has a sprained right shoulder, causing slight discomfort, with lacerations on the forehead and nose. Now since childhood the right shoulder had been Churchill's weak point. Recovery from his new injury was no simple matter. A slight attack of pleurisy in the right chest complicated it. The patient had to be given three thousand units of anti-tetanus serum. His temperature rose to 100.6.

Meanwhile the telephone rang incessantly. London calling, London calling. The King enquired. Fleet Street asked questions without pause. After a few hours cables had to be brought into the room in laundry-baskets. The faithful Thompson of Scotland Yard, once more standing guard at the door, searched these laundry-baskets most methodically. He had seen enough in the films about the ruses of American reporters. And no guests were admitted. Only Mr. Bernard Baruch and Mr. George Eustis Corcoran were allowed in for a moment.

The one most frantically excited was Mario Contasino, the hack-driver, although he was immediately exonerated. When he learned who the gentleman was who had run into his cab, he set up a real Italian—or at least Yonkers Italian—aria of despair. He finally calmed down a little when Churchill shook hands with him. The handshake too of course appeared in the tabloids. The newspapers reported that Mr. Churchill had given the Contasino family an inscribed copy of his latest book as a sign that there were no hard feelings even over a hairbreadth escape from death—how many did that make in his charmed life? All Yonkers Avenue was wild with enthusiasm. So was New York. The lecture tour through the United States, which Churchill resumed after a couple of weeks' delay, was an extraordinary success. It was the last unspoiled pleasure in his life.

CHAPTER XXIV

The Road to Hitler

IF any definite point can be established at which England's sickness passed over into a death-agony, future historians will probably choose the 25th of August, 1931, the day when the first National Government was formed, and Messrs. MacDonald and Baldwin took joint power. The ailment that hitherto had endangered the country's eyes now also affected its heart and its brain.

Mr. MacDonald was a well-meaning man. He dealt with the distresses of the times by telling a deputation from the Churches, which waited on him: "I hope you will go on pressing and pressing and pressing. Do help us to do the broad, just, fundamental, eternal thing." He did not describe this "thing" any more exactly. In the sphere of disarmament, which now dominated the international discussion, just as on domestic matters, particularly unemployment, the world's second worry, the Prime Minister was always carefully muddy, ambiguous, vague. He wanted to hurt no one. He wanted to suffer no hurt. He was a humanitarian, a very weak one.

The Disarmament Conference dragged on and on. Meanwhile, on September 18, Japan seized Mukden, and on February 18, 1932, proclaimed the establishment of the Manchurian puppet state. Sir John Simon, Foreign Secretary in the National Government, refused to take any practical steps, although for the first and last time in the post-war period America would have been willing to coöperate. Manchuria was far away, and that France too would one day go Manchu, along with the rest of the European Continent, was something that the much-admired "keen legal brain" of Sir John Simon could not foresee.

On April 10, 1932, Field-Marshal von Hindenburg was re-elected by 19,300,000 votes against the lance-corporal, Hitler, who had but 13,400,000, as President of the German Reich. London celebrated this peace-time victory for the loser of the World War as its own triumph. The German people, which, sad to say, had been creating some disturbance in the last few years, was splendidly rehabilitated. The English sense of fair play could of course no longer refuse the Teutons equality of armament with France. The French Government was put under severe pressure from London to disarm at a rapid pace.

Now not Germany was the trouble-maker, but Churchill again. The old fighting-cock, reappearing from his retreat at Chartwell Manor, made use of the Debate on the Adjournment on May 13 to present to his colleagues in the House a very simple truth. He asked those who would like to see Germany and France on equal footing in armaments, "Do you wish for war?"

Even then—in May, 1932!—he foresaw the Moscow-Berlin axis, and gave warning of "the great mass of Russia," likewise feverishly preparing for war.

The speech had but one effect: Churchill was branded as hopelessly old-fashioned. If he were to warn people of Germany or of Russia alone, all right: some basis of discussion with Right or Left might possibly be found. But in attacking both radical wings he was definitely turning against the spirit of the times. Too bad about the old warrior who could not disentangle himself from the World War!

Anyone who wanted to be fashionable at that time was touched at least with a rosy pink. The young gentlemen who would soon be Junior Cabinet Members resolved at the Oxford Union "that this house will in no circumstances fight for King and Country." On the other hand the people who had arrived, and who could smile at such innocent youthful pranks, knew that the enemy was within. It was lucky that the German block lay between their own coal-miners and Moscow. Mr. MacDonald, who had once organized the miners, was no longer dangerous. He was welcomed in the best houses.

The social revolution was brewing among nations without work, and everywhere demagogic quacks were ready to satisfy with witchcraft the hunger for which there was no regular medicine. Meanwhile the relations among members of good society continued undisturbed. British Lordships spent their week-ends at the pompous, over-decorated, vulgar villas of Rhenish Westphalian heavy-industrialists. The palatial home of Fritz Thyssen in particular was a favorite meeting-place of London clubmen. The palatial home was bankrupt from ridgepole to cellar. Dr. Brüning's government had to buy up the steel shares, Thyssen's fortune, at four times the market value to prevent a catastrophic financial scandal. Then the last, pig-headed liberal Chancellor of the Republic refused to toss the taxpayers' millions that he had spent for the shares back into the old owner's maw. A new trust was founded, in which Mr. Fritz Thyssen had but a very small share.

Consequently Brüning had to go. Under Thyssen's leadership, German heavy industry jockeyed him out. As their tool they used Mr. Adolf Hitler, "an excellent man, the one bulwark against Bolshevism," in Fritz Thyssen's own words. The industrialists had raised three million marks for his previous election campaign. For the sake of accuracy it must be remarked that the contribution made to the Fuehrer by Italy, by Mussolini personally, in order to liberate Germany was a good deal larger even than this. Goebbels now had the money for his propaganda machine, which had been penniless. The industrialists bought for old von Hindenburg the family castle of his ancestors, Castle Neudeck in East Prussia. They presented it to him as a "National gift of honor" and thus got him out of Berlin. The coast was clear.

In one last clumsy attempt to keep the reins in his own hands, the aged Hindenburg on June 3, 1932, appointed Chancellor his personal favorite Franz von Papen. Mr. von Papen looked like a gray-haired playboy, and became the Judas of Germany.

When he came into power little was known of him except that during the World War he had plotted and directed bombings in America, and that he had squandered the fortune of his wife, a member of the rich Saarland manufacturing family of Villeroy-Boch.

People in London did begin to get a little nervous when they found themselves confronted for the first time with a self-styled "National Government" in Germany. Mr. MacDonald and Sir John Simon set off uneasily for the Lausanne Conference, where the first meeting took place. At Lausanne, incidentally, a pathetic, undersized figure tried to get hold of them for a conference—Dr. Engelbert Dollfuss. Neither Sir John nor the well-groomed Prime Minister had any time for the midget Chancellor of Austria. They were under the spell of Mr. von Papen.

Franz von Papen in turn had little time for the English statesmen. He arrived, indeed, with a long list of wants headed by the total cancellation of the reparations, but he spent his days riding, swimming, motor-boating. He also spoke English better than any tourist guide in Paris, French at least as well as the headwaiter at the Savoy. He was irresistible.

Within a short time he had accomplished the formal cancellation of reparations. This was no great trick; as a matter of fact Dr. Brüning with his last strength had already gained this concession for Germany. The Nationalist Papen had only to collect for his Liberal predecessor.

On July 11 MacDonald and Sir John returned from Lausanne. All the Cabinet Members were drawn up like a row of Grenadiers at the station. Crowds cheered in the streets. In the House even the Socialist Opposition applauded the settlement. All England was jubilant now that poor Germany need no longer be bled white by extortion. There was only a small balance of three billion marks—on paper.

"In a few months the amount will not be worth three marks!" Hitler, already in Papen's time the moving impulse behind the German Government, had made the statement, and Churchill quoted it in the House on the very day of MacDonald's and Sir John Simon's "triumphal" return from Lausanne. The day is remarkable for another reason as well. On that day Winston Churchill embarked upon his violent career of speech-making—of warning Government and Parliament, England and the world, against the war Adolf Hitler was about to unloose. The last war, Churchill insisted, had by no means broken the Teutonic spirit of aggression. It had not been ended with any "Carthaginian" peace, and all talk of "bleeding Germany white" by the victors was pure rubbish. In fact the loans Germany had received, particularly from America and England, amounted to twice as much as the reparations had cost her. Since it was very clear that Germany showed no desire ever to repay her loans, the economic consequences, at least, of Versailles were a bargain indeed for the Reich.

From now on he was always to hew to the same line. Six months later, on November 23, 1932, he repeated his argument. He spoke without prejudice; as a matter of fact he delivered few public speeches until the outbreak of the second World War in which he did not express his admiration for German ability, and his desire to give this great nation justice and an equal opportunity. He was, however, the first man in England—and for years the only one—to realize that the Germans were concerned not with justice and equal opportunity, but with world power. This time he quoted exact figures. Germany had paid since the war an indemnity of about one thousand million sterling, but she borrowed in the same time about two thousand million. What was she doing with this surplus money? She was rearming.

From then until the present moment the specter of German rearmament has never been absent from his sight. It pursued him in his dreams. It lent wings to his every word. It weighed heavy upon his soul—and at the same time it spurred him to new achievements. During the years when the triumph of Nazism was announcing its coming, and then immediately afterward setting out on the road, Churchill believed that it was the last duty of his life to shout, "England, awake!" That he himself would be called

THE CHURCHILLS LEAVING BOURNEMOUTH, 1935

Mr. and Mrs. Winston Churchill with their son Randolph

to turn the words into action was a hope that he surrendered resignedly, but with spirit undaunted.

"Britain's hour of weakness is Europe's hour of danger!" he cried to the House.

Here he paused. That moment will remain unforgettable to everyone who attended that memorable session of Parliament. Mr. MacDonald's head was deeply bowed. Perhaps he was communing with his conscience. Or perhaps he was only having a little nap. It was so hot in the overcrowded chamber, and Churchill's voice went on slowly with monotonous hammer blows, without shrill accents. Perhaps he was talking the Prime Minister to sleep. But perhaps too he would shake England from her slumber. He looked around the chamber. The members were listening to him spellbound. True, it was rather with interest than with an expression of allegiance. "They are taking him more seriously now that he does not take himself so very seriously any longer," whispered a voice in the Press Gallery.

Mr. Baldwin, the Lord President, who pulled the strings of the puppet MacDonald, gazed expressionlessly into space. His own eyes were empty. Had he in secret already abdicated? A week before, Baldwin had said to English youth: "When the next war comes and European civilization is wiped out, as it will be, then do not let them lay the blame upon the old men. Let them remember that youth principally and alone is responsible for the terrors that have fallen on the earth." And yet there was not a single youthful face on the Government bench. The puppeteer could not drop the strings from his stiffening fingers. His face was still round and red. A year later people would begin to notice that he too occasionally fell asleep in the midst of parliamentary business. But his face would still stare out round and red from the high collar.

The seat next to the Prime Minister was empty. Foreign Secretary Sir John Simon was conspicuously absent. Churchill was a second-string speaker, or rather a third- or fourth-string speaker. He no longer had to be shown the honor of ministerial attention.

He spoke for no group and no party. He spoke merely for common sense.

Not only the Prime Minister and the Lord President were asleep in England. England was asleep. Now events in Germany began to tread on one another's heels. On the 2nd of December General von Schleicher was appointed Chancellor of the Reich. On January 27 he finally summoned the resolution to stave off the Nazi terror by a military dictatorship supported by all the parliamentary parties, prominent among them coöperative Nazi elements. But when the Field-Marshal-President sent for him next day, von Schleicher was not the savior of Germany, but the typical barrack-yard general clicking his heels smartly before the senile but senior officer, and accepting his dismissal without a word. Two days later Hitler was appointed Chancellor. A hundred thousand brownshirts marched into the Wilhelmsplatz. They cheered Hitler. When Hindenburg allowed himself to be pushed on to the balcony, a burst of laughter from many thousand throats received him. Taking it for the love of the people, he waved with a trembling gesture. Hitler, standing beside him, caught the bloodless hand as Hindenburg was about to raise it for the second time. Whose business was it now to wave good-bye? The State Secretary to the Marshal-President, Dr. Meissner, led the aged man off the balcony: "It is cool outside, Your Excellency!" Hitler at once took into his own service the resourceful State Secretary, who had originated in the Social-Democratic Party. In one night 8,000 people committed suicide in the city of Berlin alone. American papers printed front-page photographs showing the delirious joy of the German people. During the first week of the Third Reich 500,000 people landed in concentration camps that had sprung up overnight. The Reichstag went up in flames. In spite of this stunt the Nazis did not get a majority in the elections, which was a matter of complete indifference to Mr. Hitler. Early one sleepless morning he signed the order for general conscription; it must only be kept for a short while in his desk drawer.

In the House of Commons the Under Secretary for Air, Sir

Philip Sassoon, praised the importance of the Royal Air Force: they were most useful in combating the locust pest and in carrying blankets and other stores to certain stricken areas. Nevertheless the Air Estimates had unfortunately to be reduced. For 1933 they were £342,000 less than for 1932, and over £100,000,000 less than for 1931.

Mr. Baldwin felt that there was something not quite right about the way things were going. He delivered a speech on the bombing of open towns and the murdering of women and children. It would certainly be done, he assumed. And he was very sorry indeed that there was no remedy. Retaliation might be an answer, but not a defense. He spoke in a helpless, hopeless mood. At bottom he did not want to meddle in the affair. That was the department of his Air Minister, the Marquess of Londonderry, soon to win a peculiar world fame as England's pro-Nazi No. 1.

To the Socialists the Marquess of Londonderry was an "Ulster reactionary" of the worst sort (he actually had large estates in Northern Ireland), but the proposal that he put forward at the Geneva disarmament conference enjoyed the undivided approval of the Reds. Defeatism made strange bedfellows. Londonderry's suggestion was that the air forces of all the world should be reduced to England's level—at that time England had the fifth air armada in the world—and then all the countries were to take another step down together to the extent of 33.3 per cent. Churchill replied to his childish proposal with a savage smile. Did the Secretary of State seriously believe that the other powers would agree to such a proposition? Ought they not to be able to rise quite to the level of British comprehension?

Churchill smiled at the House. There is such a thing as a holy rage that can be expressed only with a grin. We know Churchill when the vein in his forehead begins to stand out a little, and his teeth are bared, when he speaks with a gentle voice: "We ought not to deal in humbug. We ought to deal in airplanes." Then he added, prophetically, "The sea perhaps is no longer complete security for our island development; it must be the air too."

Churchill delivered that speech on March 14, 1933. Six weeks of Nazism had convinced him that there was but one answer to Hitler: the air. Six years of Nazism convinced England that there was but one answer to Churchill: to call him gadfly.

CHAPTER XXV

The Road to England

THE startled flock in the European poultry-yard fluttered about, led by capons. The first months of Hitler produced a great deal of flapping of wings, noisy cackle, Roman conferences, Geneva interviews. Then the feathered tribe became reconciled to the new situation, and the fight for every scrap of fodder in the backyard went on. The old fighting-cock's comb rose as he sat looking on from the corner. The capons had shut him out.

And yet Churchill by no means wanted a preventive war against the new, vengeful Germany—although at that time the whole trouble could have been swept away with a single gesture—but only preparedness to avert war. He wanted England to be entangled in no more Continental conflicts. Of course he knew that the country would have to give France every help short of sending an army over in order to strengthen her defensive position. "Thank God for the French Army," he said, and it sounded just as Americans have sounded when they whispered, "Thank God for the British Navy!" His attitude toward the European Continent, particularly toward France, was astonishingly like America's attitude toward England today: Sympathy—but hands off! Churchill, indeed, was as much quicker to realize the dishonesty and untenability of that inner contradiction as the Channel is narrower than the Atlantic.

Apathy and muddling through, on the other hand, were the watchwords that guided Ramsay MacDonald. A leading neutral organ, a German-language Swiss paper, accused the English Prime Minister of deliberately indulging pro-German sympathies and deliberately endeavoring to weaken France. Mr. MacDonald did

305

not answer. He had just proposed at the Disarmament Conference that France should reduce her standing army from 700,000 to 400,000 men. On the table at Geneva he spread a vast plan for bringing all armaments down, and consequently improving relatively the military strength of Germany—as if Mr. Hitler would not have taken care of this last part of MacDonald's program himself. Mr. MacDonald had not the faintest idea of the substance and significance of his own disarmament plan. The Committee of Imperial Defense had not been consulted, nor had the Chiefs of the Fighting Services. "Unknown hands," Churchill could say uncontradicted, "have prepared these figures, and the author of the document has admitted that he has not himself mastered them, either in scope or in detail." He described the Disarmament Conference, which MacDonald dominated, as "a solemn and prolonged farce, which has undoubtedly lowered the prestige of the League of Nations and irritated many of the countries affected." And yet Churchill himself was an outspoken partisan of the League. The misuse of it was what he was trying to prevent.

In the middle of March Mr. MacDonald, accompanied by the inevitable Sir John Simon, went to Rome. On March 18, 1933, Mussolini proposed a Four-Power Pact. The date is worthy of note because the idea of Munich was first formulated on that day. MacDonald had come to Rome with dark forebodings. He knew roughly what was in store for him; a blow at the democratic majority in the League of Nations, which was to be replaced by a directorate of the great powers, half-Fascistic in its membership, entirely Fascistic under the influence of the two dictators. By what means the Duce succeeded in winding England's great Socialist round his finger is a part of secret history to this day. As a matter of fact Mr. MacDonald returned singing the praises of the Four-Power Pact. France had to push forward her small allies at Geneva in order to break up the plan. France alone was of course not equal to the coalition of Hitler, Mussolini and MacDonald.

The "isolationist" Churchill was the only man at Westminster who realized how the French must shudder if Hitler should close in on La Patrie with Italian support and official English aid. He pleaded with his government not to ask France to halve her army and air force while at the same time Germany doubled hers. "As yet their [the Nazis] fierce passions have no other outlet than upon Germans," he added.

Here the decisive fact was put in two words: *as yet*. After less than two months of Hitler—the warning was given on March 23, 1933—Churchill recognized what our world was to recognize only after nine months of the second World War: that Nazism is not a national matter of German freedom, but a fiery passion seeking an outlet, not upon its own country, not upon a neighboring country, but upon the world.

Three weeks later Churchill clashed with Germany again. April 1 had meanwhile come and gone, the day of the Jewish boycott that gave a foretaste of future pogroms. At the same time Mr. Hitler made his first appearance in world politics, outside Europe. His secret emissaries induced Japan to withdraw from the League of Nations. For Germany this action had a threefold advantage; in the first place the outlines of the great plan became visible that would divide the world of free peoples into "living-spaces"; in the second place Geneva was subjected to a strain—Berlin could see for its own information how the League reacted; in the third place this League was the child of Versailles, if a still-born child, and thus the arch-enemy.

England remained undisturbed. Very little attention was paid to the insufferable warner and exhorter who was once more making use of Hitler's latest infractions of justice to strike up his old, jarring song. "I do not subscribe to the doctrine that we should throw up our hands!" Churchill declared with profound emotion. It was a personal profession of faith.

He has, indeed, never thrown up his hands—if we leave out of account the happy accident of his capture in the Boer War. He has always seized his adversaries by the throat wherever he has found them. But where was the adversary now? Churchill was fighting against shadows. Can a man seize blindness and drowsi-

ness by the throat? Will cowardice and spinelessness fight duels?
They seemed to choke him. What he said and the way he said it
all sounded moderate, polished, with a touch of rather antiquated
tolerance, even though he called a spade a spade when it came to
the point. Eight thousand public speeches, almost a quarter-
century on the Ministerial bench, association with all the great
figures of his time had mellowed him. The droop of his shoulders
was heavier, the waistline alarmingly increasing. The heavy gold
watch-chain looped from one waistcoat pocket to the other was
almost like a relic. But his blood was still red, and his nose was as
keen as ever—only his voice no longer carried.

When Mr. Churchill spoke the House was usually half empty.
The independent Member for Epping did not get his turn until
three teams of party speakers—third teams all of them—had ground
out their commonplaces within their measured speaking time.
Half a dozen old friends, perhaps a dozen, remained true to him.
They listened; England did not listen. England stopped her ears.
It was not merely carelessness. It was conscious refusal. England
itched in every nerve to hold out her hand to the Germans who
were the new masters. The English were not taken in by the
swindle of appeasement. They dreamed themselves into it, they
wished themselves into it, they excited themselves into it. The
new master in Berlin was behaving like a drunken lackey. The
English, being the best-mannered nation in the world, knew it,
and found it most disagreeable. But iron and steel called. Not that
they wanted to take it in their own hands—anything but that!
All they wanted was to lay their heads on the block, and be left
in peace, peace!

Winston Churchill saw the procession of victims marching to
the slaughter. They had already gone much further than they
knew. He must stop them. He must rouse them, this nation of
waking dreamers who were letting the garden of the earth, England, go to ruin. His voice must reach them, his voice must re-
sound, echo all over the country!

"War-monger!" the echo sang back, "Cassandra!" or at best

CHURCHILL BOARDING A PLANE

"Good old Winnie!" rather superciliously. The echo was not even loud. Who cares about an old man with a German obsession and a French complex? Not MacDonald, not Baldwin. Possibly the village cobbler in Epping.

Churchill had never been so lonely in his life, never so little understood. What was Germany to him? What was France? Those were mere factors in the game. England, the stronghold of Christian decency, was alone at stake. No matter whether he was warning of Hitler, weighing Mussolini's words, giving the French his hand, always he saw the English turf before him, and smelled the salt air of the old fishing villages, and his heart beat with the mighty rhythm of London.

"There are a few things I will venture to mention about England," he said to the Royal Society of St. George. "They are spoken in no invidious sense. Here it would hardly occur to anyone that the banks would close their doors against their depositors. Here no one questions the fairness of the courts of law and justice. Here no one thinks of persecuting a man on account of his religion or his race. Here everybody except the criminal looks on the policeman as the friend and servant of the public. Here we provide for poverty and misfortune with more compassion, in spite of all our burdens, than any other country. Here we can assert the rights of the citizen against the state, or criticize the government of the day without failing in our duty to the Crown or in our loyalty to the King. This ancient, mighty London in which we are gathered is still the financial center of the world. From the Admiralty building, half a mile away, orders can be sent to a Fleet which, though much smaller than it used to be, or it ought to be, is still unsurpassed on the seas.

"Historians have noticed, all down the centuries, one peculiarity in the English people which has cost them dear. We have always thrown away after a victory the greater part of the advantages we gained in the struggle. The worst difficulties from which we suffer do not come from without. They come from within. They do not come from the cottages of the wage-earners. They come from a peculiar type of brainy people always found in our country, who, if they add something to its culture, take much from its strength.

"Our difficulties come from the mood of unwarrantable self-abasement, into which we have been cast by a powerful section of our intellectuals. They come from the acceptance of defeatist doctrines by a large proportion of our politicians. But what do they offer but a vague internationalism, a squalid materialism, and the promise of Utopias?

"Nothing can save England if she will not save herself. If we lose faith in ourselves, in our capacity to guide and govern, if we lose our will to live, then indeed our story is told. England would sink to the level of a fifth-rate power, and nothing would remain of all her glories except a population much larger than this island can support.

"We ought, as a nation and as an Empire, to weather any storm at least as well as any other existing system of human government. It may well be that the most glorious chapters in our history are yet to be written. Indeed, the very problems and dangers that encompass us and our country ought to make English men and women of this generation glad to be here at such a time. We ought to rejoice at the responsibilities with which destiny has honored us, and be proud that we are guardians of our country in an age when her life is at stake!"

This speech was made on April 24, 1933, six years before the second World War, seven years before the battle of Britain, when Winston Churchill was fifty-nine years old, and had found his life's task.

CHAPTER XXVI

The Londonderry Air

THE new life's work, Churchill believed, would be the last service he could do for his fatherland and for mankind. Fatherland and mankind—did not that sound a bit melodramatic? Well, the goal he set himself was thoroughly realistic. Churchill used three of the precious years still allotted to him almost exclusively in making England air-conscious.

Perhaps he and Goering were the only two men who knew as early as 1933 that the state of the world for generations would be decided in the air, and this not in generations, but within a few years. Hitler, indeed, was also air-minded from the first moment. But he believed equally devoutly in poison gas and in astrology, in assassination, espionage, secret devices, counterfeit money, mechanized men, in his rhinoceros whip, his soothsayers, his indestructible vocal cords. All were weapons in his arsenal; the bomber was but one of them. Nothing existed for Mr. Goering but castles, uniforms, and bombers. Churchill had long since lost his taste for castles and uniforms. His thought by day and night was: bombs will rain on England.

Isolated though he was in politics and in his own party, the restlessness emanating from his magnetic personality did stir up ripples. It was owing to his influence that the National Union of Conservative Associations unanimously accepted on October 5, 1933, Lord Lloyd's resolution: "That this Conference desires to record its grave anxiety in regard to the inadequacy of the provisions made for Imperial defense." This was the first time since the establishment of Nazism that any authoritative body in England had taken a stand for preparedness. The reaction, however, was crushing. A bare three weeks later the Tories lost their traditional district of East Fulham in a by-election. They went backward by more than 10,000 votes; the Socialists, preaching unbridled pacifism and defeatism, gained almost 9,000. The result of East Fulham shaped English politics for a long time. The people did not want defense; that was clearly proved.

Lloyd George scented a morning breeze. Ever since this old man, a great war lord as long as the trend and situation made it desirable, had lost his office, his party, and his following, he had been like a down-at-heel actor fighting desperately for a comeback. He still had his old instinct for sure-fire scenes, and he seemed completely equipped to lead the attack on national defense. Speaking in Parliament early in November of 1933 he once more rolled all the sweet joys of demagogy across his tongue. It was possible, he said, that the Germans might have a few thousand rifles more than was allowed by the Treaty. Maybe they had a few more Boy Scouts. What then? Look at the enormous armies of Czechoslovakia and Poland with their thousands of cannon, look at the French Army! The implication obviously was that England had no reason whatever to rearm.

Lansbury, the leader of the Socialist Opposition, came to his aid. He too was one of the antediluvian fossils who haunted postwar England like ghosts. By 1933 he could make himself understood only with difficulty when he rose from his seat. Only those sitting near him understood his superb logic: the surest way of forcing Mr. Adolf Hitler to disarm was for his neighbors to disarm. If they, however, contrary to expectations, were to be attacked by Germany, he, Mr. George Lansbury in person, would proclaim a general strike in England in order to prevent any aid from being sent to them.

Sir Herbert, later Viscount, Samuel, the leader of the Liberals, was certainly not feeble-minded. He was a patriarchal, one might almost say majestic, Jew. He did not emphasize his Judaism excessively, but neither did he ever deny it. To him it was simply an accident of birth—and to prove it, there was not a soul in the country with more understanding of the Hitler regime than Sammy. It was impossible, he asserted, to treat with blank distrust the utterances of a leader of so vast a state as Germany. To represent everything that had been said by Herr Hitler as designed only for the purposes of political maneuver would be to destroy the very means of contact and of parley between one great nation and another. And when Churchill said in Wanstead on July 7, 1934, "We ought to have a large vote to double our Air Force," Samuel replied in the House of Commons on July 13: "This is rather the language of a Malay running amuck than of a responsible British statesman. It is rather the language of blind and causeless panic."

The whole weakness of the Empire in its age of decay was embodied in the person of the Prime Minister. In his wanderings Mr. MacDonald seriously believed that he towered toward heaven. He saw himself as the savior of Europe—"savior of Europe on limited liability," Churchill called it—who was leading Mr. Hitler upon the path of righteousness, and giving peace to the world. Traveler's fever drove him all through Europe; he even went to Washington, on President Roosevelt's invitation, for a rather inconsequential conversation, but wherever he went and whatever he said, it was always the same old empty phrases; it was never a man's word, never the one word that Hitler then would still have understood: Stop!

When the MacDonald Government, in which Mr. Baldwin as Lord President of the Council was the deciding figure, and bore the real political responsibility, found itself obliged to make a gesture of preparedness, it announced on November 14, 1933, "that after anxious consideration and with much regret" two ninethousand-ton cruisers would be included in the naval program. Even that seemed too much: two days later Sir Herbert Samuel and his Liberal group indignantly withdrew their support from the Government. Six weeks later, on January 31, 1934, a White Paper was published, containing fresh proposals by the desperate government for disarmament.

Churchill demanded security, not disarmament, which so far had been entirely one-sided. On February 7, 1934, he told the House of Commons that England, owing to the inadequacy of her aerial defenses, was vulnerable as never before. No longer was she the island of twenty-five years ago.

A month later, on March 8, he stated in deadly earnest that the day of an aerial attack on England might, perhaps, not be far distant. It might be "only a year, or perhaps eighteen months." And with a bold gesture Churchill passed over the old puppet that sat in the Prime Minister's seat. He addressed a personal appeal to Mr. Baldwin, whose Chancellor Churchill had been for five long years, to use his powerful influence for preparedness in the air.

The Lord President got up amid the rapt attention of the House. A historic utterance was due. But Mr. Baldwin began with his favorite words: "If—" he said emphatically, and again, "If . . . all our efforts for an agreement fail . . . then any Government will see to it that in air strength and air power this country shall no longer be in a position inferior to any country within striking distance of our shores."

All the efforts did not fail, of course. His Majesty's Government had always still another effort up their sleeve, and Hitler still had time to prolong negotiations until the Lufthansa, the German commercial-aviation organization, could manufacture the first few hundred bombers "for freight and passenger traffic."

Undoubtedly in this time of secret armament Lord Londonderry, His Majesty's Secretary of State for Air, played into Hitler's hands. It was not long before His Lordship published a book that was a profession of faith in the Fuehrer. This was probably a mistake, for it focussed public attention on Lord Londonderry's personal policies.

Churchill had learned from his own experience in the World War that coördination of defense is the most important part of the job. He demanded the establishment of a Ministry of Defense that could be made responsible for all the three Fighting Services.

As a matter of fact at the hour of direst distress in the present war, after the Norwegian disaster, the unification of the three defense arms was actually carried out, and Churchill assumed their direction. But as long as Lord Londonderry was at the helm, and unwilling to embarrass Mr. Hitler, the simple word "unpractical" from him was enough to dismiss the suggestion of the independent Member for Epping. His Lordship also felt that he should make use of his opportunities to dismiss the anxiety Mr. Churchill was stirring up in respect to air power. On June 27, 1934, Lord Londonderry convinced the House of Lords in a rambling speech that the Government was making preparations in ample time to secure parity in the air.

Churchill was not ashamed of his anxiety. Two weeks after the German St. Bartholomew's Eve of June 30, 1934, when Hitler had some of his most intimate personal friends murdered, he pointed out that men of this caliber "might easily plunge into a foreign adventure of catastrophic character to the whole world."

This time, apparently, Churchill had not shouted quite in vain to the empty air. It was no longer possible to let the voice speaking from the depths of the English consciousness die away unheard. Six days after Churchill's speech, on July 19, Mr. Baldwin announced a new five-year air program by which the R.A.F. would be increased by 860 machines; the force at home would thus be raised to a total of 75 squadrons comprising 880 machines.

At this Sir Herbert Samuel rose with a proposal to put these measures off for at least a few more weeks in order to see what would happen at Geneva. Of course disarmament had been discussed at Geneva for eight years by then, and nothing had ever happened. The actual Disarmament Conference had been proceeding, without the slightest semblance of results, for two and a half years or more.

Now Churchill lost his patience—it was a miracle to be explained only by the incomparable wisdom of his old age that he had not lost it long since. He drily informed the House of the facts about secret air armaments, which he had collected with infinite painstaking. It must not be forgotten that in these days of his isolation the best patriots regarded Churchill as a one-man Opposition, and the whole world thought him the center of resistance against the spread of Nazism. Hence unceasing streams of information of every kind poured into Chartwell Manor from all countries. As soon appeared, Mr. Churchill spoke with far more knowledge of the facts than His Majesty's Government.

He stressed four points: First, Germany had already—in violation of the Treaty—created a military air force that was for the time being two-thirds as strong as the British. Second, Germany was so rapidly increasing her air force that by the end of 1935 she must be equal to the British strength. Third, some time in 1936 Germany would be stronger. Fourth, once they got their lead England might never be able to overtake them.

Now England knew when her hour would strike. She had two years left in which to be a happy island after Churchill had ventured his prophecy of July 30, 1934. It was another of Churchill's mysteriously exact predictions, like the one that had foreseen in the midst of peace the day of the battle of the Marne. It is hard to avoid the word prophet in looking at the Churchill of those days: a square-hewn, heavily breathing man with red spots on his prominent cheekbones, the smooth round face cut up to right and left by a deep furrow, lips tightly closed as if they had grown thinner—they had said much, and had much more to repress—the eyes more darkly gleaming than in his boyhood pictures, the firm chin resting on a little cushion of fat. There was iron will in that face, and yet also warming understanding; more resolution than enthusiasm, doggedness, with one last faint touch of Epicureanism. If any hair had remained between his temples, it would undoubtedly be constantly standing on end.

Of course there were not so much as two minutes to be lost of the two years that Churchill had allowed England before the Empire's freedom of decision would be done for. Theoretically two paths were open. One was a preventive war, which by that time would not have been prevention, but a reply to Hitler's

ON THE LECTURE PLATFORM

numerous provocations and breaches of treaties. It would have been a sure and relatively bloodless expedient. But England was not in a moral state to make use of it—and what would the public opinion of the United States have said? No risk is too great for the bystander. Let England's stake go up and up! In Churchill's view the opinion of America is a decisive factor in world politics. He had only to listen to New York—he was also listening tensely to the Middle West—and to look around him at home, in order to know that this path was not possible. And he himself would indeed have been most unwilling to take it. As he stood in short sleeves and slacks in his Kent garden, a cigar in his mouth and the peace of the English landscape in his heart, his thoughts kept returning to the League of Nations, which might after all some day be a practical tool of world understanding. The war-monger, as his opponents called him, the old cavalry officer, savored peace like a ripe fruit.

So only the second way remained: a maximum of preparedness, to make an attack appear excessively costly and unattractive. In a clairvoyant address he showed the House and the country what such an attack from the air would look like while England was inadequately defended. This was still 1934, now November 28. Yet it was a perfect description of what we since have learned to know as "Luft-Blitzkrieg." Churchill left no doubt that in a week or ten days of attack upon London "30,000 or 40,000" people could be killed or maimed. At least three or four millions of people would be driven out into the open country. The docks of London and the estuary of the Thames would be in great danger. Birmingham, Sheffield, and the great manufacturing towns might be destroyed. "Worst of all," he concluded, "the air-war is the only form of war in the world in which complete predominance gives no opportunity of recovery."

In Poland, in the Lowlands, in Norway and in France this latter prediction of a visionary has been cruelly verified by history.

Churchill moved to add to the Address the words: "But humbly represent to Your Majesty that, in the present circumstances of the world, the strength of our national defenses, and especially of our air defenses, is no longer adequate to secure the peace, safety and freedom of Your Majesty's faithful subjects."

Five Members among the more than six hundred in the House supported Churchill: Sir Robert Horne, Leopold Amery, Captain F. E. Guest, Lord Winterton, Mr. Boothby.

Mr. Baldwin, obviously reluctant, rose to make a reply in which he attempted to answer the clairvoyance with a few statistical guesses. "I think it is correct to say that the Germans are engaged in creating an air force," he said, and as the Lord President did not reprove this breach of agreement by so much as a word, he was sanctioned for the first time. Mr. Baldwin estimated the German strength as "between 600 aircraft and something not over 1,000. In the United Kingdom," he continued, "560 are at present stationed." According to his own estimates, therefore, England was already overmatched in the air. How things would go on Mr. Baldwin did not know. "I cannot look further forward than the next two years. Mr. Churchill," he wound up peevishly, "speaks of what may happen in 1937."

But what was that to him? In all human probability there would be no 1937 for Mr. Baldwin, certainly not in politics. A year before that he would reach the age-limit of seventy, and retire to take his ease.

Meanwhile poor Mr. Baldwin was allowed no ease even during his annual stay at Aix-les-Bains. One day he was just about to descend into the curative bathtub when the attendant announced Mr. Winston Churchill from London. "The air armaments!" the Lord President murmured in horror, wrapping himself closer in his red dressing-gown. This time the gift of prophecy was on his side.

Churchill had brought along another gentleman—Mr. Lindemann, Professor of Experimental Philosophy at Oxford University, inventor of the mysterious Lindemann Cigar. This was a cigar not to be smoked, but fired off in the air. It made a considerable area very perilous to airplanes for an appreciable period of time, say, five minutes. If a number of these cigars were fired at the same time, a large space would become deadly to airplane invasion.

Mr. Baldwin listened to the idea with enthusiasm. Of course something must be done about the matter at once. An Air Ministry Committee must be appointed to study the problem. At once. No, not at once. First Mr. Baldwin must take his bath. And as the lukewarm medicinal waters of Aix-les-Bains rippled around him, Mr. Baldwin forgot the Lindemann Cigar. He himself was a pipe-smoker.

In response to repeated urgings from Churchill the Air Ministry Committee for study was finally appointed after all, with scientists exploring the matter. A vast number of letters passed to and fro. But at about this time Lord Londonderry advised Mr. Baldwin to deliver the famous speech in which he said that there was really no defense against air attack. It looked as if the Department simply wanted to let the affair die a natural death. The Committee was indeed still formally at work, but no real hope stimulated its progress.

Churchill secured the support of Sir Austen Chamberlain. The two men demanded that the Committee of Imperial Defense, the supreme authority, to which the heads of the Government belonged, should interest itself in the affair. The investigations would cost £100,000 a year, but what did that amount to if you could discover some method that would make the world more secure from the present disturbing menace to civilization? This pacifist touch moved Mr. MacDonald's heart. He was very much interested. But, he objected, there was already a committee occupying itself with the Lindemann Cigar. Still he would turn the matter over in his mind.

A few weeks later Sir Austen Chamberlain had a second interview with the Prime Minister. At it Mr. MacDonald confessed that jurisdictional difficulties made by the Air Ministry—Lord Londonderry, of course—seemed almost insuperable to him. Nevertheless he would appoint a special sub-committee of the Committee of Imperial Defense; but the Air Ministry would still play the decisive part. Three months later Churchill learned in response to an enquiry that this sub-committee had held all of two sessions in the meantime. There was no further experiment under way. Practically nothing at all was being done. Helped by the complacency of Messrs. MacDonald and Baldwin, Lord Londonderry had got his way once more.

England was simply not to be awakened from her wishful dreaming. On March 19, 1935, Lord Londonderry's Under Secretary Sir Philip Sassoon, whose personal fairness was quite above question, declared: "We have no official statistics, but according to the latest information in our possession, it is not correct that Germany is already stronger than this country. We have a substantially stronger air force. It is also not correct to say that at the end of the present calendar year the German air force will be 50% stronger than ours. So far as we can at present estimate we shall, at the end of this year, possess a margin of superiority." This was an official statement against Churchill's panic-mongering. The accuracy of his facts and his prestige received a terrific blow.

Five days later Churchill was splendidly rehabilitated—and this by Hitler himself. On March 24, the Fuehrer received Sir John Simon, the Foreign Secretary, and informed him that Germany had now achieved parity with Great Britain in the air. Consequently he, Mr. Hitler, had no further interest in a collective system of peace and security, and he rejected the proposed Eastern pact. He would give no guarantees with regard to Austria. He would not hear of withdrawing the conscription order.

As a matter of fact that day brought the open declaration of war. Sir John Simon, reporting three days later to the Cabinet, merely called it "the disclosure of considerable divergences of view." He pocketed the slaps in the face, and his stone smile froze even harder.

Of course the governments of Europe were now alarmed. The Stresa Conference, which resolved to guarantee the independence of Austria forever, followed on April 12. On April 17 the League of Nations Council, on a French motion, condemned Germany's deliberate repudiation of her Treaty obligations; on May 2 the Franco-Soviet Pact was signed in Paris. But as it soon turned out, it was all shadow-boxing, backed up by no good faith and no resolution. Everyone tried to cheat everyone else. No one tried to cleanse the poisoned air.

Lord Londonderry was not put on trial; on the contrary, he was able in the full consciousness of his power, his office and his responsibility to caution the House of Lords on May 22 against taking an exaggerated view of Germany's air strength. "Herr Hitler's information to Sir John Simon on the subject of German air strength came as a rude shock to the British public," he admitted. Then he went on: "The uncertainty of the situation, accentuated by a Press which had long viewed with alarm the apparent complacency of the Government in view of the increasing menace of Continental reports, had its effect on the Prime Minister and his nearest colleagues, and my task was transformed . . . into the very necessary attempt to allay the growing anxiety of those chiefly responsible for the security of the realm, who appeared to imagine that a German air force of trained pilots and up-to-date machines had developed in two years far superior to our own."

The one man who kept urging a clear accounting was Churchill. All his premonitions and warnings had now come true. All his predictions were confirmed. And now too he shed his last personal hesitations. In a series of sensational speeches delivered in quick succession in Parliament he held up to his old friend and superior Mr. Baldwin his mistakes and his inadequacy.

On March 19 he gave the figures and facts on which he based his statement that the German production would add 1500 military aircraft in the financial year of 1935-1936, while the English estimate was concerned with an increase of 150. This would be a complete reversal—Churchill made it crystal clear—of the position that Baldwin had predicted in Parliament for the end of the year. Churchill expressed the recognition of this danger in the fateful words: "We are no longer safe behind the shield of our Navy. From being the least vulnerable of all nations, we have, through development in the air, become the most vulnerable."

Would England still not listen? Two and a half years of suicidal carelessness had passed, as Churchill pointed out to the House on May 2, 1935. He was the only one who had spoken in that time. He did not boast of it. It was an old story to him. As old as the story of the Sibylline Books.

In a weary voice Mr. Baldwin, his face strangely pale, his hands trembling, tried on May 22 to explain his position. It was not even a real attempt at defense any more. It was a confession of guilt: "Where I was wrong was in my estimate of the future. There I was completely wrong. We were completely misled on that subject. . . ."

Who had misled him?

Mr. Baldwin himself furnished the answer. "I think it is only due to say that there has been a great deal of criticism about the Air Ministry. But I want to repeat that the responsibility is not that of any single Minister; it is the responsibility of the Government as a whole, and we all are responsible and we all are to blame." Thus he shielded Lord Londonderry.

Churchill in his answer put the responsibility where it belonged. He pointed out the broad stream of information about the German effort in aviation that came from almost all the European countries—and from Germany herself. He reaffirmed his belief in the British Intelligence Service. Who, then, was guilty of England's negligence?

If the country woke up to find herself suddenly inferior, everyone was equally guilty: a misinformed government, an inefficient bureaucracy, an uninstructed public opinion, a coward Parliament, a specious foreign policy.

Never had a man to fight against heavier odds. Never was a single man, summoning the people to come to their senses, faced by a worse conspiracy of blindness and stupidity. Never—until the near-repetition of the case in America just now—had a great country been lulled into so complete a feeling of false security.

On June 8, 1935, the Government was at last reorganized. But no new blood was added with the exception of Sir Philip Cunliffe-Lister, now Lord Swinton, a friend of Churchill's and an excellent man who replaced Lord Londonderry. For the rest, the ciphers simply changed places. Messrs. Baldwin and MacDonald exchanged offices, and Sir John Simon left the Foreign Office to move into the Home Office. Here he was to set the machinery of the Committee of Defense going again. In the first eight months of his tenure of office not a word was heard of the matter. Sir Samuel Hoare became Foreign Minister. He soon became known as "the whispering baritone."

The reorganized Government showed its vigor ten days after its accession to office by signing the Anglo-German Naval Agreement, condoning and even praising German treaty-breaking in fleet-building. A week later it offered a strip of British Somaliland to Mussolini if he would relax his demands on Abyssinia. A new voice was raised in British foreign policy. It had a nasal, God-fearing, self-satisfied sound. "This matter with Mussolini will be one involving a long strain which will require a cool and phlegmatic temperament." The Chancellor of the Exchequer who spoke thus was soon to prove that he was endowed with a cool and phlegmatic temperament. It was Mr. Neville Chamberlain.

Churchill was no longer cool and phlegmatic. When he was making a speech he marched up and down the platform with a restless stride, like a caged tiger. His waist-line had spread alarmingly, his face was alarmingly red. He looked as if he were about to explode. But he was not the one who exploded. England, Europe, the world would fly to pieces. Churchill was the only one who heard the ticking of the infernal machine. As early as the summer of 1935 he knew that it was no longer to be halted.

CHAPTER XXVII

Cassandra

CHURCHILL, says an American paper, understood the Nazi virus sooner and better than any other man. This is certainly true in respect to the political substance of Nazism. In 1935 he published his first analysis of the Fuehrer, "The Truth about Hitler," in the London *Strand* magazine. There was no name-calling in this essay, no hostility, but rather a desperate effort to guide back into its proper orbit a planet that had gone astray. Whether this was a diplomatic venture, or was due to the fact that a scion of the Marlboroughs simply could not conceive of the abysses from which a Hitler came, is a question that must be left unanswered. To Churchill Adolf Hitler was a fanatic for the German people, not a world revolutionist; an avenger of German honor, not an anomalous animal seeking revenge on the world of normal and comely people for the misfits of the whole universe. He did not observe that Hitler was surrounded primarily by cripples—Goering, Goebbels, Roehm. He wrote not a clinical but a political study. As such, however, the article was calculated not merely to explain history, but to make history. It was a last warning signal.

In Germany, Churchill observed, the great wheels revolved—"The rifles, the cannon, the tanks, the shot and shell, the air bombs, the poison gas cylinders, the aeroplanes, the submarines, streamed from the already largely war-mobilized arsenals and factories."

At the same time all the wheels in England stood still. The general confusion was an even worse hindrance than the general lethargy to the execution of any orderly plan of armament. Each Department had its own scheme; they all interfered with one an-

other. It was high time for the appointment of a Minister to concert the action of the three Fighting Services. This realization
took hold even in the House of Commons, cutting through party
lines. Churchill was its spokesman. In August he led a Parliamentary deputation to Mr. Baldwin in order to express the anxiety
the House felt about national defense. Simultaneously he made
his statement on the condition of the Air Force, to the careful
preparation of which he had devoted several weeks.

Mr. Baldwin listened to the statement, whose reading lasted an
hour, with his well-known Olympian calm. For seven months this
calm did not desert him. It was only on March 13, 1936, that
Attorney-General Sir Thomas Inskip was appointed Minister for
the Co-ordination of Defense. Sir Thomas knew how difficult was
the legacy he was inheriting. He spoke of "the years that the
locust hath eaten."

The gravest burden was the Anglo-German Naval Agreement.
In particular there was the mysterious U-boat clause. While the
Germans were contented with a parity of 35% in general, for
the U-boat arm they demanded 45% in the beginning, and 100%
in the long run. Why? Admiral Lord Beatty stated that the battle
fleet was now practically secure against submarines if properly
protected by flotillas. Germany declared that she would never
again use the submarine against commerce. "Strange that the
Germans should dwell with so much reiteration on the possession
of this weapon!" Churchill remarked.

And what were the world-wide results of the treaty? "A wind-
fall to Japan!" as Churchill put it. Of course the reëstablishment
of Germany's naval power, now legitimate and encouraged by the
treaty, must hamper the British Navy in the Pacific and almost
destroy the usefulness of Singapore. In the Mediterranean, too,
the British Navy's increased occupation in home waters would
soon be felt, Churchill predicted.

On October 4, 1935, Mussolini started his raid on Abyssinia,
as if to prove how right Churchill had been. The latter immediately expressed his conviction that the Duce would never have

embarked upon the venture if he had not been convinced of the "supposed military and naval weakness of Great Britain."

Churchill's is the unique gift of grasping the essential elements in the flight of events—not seeing merely the shifting evils but finding the source of all evil. With a sure logic that did not make him popular in the Baldwin-MacDonald era he pointed again and again to the "dominant factor, the factor which dwarfs all others," as he expressed it: German armament.

England's last resort he saw in steadfast coöperation with the League of Nations. "The fortunes of the British Empire and its glory are inseparably interwoven with the fortunes of the world," he insisted. "We rise or fall together." It is the same deep conviction that guides Winston Churchill's war leadership.

Even in those days it was a confession of his humanitarian feeling for England's world-wide mission. It was a straightforward profession of faith in it. But when the country was summoned to new elections in November of 1935, attacks upon the "trouble-maker" poured down from both sides. Mr. Lansbury, the old pacifist, had had to give up the leadership of the Labour Party a few weeks before, because he would not sanction the sanctions against Italy. What he called his "regained political freedom" he used chiefly for malicious attacks on Churchill. "He is haunted by German ghosts!" he kept repeating with a senile leer.

The exalted Mr. Baldwin of course never lost his poise. But he too turned against Churchill's armament program. "I give you my word, there will be no great armaments in this country!" he promised the voters; and apparently with this one promise he gained a majority of 247 for his Conservative Party. As a matter of fact the majority represented merely a choice of evils. In these disturbed times the English people did not want to expose themselves to the uncertainties of Socialist leadership. The two Mac-Donalds, father and son, were pitifully defeated in their old constituencies. Mr. Baldwin, on the other hand, did not want to lose his ally; he wanted his Government to preserve a "national" tinge, and not to look outwardly like a mere Tory Government. Consequently he put pressure on the Conservative machine to free two safe Scottish seats for the MacDonalds. The machine obeyed, though on condition that the two gentlemen should not use the words "socialist" and "labor." Thus Father MacDonald was parting from forty years of his past, to wither away for a little while longer on the Government bench. The change suited young Mac-Donald better. In the course of years he has made for himself a generally respected position in the House and in changing Governments.

He owed it all to Baldwin. The Prime Minister was now at the zenith of his power. He basked in the noble consciousness of being the lesser evil.

A month after the elections the Hoare-Laval proposal was published, laying the greater part of Abyssinia at Italy's feet. But this piece of desertion was too much for the English. The nation was not yet ripe for Munich. All over the country a storm blew up that swept away Sir Samuel Hoare. Five days later he resigned from the Foreign Office. "We must go back to the policy of Sanctions, and in due course I trust that the League of Nations will show, as I believe they will show, that they are prepared to make themselves ready to resist any attack that may be made on any one of their members," said a manly voice from the Conservative camp. The speech came, of all places, from Birmingham. And of all people the speaker was Mr. Neville Chamberlain.

Mussolini dared the sanctions. They were probably quite welcome to him as a form of education for his Italian people. Let them learn to do without their modest luxuries. It would harden them for the great war. Though if sanctions ever interfered with the import of war materials he would blow the British Mediterranean Fleet out of the water. Of course it is hardly customary for the jackal to open the attack, but behind him stood the lion—at that time perhaps a circus lion—Hitler with his moustache.

The League of Nations shut off the import of aluminum to Italy. Aluminum is a raw material important in war. It is the only one of which Italy produces more than enough for herself.

All the other raw materials Italy might continue to receive unhindered.

Mussolini's bluff worked splendidly. Hitler could see what diaper-white adversaries the dictators had to deal with. On March 7 he reoccupied the Rhineland, denouncing the treaties of Versailles and Locarno, but affirming that the reoccupation was purely symbolic—a brilliantly successful speculation on the pacifists of England and America—and that Rhenania should never be fortified. He still kept a line of retreat open. His generals had sealed orders ("To be opened at the first shot") to withdraw German troops without a battle if the English or French should march. For this emergency Mr. Hitler wore a conspicuous revolver spanning his alarmingly increasing girth. Everyone close to him knew that the Fuehrer would shoot himself if things went wrong. Storm-Troop Captain Richter, who was later liquidated in the concentration camp at Sachsenhausen, knew that the weapon was unloaded. Otherwise one careless movement might have discharged it.

To make assurance doubly sure, Mr. Leopold von Hoesch, then German ambassador in London, a beautiful man who adorned himself with orchids, handed to Mr. Eden, the new Foreign Secretary, proposals for a twenty-five-year non-aggression pact between Germany, France and Belgium, and probably Holland, with Great Britain and Italy as guarantors. He offered a Western Air Pact too, and promised Germany's return to the League of Nations. Sweet murmurs of peace rippled from German lips until Hitler could feel his head settled quite firmly on his shoulders. The echo, indeed, was the rumble of German armament factories, shipyards, arsenals.

The raging and roaring of German armaments disturbed Churchill's sleep. Lansbury was right: he *was* haunted. Baldwin must not be right: England must have great armaments.

Again he stood up in the House. Again his voice drummed up the country. Again he surveyed the scene. He could simply talk of nothing else but of the German armaments that had devoured more than eight hundred million pounds sterling in 1935. Such expenses could not go on. But how would they stop? Nazism, Churchill was positive, would soon have to choose between an internal or an external catastrophe. Could there remain any doubts in the minds of the honorable members which course a man like Hitler would choose? Or did anybody believe that Hitler would hold back his blow until England was ready to meet him? Why did they not put their house in order? Was England always condemned to be too late?

Every word in Churchill's speech of March 10, 1936, was laden with fate. Much of it still teaches a lesson that even belligerent England today—and neutral America—might take to heart. But Mr. von Hoesch could confidently report to Berlin that there was no need to worry too much about the old fool's "incendiary speeches." His Parliamentary following was small, his popularity in the country confined to personal liking, his influence on the Government zero. As a matter of fact England's Parliament, nation and Government did not take the slightest step to call the bluff in Rhenania. On the contrary, when Herr von Ribbentrop came to London on March 14, 1936, for an extraordinary session of the Council of the League of Nations, he was received with honors not due even the Pope of Catholic Christianity.

Mr. Joachim von Ribbentrop was not particularly distinguished for Christian qualities. He took all the night clubs and bottle parties of the West End by storm. Here he could feel at home. For only recently he had been a champagne salesman. He had married the boss's daughter—Henkel & Co., the leading German champagne house—which after all was a proof of business ability, and he was the originator of the proud saying: "I am the only man who can sell German *sekt* at the price of French champagne!" London society took him enthusiastically to its bosom. It is no exaggeration to call Mr. von Ribbentrop—the nobleman's *von* came from a distant aunt, and had been appropriated by adoption —the darling of the London season. A wave of political perversion broke over polite society.

Mr. von Ribbentrop spent his cocktail hours in the palace of the Marquess of Londonderry. Over the week-end he was invited to Cliveden by Lady Nancy Astor. No one in the drawing-rooms suspected that he "would wage a war to exterminate the English gentleman," as his party associate Alfred Rosenberg, the Nazi philosopher, later formulated it. Or did they have forebodings of the inevitable? Were they, like their French fellow-noblemen in the dying age of rococo, dancing their way to the Bastille?

"There is an extreme volume of Nazi propaganda in this country," was Churchill's farewell to Ribbentrop's visit. He had discovered the newest weapon in the arsenal of German secret armaments: the Fifth Column was established in London.

It was a foul weapon, like poison gas. But the germs flourished on the most fruitful soil. Subconsciously, half-consciously, England had fallen into the clutches of the Germans. Why, they were awfully nice people, weren't they, the nation of Goethe and Beethoven? But that Goethe had despised the Germans all his life, and Beethoven had had to flee from Germany to find a resting-place for his genius in the extremely un-German imperial Vienna, was not taught in the Public Schools. The English "intelligentsia" particularly was not to be cured of its secret, its mysterious admiration for the Germans. They were convinced that what was going on in the Third Reich did not suit the Germans themselves. It was not the people, it was Hitler—and even he would have used up his energy some day. That thousands of German children were delivering up their parents to the Gestapo as "enemies of the State," that hundreds of thousands of German youths were working off their sadism on the victims of the concentration camps, that millions of German men were preparing for the day when the "slave races"—Poles and English, French, Huzules, and Latin-Americans—would be laboring for the lords of the earth, that millions of German women were looking up with hungry eyes to the Fuehrer's picture over their beds, that except for a handful of émigrés not a single voice was raised in the nation against the bestialization of man—all this was something that the kindly, slightly inhibited English could not understand. This was England's tragic unpreparedness, and the men who translated this lack of instinct into lack of planes and tanks, the MacDonalds, Baldwins, Chamberlains, the Sir John Simons and Lord Londonderrys and all the rest, were—though their extreme guilt for misleading their nation cannot be denied—fundamentally only the executive organs of the Nemesis that gripped England.

"There is much goodwill in England," Churchill stated on March 13, 1936. He protested his own goodwill as well. But he remarked that Hitler was continuing his efforts to separate British public opinion from the British Government and House of Commons. Still courteously, but with uncompromising clarity, he revealed the tactics of Nazi propaganda which tried to obfuscate actualities, and the gravest actuality of all: German armament.

Some well-meaning friends began to wonder that Churchill was not yet tired of his obsession with German armament. But as long as Hitler did not grow tired of arming, there was no tiring for Churchill, either. The duel had to be fought out to the bitter end.

On March 26, 1936, Churchill explained in Parliament what a terrific danger the violation and fortification of the Rhineland was, not to France alone, but to Holland and Belgium as well. On April 6 he predicted the Blitzkrieg through the Lowlands with truly prophetic accuracy, again in Parliament. He showed how inevitably all the northern, eastern and southern countries of Europe must be affected by the fact that Germany's Western border was now to be an unimpregnable fortress. He foresaw that the neutrals would simply have to fall in line with the German masters—unless, at this final moment, England and France stopped the attempt at German overlordship by halting her illegitimate armament, particularly in the Rhine zone. "All the signals are set for danger!" he exclaimed. "The red lights flash through the gloom!"

Sir Thomas Inskip, the recently appointed Minister for the

Co-ordination of Defense, shrugged his shoulders. Whatever the Germans might be doing—"I am working under peace conditions!"

Churchill insisted that Labor should be included in the great task of counter-preparation. He blamed the Government for not yet having sought contact with the trade unions, and having done nothing effective about profiteering. "You will not get the effective coöperation of the working people so long as they think there are a lot of greedy fingers having a rake-off!"

This time he did not speak quite in vain. The working men pricked up their ears. For years they had been taught to hate Churchill as a red-baiter. Memories of the munition workers' strike at the end of the first war clung to him, as did his energetic attitude in the General Strike, and his anti-Bolshevik record. Their own leaders had pitilessly denounced him. But the prestige of those leaders meanwhile had considerably declined.

What? Churchill a Marlborough, representative of the large estates, of the vested interests? He lived in a country cottage, larger and more comfortable than their own, to be sure, but by no means fundamentally different. All his life he had spoken of the "English cottage home," the house of the little man from whom the strength of the great nation issued. His descent, after all, was no shame. Their own forefathers had been soldiers of Marlborough. With Mr. 'Itler breaking up the unions over there, and degrading the worker into a tin soldier, perhaps it was not a bad thing to remember. Churchill began to gain his first following among the small people, less subject to the whims of fashion, who had little more than the pub on Saturday evening and the Church Sunday morning, and a tiny bit of English soil under their weary feet. When he pulled to pieces the contradictions and half-heartedness of the Government, the applause—except that from his handful of honest but uninfluential friends among the Conservative back-benchers—came from the ranks of the Opposition. The Socialist intellectuals did indeed still keep painfully aloof, but the old Union leaders nodded portentously, and "good old Winnie" was recognized again as a friend of the people.

Churchill needed it. Personally he felt anything but at ease in the role of Cassandra that Fate imposed on him. It was extremely disagreeable to be a marked man whose voice made people start and the sight of whom caused them to cross themselves. At bottom he was a sociable, warm-hearted man, loving his neighbor, and cutting a rather unhappy figure as the prophet of doom. Must he be an outcast simply because he could not let this sociable, neighbor-loving, warm-hearted world of humanity drift into the abyss without a word?

The approval that he enjoyed among the little people straightened him up again; he had been quite bowed down. Perhaps he knew that this approval was soon to become a resolute fighting fellowship. And that when all the lights of England were shining most brightly in England's deepest night the specter would be banished—the Cassandra business . . .

CHAPTER XXVIII

Cause of Death: Sleeping Sickness

ODDLY enough a word of agreement came from the other side as well. "We can already feel the heat of the flames upon our faces," said Mr. Neville Chamberlain. For a man so characteristically restrained in his language this was a formidable expression. It explained one half of the man who led England the last few steps into the abyss. Before Mr. Chamberlain became so grimly involved in his hopeless appeasement experiment, we must not forget that he was the best and most successful Chancellor of the Exchequer England had had for years. In the summer of 1936, when Mr. Baldwin had to take three months' leave on account of ill-health, and Mr. MacDonald, the Lord President of the Council, was no longer able to take the Prime Minister's place, Chamberlain was the driving power of the Government, the only man who could keep together the diverging elements. His two most pronounced qualities, stubbornness and distrust, at that time contributed as much or as little to the maintenance of English power as was maintained at all.

Undoubtedly as Chancellor he was already the strong man of the nation. Unluckily he had no room for extraordinary men beside him. When he needed their advice and their supervision most desperately, Churchill was banned to the farthest corner.

The thing about Churchill that probably most disturbed the cool and punctilious Mr. Chamberlain was his clairvoyant imagination, an unbusinesslike quality in Mr. Chamberlain's eyes. For when Churchill predicted unparalleled German armaments, and demanded similar exertions in England, Neville Chamberlain, a business man and no visionary, replied: "The expenditure will rise to a peak, then fall a little, and then remain level, but at a much greater height than at the present time."

Churchill, the old warrior, knew that guns impelled by their own magic go off of their own accord. Neville Chamberlain, the Birmingham business man, knew the balances, and believed that some day they must be settled. That was the difference between the two.

Churchill's instinct was surer than Chamberlain's calculation. On May 21, 1936—once again we must notice the early date— he put some questions in the House. They were to have their gruesome answer years later. He asked for an answer to the question of the air-bomb versus the battleship. Was England in danger of invasion from the air? Was it possible now, or might it be possible soon, to land from the air substantial forces? How was the Government "going to provide for the overseas supplies for 45,000,000 people whose shipping has been greatly reduced since the last war? What about gas masks and the defence of the civil population from aerial attack by chemical means? What, for instance, will be the strength of the German Air Force in 1938 or 1939?"

In July, 1936, the first session of the new—the present—Parliament drew to a close. Thirteen years had now passed since the fall of the Lloyd George Coalition had brought the "Baldwin-MacDonald regime," as Churchill called it, into power, eight years since he himself had been relieved of responsibility. What had happened to England in that time—how low the fortunes of the country had sunk!

In one of his news-letters Churchill summed up the tragedy. He called the MacDonald-Baldwin team "two nurses, fit to keep silence around a darkened room." They were perfectly equipped to give the country a rest-cure, which could be prolonged indefinitely, if only the British Isles were not situated ten minutes by air from the stormy continent.

A few sentences described the autopsy of a system on which a world empire rests. The cause of death: sleeping sickness.

Mr. Baldwin still believed he was alive. On July 2 he assured a dinner of the City of London Conservative Association that he had not the slightest intention of retiring.

To Mr. Hitler this declaration was a tonic. He ordered Austrian negotiators to Berlin, and on July 11 forced upon them the Pact of Berlin, which opened wide the gates to Nazism in Austria, and thus made the last bulwark of civilization in Central Europe untenable. The bulwark, incidentally, was already alarmingly undermined within. The Austrian negotiator was Dr. Guido Schmitt, Secretary of State for Foreign Affairs, whom Dr. Schuschnigg described as "my only personal friend." Dr. Schmitt was a bribed tool of Nazism. During the overturn in Vienna he silently vanished, to reappear a few days later as director of the Hermann Goering Works. Today he is one of the most important industrialists in the armament industry of Hitler's war machine. But as he had agreed with his Nazi bosses to play the independent Austrian at the Berlin negotiations of July, 1936, he said for the record: "You mustn't ask too much of us, gentlemen. England will not allow our sovereignty to be suppressed."

"Your sovereignty, did you say?" Hitler could not help laughing at this. "England, did you say?" he laughed yet louder. Finally he rocked with laughter: "You mean Mr. Stanley Baldwin?"

Mr. Baldwin had other worries. So had England. In the summer of 1936 the first rumors about the new King's intention to marry beneath him began to circulate. The High Church and the middle class were against the divorced American woman whom Edward loved. Churchill was among the few friends of the sovereign who upheld his King's right to his own choice. Perhaps he recalled another American lady who burst into London society like a whirlwind—even though Lady Randolph had not been divorced. Perhaps his American blood was aroused. Probably, however, his sense of fair play was involved. If Mr. Baldwin thought the union impossible for reasons of state let him speak up as soon as the question became acute—that is, in August. But as a matter of fact, the Prime Minister waited until October, old chess-player

THE PRIME MINISTER VISITS BRITAIN'S FRONT LINE

Winston Churchill inspecting air raid damage to Ramsgate by Nazi bombers in the present war

that he was, before moving to checkmate the King, an event which finally took place on December 10.

And so the greater part of the year was occupied almost exclusively with the quarrel over the Crown. England's energies were canalized. Mr. Neville Chamberlain shrugged his shoulders: "The idea of continuing the policy of Sanctions is a midsummer madness," he said, addressing the 1900 Club. A week later Mr. Eden had to admit in the House: "Whatever view we take of the course of action which the League should follow, there is one fact upon which we must, of course, be agreed. We have to admit that the purpose for which the Sanctions have been imposed has not been realized." On July 1 at Geneva he proposed the abandonment of Sanctions.

These were good times for the dictators, bad times for those responsible in the democracies. Even Lord Londonderry could make bold to open his mouth again. Speaking at Newcastle-upon-Tyne, he asserted without batting an eye: "Mr. Baldwin announced to the House of Commons that he had been misled in relation to German armament. Mr. Baldwin was never misled."

In the summer of 1936 the European Dance of Death went into feverish spasms. Churchill recognized that Stalin's series of murdering trials opened the way for the Nazi-Communist world conspiracy. He asserted that Stalin had now come to represent Russian nationalism in "somehow threadbare Communist trappings." In his news letters he reviewed the consequences of the German-Japanese agreement, and he faced the fact that the smaller nations were anxious to put themselves on good terms with the stronger power. Most disastrous of all seemed to him the illusion in which Italy was reared. Rome began to regard Great Britain as a worn-out, dying power, whose great possessions and foremost place in the Mediterranean were the future inheritance of Fascism. He predicted clearly what President Roosevelt later termed "Mussolini's stab in the back."

The start of 1937 was no more encouraging. On January 27 Churchill proved in the House of Commons that Germany had already 2,000 front-line machines, including 200 so-called commercial planes that were disguised war machines—a figure that agreed with statements made in the French Chamber. The previous November, he declared, he had had to complain that the British Air Force amounted to but two-thirds of the German strength. Since then this proportion had increased to 1:2 in favor of Germany.

When Mr. Hitler declared on January 30, 1937, "The German Government have assured Belgium and Holland that they are prepared at any time to recognize and guarantee these States as inviolable neutral territories," Churchill remained skeptical. He knew that the existence of all the little states in the neighborhood of the Third Reich was threatened. He knew—and declared openly—that it was threatened by the helplessness and subservience of democracy in the hands of ambitious and commanding men, aided by the facilities of modern propaganda. There is no clearer anticipation of the hideous work of the Fifth Columns than as he presented it. The will of a single man with a handful of deeply involved confederates and a host of valiant and obedient agents, he asserted, might in a few weeks turn the same blast of propaganda, to which Czechoslovakia was just then exposed, against Holland, or against—the British Isles.

Churchill openly pointed out—on March 4, 1937—the devastating activity of a Fifth Column if things should come to the point of a battle for Britain. He spoke about "the presence in this country of the large number of foreigners who are all held together by bonds of Nazi or Fascist organizations." Probably some foreign General Staffs were better informed about a number of facts in England than her own Parliament.

In just one point the perpetual outsider could agree with the Government. Hands off Spain! was the advice he kept persistently giving his country, month after month. In face of the shameless, perjured intermeddling of the dictators it was hard to remain quiet and watch Spain, vital alike geographically and economically for England, sinking into vassalhood to the Axis. But the Loyalists were falling more and more under the spell of the red terror, and Churchill could foresee the day when Comrade Stalin would follow the call of his heart, his obsession for his model, Hitler. England, he felt, had no business in the fratricidal strife of the tyrannies. "I will not pretend that, if I had to choose between Communism and Nazism, I would choose Communism. I hope not to be called upon to survive in the world under a Government of either of those dispensations."

"You would not!" the independent Laborite Maxton shouted at him. A black forelock hung down over his bloodless face. It would be a great day when the comrades stood the counter-revolutionist Churchill against the wall—for smoking fine Havana cigars, owning an anti-proletarian wine cellar, and loving the fatherland of exploiters.

The King of the Belgians had just arrived in London on March 22, 1937. It was a wholly private visit. Handsome Leopold had expressly insisted that he should not be received with the honors of a state visit; presumably Mr. Hitler might object. Everyone knows that the Fuehrer is so sensitive. In his negotiations with Mr. Eden, the Foreign Secretary, he expressed the desire for effective safeguarding of Belgium's neutrality.

With pleasure, replied Mr. Eden. The Franco-Belgian Agreement of 1920 bound the French ally; the Treaty of Locarno also bound England to come to Belgium's assistance in case of German aggression. The obligation was of course reciprocal. Certainly it was time to start three-cornered General Staff conversations.

But no, that was not exactly what His Majesty meant. What he really meant was that he felt obliged to cancel the treaties with England and France. Hitler is not the naughty boy; that is all slander. The Fuehrer has promised not to hurt a hair of the Belgians' heads. He will respect their independence. It was disagreeable enough that the Belgians owed this independence to French and English mass sacrifice on the blood-soaked fields of Flanders.

Leopold was tall, dark blond, with brightly shining blue eyes.

He was the hero of a famous royal romance, the chivalrous ruler of "heroic little Belgium." The streets of London waved him a jubilant farewell when he had talked himself out of his obligations —Mr. Hitler does that sort of thing much more simply.

Only the old trouble-maker struck another discordant note. He frankly confessed that Leopold's change in Belgian policy caused him regrets and misgivings. He hoped the French would now draw their fortress line equally strong behind Belgium— which, disastrously, they never did. Does the decision of Belgium not almost imply acquiescence beforehand in their absorption by an aggressive Germany? Churchill asked.

They did worse than acquiesce, as was shown by a very near future that is now already in the past. They surrendered as soon as they had got English help on the spot, thus trapping the better part of the heroic B.E.F. and exposing it to untold horror. The English, of course, had come to rescue Leopold; so did the French, instead of their both remaining behind the French defenses, which were now thrown wide open. The English could be as naive as that. And the most clairvoyant of all Englishmen could be so naive as to receive the news of Leopold's surrender with the sole comment: "Thou shalt not judge."

When the European scene darkened, Churchill looked toward America. He was seeking for clarification more than for help and support. He realized the limits of American readiness to help, but also its importance. He warned of assuming that America's "friendly declarations" implied "any intention on the part of the United States to become involved in the quarrels and combinations of Europe." On the contrary, he felt the main movement of opinion in America was "more set on avoiding foreign entanglements and keeping out of another world war than ever before." Yet he considered it "a settled maxim of British policy that without the goodwill, or at least the acquiescence, of the United States the famous weapon of the blockade cannot be used."

On May 28 Mr. Baldwin resigned. This marked a momentous epoch in British politics; as a matter of fact Earl Baldwin of

Bewdley—he was elevated to the peerage on his retirement—was the last figure in London whom we still identify with peace-time. But the change took place in perfect calm. Everyone had expected it. Mr. Baldwin himself had announced it on April 11, speaking at Bewdley. Everyone knew that Mr. Neville Chamberlain, already for months past the driving force behind the scenes, would be in the driver's seat.

With unpretentious casualness he stepped into the foreground. The consuming egocentricity of a man to whom power came late in life remained concealed behind a rigid reserve that could be interpreted either as arrogance or as a retiring disposition. With his black hair surrounded by a band of silver, bushy eyebrows arched over dark eyes, prominent nose jutting from the thin face, his thin lips, his upright carriage, his invariable black suit with black tie, he looked like a raven. He had the dark pink complexion of the healthy elderly Englishman; not for two years was anyone to see how mortally pale he could turn. He looked ten or twenty years younger than his age. Probably in his youth he had looked ten or twenty years older. It is impossible to tell whether he was ever young. For the first fifty years or more he stood in the shadow of his great father, Joseph, and his brilliant half-brother, Sir Austen. He had to look after the family business while they were building an empire. They sent him to a desolate island in the Bahamas to plant hemp for seven years.

That same perseverance had survived. With admirable energy he steered again by the wrong compass. He and he alone was the skipper. The son of Joe the Olympian and the brother of Sir Austen with the gold-rimmed monocle no longer wanted any splendid figures about him. He surrounded himself with men who had a "passion for anonymity." His associates might neither appear nor be mentioned in public. The most important of them was Sir Horace Wilson, who soon rose to the gray eminence of Downing Street. Sir Horace had begun as a petty clerk in the Civil Service. He had not even attended a Public School. Along with Chamberlain he became the co-author of the Pact of Munich.

The old guard did not die and did not surrender. Sir John Simon was shifted to the Chancellorship. All England shuddered, for according to old tradition the next Prime Minister would be groomed there—and of all people in the country he was the most unpopular. Sir Samuel Hoare left the Admiralty for the Home Office. Here, while Nazi agents were flooding the United Kingdom, he fought stoutly for the abolition of the cat-o'-nine-tails. Mr. Duff Cooper took over the Admiralty, and Mr. Hore-Belisha became Secretary for War. Both were young blood, fiery patriots —and without influence in the highest councils.

Neville Chamberlain would put about the helm at his own discretion. He understood as well as anyone else that there was no going on with the old laissez-faire. But he shared his secret formula with no one. He had done an excellent job as Chancellor, and now he would triumph in history. As a matter of fact it was only an outward change. Baldwin's pipe was replaced by the umbrella as the national symbol. Mr. Chamberlain was proud— if so vain a feeling could be allowed—of the jokes that everyone made about his umbrella. It was the best defensive weapon. It was an old-fashioned article, admitted. But that was just what he wanted to be: a gruff, kindly, omnipotent pater familias. Thus he came close to the dictators. But he hoped that this would give him the reputation of an old-fashioned thoroughbred Englishman. He liked to be called "British like beef." Actually he was British like the slightly awry Englishmen who wear boiled shirts with their evening clothes for dinner in the middle of the African jungle, or like the missionaries who fish for heathen souls in the South Sea Islands. He was an eccentric figure behind a disguise of excessive normality. He was an introvert.

Churchill is an extrovert. He has nothing to conceal, nothing to suppress, nothing to compensate for. Although basically he has had to keep to himself the secret wealth of his visions, he feels comfortable only in company. Although he has spent his nights over figures, statistics, formulas, he laughs good-naturedly when they call him the perpetual dilettante. From the Indian polo championship to the last duel, the combat with Hitler, it has been an embattled road. But he has galloped irresistibly along it. Perhaps he is a Renaissance figure, perhaps the last Roman. Certainly he is a thoroughgoing Englishman, British like beef. He needs space, air, freedom to breathe, discussion and an audience. Of course he was instantly banished from Mr. Chamberlain's view. Thus began the hardest two years of his life.

He could not be silent, although he now sat in the furthest corner of the House, and got the floor only when no one was listening. Mr. Chamberlain exercised a stronger pressure than anyone ever before on the Conservative machine. He had all the whips in his pocket as no leader before him had ever done. Seats depended on the baring of his teeth, which some people could interpret as agreement, others as disapproval; at least so it seemed. The baring of his teeth when the Honorable Member for Epping spoke was always unmistakable. The Prime Minister wanted tranquillity in the country, and above all in the Party.

Churchill found no tranquility. After Mr. Chamberlain had been in office for two weeks, and the great opera of the Coronation was also past, he declared: "I, personally, have never been able to forget Europe. It hangs over my mind like a vulture."

While his own country slept, he put unshakable trust in France. "France is not going to be the country to betray the cause of Democracy." Here Churchill erred.

Sometimes he even still hoped for an understanding with the German people. His sole mistrust was directed at the Nazi Government. He could not understand, he confessed, why they seemed "resolved to isolate themselves morally as well as economically from the other great nations of the West." He could not keep his eyes shut to the fact that the Nazi Government followed the example the Comintern had set. He strongly felt the constant menace from the Fifth Column in England, those regimented Nazis in his own country. Why did not the Germans understand that such organizations were an affront to the national sovereignty of England?

The Nazi Press answered with a chorus of revenge. Churchill was now singled out in the Berlin Ministry of Propaganda as Nazism's enemy No. 1. Even "the Jew Rosenfeld"—the German translation of Roosevelt—was never so shamelessly slavered over.

Patiently Churchill replied that it was quite untrue to depict him as an enemy of Germany. To feel deep concern about that country's armed powers was in no way derogatory. One might dislike Hitler's system and yet admire his achievements.

One could not, obviously. Hitler's much-admired "achievements" were the direct consequence of his inhuman system. Churchill certainly understood this simple truism. But as the storm was raging he made a desperate effort to "appease" the Nazis in his own way: not by suicidal concessions, but by frank discussion. The storm of slander and abuse from Berlin taught him that no man and no country could escape its fate.

Mr. Chamberlain preferred other methods of appeasement: not direct public discussion between man and man, but secret diplomacy, for whose results the omnipotent head of the Government was not accountable even to his own Parliament. He strove not for an understanding of the peoples—perhaps he recognized that this was impossible in the state of mind of the Nazi nation—but a division of spheres of influence between great lords. He was not a Fascist himself—just the next thing to it. Out of a profound love of peace he struggled into the iron armor of dictatorship. It did not attract him, but neither did it repel him. Only he forgot that iron armor demands a sword, not an umbrella.

On November 16, 1937, he sent Lord Halifax to Germany. It was only a hunting party at Goering's forest of Schorfheide near Berlin. Unexpectedly it turned into a visit to Hitler at Berchtesgaden. After the shock produced by Sir John Simon's visit to the Fuehrer, such a repetition could of course never have been announced to the English public. But Mr. Chamberlain had made up his mind not to ask the children whether their diet suited them.

Lord Halifax's visit to Berchtesgaden was of course but one

more act of submission, for which Mr. Chamberlain, with great personal courage, had to assume the responsibility. The visit took place after Baron von Neurath, Hitler's conservative Foreign Minister, who was already at his last gasp—as Lord Protector of Czechoslovakia today he is the virtual prisoner of the Gestapo in the Hradschin at Prague—had declined to come to England. "The Angel of Peace is unsnubbable," as Churchill described it. He was not offended. He was always for talking. But he reminded the Government "how very sharp the European situation is at the present time."

Mr. Hitler too knew this perfectly well. Mussolini flashed the green light. The Duce introduced the Prussian goose-step in the Italian Army on February 3, 1938. This was one of the small attentions that passed between dictators—perhaps not outright professions of love, but at least signs of a working business agreement. With Mussolini in a good humor, or maybe trembling in his boots at his Frankenstein monster, Hitler could venture to inflict on him the greatest outrage Il Duce has ever had to endure. Hitler strengthened himself for the rape he intended by making the champagne salesman Ribbentrop Reich Foreign Minister a few days beforehand, on February 5, and turning out the two highest-ranking generals of the German Army, Minister of War von Blomberg and Army Chief von Fritsch. Both had warned the boss against adventures. On February 12 he summoned Dr. Schuschnigg to Berchtesgaden, and snatched Italy's Austrian protectorate.

In his eyrie up in the purer mountain air Hitler raged for seven hours. Not *like* a madman—during those hours, while the dream of his youth was being fulfilled it *was* real, open madness. "Vienna will be blasted from the earth if you keep on holding out, you damned Jesuit!" he bellowed at the Chancellor of Austria, the sovereignty of which he had voluntarily guaranteed six months before. "Do you want a witness to show that I really mean it?"

The Fuehrer was foaming at the mouth. "Keitel! Keitel! Keitel!" he raved. The new German Army Chief, General Keitel, must have been listening at the keyhole for his cue. He clicked his heels. "Correct, Sir," he agreed in curt Prussian. "All the plans for the aerial bombardment of Vienna are made."

With a despairing gesture Dr. von Schuschnigg reached for his cigarette-case.

"Do you want to poison me?" the Fuehrer bellowed at him, grabbing the cigarette from his hand.

Dr. von Schuschnigg got across the Austrian frontier with a couple of hours' delay. His companions no longer expected him. He slept like a dead man for twenty-four hours. Then he said: "It was a hard day." Then he appointed as his right-hand man Dr. Seyss-Inquart, the Nazi Gauleiter, Hitler's personal choice, who had hitherto professed to be a good Austrian Catholic. (To-day he is the Nazi Viceroy of Holland, Lord Protector of the country's Fifth Column, a traitor from first to last.) Then he made his will. And then the people of Austria rose to its old greatness for the last time in its two thousand years of history. The Austrian flag waved red, white and red in the wind from every house. The Nazis were gone from the streets of Vienna.

Mr. Eden was gone from Downing Street. Four days after Berchtesgaden, to which he wanted to reply with a show of energy, Mr. Chamberlain dropped him from the Government. Hitler had personally and publicly insulted him. Mussolini had his hench-man Farinacci write: "Our opinion will not change until London's foreign policy ceases to be directed by Mr. Eden." Mr. Chamberlain complied with the command. Even so he was a brave man—against his own Englishmen. He put the cause above the man.

Churchill shook his head. There was not much more that he could do while out of power. He could but try, try desperately to act as a guiding angel, unwaveringly and unshakably reminding the Government of the right path.

But Mr. Chamberlain had no use for a tutor in his family. He was pater familias himself. The guiding angel was just another undisciplined back-bencher to him. What did he care what Winston Churchill had to say?

Winston Churchill spoke most reasonably. He would go "as far as many a man" in making concessions, he asserted. He would not mind sacrifices, even, it was implied, the loss of a personal friend, and of much British prestige, provided such concessions would be reciprocated. There was only one possible reciprocation: the breaking of the Rome-Berlin axis. But Lord Halifax had just told the House that there could be no question of having the axis altered in any way. So why this complete defeat? Why this departure from power of a man whom nation and Parliament had entrusted with a certain task?

Again Churchill delivered one of his most memorable speeches. It was no use; he knew that his audience would not listen. Perhaps he only spoke to relieve himself. There was not much time left to speak.

The Navy, Churchill pointed out again and yet again, was no protection against the air. Was Europe confused, as Lord Halifax had said the other day? Certainly not on the side of the dictators, Churchill replied. Unless England woke up immediately, he foresaw a terrible fate.

Fate racing at express speed has confirmed every word of the prediction in this speech. The Prime Minister, falling under the wheels of Fate, forgave the prophet not a single word. Chamberlain took revenge upon Churchill for the slaps pocketed with aplomb from Hitler and Mussolini. This one man must now be banished and outlawed. His connection with the Conservative Party hung by a hair. The boss would break the hair with a single snap of the finger.

He was still the boss. Stubbornly Chamberlain clutched his power. England, he knew, was more powerless than ever. There were seven anti-aircraft guns in London. Churchill years before had demanded 1,500, as many as Germany had. Churchill must be crazy. The Prime Minister's tight lips were marked during those days by a smile that did not look altogether untroubled.

He still had his trump up his sleeve. At almost seventy the respectable business man of Birmingham, who had never bet more than half a crown on a horse, became a reckless gambler.

If only the time would not pass so swiftly! Chamberlain was seventy years old . . . and Hitler might wait scarcely a few weeks. Mr. Neville Chamberlain plunged into a breathless race against time. Outwardly he remained cool, calm and self-possessed. Every morning at ten he went for a casual stroll in Hyde Park. Annie, his wife, the only person who understood him, would be on his arm, with the Downing Street cat walking behind. Passers-by were surprised that he smiled so serenely while the earth trembled. Good old Neville . . . He knew what he was doing. As long as the Prime Minister was smiling, the nation could play cricket.

Certainly Mr. Chamberlain knew what he was doing. It was a devilishly clever idea. He would make time stand still by smashing the clock. Churchill, whose voice sounded like the bells of Big Ben, must be silenced.

CHAPTER XXIX

Winnie Is Back

Now no dog would take a scrap from his hand. Not when he parted in his youth from the Party he was born to, nor again at his noonday when he left the Liberals, with whom he had been twenty years in power, had he been so alone as now, raising his voice for the last time as an old man to snatch England back from the abyss into which she was reeling, drunk with sleep.

Thirty-five years before, when he first crossed the floor, Joseph Chamberlain had hated to see him go. Remember the Olympian's remark to Lady Oxford: "Arthur's mistake was in letting Winston go"? The son of the Olympian was different. He was a family man who took his flock under his wing—under the umbrella. "Père de famille est capable de tout." He shut Churchill out of all councils, cut him off from contact with the Party, never deigned to reply to his criticisms. Let Big Ben rumble itself hoarse in a vacuum.

It took courage now to stand by Churchill. The little lost legion in Parliament had courage. It stood by him. The world listened to him. American correspondents cabled his speeches at length to the other side. Though of course to avoid misleading their readers they had to add: However, it should not be forgotten that Mr. Churchill is only speaking for himself and, at best, for a handful of dutiful back-benchers. With this annotation the voice of England, her only one, crossed the ocean. The London press devoted a mere few lines of Parliamentary report to his statements.

And yet Churchill, who did not want to aggravate the situation, was speaking more cautiously than ever. Even to the hostility of Neville Chamberlain he replied courteously, as if he did not understand it, as if it did not shut him out from the responsibilities that awaited him. This was no time to be sensitive; this was the hour of doom.

On March 11, 1938, German troops invaded Austria. Now the swastika waved from every house in Vienna—or else. Field Marshal Goering gave his word of honor as an officer for Germany's determination to respect the territorial integrity of Czechoslovakia. As a matter of fact the second World War had already begun.

Mr. Chamberlain made a speech in the House on the rape of Austria that betrayed both despair and determination. Churchill resolved to hear only the determination. He had no voice left for personal feuds. Even if he was almost a political outcast he would put at the disposal of his Government whatever weight he still carried.

"Certainly not since the war have we heard a statement so momentous, expressed in language of frigid restraint but giving the feeling of iron determination behind it," he greeted Chamberlain's statement.

For two minutes he dutifully blew the horn of appeasement. Then the tune changed. He could not help it. He could not lie. "Why should we assume that time is on our side?" he asked, just having advised that no hasty decision should be taken. It was a cavalry-charge that he rode in the House. What good was it to deceive oneself any longer? Europe was confronted with a program of aggression, precisely unfolding. The choice between two decisions was left: to submit or to cope with the danger.

But could England still stave off the disaster? Where was she now? She had lost round after round of the armament competition. Ugly rumors about differences of opinion among the leading Ministers in respect to the development of the Air Arm circulated in the country. True, Mr. Chamberlain kept those differences down with an iron hand. He alone was in authority; all other opinions were unimportant. Nor would he tolerate any leakage to the public. For the first time the newspapers were warned to be careful in their reporting. But the young people of the R.A.F.

refused to be censored. Nothing was getting forward, they murmured. They received no arms, no planes; the aircraft manufac-
turers complained that no broad layout of the British aircraft
industry had been made at the beginning of the expansion; that
orders were given piecemeal in little packets; that plans were
repeatedly altered, that they had never been able to prepare their
works for mass production. Some of the aircraft firms were working at only two-thirds of their capacity; skilled workers were being
paid off in appreciable numbers in many places.

Unrest stirred in the country. Secret grumbling was heard even
in the acquiescent Parliament.

Churchill suggested placing the largest possible orders in the
United States and Canada. He had made that proposal two years
before, but then Mr. Baldwin of Sheffield did not want to com-
pete with home industry. Now Churchill pressed his idea once
more. Again and again his eyes turned to America—and again and
again he warned his country not to look at America with European eyes.

America was far away. But to the average Englishman Central
Europe was still more remote. People twisted their tongues around
Cze-cho-slo-va-kia. Were they to have their heads broken for it as
well? The innate anti-Continentalism of the island people was one
of the strongest trumps in Hitler's hand. Churchill again made
himself universally unpopular by trying to show his nation how
tremendously the map has shrunk. He warned of the time that he
saw coming, and that did indeed come, when Germany would be
undisputed master of the entire European continent. At present,
he asserted in those last days before the fall of Czechoslovakia,
Germany might contemplate a short war. But once she had swal-
lowed the continental powers the Nazi regime might be able to
feed itself indefinitely, however long a war lasted.

He was tired now of his everlasting prophecies, and still more
thoroughly tired of the awful consistency with which they were
fulfilled. He looked back to the five years he had talked to the
House, almost always about the same matters: about the danger

that the fate of Rome and Carthage might repeat itself. And repeat itself so senselessly. If Fate overtook us, he said, "Historians in a thousand years will still be baffled by the mystery of our affairs!"

Now was the last moment to rouse the nation. With hands upraised Winston Churchill stood before his people.

"The time is now!" unfortunately, was an expression that the English did not understand. It was more like words from Hitler's stock. The world had not yet recovered from the Austrian shock when a drum-fire of Nazi propaganda unparalleled in history was hurled against Czechoslovakia. Hitler himself fired the biggest gun. "Liar!" he shouted at the President of the Czechoslovakian Republic. "Miserable liar, low, vile liar," he repeated in a radio speech. Like a flood of slime there poured out of him the whole vocabulary that he had picked up at the Vienna flop-house.

At the same time his soldiers were marching, marching day and night. The entire German-Czech frontier was lined with a million and a half German troops. Tank regiments led the field-gray columns. Thousands of battle planes were mobilized. The plump Goering, reminded of his word of honor as an officer, said to the British ambassador, Sir Nevile Henderson: "Maneuvers, nothing but routine maneuvers!" He held out his hand, grinning. Sir Nevile shook it.

Neville Chamberlain at home was wringing his hands. With the existence of Czechoslovakia the honor of the Allies was at stake. Did the honest merchant from Birmingham understand it? Did he know that a firm dare not lose its credit? Mr. Chamberlain remained impenetrable. No man could see through his forehead. There are various conceptions of honor. Not of the existence of the Empire. What Mr. Chamberlain certainly did not understand during the days that led to Munich was that its existence was imperilled at the moment when the Nazis should become lords of the European Continent. In this historic stroke of stupidity lies his tragic guilt.

He suffered from a single obsession: the whole London area

GUNNING FOR NAZIS

Winston Churchill inspects an American-made "Tommy" gun

was protected by seven anti-aircraft guns. That idea might have driven even a younger man to madness. Under its pressure the Pact of Munich was solemnly signed on September 28, 1938. Cheers received the old man on his return to Croydon from signing away the safety of the British Empire. Strangers embraced in the street. Parliament held a triumphal demonstration in honor of its leader. John Masefield, the Poet Laureate, compared him with Priam, who went to the tent of the enemy to beg for his son. Thus Mr. Neville Chamberlain had begged in the tent of Munich for the sons of England.

Churchill? Thank goodness that old chatterbox could now be forgotten!

He would soon be not only forgotten but buried. New negotiations were announced between Chamberlain and Hitler. The return of the former German colonies was now in question. The Prime Minister was convinced that the Nazis' appetite would be satisfied when they had broken Czechoslovakia and got back their colonies. Then some treaties of friendship could be concluded—for instance an air pact including the abolition of the long-distance aeroplane. This might sound very pacifistic, but in practice would mean that Germany with her medium aircraft could easily reach London, while the R.A.F. could no longer reach Berlin. Then Hitler had another plan. He would demand that general elections in England should sanction the new agreements to be made. The British Government must prove its ability to deliver the goods. How could it prove that ability? Only by excluding certain parties and personalities from the elections. Gentle pressure from the Conservative machine would be enough to put out of politics for good the one man whom Mr. Hitler would no longer tolerate in the House at Westminster.

It was a diabolical scheme. Perhaps its execution failed only because Hitler could not observe even the pacts that he signed in bad faith. On the Ides of March his troops entered Prague. It all went so swiftly that the world was still rubbing its eyes while the Czechoslovakian Republic was already annexed, its army disarmed, its gold reserve, its armaments, its raw materials and food staples stolen. Without a single hour's pause for the change its industry went on working—for Germany; especially the Skoda Works, the greatest munitions factory on the Continent.

Now even Mr. Chamberlain awoke to the danger. He flung the helm all the way over. Poland and Rumania received guarantees. Other diplomatic negotiations were begun, particularly with Russia, and there were General-Staff conversations with France. A truce was declared in domestic politics. The Opposition was cordially urged to join in. Defense and preparations! was the new program. Only the man who had shouted himself hoarse for defense and preparation, Churchill, was excluded.

For the second time Mr. Chamberlain traveled the road alone— though this time he was going in the opposite direction. He was the weakling with the gesture of violence. Now he would show the world and show Hitler that they couldn't fool him! Public opinion, indeed, was outraged. The pillars of the system had to pull out all the stops to keep down the indignation for a while longer. The fall from the pacifist fool's paradise was too abrupt, the depth too great. "Crucify him!" took the place of "Hosanna!" Many people mistrusted Mr. Chamberlain. They suspected him still of having secret appeasement plans. They did him an injustice. This unassuming, inconspicuous gentleman, with his permanent, respectably black, protective coloration, had been hit at his most vulnerable point—his vanity. If he were to allow Churchill at his side now, as the rising clamor throughout the country demanded, the man would mar his own rehabilitation. Inevitably Churchill would steal the show that Mr. Chamberlain was determined to stage. This was the only visible reason why he still resisted, with the tenacity of a nine-lived cat, taking Churchill into his Cabinet.

The by-election at Westminster that had forced Churchill on the Conservative Party again had been a dress-rehearsal. The case was repeated. In the summer of 1939 all the elements that cut any figure in the intellectual and cultural life of the nation rose to demand Churchill's return. Lord Derby, England's Grand Old Man, the most popular figure in the realm next to the King, pulled the strings without emerging from his august retirement. The young Conservatives were his most heated advocates. The Liberals had no masses to put at his disposal, but there were a few excellent minds, among them Sir Archibald Sinclair, his friend of the Flanders trenches. But now it was no longer education and property alone that demanded Churchill. It was the people, the family in the cottage home, the beer-drinkers at the bar of the village pub, the fishermen, farmers, yes, even the munitions workers. The Labor Party had buried the hatchet. It realized that Winston Churchill was no longer a Party adversary. He no longer saw red, and the fact that he had been true blue all his life under the changing banners and colors was no reason for opposition now. The Labor Party sent its membership to attend when he got up in the House.

He got up but seldom. Perhaps he felt that he had grown beyond it all—even beyond the Parliament that had been his only true home since his twenty-fifth year. After this by-election in the summer of 1939, with all England one great constituency, he was a figure, almost an idea, not a man of parties and majorities.

He spent the summer at Chartwell Manor, seldom coming to town. He scarcely joined in the discussion, even in international discussion. The time for words was past. Was he to dispute with Mr. Chamberlain? Ridiculous! His was the duel with Hitler.

Beside this light the black shadow of Chamberlain vanished. True, the Prime Minister still had time to make what he called his feverish preparations in case of need. It was all too little and too late. Irreplaceable months were lost. And every soul in England knew that if it came to a war, Winnie would come back. Perhaps he would take over the Navy.

Every soul knew that war would come. Hitler swamped Poland. It might equally well have been Belgium, Norway, Switzerland, England herself—each country would have its turn in the end.

On September 3, at eleven-fifteen in the forenoon, Mr. Chamberlain had an important announcement to make to the country over the radio. War was declared!

At the same instant a wireless message went out from the Admiralty to all the English ships on the seven seas: Winnie is back.

CHAPTER XXX

On the Bridge

THERE he was again in his old place. Nothing had changed at Admiralty House since he had left it almost twenty-five years before. Only the crowds standing in front of the building, jubilantly cheering and welcoming old man Winnie back, where he so obviously belonged, had considerably increased since 1914. Then it had been Kitchener whose appearance at the window of the War Office had both excited and reassured the people of London. Acclaiming him they knew that victory would ultimately be won. This time the spontaneous ovation of the masses went to Churchill. Nobody considered that after all he merely held a post in Mr. Chamberlain's re-formed cabinet. That inexplicable understanding which in crucial moments unites nations and their true leaders— elected, appointed, or just God-given—swept the streets of London.

Here, behind the window of the old building, stood the man who was destined to be their war lord. He was no longer the familiar figure in the old-fashioned black suit, the polka-dotted tie, and the antediluvian hat he has worn for forty years. This hat, incidentally, was a combination of three chimney-pot styles, the Russel, the Sandringham and the Cockburn, as Lock's, his hatters of St. James's Street, once divulged. But now he has donned his world war uniform again, a simple blue outfit, and his square face with the double chin, the pugnacious nose, the heavy mouth, was overshadowed by a white naval service cap.

He lost no time in assuming his leadership. Immediately after Mr. Chamberlain in a grave, determined voice had declared that a state of war exists with Germany, Churchill spoke to the people

of the British Isles. His was but a short resounding address—
"pep talks" these speeches were soon to be called—but it contained all the elements of that high oratory that was soon to carry
Churchill's wartime speeches all over the world. The mixture is
always identical: excitement and warning, enthusiasm and scepti-
cism, sober horse-sense and unbreakable trust in the cause. There
is a touch of vision in these speeches, but hard-boiled realism, too,
and, above all, confidence that right will prevail. Since Winston
Churchill has outgrown himself he is, as a speaker as well as a
fighter, first and foremost a moralist.

"Outside the storms of war may blow and the land may be
lashed with the fury of its gales," he addressed England on September 3, 1939. "But in our hearts, this Sunday morning, there is
peace. Our hands may be active, but our consciences are at rest.
We must expect many disappointments and many unpleasant surprises," he added as a warning which any other speaker would
certainly have skipped at this moment of general elation. "This
is not a question of fighting for Poland," he continued, thus stat-
ing at the very beginning the British war aims which today still
excite so much curiosity among American business-appeasers. "We
are fighting to save the whole world from the pestilence of Nazi
tyranny and in defense of all that is most sacred to man. This is
a war to establish on impregnable rocks the right of the individual, and it is a war to establish and revive the stature of man.
Confidently we look forward to the day when our liberties and
rights will be restored to us, and when we shall be able to share
them with the peoples to whom such blessings are unknown."

Berlin did not miss this flourish of trumpets. "There stands the
enemy!" the spokesman in the Wilhemstrasse said, commenting
on Churchill's first declaration. Grand Admiral Raeder, C.I.C.
of the German Fleet, and the only officer in the German High
Command about whose personal faithfulness to Hitler there is
no doubt, kept silent. He had prepared his answer already. A few
days before the start of hostilities German U-boats had been dispatched to the shipping lanes on the high seas. One of them tor-

pedoed the *Athenia,* carrying hundreds of Americans back to their homes. This assault on an unarmed merchantman with a cargo of civilians, mostly neutrals, was just the opening shot in the German propaganda barrage. Presently the second stroke followed. Residents of New Jersey, many of whose names appear on Goebbels' mailing lists, were deluged with letters from Berlin accusing Churchill of having deliberately sunk the *Athenia* in order to create a new *Lusitania* incident. Winston Churchill was singled out as the arch-enemy of humanity, which Hitler was about to defend. Thus the German assault on the freedom of the seas started with a crime and a lie.

Churchill conducted the war at sea from Admiralty House which had not changed in two hundred years, though it was now but a small part of the Admiralty Buildings. The First Lord still presided as he had for two hundred years in the same old Board Room over the dinners and decisions of the Sea Lords. In the middle of this room stands a big directors' table with a great elliptical seat carved out at one end to provide greater comfort for a stout admiral. Undeniably Mr. Churchill had to use this seat. Today, if he still were at the Admiralty, he would no longer need it. He has lost fifteen pounds.

The room is panelled in dark oak with pilasters spaced along the walls. Over the fireplace hangs the famous wind-dial connected to a vane on the roof. Mapped on the face of the dial are Britain's seas full of whales and other allegoric figures, and each of the neighboring countries bearing its heraldic symbol. From one end of the room looks down the picture of William IV, from the other Nelson after the battle of the Nile. A little ivory desk in wood panelling is near the fireplace. It is five feet four inches from the floor: Nelson's height, and since his day, the minimum height for enlistment in the navy. At this desk the decisions are signed. So it was in Nelson's time.

The idyllic life of the country squire in Chartwell Manor is gone. Churchill no longer presides over the five reception rooms of his country seat, the nineteen bed- and dressing-rooms, the large studio—in which some of his greatest works of literature were written—and the three cottages (one of them built personally by the squire with the help of his daughter Sarah and her husband Vic Oliver, the comedian). He now confined himself to a narrow bedroom on the ground floor at the far left corner of Admiralty House, along with the suite of rooms for entertaining the government. He did not miss too much the comfort he had previously enjoyed. When friends reminded him of the floodlit swimming pool in Chartwell, the First Lord's answer was: "The seven seas are bigger!" The large studio with its north light, where he used to paint, had to be forgotten—and the painting, too. The blue sitting room with doors on to a tiled terrace and with the wonderful view from the windows of the Kentish Weald was now a memory. There is one pleasure of private life, however, which Winston Churchill cannot forget. He remembers his personal friends, the ten thousand tropical fish in the seven ponds on his estate. In peaceful times he used to watch them for hours, to feed them, and call some of them by name. He remembered them when Hitler's attacks on man and beast in England grew ever more ruthless. The First Lord of the Admiralty took care to have them moved to safer ponds.

Exercise, of course, had to be given up. From bed to desk was about all. For centuries it had been the same desk and the same old oak chair in front of it, and Samuel Pepys' picture smiling cryptically down. In other rooms, around him, the telegraphists were working on their codes, the experts drafting blueprints for naval improvements. The wireless atop the Admiralty is used only for picking up messages. The real transmission points for messages to the Fleet are elsewhere in England. But in Churchill's room beat the pulse of the world. Sea battles in the South Atlantic and Eastern Mediterranean were directed from his desk.

Already in the first days of the war his impact on the country was terrific. He talked, a cabinet colleague observed, with the accents of a war leader. There was no regret over the past, no trace of weariness in his voice and manner. His hammered sentences sounded like the bark of field guns. "He has an imaginative grasp of strategy!" the *New Statesman and Nation* welcomed him. Others were afraid that under Churchill's conduct the Admiralty's share of the war would overbalance the army's side. But would he remain at the Admiralty? Suddenly a word was again circulated, a word that Sir Edward Grey had said at his own dinner table as far back as 1909: "Winston will very soon be incapable, from sheer activity of mind, of being anything else in a cabinet but Prime Minister." And another sentence, coined long ago by Lord Birkenhead, made the rounds of Whitehall again: "Churchill's tastes are simple. He is easily contented with the best of everything."

However soon these predictions proved to be justified, there was no doubt of Churchill's naval single-mindedness at the outset of the war. He was aware that he had picked out the hardest job for himself, and that the survival of the Empire depended on England's maintaining her supremacy at sea. The development of the war so far has fully confirmed this view.

On September 26, 1939, Churchill delivered his first statement as a cabinet member. Old-timers in the House were touched as he rose not from his already historic modest seat below the gangway, but from the front bench. Aesthetes objected. "No longer shall we see him in that famous corner seat," the *Sunday Times* wrote lyrically, "drawing his sword and urging the entire Ministry to be on guard. The brigand chief is in chains, the buccaneer in irons. It did not seem right to see him rise and make a statement from the dispatch box with an almost deferential air."

This deferential air, it seems, was worn to cover strong emotions. Churchill was subject to little tongue slips, such as had never occurred to him in forty years of parliamentary oratory. He spoke of December instead of September; he used the figure of fourteen instead of fourteen thousand; occasionally his Parliamentary Under Secretary, Geoffrey Shakespeare, had to come to his aid. It was the old skipper's first day on the bridge, an important day in Churchill's life indeed. His first governmental declaration confirmed that he had made peace with the powers that be, and that he had buried his conflict with Chamberlain, whom, incidentally, he overshadowed from the first moment he joined the government. But of course he did not touch upon personal affairs. "The war at sea has opened with intensity," he stated. "Ships were set upon by U-boats carefully posted beforehand. In the first week our losses were half of the losses in 1917, the peak year of U-boat attack. The convoy system is a good and well tried defense, but no one can pretend that it is a complete defense. Other forms of attack on our shipping are attack by surface craft and attack from the air. I must warn the House that we cannot guaranty immunity. We must expect further losses."

Again a prediction of Churchill's became stark reality. A year later the U-boat was to be the deadliest menace to England's conduct of the war. However, the First Lord was not disheartened by difficulties. He promised that soon the entire mercantile marine of the British Empire—two thousand ships on the salt water every day—would be armed, and that the "hunting forces," the destroyer flotillas, should rapidly increase. "One German captain signaled to me personally the position of a British ship which he had just sunk," Churchill continued. "Since his message was only signed *German Submarine* I was in doubt at the time as to what address I should direct my reply. However, the captain is now in our hands, and will be treated with all consideration."

The House roared with laughter. The Nazis displayed less sense of humor. U-boat Captain Herbert Schultze—which means John Doe in German—replied over the CBS network in Berlin that he had sent this particular message to Mr. Churchill, after having sunk the British steamer *Firby,* and he stressed that he still enjoyed his liberty.

Again German propaganda miscarried. The U-boat captain, who had indeed sunk the *Firby* off the Scottish coast, had been kind enough to invite Mr. James Woodruff, chief officer of the torpedoed boat, to a stiff drink and a friendly conversation. Mr. Woodruff listened to the radio boast of "Captain Herbert

Schultze," and stated with absolute confidence that this was an impersonator's voice. The right U-boat skipper, in fact, enjoyed—and still enjoys—British hospitality somewhere in Canada.

There are not always cordial chats and friendly drinks when U-boats torpedo merchantmen. Outraged, Churchill in his first account of the war at sea told the House of the sinking of the *Royal Sceptre,* whose crew of thirty-two were left in open boats hundreds of miles from the nearest shore. Then there was the case of the *Hazeltide,* an ordinary merchantship, twelve of whose sailors were killed by surprise gunfire. "We cannot recognize this type of warfare as other than contrary to all long acquired and accepted traditions of the sea," Churchill said.

Today Hitler does not mind admitting that his U-boat campaign by no means conforms to international law. With gusto he boasts the "packs of wolves" which he unlooses upon the shipping lanes. At the beginning, however, the German war conduct still pretended to decency. In defense of his decency Hitler, answering Churchill in Saarbrücken, called the First Lord a "warmonger." That was his only explanation of the U-boat's crimes.

After five weeks Churchill was undisputedly recognized as the most inspiring figure in the cabinet. He was in his element. The English people sensed it. They had forgotten his family name. Even the doorman at the Admiralty spoke of his boss tenderly as Winnie. A secret service man in Number 10 Downing Street seemed to be the last die-hard. When the First Lord rushed by him, at sixty-five still the young man in a hurry, he was suddenly stopped.

"Your pass, sir!"

"My face is my fortune!" Churchill answered and stormed along.

The pubs approved of him. The streets were jubilant when he appeared. He stole the show when he accompanied his son Randolph to church in Westminster. At this marriage, on October 7, 1939, not the beautiful bride—the Honorable Pamela Beryl Digby —but the bridegroom's father was the star.

The Cockneys loved him, when they caught a glimpse of him walking like a happy old tugboat captain with a sailor's cap on his head and a dead cigar between his teeth. The two pictures he permitted to be taken of himself during the first weeks of the war were carefully chosen. The first showed him with his unbreakable "Just let me handle this job" smile entering the Admiralty, the second in an old battered hat, after an inspection of the fleet, somewhere in Scotland. He was the first First Lord of the Admiralty whom the army, too, admired, in spite of some traditional rivalry between the fighting services. On October 20 he was promoted to the rank of Honorary Colonel of the Royal Artillery of the Territorial Army.

His words electrified the masses. "Hunting German submarines not without relish" immediately became a household expression. About the Soviet Union he coined the phrase: "a mystery wrapped inside an enigma." But he by no means confined himself to coining popular phrases. His speeches were heavy with serious forebodings, none of which, however, could seriously affect his confidence in the future. "Britain," he declared on October 1, "accepts whatever sacrifices are necessary to protect her way of life and the ideals she cherishes. . . . It may be that great ordeals will come to us in this island from the air. But we must remember that the command of the seas will always enable us to bring the immense resources of Canada and the New World into play as a decisive ultimate air factor beyond the reach of what we have to give and take over here." These prophetic words were borne out by events a year later. We have witnessed "the great ordeal from the air" that came to England, and we are witnessing the New World mobilizing at top speed.

Early in November Churchill assured his country that the final victory on the sea was assured. But it would take enormous efforts, he added, to overcome the U-boat menace. He ventured to predict that Germany would have a hundred or more new submarines in action toward the turn of the year, information which proved to be accurate. A U-boat had torpedoed the *Royal Oak* at

Scapa Flow on October 14. Discussing this tragic incident in the House on November 8, Churchill did not conceal the flaws in the defenses of Scapa Flow, and what he termed the "overconfidence" which led to the loss of the *Royal Oak* through sheer neglect. He did not, of course, stress that he had inherited this sad state of affairs from his predecessor at the Admiralty. He extended his chivalry even to the enemy. "A remarkable exploit of professional skill and daring" he called U-Boat Captain Guenther Prien's action. But it should not happen again, and indeed it did not happen again. "Utmost fish!" was Churchill's slogan. "Utmost fish" is navy slang. It means: action is urgently requested.

To stave off the U-boat danger Churchill suggested more intimate collaboration with the French fleet. He took a day off from his office, flew to Paris, and dined on November 3 with Cesar Campini, the French Minister of the Navy. He interviewed Daladier and held rapid conferences with Gamelin, Air-Minister General Victor Vuillemint, and Admiral Jean Darlan, who would have liked to become Supreme Commander-in-Chief of the inter-Allied navies. Since he did not reach this ambitious aim, he chilled considerably toward England; later, as Pétain's minister, he commanded the fleet of Vichy. Churchill's interest in and sympathy for the French ally was as keen as during the first World War, when he had been the pillar of the entente cordiale on the British side.

To Hitler this stressing of the intimacy between the two great Western democracies, that then still existed, was the most disturbing of Churchill's various activities. The Führer undoubtedly had already entered the war with the intention of forcing France out of the alliance, down the road of treason, surrender and suicide. Again it was no other but Winston Churchill who endangered this conspiracy. The Nazis reacted true to form. As soon as Churchill returned from Paris, he was singled out by their propaganda as public enemy number one.

A man hunt started. The Berlin Telefunken broadcast the following warning: "If something should happen to our Führer we should have no one left in Germany to keep us calm. That, Mr. Churchill, might cost you your life!" German mines were inscribed in white paint: "When that goes up, up goes Churchill!" Mr. Thomas, fireman aboard the torpedoed steamer *Darino*, stated that the torpedoes which had blown up his ship carried the inscription: "For Churchill!"

Churchill did not answer in kind, but now he dropped the vestige of politeness with which he so far had treated Hitler personally. In a radio speech on November 12, he called the Führer a cornered maniac and a monstrous apparition, and for the first time in this war he used the last war's favorite expression: Huns.

The battle of words, of course, echoed as far as America. On November 30, thousands of surprised Americans found in their morning mail leaflets from an unknown German friend, Herr H. R. Hoffmann, Starnberg, Bavaria—whose propaganda barrages on America were recently disclosed by the Dies Committee—who had taken the liberty of sending, via Siberia, his pamphlet "News from Germany" which carried obscene attacks on Churchill. The headline shouted piously: "And ye shall know the truth, and the truth shall make you free!" What Herr Hoffmann called the truth is not fit for print. Remarkably, his England-baiting and his furious assault on Churchill was not interspersed with a single word against France.

While American onlookers were still joking about the "Sitzkrieg" the fate of France was already in the making. From the British side, it was an underground battle which Churchill led. He hoped that the scuttling of the *Graf Spee*, which occurred in the middle of December and which spread joy and new confidence all over England, would encourage the French also. Not quite without contempt, Churchill emphasized in his report that the *Graf Spee* had scuttled herself to avoid a showdown—a sacrifice to the headlines rather than to superior tonnage and firing power, he termed it. The "reinforcements," which the Admiralty had announced to frighten the *Graf Spee* commander, in fact consisted solely of the light cruiser *Cumberland*, which took the

Exeter's place. The *Graf Spee* could still have outgunned and outsped the light British craft she had to cope with.

The victory of Rio Plata did not fail to impress the French. M. Campini, Minister of the Navy, returned Churchill's visit on December 20 in London. He assured his British colleagues of France's eternal fidelity.

Churchill wanted to find out for himself. On New Year's Day, 1940, he flew to Paris once more. With him went Mr. Chamberlain and Viscount Halifax to meet their French colleagues of the Supreme War Council. On their way they saw German mines floating down the Channel. They were detained a bit. Churchill, of course, had to watch the destruction of these mines by British mine-sweepers.

He used the occasion of his flying visit to France to inspect the British forces on the Western Front. He dined with the leaders of the R.A.F. He was accompanied by Professor Lindeman of Oxford, the inventor of the "Lindeman cigar" to combat the airplanes. A few years previously, as has been mentioned, Churchill and Lindeman had in vain tried to interest Earl Baldwin, then vacationing at Aix-les-Bains, in the invention. Churchill does not forget his friends. On assuming the First Lord's job he made the professor chief of the Admiralty department that examines the inventions submitted. The professor, now Lieutenant Colonel, is among the greatest living authorities on secret weapons.

On the surface these early days in January passed in perfect harmony. Sir Edmund Ironside, then Chief of Staff of the B.E.F., was decorated with the Grand Croix of the Legion d'Honneur, and Churchill watched the ceremony with a bright smile which could not escape the photographer's attention. There were dinners in the headquarters of the B.E.F. and the R.A.F., at which the First Lord and the French leaders exchanged highly complimentary toasts. But before and after dinner there were serious conversations. Churchill was intuitively aware that the French nerves were cracking. His French friends explained to him that they wanted to relieve from military service their own older men.

Why was the B.E.F. not reinforced to offset the balance? The British War Minister at that time was Leslie Hore-Belisha. He opposed the idea of calling up masses of untrained and unequipped men and sending them over to France. Churchill tried to bring about a compromise. He understood the tremendous importance of keeping France in line. He did not see eye to eye with Hore-Belisha in all problems of war conduct. But he was handicapped by his position in the Admiralty. It was indeed unusual that the First Lord should inspect the expeditionary forces and review the air-arm, that he should conduct diplomatic negotiations with the allies, that, in fact, a department minister should run the show.

In these days the first rumors started that Churchill would coordinate the British defense. The experience of the last war had unmistakably shown the necessity of such coördination, which, indeed, should have gone beyond national boundaries and been inter-allied. There is no possible doubt that the blitzkrieg, the success of which was due far more to the weakness of defense than to the German offensive power, could never have crushed Holland, Belgium and France had the resistance been better organized and centralized. There was one man on earth for this job.

But, in addition to French jealousies, at home Mr. Chamberlain balked. He was no longer an appeaser. On the contrary, his outraged honesty was infuriated against Hitler, who had double-crossed him. Now it was his personal holy task to break Hitler. He would not share his task with anybody. It was a question of his personal vindication. So Mr. Chamberlain decided that coördination of defenses would lead to dual control of the British war conduct. It could not be done.

Of course it could have been done had Churchill insisted on a showdown. United, England stood behind him, and Chamberlain was entirely dependent on his coöperation. But Winston Churchill remains a Victorian gentleman also in a rather shabby world. Domestic troubles at a moment that demanded closest national concentration would have been unthinkable to him. Besides, he must have sensed—while onlookers on both sides of the Atlantic still joked about the Sitzkrieg—that an unparalleled assault was in the making. He knew the hour was coming. It would be his hour. Gay, jovial, expansive Winnie was a secluded, a lonesome man in these nerve-racking days of lull and silence. He leaned on a friendship that was rapidly becoming increasingly important to him— the friendship with his son, now his constant companion.

Winston Churchill does not wait for the enemy to strike. He has never accepted Hitler's boastful claim that he, the Führer, alone dictates the law of action. "Prepare for very rough sailing!" Churchill admonished his nation on January 13. He did not want to be misunderstood. He did not demand any glorious side-shows. What he demanded was full concentration on the world's neuralgic spot: the Western Front.

On January 20, he delivered a radio address which remains so far his most striking utterance of the war. He appealed to Europe's neutrals to side with the Allies, not in the interest of the Franco-British cause, or even of the world cause of democracy, but simply to save their own skins. His hope was to concentrate all the forces of European civilization in a powerful counter-attack against aggression and oppression. It was the old League of Nations idea, adapted to the necessities of winning the war and creating a better order. He said, in part:

"For several months past the Nazis have been uttering ferocious threats of what they are going to do to the British Empire. But so far it is the small neutral states that are bearing the brunt of German malice and cruelty. The plight of the neutrals is lamentable. It will become much worse. They bow humbly and in fear to German threats of violence. Each one hopes that if he feeds the crocodile enough, the crocodile will eat him last. All of them hope that the storm will pass before their turn will come to be devoured. But I fear greatly that the storm will not pass. It will rage and it will roar, ever more loudly, ever more widely. It will spread to the south, it will spread to the north.

"Neutral ships are sunk without law or mercy. A German major makes a forced landing in Belgium with plans for the invasion. In Rumania there is deep fear lest by some deal between Berlin and Moscow they may become the next object of aggression. German intrigues are seeking to undermine the newly strengthened solidarity of the South Slavs. The Dutch stand along their dikes. All Scandinavia dwells brooding under Nazi and Bolshevist threats."

The little neutral's reaction to this appeal to their sanity was disappointing. Some of them furiously attacked Churchill as the aggressor. "A strange reprimand of neutrals," the semi-official *Nation Balge* termed his speech, declaring: "Belgium does not feed the crocodile, and is ready to defend her territory against foreign invasion. May we say that our King and our government and our Parliament approving the reasons for remaining neutral are better placed and qualified to judge the interests of our country?"

In Holland the reaction was similar. "Churchill's broadcast was a sharp attack on the neutrals," the *Rotterdamsche Courant* wrote. "The Dutch government remains sure that Germany will not attack the Netherlands." The *Telegraaph*, Holland's largest circulation daily, echoed: "Our government's determination to maintain neutrality at any cost is so well known that Churchill himself cannot doubt it." And *Het Volk* of Amsterdam, the socialist mouthpiece, added: "Churchill's statement is unfriendly and wide of the mark. It is a piece of eloquence rather than a political argument."

The Dutch parliament indulged in a full-dress debate on Churchill's speech. Unanimously speakers of all parties rejected it. Vigorously they assailed Churchill. Dr. Lohmann, speaking for Prime Minister de Geer's Christian Historic Party, declared: "Churchill's speech has killed collective security."

In Copenhagen the powerful *Politiken* accused Churchill of "trying to whirl the remaining neutrals into savagery. The small neutral states will feel no gratitude to Mr. Churchill," the paper continued, "because he is dragging them in. Mr. Churchill's speech will be considered a dainty morsel for the German Propaganda Ministry." And Copenhagen's *Ekstrabladet* added: "Churchill's appeal will meet with definite opposition from this group of neutral states to which Denmark belongs. The war aims of either side are irrelevant to her."

The Norwegian *Dagbladed* summed up: "Mr. Churchill's moral exhortations are unwarranted."

The papers quoted above and all the countries they spoke for were liquidated a few weeks later. The official German comment which Churchill's speech evoked reads ironically in the light of events that followed immediately and that are history today. Said the *Deutsche Diplomatische Correspondence,* the German Foreign Office official organ: "Everyone knows that Germany desires no open or camouflaged inclusion of any kind of the neutrals in the war. The invitations to the neutrals to join the Allies in their crusade against aggression and wrongs aroused more suspicion than sympathy. The speech has been disavowed in Churchill's own country."

Indeed, Viscount Halifax, the Foreign Secretary, had not been slow in reassuring the neutrals—in a speech delivered at Leeds—that no changes in British foreign policy were planned. In no neutral country, the Viscount perfectly well understood, was there a tendency to take up arms to bring about termination of hostilities.

Again, as so often in his life, Churchill had been ahead of his times, if, on this occasion, only for a few weeks. Again he stood alone. The fifth columnists—a handful of Communist and Nazi sympathisers who soon were to be effectively dealt with—sensed their opportunity. They tried to disturb the big meeting in Manchester on January 27, 1940, at which Churchill spoke.

Manchester is a well-tried battleground for Churchill. Here he won his spurs as a youngster in politics. From here he was sent to the House. Here his name resounded with memories from the old days. True, the slogan "Manchester versus Birmingham" has long lost its meaning. Yet the burgesses of Manchester still proudly remember that Winston Churchill made the name of their city an international slogan, known all over the world as a by-word for Free Trade. It was most uncautious on the part of the fifth columnists to challenge the old lion in his den.

The chairman of the meeting was for calling the police when the hecklers began to interrupt. But Winston Churchill needs no police in Manchester. "It's all right," he told the chairman, "I'll hold them. I've forty years' experience addressing rowdy meetings." Undoubtedly, he still liked a fight.

"Resistance is not enough for victory," he declared. "Not national defense but only annihilation of Hitler's system will save England. The Germans are responsible for the Nazi cause. Economic warfare alone cannot accomplish Hitler's defeat. The Germans are a tough lot, able to endure privations indefinitely. The German army is a formidable machine, still unimpaired. The Allies must force Hitler to accept battle whenever it suits them. Exercise of ceaselessly growing pressure on the Germans is what the nation now expects to be done. Not Germany must be destroyed, but her armed might."

From the outset to this day Churchill has remained the one man in England whom the Nazis could not fool, neither about their tactics, nor about their nature. They used desperate means to discredit him. Berlin recorded Churchill's Manchester speech. It was doctored with boos, catcalls and whistling. "England is at the brink of revolution!" the German radio speaker announced. "Listen what sort of a reception the warmonger Churchill gets from his own people. . . ."

The reception, in fact, had been enthusiastic. Not Manchester alone, but all England cheered. They hearkened to the voice. Churchill had already established his supreme authority in Britain.

Mr. John McGovern, independent Labour M.P., raised the only dissenting voice: "Churchill is prepared to carry on the war for the next fifteen years," he declared, "and then to hand it over to his son Randolph or to Vic Oliver."

Churchill made no objection. On this particular day he was engaged in more important business. He was deeply in conversation with the American Under-Secretary of State, Mr. Sumner Welles, President Roosevelt's personal emissary.

The conclusions to which Mr. Welles came after his peace mission to the belligerent capitals are still a strictly guarded secret. It can be assumed, however, that his meeting with Churchill left him under no illusion about the latter's decision to carry the war to a victorious, if probably distant, end.

"The small nations," Churchill explained on March 30, undaunted by the rebuke he had just received from them, "are still forced to supply Germany with the means of future aggression. This is a fantastic situation. While it is, to quote Lord Balfour, a singularly ill-contrived world, it is not so ill-contrived as that. Europe is in for a long war. In part this is due to the failure of the little neutrals to recognize the common peril and to see on which side their bread is buttered. At any moment those neutrals may be subjected to an avalanche of steel and fire. The decision rests in the hands of a haunted, morbid being whom, to their eternal shame, the German people in their bewilderment have worshipped as a god! . . . The war will be long and not an easy one. To dilettante or purblind worldlings who ask why we are fighting I say: If we left off fighting you would soon find out!"

He did not leave off fighting. Invisible to most, but watched by Churchill with every breath and every throb of his heart, the catastrophe closed in upon neutral onlookers and half-hearted allies. Churchill decided to attack in defense. On April 1 he issued an order to tighten the blockade. The contraband control should be extended to the Pacific. He pointed out the spectacular rise in export of U.S.A. war-materials to the Soviet Union and other neighbors of Germany; of course these goods were re-shipped into the Reich, although some of them had previously been bought in British colonies for American consumption alone.

This radio speech, largely addressed to Canadian and American listeners, caused healthy reactions across the Atlantic, but Europe's little neutrals remained on the fence. An official Dutch comment argued that deliberate restrictions of the Netherlands' trade with Germany would not decisively contribute to an Allied victory, but only anger Germany. More violent was the repercussion in Norway. Churchill had suggested that the Norwegians stop supplying Germany with Swedish ore along their waterways. Such a measure, he insisted, would certainly shorten the war. He preferred to avoid intervention, he asserted, but the traffic with Swedish ore must be stopped.

"Norway will protest!" the answer came like a flash. "She will seek to prevent any violation of her territorial waters with whatever show of force she can display." Indeed, Norway threatened England with war, while a few thousand German "tourists" were already occupying the country's strategic key positions.

Most likely the difficulties with Norway finally induced Mr. Chamberlain to promote Churchill to the rank of director of the armed services, simultaneously retaining his office as First Lord.

Berlin raged. "The power in England is now in the hands of fanatics who have no inhibitions." It sounded strange indeed from Hitler's mouth. Besides, it was an overstatement. In fact the roles in London were little changed. Churchill's promotion was merely a governmental affair. His new rank had no standing, either in the political conception or constitutionally.

"Does that mean that Churchill has taken over the war conduct?" a frightened foreign diplomat inquired. He received a reassuring answer: "Two men run this war, Chamberlain and Halifax!"

True, Churchill was now recognized as the Prime Minister's powerful adviser on military affairs. But his promotion was still a half-hearted business. It was like every act of Mr. Chamberlain's during the years of his unrestricted control, too little and too late.

Churchill, on the other hand, has never lost time. Four days after his modest promotion he ordered the laying of mines in Norwegian waters. Thus the German shipping of Swedish ore would be forced into the open seas, where the British navy was waiting to interrupt the flow of Germany's vital war commodity.

London was not astonished. The English considered Churchill's measure as the logical outcome of the cabinet reshuffle. But Norway protested in London. Her last act of independence was to assail the very power on which she depended for protection.

Two days later, on April 9, there was nothing left of Norway's independence. The German invasion had started with clockwork precision. While Hitler's legions were already marching, Goering's pilots dropped pamphlets all over Norway and Denmark. They read: "Churchill wanted to police the Norwegian and Danish waters against the will of the two countries. He is responsible for your lot. He is the century's greatest warmonger."

And to the Gestapo chief in Narvik, who had muscled in with the spearhead of the attack, went a cable from Berlin, right from the Führer's private secretariat: "Seize Giles Romilly, Daily Express reporter. He is Winston Churchill's nephew."

CHAPTER XXXI

Falling Upstairs

AND so, after seven months of indecision, London was aroused to the reality of war. Mr. Chamberlain had received the news of the German invasion at 7 A.M. He immediately summoned a cabinet meeting. Churchill was first to arrive, at 8:30 sharp. The deliberation of the cabinet was interrupted, at 10:15, by a visit from Eric Colban, the Norwegian Minister. He looked disturbed—a few days ago he had presented his country's protest to the same men whose assistance he now frantically implored. Viscount Halifax gently took him aside. When they had finished their chat, Mr. Colban smiled: "Nobody is so agreeable to talk to as Lord Halifax when a minister has lost his country."

At tea time Ambassador Joseph Kennedy called at the Foreign Office. Meanwhile Messrs. Reynaud and Daladier had arrived by plane from Paris. Whitehall was teeming with activity. What did they talk about? What was the decision?

The *Daily Sketch* next morning presented the main topic of conversation, as Norway and Denmark fell. "Winston Churchill now faces the greatest opportunity of his life!" the paper's headline screamed.

The opportunity was supposed to be primarily naval, and it developed into high politics. The naval opportunity, to tell the truth, was non-existent. In vain the *Daily Sketch* had written: "Our navy at last will have her chance. It is an opportunity such as has not been afforded to us since Trafalgar destroyed Napoleon's last claim to mastery of the seas." In the days of Trafalgar the narrow waters were not yet dominated by aircraft. Now the exposure of heavy battleships in coastal waters would have been naval suicide.

The British navy, however, gave a good account of her fighting spirit in the Kattegat and in the North Sea. She inflicted heavy losses on the German fleet, sinking enemy warships and many troopships. Exactly to what extent the German fleet was crippled will probably not be known until the end of the war. Certainly her appetite for another encounter was spoiled. The German High Sea Fleet, up to this writing, has not again left home ports and coastal waters. The situation, of course, will forcibly be changed, if and when Hitler actually attempts invasion of England.

The battle of the North Sea raged four days: from invasion day, the seventh of April, to the eleventh. For Churchill these were days and nights of almost superhuman tension. He spent them at his desk in the Admiralty. There he was the all-powerful Commander in Chief, yet, by the same token, only an onlooker. Hundreds of miles of stormy sea separated him from the actual fighting, yet he was every minute and every second informed about it. The radio station atop the Admiralty picked up signals, commands, messages. At times the man at the receiving end could hear the spattering of shells and the burst of broadsides. But Churchill had to pace a room—a spacious one, admittedly—and that felt like being in a prison cell.

Churchill paced the Admiralty operation room from the moment when reconnaissance aircraft of the R.A.F. had spotted the German High Sea Fleet at sea, that Sunday night. He had immediately established contact with Admiral Charles Forbes, commander of the Home Fleet, and the latter had taken his ships out without delay. As in 1914, Churchill's navy was ready.

Admiral Forbes's units swept south and east to place themselves between the German expedition and their base. North of the Germans' probable course lay the strong British force that was covering the mine-laying activities. Grand Admiral Raeder was caught between the British pincers—or so it seemed on the charts. "All the German ships in the Skagerrak and the Kattegat will be sunk!" Churchill declared. His face was flushed, his nostrils trembled. The old war horse listened to the signals.

Minute by minute the signals came from the destroyer *Glow-worm*, which, engaged in mine-laying, was the spearhead of the British navy's expedition. Yes, the *Glowworm* reported, the Germans are steaming ahead. They are sailing right into the trap.

Churchill crouched over his charts. Patience was all-important. Patience while the hours were racing: the clocks, it seemed, could not catch up with them. Would this Sunday evening last until the end of time? Would this night never be over in the darkness of which the enemy could move uncontrolled? A tense group gathered in the operation room. His Majesty's Sea Lords smoked too much, they drank innumerable cups of tea. They did not speak.

Again the *Glowworm's* message came: No news. The next call would come in fifteen minutes.

Churchill smiled happily. No news is good news. There was a quarter of an hour to wait and waste. Someone insisted later that he had heard Winnie snoring. He can force himself to fall asleep at any moment and for exactly as long as he pleases: for five minutes, ten minutes, a quarter of an hour. But after fourteen minutes the First Lord said very clearly: "Now we must hear from them again!"

They did not hear from the *Glowworm* until considerably later. Then it was disclosed that the courageous destroyer had been sunk while stopping for a moment to pick up a man who had gone overboard. Thus the fight began.

The German High Sea Fleet definitely showed no taste for fighting. And the night, indeed, seemed never to end. The dawn of Monday was blacked out by dense fog. A heavy gale lashed the North Sea, making the spotting of the German ships extremely difficult. "Hitler weather" the Nazis call the pea-soup skies that helped them to escape. In the last war blue skies and a shining sun were called "Kaiser weather." Times change, and their symbols, too.

Admiral Forbes's ships patrolled the North Sea until Monday late at night. Grimly the operation room watched. Kitchener had an expression for such a situation: "It is easier to kill Germans than to kill time."

Tuesday morning the great kill began. Clouds of German bombers swarmed above the North Sea. For the first time the locusts displayed their sinister force. They subjected the Grand Fleet to merciless bombardment. Churchill was on the alert. The decisive moment had come, which he had for years predicted: aircraft attacked the battleship. It was a test case. The outcome of the war was at stake.

From the top of the Admiralty Building came the message, cool and mechanical: "A thousand-pound bomb has struck the *Rodney!*"

Was England doomed?

"The *Rodney* is undamaged," the voice from the rooftop announced a little later. "The bomb did not pierce the ship's steel. But three officers and seven ratings are killed."

And so the battleship, the mainstay of British seapower, had another lease on life.

Three British cruisers were slightly injured by bombs, but none of them fell out of line. The destroyer *Gurkha* was sunk. She fought with her guns until the last moment. All but fourteen of her crew were saved.

On the same Tuesday, off the Orkneys, the *Gurkha's* sister ship *Zulu* sent a German submarine to the bottom. An hour later the battle-cruiser *Renown,* one of the five heaviest and fastest ships in this war, sighted two of Germany's strongest units, the 26,000-ton *Scharnhorst* and the 10,000-ton pocket-battleship *Admiral Hipper,* off Narvik.

Churchill immediately knew that his *Renown* would attack singlehanded both the German men-of-war. Indeed, she opened fire at 18,000 yards.

Three minutes passed, thrice sixty seconds, an eternity.

Then came the first report from the *Renown:* "*Scharnhorst* just returned the fire and immediately turned away. Following her."

The *Renown* can do twenty-four knots. A German shell struck her right above the waterline. But the shell passed without exploding. The *Exeter* in her battle with the *Graf Spee* had the same piece of incredibly good luck. Some in the British navy believe that Churchill's sailors have their skipper's charmed life.

The *Renown's* foremast was slightly damaged. That is all the injury she received. There were no casualties. But both the German heroes of the blue waters escaped.

Again the skies darken. It is evening. But there shall be no night after this crucial day. Captain B. A. W. Warburton Lee, a veteran sea-bear if there ever was one, takes five over-age destroyers out on a suicide expedition.

The Germans have assembled their store-ships in the harbor of Narvik. If they are sunk, the northern army of invasion is cut off from their ammunition and supply, and lost.

Six German destroyers defended the harbor of Narvik. A terrific barrage from the coastal forts greeted the English expedition. Two of the attacking destroyers went down. Captain Warburton Lee fell on the bridge of his ship. But all the German destroyers were heavily damaged, and the assembled fleet of store-ships was sunk.

Next morning the British Naval air-arm took up the raiding. At dawn two waves of air force bombers, twelve each, went after German ships in the Bergen Fjord. They damaged two German light cruisers. Thursday the fleet air-arm flew for the last attack. They bagged a German destroyer in the harbor of Trondheim.

Trondheim was the key position in the battle for Norway. Admiral Sir Roger Keyes, long retired but now again in active service, offered to attack and take the port of Trondheim with as many over-age ships as the navy was in a position to lose. Of course none of the ships would have had a chance to come back from the perilous venture. Trondheim is the most strongly fortified harbor in Norway. The government refused Sir Roger's offer. The situation in Trondheim was well in the army's hand, the admiral was told. In fact Churchill probably did not want to lose valuable units of his fleet as the war was just starting.

The good companion Churchill has to pay the price of greatness: solitude. The man at the helm can share his thoughts with one, his activities with another, his joys with a few, his worries with a nation. But he can no longer share his life, which is friendship's deepest meaning. How was he to explain to his old friend Roger that he, the First Lord and elder statesman, could no longer be the rough rider of Antwerp? He was twenty-six years older than he had been when he occupied the same chair in the same room at the outbreak of the last war, and centuries wiser. Sir Roger Keyes may easily have remained the same: once a firebrand, always a firebrand. He was not, like Churchill, about to take the load of an Empire battling for her life, on broad, if somewhat stooping, shoulders.

Discipline is an essential part of age's wisdom. The morning after the battle for the North Sea nobody who came to call on the First Lord would have noticed anything of the storms that had raged. As always the room looked tidy. No paper littered the desk. The only decoration was the map of the West Front and of the Maginot Line on the wall, and Samuel Scott's famous painting of Westminster that was presented to Churchill while he was Minister of Munitions in the last war. Undisturbed, a globe stood in the left corner.

As if nothing had happened in the last four days and nights, the First Lord went about his business. It was a day like other days. In the forenoon he dictated his letters and the speech he was about to deliver to the House. Incidentally, he dictates correct and complete sentences to a secretary at a noiseless typewriter in a calm, restrained voice. Lunch came on a tray which was put on his desk. Since Churchill strictly observes the regulations of rationing and, besides, watches his waistline, his lunch usually consists of a few slices of cold roast beef. When there are oysters, his favorite dish—they are, alas, getting ever rarer—he does not refuse them. The meal ends with coffee and brandy.

Work continues in the afternoon, through the evening, and long into the night. If no event occurs that keeps him longer at his desk, he is through with his daily work at 2 A.M. Never as long as he was First Lord did he retire before having visited the operation room for a last time to check up on the dispositions of his and the enemy ships. Some intimates insist he just looks for an excuse to light another cigar, definitely the last one of the day.

Had he become a different man, as disappointed Sir Roger Keyes obviously believed? When Winnie was a little boy at Harrow, his headmaster said a remarkable word about him: "His style is unorthodox but effective." Indeed he had, in spite of a hundred changes, remained true to this style. In the first days of the lamentable Norwegian campaign all London was in danger of losing its head. Churchill alone remained unperturbed. Indeed, as he walked from his office to Parliament, he stopped to watch a few bricklayers working on a building. Suddenly he took off his coat, and joined them for half an hour in their work. Here he was at his old hobby again. He smiled happily. He even whistled. He was so gay and cheerful that one might almost have guessed that he was trying to overcome a feeling of uneasiness.

The uneasy feeling spread rapidly. The Chamberlain government faced growing criticism. Hore-Belisha, recently dismissed as Minister of War, voiced violent opposition. Some of Churchill's oldest and most trusted friends in the House, like Leopold Amery, his school-fellow at Harrow, and Sir Archibald Sinclair, the comrade from the Flanders trenches, joined the attack. Major Attlee, then leader of the opposition, refused point-blank any coöperation with the Chamberlain government. A few days before, Mr. Chamberlain had coined the unfortunate phrase: "Hitler has missed the bus!" Now this expression followed him wherever he went. Dissatisfied crowds gathered in Downing Street. "Where are our soldiers and ships?" they shouted. These were, of course, highly patriotic demonstrations of dissatisfaction. But the Nazi propaganda falsified them into defeatism. "Churchill can no longer show his stout face in Downing Street!" gibed Lord Haw Haw.

In fact, Churchill was Parliament's and the people's only hope.

They did not pin the responsibility for the Norwegian disaster on the First Lord, who time and time again had pointed out the inevitable consequences of neutral temporizing. The popular feeling was: we should have followed him years ago.

At this moment Churchill could make or break the regime. He had every reason to part from Mr. Chamberlain, whom only the mysterious influence of the then Tory Chief Whip, now Minister of War, Captain David Margesson, kept in power. But Churchill cast his lot with Chamberlain. There has never been a more glorious revenge.

The House met on May 7. A decision was due. Critical, hostile faces stared at the Prime Minister as he rose to speak. Chamberlain appeared tired, nervous, discouraged. Previously he had had to swallow many defeats. But he had always taken them with good grace. Now for the first time he lost his poise. His apology neither convinced the majority of his own party, nor the opposition.

Attention was centered on Sir Roger Keyes. There he sat on his seat in the Conservative benches, which he only rarely occupied. But today he appeared in his uniform as an Admiral of the Fleet, wearing the medals of Zeebrugge and the Dardanelles. He disclosed to the House his offer to take Trondheim, irrespective of the losses, and how shamefully it had been rejected. He did not mention Churchill. Yet the tragic case of John Arbuthnot, Lord Fisher was repeated.

Chamberlain had finished his speech. He sank back into his seat. At this moment Churchill entered to take place next to the Prime Minister on the front bench. He glanced rapidly over the House. He found Parliament in an uproar. That was the last thing the situation permitted. For a short moment he let his head fall despondently into his hands. But immediately he jumped up. "The country does not yet realize the gravity of the peril before it now!" he exclaimed.

"Do you?" a voice answered.

Then Churchill spoke. His lisp was a little thicker than usual, and if you stood near him you could hear his heavy breathing.

Yet, in a few minutes he exercised that magic spell again, with which he had so often mastered the House. The Speaker, who had had to interfere frequently during Chamberlain's address, to restore order, could comfortably sit back again. The opposition calmed down. Everybody listened.

Churchill reviewed the consequences rather than the causes of the Norwegian disaster. As usual he was ahead of the discussion. France, he observed—and only those very close to him could hear a faint uncertainty in his voice—remained remarkably steady. The effect of the reverse on Sweden, on the other hand, was very bad. Of course Sweden must bear a large part of the responsibility for the plight in which she would find herself after Norway's fall, since she had failed to coöperate with the Allies. Swedish coöperation on the spot would immediately have remedied the situation. However, the fight in Narvik continued.

"It is folly to talk of continuing the operations in Narvik!" Major Attlee, the leader of the opposition, interrupted. Sir Archibald Sinclair minced no words. "It is all due to your bungling!" he attacked the front bench.

To all this Churchill gave a summary reply. "We do not take the initiative because of our failure in the last five years to retain air parity with Germany. Our numerical deficiency in the air will condemn us for some time to come to a great deal of difficulty, suffering and danger. The immense enemy air strength made naval domination of the Skagerrak much too costly. The losses which would have been inflicted on the patrol would undoubtedly very soon have constituted a naval disaster. Therefore we had to limit our operations in the Skagerrak to submarine activities. The decision to abandon an attack on Trondheim saved us from a most disastrous entanglement. The spectacle of our fleet being completely absorbed would have brought new adversaries down upon us."

Every word was the confession of the gravest crisis in English history. Yet every word was a vindication of Winston Churchill's years-old, singlehanded fight for preparedness. He did not draw any personal conclusions. But Mr. Chamberlain saved his Prime Ministerial skin for the last time when he announced that Churchill from now on would control the day-to-day operations of all the fighting forces. A murmur of approval answered, and a small majority—281 to 200—absolved Neville Chamberlain. His prestige, however, was irrevocably gone.

Believing that England was in the throes of grave political crisis, Hitler struck for the second time. Three days after the fatal debate in the House his legions invaded the Lowlands. In the first hours of this new invasion it seemed as if Hitler had succeeded in saving Chamberlain. The Labour Party now forgot the opposition.

But Neville Chamberlain understood that the game was up. Perhaps he had just to look into the mirror. He submitted his resignation to the King. There was no question about the only possible successor. On May 10, 1940, while the Allied armies raced across Belgium, Winston Churchill was appointed Prime Minister. Of course he retained his office as Minister for the Co-Ordination of Defense.

CHAPTER XXXII

The Tide Turns

"I HAVE nothing to offer but blood, toil, tears and sweat." With these words Churchill introduced his cabinet on May 13. The resounding phrase struck. It is the most famous and most popular battle cry Churchill has coined. "He has brought back the splendor and the arrogance of Elizabethan language," a highly placed listener commented. Churchill's own utterance was an understatement.

Winston Churchill, now undisputed war lord of Great Britain, had new spirit and speed to offer. He electrified the nation. The task he had undertaken was nothing less than the rebirth of the British Empire. There is little doubt that his appointment, had it come a few years earlier, would have prevented the war by breaking the aggressor in time. There is no doubt that his appointment, belated as it was, changed the course of war.

He introduced a coalition government in which Tories and Labour approximately balanced their power and in which the last Liberals were not forgotten. The Independent Socialist McGovern, with three followers, represented all that was left by way of opposition. The national emergency allowed no room for personal grudges. Neville Chamberlain remained in the war cabinet, the inner circle of five. His office as Lord President of the Council was more decorative than decisive. But the old gentleman was permitted to give his last strength to the struggle for his rehabilitation—the struggle against Hitler. He was even permitted to retain the leadership of the Conservative Party. True, the Party Committee had approached Churchill, their prodigal son, with the offer of leadership. Politely Churchill refused. As head of a coalition government, he explained, he would rather not carry partisan responsibilities. The prize of forty years of parliamentary struggle lay at his feet. He no longer had use for it. Now parties did not count. Now only Britain counted.

The rapid establishment of the Churchill government, which united so many divergent elements in perfect harmony, had a tonic effect on the country. Germany accepted it as a challenge. Years ago Hitler had raged that Churchill as Prime Minister would constitute the *casus belli* for him. He could not declare war for a second time. So he declared that "democracy was done for in England because all parties had united and the democratic principle of opposition was violated." Churchill is no doubt the only man who could have converted Hitler into upholding democratic principles.

France was delighted with the new choice. Churchill's record as a pro-French, as an admirer of the *grande nation,* her civilization, language and spirit, had been well established for many years. The French still banked on this old predilection in the days in which their civilization deteriorated, their language became a dangerous whisper, and their spirit broke.

It did not take much of Churchill's visionary gift to see that a French catastrophe was imminent. Yet he challenged fate once more, and threw himself, two-fisted and broad-shouldered, into the losing battle. Both in the first and in the second week of his Premiership he flew to Paris. "A talk with Churchill is a shot in the arm," an American visitor had once expressed it. Did he hope that his personal magic would once more sway the wretched French leaders?

His conversation with Paul Reynaud went off well. General Weygand, the veteran, impressed him by his youthful energy. At a certain moment in their three-cornered conversation an important document was missing. "Wait a minute," said Weygand. "I think I have it in my office." Up he jumped, and raced to fetch it. Churchill watched the old warrior, aged seventy-six, and turned around to Reynaud: "Don't you think we are reckless in entrusting the fate of our two countries to such a young man?"

But after he returned to London France collapsed. Weygand called the miserable show the French were putting against the German offensive "the battle of France." Churchill, for his part, defiantly termed it "the battle of the bulge." He explained the two fundamental reasons for the collapse on the Western Front. The first was the surrender of Leopold, King of the Belgians, which, as Churchill clearly stated, had not previously been announced to the Allied High Command. The second catastrophic mistake was the failure of the French General Staff to withdraw their troops from Belgium and throw them into the battle before Amiens, where the Germans, almost unopposed, were permitted to dent the French lines and to create the fateful "bulge."

As early as May 19, when the fighting in France was still in full swing, Churchill exhorted the people of England to "steel themselves for a major battle for our island." Invasion, he foretold, was near. Two days later he issued regulations to deal with all possible dangers. Since German parachutists, disguised as civilians, frequently even as women and priests, had played a major part in the assault on the Lowlands, the Prime Minister informed the world, particularly Germany, that in England such chutists in mufti would be dealt with as spies, and immediately shot. Hitler countered with the announcement that his troops would consider the Home Guards—a force of one million men, of course a strictly military force—as snipers and franc-tireurs and that he would "blow life out of everyone." The Home Guards, mostly veterans from the first war, laughed. At this writing eight months have passed since the Führer uttered his threat of "Schrecklichkeit"—frightfulness—and although the British Isles have meanwhile become the target of barbaric German atrocities from the air, the old Home Guards are still laughing.

The end of the world seemed near. Some American onlookers had already written off England. But Churchill maintained a serene expression which even his friends could hardly understand.

It was rather a smile of determination and defiance, the expression of a man who was at war with half the world, but at peace with his innermost self and with his own people.

Now the people of England had to learn what ultimate preparedness really means. Individual privileges were voluntarily and joyfully sacrificed to the common welfare. On May 23 all the airplane, munition, and subsidiary factories were taken over by the state, and not a single industrialist complained. By the same token the decisions on labor questions were transferred to a national board, and British labor cheered. These were no days for great words. When an M.P. asked the Prime Minister whether the government still stuck to its predecessor's declaration that no separate peace should be considered, Churchill answered with a single word: "Yes!" He did not even bother about the traditional: "Yes, sir!"

Probably this question had been pre-arranged. It served to remind the French that both the Allies were in the same boat. "Heavy tidings," Churchill admitted. On May 23 he informed the House that the German Channel drive was apparently succeeding. The invaders had already reached Boulogne. Two days later he said, "The gravity of the situation deepens from hour to hour." Reynaud, still full of fight, had visited him by airplane, but obviously Churchill sensed that France was lost before the French Premier himself had realized it.

Churchill's last endeavour to save what was left of France— the Colonial Empire, the navy, and, most precious of all, the fighting spirit—led him to offer the Third Republic complete amalgamation with the British Empire. The dream was too beautiful to come true. It was a genuine Churchill dream. Once more this last defender of the old world and the first pathfinder in a new one was ahead of his time.

Dunkerque brought the German success to its climax, but it was, for Hitler's ambitions, an anti-climax, too. In orderly fashion the B.E.F. and such French and Belgian units as chose to continue resistance were enabled to cross the Channel. The epic of

Dunkerque remains unforgotten. To a hushed House, some of whose own members had fallen on the field of honor, Churchill told the story of heroism and sacrifice of the British army in Flanders. "The bulk of this encircled army was betrayed by King Leopold of the Belgians," he stated. He frankly admitted that a catastrophe had occurred. "Wars are not won by retreats and withdrawals of armies," he said. But his credo followed: "We shall go to the end. We shall fight on the seas and the oceans. We shall fight with growing confidence of strength in the air. We shall fight on our beaches. We shall fight on our landing grounds. We shall never surrender and even if—which I do not for a moment believe—this island or a large part of it is subjected and starving, then our Empire beyond the seas, armed and guarded by the British Fleet, will carry on the struggle until in God's good time the New World, with all its power and might, steps forth to the liberation and rescue of the Old."

Today these words are history. They were an epilogue to the first part of the war. Democracy had lost the first round. But immediately Churchill girded himself for the second. He did not need a breathing spell. Not for one heartbeat did he waver. Uppermost in his tireless mind was the bugbear that a search for culprits might tear to pieces the last vestiges of democratic unity.

"I spoke the other day of the colossal military disaster which occurred when the French High Command failed to withdraw the northern armies from Belgium," he reminded the House on June 18. "But no recriminations!" he proclaimed, and added forcefully: "This also applies in a small way to our affairs at home. There are many who want to hold an inquest upon the conduct of government and Parliament during the years that led up to this catastrophe. They wish to indict those who were responsible for the guidance of our affairs." Such an inquest, of course, could not but have ended in a perfect vindication of his own unrelenting strivings and in a severe condemnation of all his opponents. Yet Churchill prevented the inquest. "It would be a foolish and pernicious process. There are too many in it. Let every man search his conscience and search his speeches as I frequently search mine. Of this I am quite sure that if we open a quarrel between the past and the present, we shall find that we have lost the future."

His words struck home. Mr. Chamberlain, whose immediate retirement even from the shadowy position he now held, was urgently demanded in the days after Dunkerque, could breathe a little easier. Truly he had found a generous opponent.

But France was already beyond the reach of Churchill's words. On Sunday, June 23, the message came that France had concluded an armistice with the victor. The terms of this armistice indicated to Churchill, who knows his Hitler, that France sooner or later should be transformed into an active enemy of Britain. The hardest blow was not so much the danger that the French fleet and Empire might join the aggressors in their triumphal hour, as the grief of having lost a national friendship Churchill had treasured during his entire political life. For his part he was not willing to give up the friendship. "Great Britain," he declared immediately, "grieved and amazed at France's acceptance of German armistice terms, appeals to all Frenchmen to continue the fight. Victorious Britain will cherish the cause of the French people. A British victory is the only hope for the restoration of France and for the freedom of its people."

These words have not been forgotten during the months that have elapsed. But their immediate effect on the Frenchmen then in power was nil. Only one man rose, a tall young general, whom Churchill had casually met at his last conference in Paris. He was Under-Secretary of War in Paul Reynaud's cabinet, and today he is the leader of all Free Frenchmen—Charles De Gaulle. "The armistice," the general declared, "is submission and slavery. The present government has no right to surrender. France cannot honorably do less than Poland."

To stress the importance of these words General Sikorski, Polish Prime Minister in exile, called upon Churchill on June 25 to emphasize the allegiance of the subjugated nations.

Even Mr. Chamberlain came out of his semi-retirement. On June 28 one could have heard his voice distinctly saying: "We are just beginning the struggle." And now it was clear that Churchill, in the middle of crisis and catastrophe, had succeeded in turning the tide.

The path up which he led his nation out of disaster, was hard and stony. The danger of the French navy's joining the Axis fleets loomed dark over the horizon. If this happened the British navy would be outnumbered and England would lose her supremacy at sea. It must not happen, and it did not. The action of Oran prevented it. Churchill did not command this action light-heartedly. Vice Admiral Sommerville, commander of the British Fleet in the Mediterranean, was a trusted friend of France, who had just rescued 100,000 French soldiers from Dunkerque. He tried to persuade the French Admiral Gensoul to sail his ships into neutral American waters. Only the French Admiral's insistence on keeping his fleet where she might easily have fallen prey to the Axis necessitated the action. On July 3, at 5:58 A.M. Vice Admiral Sommerville gave the order to open fire. At 7:30 A.M. the two most important units of the French Mediterranean Fleet, the *Strasbourg* and the *Dunkerque* were *hors de combat*.

The House cheered when it heard Churchill's account two days later. But for once his face was drawn and careworn. He did not care that M. Baudoin, one of the grave-diggers of France and short-lived Foreign Secretary of Vichy, raged: "Churchill is guilty of an act of aggression without precedent in history." His mind was at that moment occupied by a single thought: now the entente cordiale was definitely dead—after thirty-six years.

Vichy let off some steam in ordering French pilots to join an Italian air-raid over Gibraltar. The French pilots submitted to the command. But they dumped their bombs right into the sea. More disagreeable was Marshal Pétain's decision to release four hundred German pilots, most of whom the R.A.F. had shot down, from French captivity. "We will have to shoot them down once more," Churchill said philosophically.

Personally he was—and he remains—entirely unafraid of German pilots. On July 12 he was just inspecting British troops on the southeast coast, when Jerry's raiders came. In those days they came in smaller waves; the all-out assault from the air was still in preparation. Churchill refused to take shelter with his troops. He pressed the blue steel helmet, a memory from his service in the trenches of Flanders, a little more firmly upon his big, stubborn head, and curiously he watched the approach of the birds of prey.

Somehow or other the enemy must have heard of this newest proof of Churchill's defiance. Next morning the Stockholm *Tidningen,* a Nazi-controlled Swedish sheet, exulted: "Churchill injured by German raiders!"

Once and for all he clarified his attitude to Hitler and to whoever was listening in. "Britain seeks no peace terms," he stated on July 14, "tolerates no parleys, asks no mercy. The world shall cease wondering whether Britain will survive. We will defend every village, every town, every city. The vast mass of London itself, fought street by street, could easily devour an entire hostile army, and we would rather see London laid in ashes and ruins than that it should be tamely abjected and enslaved."

It was long since the British people had heard such accents of leadership. Toward the finish of the speech some listeners kept wondering whether sirens would not be sounding before Churchill had got through.

But the Germans cautiously delayed their attack: hour to hour, day to day, month to month. "The longer the Germans wait, the more guns, concrete, sandbags and barbed wire they will face," Churchill assured his people. And when he was informed that Virginio Gayda, Mussolini's parrot and mouthpiece, had definitely announced the invasion for Friday next, he grinned: "Friday is as good as another day."

It was of course not all grinning and wisecracking. Problems of tremendous importance demanded solution. One of them was what to do about London's children, as everybody was expecting the blitzkrieg from the air. Rather wild schemes for their mass exodus were circulated. Churchill had to appeal to sound reason. He termed the proposed exodus to the United States and to the Dominions both undesirable and physically impossible. But he fostered a "decentralization" of children overseas within the limits of possibility, insisting that no difference should be made between the duke's son and the beggarman's.

He radiated fighting spirit and confidence. Both were contagious. Everyone who came in contact with Churchill in those days in which England had found herself again was inspired by the old man's second youth.

When Churchill moved into Number 10, he celebrated the occasion by cutting his sleeping hours from six to five. Now he could assemble his ministerial colleagues at his bedside. They had to be constantly available. First, because the German invasion could materialize at any moment. Second, to improve the attendance at the "breakfast cabinet meetings," a custom Lloyd George had instituted toward the end of the first World War, and Churchill cheerfully revived. Third, he wanted to have the proper audience ready, whenever ideas rose in his head.

Some of the ministers and high officials—among them Sir Archibald Sinclair, Air Secretary, Mr. Alexander, Churchill's successor as First Lord, and General Dill—already slept in their offices. Most of the other government members had their suites in hotels around Whitehall. Churchill admonished them all to use their offices as night quarters. They should get a little expense money, he said, but he expected they would not take advantage of the Chancellor of the Exchequer's dwindling funds. Some senior ministers shook their heads over this newest Winston folly. Would he never mature? It took those gentlemen a little while to understand that the chief just wanted to assure them the best available air-raid protection. While he lay in his bed, the cigar in the corner of his mouth, chatting with friends, interspersing world-embracing decisions with good-natured jokes, he was perfectly aware that the skies were rapidly darkening, and fire and death would soon rain over London.

There was no way of avoiding the crucial test. It was evident that the war would increase in ferocity when Hitler started that peace-offensive which always precedes his assaults. Did Hitler in his disturbed mind seriously believe that he could bluff Winston Churchill into submission and England into subjugation? "Hitler's peace offers are not worthy of comment," Churchill said on July 19, after the Führer in one of his bombastic speeches had exhorted Britain to "make overtures." Churchill's defiance was now shared by the country. Viscount Halifax, whom he had inherited as Foreign Secretary, hurried to remake his reputation in refusing—perhaps, as a devout churchman, primarily for religious reasons—any thought of appeasing the Antichrist.

The general feeling in England had so completely changed for the better since Churchill stood on the bridge that he could now allow the "hush hush" rules to be eased. All sentences for careless talk, he promised the House, would be reviewed. It was a great proof of that liberal spirit to which Englishmen are born and bred, and an assertion of the democratic way of war-making. The only topic still subject to censorship remained, for obvious military reasons, aerial activity. When the Conservative M.P. Lewis questioned the Prime Minister whether the German bombing should evoke British reprisals, Churchill countered with a paternal smile: "If the answer were in the negative it would remove a deterrent for the enemy. If it were in the affirmative it might spur him on to increase his preparations, and add to the difficulties of our airmen. If it were non-committal it would not add to the enlightenment of the honorable member."

Mr. Lewis was fully satisfied with this answer. Mr. Churchill himself was not. Suddenly he had caught himself speaking that "officialese" which he, an orator with an artist's sensitiveness, had always ridiculed. "In the affirmative . . . to the negative. . . ." Good God, the words were Yes! or No! On August 22, Churchill issued an edict of self-censorship. Officialese was strictly banned.

Answers were no longer "in the affirmative" but simply: Yes! A man was no longer "conveyed to his place of residence in an intoxicated condition." The good man was carried home drunk.

It is the privilege, and perhaps the compulsion, of genius to relieve the constant pressure on the mind by roving a bit along sidelines. But Churchill's good-natured jokes never distracted him from the danger on which his attention was fixed. On August 4, in an official statement released by his office, he warned the people that tremendous air attacks were to be expected, and he recalled to them that the danger of the blitzkrieg had by no means passed away. Next day he delivered a speech warning his audience to beware of relaxing vigilance. He never assumed the severe paterfamilias air of his predecessor. But he never tired in giving every man, woman and child in the British Isles his guidance and something of his experience. His popularity rose immensely. It was rather expressed in popular jokes than in hero-worship. Sir Kingsley Wood, Chancellor of the Exchequer, said in the House: "Maybe in a few months when we see somebody wearing a shabby hat, we will say: This is a patriotic man!"

"Does that apply to the Prime Minister?" a member asked. The House laughed, and England echoed the laughter.

British democracy conducts the war with full respect for personal liberty. Churchill, who has spent so much of his life in the House, truly his spiritual home, sees to it that Parliament should continue its function as watchdog. He accepted the decision of his own majority that the government should withdraw the proposed taxes on books and newspapers, which some members viewed as a danger to free discussion. Following the feeling of the House, Churchill ordered modification of the treatment of enemy aliens. More than half their number were released from internment camps. Churchill stopped his Home Secretary's effort to establish columns of eavesdroppers who would report to the police anyone spreading gloom and despondency. "This measure was an error," Churchill frankly confessed.

Yet Scotland Yard and the British Intelligence Service had to maintain a ceaseless watch for fifth columnists, which both Nazi and Communists frantically tried to plant on English soil. Churchill centralized this work under the control of a commission headed by Lord Swinton, who was not too popular with the Left. His appointment led to turbulent scenes in the House, in the middle of May. But Churchill stood his ground. Of course he could not divulge even a part of the Swinton committee's activities. He had to confine himself to a few allusions. The investigation, he declared, had discovered that confidential diplomatic reports on British official affairs, in a code known only to friendly nations, had reached Berlin. An embassy in a neutral country had served as relay point. The friendly nation acquainted with the British diplomatic code was the U.S.A. and the traitor, who did the dirty work, the clerk in the U. S. Embassy in London, Tyler Kent, an American turncoat in the pay of the Gestapo.

Furthermore, Churchill disclosed, the Germans had been informed of secret signals used by British planes to identify themselves as they passed over the home coast. Naturally the German knights of the air used these signals to protect their skins. Persons on the ground were signalling the British codes to Nazi airmen with colored lights. These persons were jailed, the Prime Minister added. Finally a trick to direct enemy raiders to an ammunition factory had been disclosed by an R.A.F. officer. Red tile roofs were put on a row of houses, forming a mammoth red arrow that pointed to the ammunition plant. "But the danger is now reduced to proper proportions," Churchill ended his report with grim satisfaction. Hitler had attacked England below the belt. He had lost this round, too.

Such are the minor worries Churchill has to cope with in war times. A major pleasure came to him when he could publicly offer 99-year leases for air and naval bases to the U.S.A. on all British islands between Newfoundland and Guiana in return for fifty over-age destroyers from the American navy. The much too long delayed Anglo-American coöperation began in earnest. Churchill, who in previous times had been scoffed at as "half American," rejoiced in the success—a proof of the good sense of both the high contracting parties, but also a personal success of the son of an American mother and an English father.

After the American deal he could for the first time survey the war with a note of unalloyed confidence. For three months, he pointed out his government had had to face a "cataract of disaster. Three weeks ago," he continued, "nobody would have believed in our victory. Few have believed that we could survive." But now confidence was everywhere restored.

There still loomed grave dangers, and Churchill did not minimize them. "The puppet government in Vichy may at any moment be forced to become our foe. But we will be able to continue the struggle, particularly the air-struggle, indefinitely."

The first signs of American awakening gave him strong hope. Certainly the solution of many problems would require a large amount of good will. England needed more naval vessels from the U.S.A., Churchill declared. Then there was the Hoover plan for relieving Hitler of his obligation to feed his serfs in the subjected countries, a plan that would have wrecked the British blockade.

But Churchill did not worry over new difficulties. Everyone would be dealt with in God's good time. He has saved England from worrying herself to death.

Two things were on his mind: the impending German air-attack and the American help that would probably not come as rapidly. Both were decisive problems. He discussed them, on August 28, with Vice Admiral Robert L. Ghormley, President Roosevelt's naval observer, as the two men walked along the coast of Dover, intensely watching the aerial fight that went on in the skies over Dover and Ramsgate.

Suddenly Churchill realized that he had a guest for whose safety he felt responsible, and, against his personal custom, he urged Admiral Ghormley to enter a shelter with him.

The shelter warden received his war lord with the words: "No smoking inside, sir!"

Churchill had just lit a fresh cigar. Instantly he dropped it, if with a sigh. "All right. Here goes a good one."

It was the only time during this war that anybody has heard Churchill sighing.

CHAPTER XXXIII

Man of Destiny

ON the cliffs of Dover a man stands all alone. His heavy profile grows out of the earth. If you look at him from a distance, it seems as if it wanted to grow into the skies. His head is held erect. The expression of his rotund and rubicund face is inscrutable. Not a muscle moves in this deeply lined quadrangular mask. Only his eyes, red-rimmed by lack of sleep, are ever on the alert. You see him tirelessly watching the skies. An eagle-hunter has this sharp, determined look. Or a tugboat skipper who steers his smack into the safety of the harbor before the gale rises to full fury.

But the storm is already unleashed. A hail of explosives falls on the white British coast. Roaring thunder and yellow lightning tear the skies to pieces. Clouds burst in volcanic eruptions: clouds of German bombers.

Slowly, as if it were difficult to turn away from this hell in heaven, the man looks to the other side. Clouds again, white clouds. Or are they silver birds? The Spitfires are racing along. They are fewer than the German bombers—many fewer—but they fly higher, they'll have the advantage. As far as one can judge from the ground, they also race faster. Black clouds clash with white ones. Why, in Heaven's name, does one call this a dogfight? Perhaps because the boys in the Spitfires have no use for resounding words. If you say "courage" when all is over and they drink their cup of tea in the airdrome's modest canteen, the next round is on you. And if you utter heroics you are quickly but effectively silenced.

Immovable as a monument Churchill has watched the first mass assault of German raiders on England, on September 1, on the chalk cliffs of Dover. Alone and unprotected he stood gazing at the fight while it lasted. He is incorrigible, at sixty-six more the despair of his friends than he was half a century ago the despair of his Harrovian schoolmasters. He has made up his mind not to bother about Goering's raindrops. By temperament he simply cannot be fettered in his movements. And he cannot run away. It is not in his dictionary. The German raiders came for the first time in droves over London as the first anniversary of the war was observed in Westminster Abbey, on September 3. Of course, the Abbey was the most inviting target. But no one thought of interrupting the service. Churchill, to whom all eyes were directed, simply nodded. All England knows his nod. "Carry on!" it says.

Almost daily Churchill spoke to his people. "Britain's might grows," he assured them the day after the service in the Abbey. Next day he spoke during a heavy air-raid. He dared Hitler to do his worst. "We can stand it!" he thundered, raising his fist against the embattled skies. Personally Churchill supervised the construction of air-raid shelters, their equipment and constant improvement. Unfortunately the previous government had not taken sufficient precautionary measures in good time. London had to meet the sudden emergency with preparations uncompleted. Churchill remembered his "Utmost fish!" from the navy slang he will never forget. He insisted on immediate action. He advised carefulness and caution. But he succeeded—and it was no mean success—in staving off panic and hysteria. "Blackout without gloom" was his slogan.

Grimly and gaily London carried on. Churchill inspected every part of the city that had borne the brunt of the attack. On September 9, he was visiting the East End with Brendan Bracken, the chief of his personal secretariat, when a passer-by suddenly turned to him: "The people of England are the bravest in the world," the stranger exclaimed. Churchill smiled proudly.

It is difficult to conceal that he, personally, is the bravest of the brave. As in peacetime, he quietly announced the speeches he would deliver, the place and the hour. Such announcements sounded like an invitation to the Luftwaffe. "We will stop this man speaking!" Goering told reporters. The fat Marshal himself, like his Führer, is of course very careful that his harangues never receive pre-arranged publicity. Life in Germany is too beautiful, at least for the bosses.

On September 11 a furious German assault from the air attempted to silence Churchill. He did not interrupt his speech for a moment. Believe it or not, he outroared the bombs. Next day he gave an important message to the nation: "Heavy convoys of German troops presage full scale invasion." In a few seconds his words flashed across the seven seas. The New York Stock Exchange was chilled. But the Cockneys remained undaunted. All right. They were ready.

The days, the hours that came then were to decide the fate of England—the fate of the world. Hitler was all set for the kill. On the British side, Churchill stated on that fatal Friday, September 13, that every possible precaution had been taken. He did not forget to add that the Mediterranean navy had been doubled in the last weeks and that troops had been provided for the southern theatre of war. Mussolini was kindly invited to join in the all out.

Saturday was a day of merciless air battle. Sunday brought the German attack to its peak. Undoubtedly the Luftwaffe was bent on breaking up the R.A.F., on winning undisputed supremacy over the British skies, and on facilitating the landing of troops on the English coast.

But on this memorable Sunday, September 15, 1940, 185 German airplanes were downed against British losses of 25; and among the 25, the pilots of 14 could safely land on British soil. The grand scale daylight air attack was stopped. The British skies remained blue and free, if only in daytime, and Hitler suffered the worst defeat of his life so far.

For the time England was saved. She owes her rescue primarily to a score of Coastal Command fliers who intercepted the German raiders as they came, fighting one against ten, fifteen, twenty, and chasing them back from the approach. Monday morning Churchill congratulated the Coastal Command fliers on their unprecedented bravery. To them his words go: "Never has so much been owed by so many to so few."

But he was the object of congratulations, too. All England understood that without his guidance such feats as the repelling of the overwhelmingly powerful German air attack would never have been possible. Even the "Conservative Committee of 1922" accepted this obvious truth. This committee is a small but influential group of those Tories who in previous years had made life particularly hard for Churchill, the party-traitor. But on Wednesday after the air battle for Britain they resolved to "appreciate Mr. Churchill's leadership." This resolution was another invitation to him, thinly disguised, to assume the guidance of the party. Unfortunately, Mr. Churchill at this moment was too busy for party politics.

Another deputation, an informal one, that came to him, consisted of his personal friends. They implored him no longer to be as reckless as he had showed himself in recent days. They were seriously worried over his habit of donning a tin hat and sauntering out into the street to watch the German attacks and listen with gusto to the salvos from British anti-aircraft barrages.

Does Churchill court death? Quite the contrary. He lives his life to the full. Never, he insists, was there more reason to be grateful for one's life and never had a generation of British people a prouder task to carry out than the present one. His defiance of death has never led him to forget the sanctity of life, and his foremost concern remains the protection of his fellow-citizens. Outraged, he published the figures of casualties during the first half of September, the time of the worst German day raids. Two thousand civilians had been killed and eight thousand wounded, four fifths of them Londoners, as compared to two hundred and fifty men, the total losses of the armed forces during the same period. Hitler, it is obvious, leads his war less against soldiers, who might shoot back, and more against women and children.

The women and children of London, and the rest of the city population in addition, were now handed over to the care of "Evans of the Broke," one of Churchill's oldest friends. On October 1, Marshal Sir Edward R. G. R. Evans, hero of the Dover patrol in 1917, later commander of the Home Fleet, received from the Prime Minister's hands his assignment as shelter dictator.

On the same day Mr. Chamberlain resigned from the cabinet. Friendly letters of mutual admiration exchanged between him and his successor closed what had been an important chapter both for England and for Churchill. "I feel warm appreciation of your kindness and consideration you have constantly shown me since the formation of your government," Chamberlain wrote to his "dear Winston," and the latter replied to dear Neville: "I and all of your colleagues have admired your unshaken nerve and persevering will. You did all you could for peace. You did all you could for victory. I trust that we shall rejoice together in the better days that are to come."

For Neville Chamberlain the better days have already come. He rests in Westminster Abbey. Churchill demanded this last honor for his dead antagonist.

Now Churchill could no longer refuse the orphaned Tory leadership. Viscount Halifax, another ex-appeaser, had the privilege of eulogizing him amidst general loud applause as Churchill assumed his new post of dignity. It had been his boyhood dream, and it had been withheld from him for many years. Now he accepted it with a few amiable phrases, but with the unmistakable sentence sandwiched in: "In no other way can we save our lives but by recognizing that this is no time for partisanship."

This is the time for fighting, and for nothing else. "The Prime Minister is getting on with the war" was the official statement on his sixty-sixth birthday on November 30, 1940. Indeed, since the start of the war Churchill had only one day off: Christmas, 1940. He spent the better part of this holiday watching the antics of

Winston Churchill, II, the son of Randolph, who last Christmas was aged eight weeks.

As a rule Churchill's day begins at 7:15 when the alarm bell rings. A quarter of an hour is "wasted" idling around in bed, stretching the formidable body, yawning occasionally—and thinking rapidly. In these comfortably squandered fifteen minutes Winston Churchill makes his plans for the day. At 7:30 he rings the bell. The servant appears, not with the breakfast tray but with the box of cigars. Churchill lights the first one, and that is the sign for the secretary in waiting to appear. Without pause, uninterrupted, Churchill now dictates his speeches and letters. At half past ten he is dressed for the daily cabinet meeting. He always wears the same short black coat with striped trousers. His choice of shoes is more catholic. But they have one peculiarity in common—they look so outworn that they, like his hats, have often been the object of jokes.

Churchill never leaves his house without his cane. Among his collection of sticks the one King Edward presented him with at his marriage is his favorite. Another of Churchill's canes has a piece of mechanism in the knob. It is, insiders hinted, an automatic pistol for self-defense. They were scared to death when the Prime Minister on an evening stroll along blacked-out Whitehall for the first time pressed the button of the concealed machine. A flash followed immediately, but no detonation. A noiseless gun? No, just a pocket battery for finding one's way in the dark.

The cabinet meetings usually last until noon. Lunch follows. In the afternoon he receives visitors or spends his time in the House. Before dinner—toward 6 P.M.—he returns to Number 10. He undresses and goes to bed for exactly forty-five minutes of sane and undisturbed sleep. At seven he appears in dinner-jacket for dinner, which is regularly attended by friends and co-workers. Mrs. Churchill does the honors during the simple meals. She retires immediately afterward, and the conferences continue until 2 or 3 A.M., sometimes until dawn.

He is at his best during his nightly conferences, and that is when most decisions are made. One night in November he decided to take a chance with Marshal Graziani's Fascist hordes, which had penetrated Egypt, if not very far, and a few weeks later they were driven out of their own Lybian strongholds. Another night Churchill decided to re-open the Burma Road to bring help to the hard-pressed Chinese democracy. The Japanese would let loose hell, he was warned. Sometimes he manages not to hear the friendly warnings coming from more anxious souls. Many a night Churchill ponders the future of Anglo-American relations, on which, he feels, depends the future of the world.

Is it as simple as that?

It is by no means simple. It was the road to Calvary. But salvation came when the British awoke. Fighting with their backs to the wall they realized their destiny. There stood the man of destiny before them. He bore a Herculean burden on his stooped shoulders. But he did not fall. He could not fall. He drew his strength from the green soil of England. At the end of his long pilgrimage Winston Churchill was a national symbol.

The French in a similar extremity had a prophetic goose-girl hundreds of years ago. No saint comes down to the English now. Instead of a Jeanne d'Arc they followed the old man whom they themselves had begotten through a long series of generations, flesh of their flesh and blood of their blood.

For twenty years the English people and the English leadership had underbid each other, sinking deeper and deeper. Now they were on the way up. Now the plump, old-fashioned, much-loved figure could sit at the helm. Now, at last, the factories were working twenty-four hours a day; now, at last, millions were called to the colors. Now, at last, with the billows breaking over their island, they remembered that in this war, which decides not frontiers but the fate of mankind, they were the chosen fighters for humanity.

The odds still weigh heavily against Churchill's England. At the end of all things stands the great question-mark. But everywhere millions of hands are busy for him and his cause, and out of millions of hearts surges the prayer that God might be for him—for His staunchest, most picturesque and humblest warrior.

INDEX